SECOND CANADIAN EDITION

NEW MEDIA
AN INTRODUCTION

Terry Flew and Richard Smith

OXFORD

UNIVERSITY PRESS

OXFORD
UNIVERSITY PRESS

Oxford University Press is a department of the University of Oxford.
It furthers the University's objective of excellence in research, scholarship,
and education by publishing worldwide. Oxford is a registered trade mark of
Oxford University Press in the UK and in certain other countries.

Published in Canada by
Oxford University Press
8 Sampson Mews, Suite 204,
Don Mills, Ontario M3C 0H5 Canada

www.oupcanada.com

Copyright © Oxford University Press Canada 2014

The moral rights of the authors have been asserted

Database right Oxford University Press (maker)

First Canadian Edition published in 2011

Original edition published by Oxford University Press,
253 Normanby Road, South Melbourne, Victoria, 3205, Australia
Copyright © 2008 Terry Flew

Library and Archives Canada Cataloguing in Publication

Flew, Terry, author
New media : an introduction / Terry Flew and Richard Smith. – Second
Canadian edition.
Revision of: New media : an introduction / Terry Flew & Richard Smith. –
1st Canadian ed. – Don Mills, Ont. : OUP Press, 2011.

Includes bibliographical references and index.
ISBN 978-0-19-900550-5 (pbk.)

1. Mass media–Technological innovations–Textbooks. 2. Mass media–
Influence–Textbooks. 3. Mass media–Social aspects–Textbooks. 4. Mass
media–Political aspects–Textbooks. I. Smith, Richard Keith, author II. Title.

P96.T42F64 2014   302.23   C2013-908207-7

Cover image: roccomontoya/iStockphoto

Oxford University Press is committed to our environment.
This book is printed on Forest Stewardship Council® certified paper
and comes from responsible sources.

MIX
Paper from
responsible sources
FSC
www.fsc.org
FSC® C004071

Printed and bound in Canada
7 8 9 — 18 17 16

Contents

Chapter 3　Approaches to New Media　56

Chapter 4　Mobile New Media　79

Chapter 5　Social Networks and Participatory Culture　106

Preface to the Second Edition

Revising *New Media: An Introduction* has been an amazing experience, for several reasons. As I noted in the preface to the first Canadian edition, the pace as well as the amount of change in the industry challenge authors of new media books. This happens in both the technology and the ways in which people use it. New media is, by its nature, extremely malleable and fluid in how it is used. Many of the same bits and pieces that go into making web pages also bring streaming radio and video, for example, Google Glass is built on top of the Android operating system for mobile phones.

When you add to this mix the creative output of billions of people, the possibilities are endless. From LOLCats to "Gangnam Style" to the Arab Spring, new media content is amusing, entertaining, and inspiring change around the world. New issues like cyberbullying, and the latest reconfigurations—such as augmented reality games (e.g., *Ingress*)—have also been included in this edition.

This is not to say that technology is lagging behind user behaviour or that issues arise only from social circumstances. Google Glass (privacy implications), 3D printers (gun parts being manufactured in the home), and low-cost robots (cleaning our houses, helping with surgery) are all examples of enabling technologies that humans are just starting to understand and use. We touch on these and many other aspects of new media in this second Canadian edition.

As a result, the book is considerably larger than the first Canadian edition, with longer chapters and plenty of new material. I have added boxes to address new media theorists, and a series of interviews with leading scholars of new media in Canada. In keeping with the pedagogical objectives of the first Canadian edition, I've also positioned the book as an explicitly pedagogical project, with chapter objectives, questions to ask yourself, discussion questions, and further reading included in all of the chapters. This isn't to pre-empt the work of instructors. Rather, I hope these elements contribute to their repertoire of material as they seek to animate the text for their students and guide the use of the book in lectures and tutorials. In this vein, debate questions were added in this edition. I hope they are useful to you. In most cases, the "Useful Websites" and "Further Readings" have been updated as well.

In this edition, I have added even more Canadian content and updated key elements. While Canadian readers are familiar with international trends and events in new media, it is sometimes more interesting and salient to see how these play out in the national, regional, and local scene. This book is explicitly and proudly Canadian in its approach, examples, and almost all of the case studies. Without making it parochial, I have tried to position this book as a Canadian exploration of new media. Some things, such as our specific regulatory and legal history in relation to new media, are distinct and require a specifically Canadian treatment, keeping in mind, of course, the international context in which all new media operate.

Other facets of new media (and the history of new media) are, in fact, Canadian contributions to the global environment. Despite its recent troubles, it can be argued that BlackBerry, for example, popularized smartphones in North America and changed the way business, government, and social life were conducted in this country, as well as around the world. The constantly in-touch executive, socialite, or student is both a caricature and a reality because of BlackBerry, a Canadian company. Reading about them, or Kelowna's Club Penguin, doesn't just bring the world of new media alive to Canadian students but—potentially—it can also inspire interest in the larger topic and demonstrate how Canadian new media inventions fit into global media empires.

Many of the updates to this edition came as a result of suggestions from reviewers as well as the faculty and students—including my own—who are the primary users of the book. And a tip of my hat has to go to the clever students who caught errors and omissions in the first version. You know who you are, and thank you! Keep those contributions coming in.

Although the revisions have been an extremely challenging task, I have been aided immeasurably in the process by a number of colleagues who have contributed to this book by participating in interviews, reviewing drafts, and making suggestions. Jon Festinger, and Kimberly Voll, colleagues at the Centre for Digital Media, helped with suggestions for Chapter 6 on games, as did former Ph.D. student and newly appointed professor at Loyola University, Florence Chee. William Leiss, Philip Savage, Charles Davis, and Jeremy Shtern also contributed greatly by participating in interviews.

As before, the team at Oxford University Press Canada has been wonderful. In particular, I appreciate the excellent guidance from developmental editor Tanuja Weerasooriya, who ensured that the project stayed on track both from a time and blueprint perspective. I could not have finished this book on time while taking on the responsibilities of a new job without the enormous support of my wife, Deborah Kirby, who has been extremely supportive of the late nights and weekends that went into this project. Many of those late nights and weekends were productive, and even fun, because of my secret weapon in completing this manuscript: my daughter (and English major), Eleanor Smith. Her editorial assistance made this project possible. Without her, I would still be back at Chapter 2, wondering how I would get organized. All errors and omissions fall to me, of course, and I encourage you to call me on them: smith@thecdm.ca.

Richard Smith, Vancouver
September 2013

Introduction

This second Canadian edition of *New Media* is intended to be used in undergraduate courses on new media in a range of disciplines in the arts and social sciences, including (mass) communication, journalism, sociology, and anthropology. It could also be used as a supplement to a business or marketing course, given our attention to innovation and the business setting for new media. We don't assume a great deal of prior knowledge about theories, approaches, or technology and we attempt to cover new media from a variety of perspectives.

Throughout the text, we pay special attention to the role of the new "read-write-Web" or Web 2.0 as it is commonly called, which has both captured the popular imagination via sites like Facebook (http://facebook.com) and demonstrated the political and economic power of new media as we saw in the use of YouTube (http://youtube.com) videos following the 2010 G20 protests in Toronto, the Idle No More campaigns, or the incredibly successful Old Spice videos. We do not sugar coat new media, however, and show the negative as well as the positive cultural, social, environmental, and civil rights implications of the widespread adoption of new media tools. Our objective is to help readers become critical and analytical users and students of new media.

The first chapter asks the question, "What is new for society in new media?" Then we look at the role of new media in social change. New media is already deeply embedded in the debates, processes, and practicalities of our society. We explore new media as an outcome "convergence"—the process by which media technologies, industries, and services are merging—through changes in computing and communications networks and content. Although convergence is important, we attempt to put these changes in perspective and recognize that long-standing social, cultural, political, and economic forces remain significant factors affecting technological change. We then examine the characteristics of digital information and how those characteristics result in interactive communication and communication practices. Since the Internet is one of the most important new media forms of the late twentieth and early twenty-first century, we review the history of the Internet, its social implications, the recent growth of Web 2.0, and the importance of search engines. We also look at the importance of online encyclopedias, status updates, friend lists, and online video, in the context of a growing and globalizing technology. Chapter 1 concludes with a review of the implications of convergence and Web 2.0 for the creation and consumption of media content.

Chapter 2 provides the historical context for new media. Connections are drawn between current network technologies and prior inventions such as the telegraph, radio, and television. Although the path has been twisty sometimes, ever since we have been able to send messages without moving physical objects (the first telegraph), that immediacy has forever changed our expectations about communication media. With new capabilities came new institutions and social arrangements and these have proven to be foundational and influential for subsequent generations of media. Journalism, politics, and business were all transformed by their use of the telegraph and the telephone, as Chapter 2 demonstrates. The radio and, later, television provided a testing ground for key elements of new media and in particular the business model in which the content could be accessed for free, if one was willing to accept a little bit of advertising. We conclude the chapter with a brief discussion of the educational potential of earlier new media.

Chapter 3 is premised on the notion that a well-rounded view of the role and effects of new media in society can only be gleaned by considering a number of perspectives. For this reason, the chapter presents several theoretical approaches to new media while providing insight into their strengths and weaknesses. For example, we critically examine technological determinism, and point out its weaknesses while acknowledging that existing technological configurations inevitably influence society once they are widely adopted. Particular emphasis is placed on a "social shaping" perspective, in which groups and individuals are understood as able to influence how media is used and how it evolves. We explore some of the hype that surrounds new media and try to understand why science-driven messages are so compelling, while critically examining both the overly positive and the unnecessarily negative (frequently deterministic) portrayals of the effects of new media. Both cultural context and media forms are explored as ways of understanding new media, along with social, psychological, and economic explanations.

Chapter 4 focuses on mobile technologies as a vital and important part of new media today. In this chapter, we explore the mobile phone and related technologies, such as the tablet computer, from historical, technological, and economic perspectives. Some of the key technical features of mobile phones are explained and examined with an eye to making this sometimes mysterious technology more comprehensible. We also look at how social media services such as Facebook or Twitter are deployed on mobile devices, and the implications of location on these services. We examine, as well, some of the cultural impacts of mobile new media technologies as well as social, health, and environmental implications.

Chapter 5 is about social networks and the use of these networks for the production of culture and cultural goods. In the first half of the chapter, we consider the concept of social networks and how these enable a culture of mass participation—a "participatory culture." We also examine how these networks enable and enhance many other social processes. Although networks are not new phenomena, they are enhanced and extended by new media and we explore this process in more detail here. Networks are economic and political as well as social phenomena and, given their importance, it is not surprising that new research methods have arisen to study them. One of these, social network analysis, is considered in detail from both a practical and an historical point of view. Social network theories are also critically examined in this chapter. In the second part of Chapter 5, we look at social production and participatory culture as it has emerged in information and communication technology enhanced social networks.

In Chapter 6, we present a rounded and broad examination of computer games. Game play and the game industry are a prime example of new media in the twenty-first century. We examine games as a significant part of popular culture, extending beyond their economic impact. We also look at how the immersive nature and rapid pace of change places online and computer games at the centre of debates about gender roles, culture, childhood experiences, and intellectual property. We take a look at the economics of the game industry, including its dependence on subcontractors. This is followed by a consideration of the tension between the creative side of the business and the investment side, as well as the complex value chain between production and distribution. In the last part of the chapter, we look at some of the most significant gaming developments in the early years of the twenty-first century, such as the role of producer-consumers "modding" games, mobile gaming, smaller indie game studios, and free-to-play games. We conclude the chapter with a discussion of the political economy of the game industry, as well as a look at the game industry in Canada.

Chapter 7 is about the creative industries generally and how digital media has accelerated, broadened, and deepened the industrialization of creativity. We begin with an examination of the concept of creativity and, especially, under what circumstances it can flourish. We next consider the notion of "creative industries" and how and why they have become a policy objective of cities, provinces/states, and countries around the world. The rise of a creative economy, creative cities, and the creative class, both as reality and as vision or ideal, is considered and debated.

In Chapter 8, we look at the global knowledge economy and new media as a powerful force for globalization. Here, we explain the complexity of globalization and review some of the main criticisms of these developments as part of an overall knowledge economy. We examine both technological change and its role in the economy as well as more practical matters such as e-commerce strategies and the role that new media play in "disintermediation" in order to better understand the forces that drive the global knowledge economy. We look at the nature of digital goods and how they have disrupted many industries that relied on the expense of reproducing and transporting ideas (e.g., news, music, movies) for a competitive advantage and now find themselves without their former basis for extracting value. In this context, we return to some of the themes on creativity from Chapter 7 and examine the creative economy more closely from a business perspective. Here, we examine topics such as technological innovation and innovators' dilemmas.

In Chapter 9, we examine law, policy, and governance for new media, and then consider the interesting and sometimes difficult issues that have arisen in a world in which two of the foundational principles of law—property and the state—are significantly altered by digital and global information flows. In the absence of a strong legal foundation for new media, nations have attempted to use policy initiatives to establish priorities and create programs that will boost the power and role of their own citizens and corporations in the use of information and communication technologies. Governments have also intervened by subsidy or procurement strategies. We examine these issues along with implications for copyright and property rights, and the open-source software movement. While it is still early days in the interpretation of the 2012 ruling by the Supreme Court of Canada and 2012 revisions to the Copyright Act in Canada, it appears that *users' rights* are getting greater recognition in this country.

In Chapter 10, the concluding chapter, we consider how new media are evolving in the early 2000s. We look at several additional topics that are particularly relevant in considering the continued evolution of new media, including the future of mobility, the growing presence of an *Internet of things*, and our reliance on the Internet as something that is always on and always there. We also return to look further at social media and their implications for social interaction, whether for personal, business, political, or other purposes, and we review in some detail the surveillance implications of our networked, digital new media. New and digital media are moving beyond the screens and out into the world through innovations such as 3D printing and scanning, robotics, and augmented reality. These topics, as well as some emerging themes for new media scholars, are part of the Chapter 10 conclusion.

Abbreviations

3G	third generation (in the context of mobile telephony)
4G	fourth generation (mobile phones, Internet protocol based)
ACTA	Anti-counterfeiting Trade Agreement
API	applications programming interface
ARPA	Advanced Research Projects Agency
ASCII	American Standard Code for Information Interchange
B2B	business to business
B2C	business to consumer
BBC	British Broadcasting Corporation
CBC	Canadian Broadcasting Corporation
CC	Creative Commons
CCI	creative industries and innovation
CDS	Center for Digital Storytelling
CED	Committee for Economic Development
CERN	Conseil Européen pour la Recherche Nucléaire (European Organisation for Nuclear Research)
CMC	computer-mediated communication
CRTC	Canadian Radio-television and Telecommunications Commission
CWTA	Canadian Wireless Telecommunications Association
DIY	do-it-yourself
DRM	digital-rights management
EA	Electronic Arts
EFF	Electronic Frontier Foundation
ESA	Entertainment Software Alliance
EULA	end-user licensing agreement
FPS	first-person shooter (video-game type)
GATS	General Agreement on Trade in Services
GII	global information infrastructure
GPS	global positioning system
GUI	graphical user interface
HTML	hypertext markup language
HTTP	hypertext transfer protocol
ICANN	Internet Corporation for Assigned Names and Numbers
ICTS	information and communication technologies
IHAC	Information Highway Advisory Council
IP	Internet protocol
IPR	intellectual property rights
ISOC	Internet Society
IT	information technology
ITCP	IT-related creative practice
ITU	International Telecommunications Union
LAN	local area network
LTE	long-term evolution (mobile phone technology)
MIT	Massachusetts Institute of Technology

MMOG	massive multiplayer online game	**RSS**	really simple syndication; rich site summary
MOO	multi-user object-oriented domain	**RTS**	real-time strategy
		SMS	short message services
MMORPG	massively multiplayer online role playing game	**TCP/IP**	transmission control protocol/Internet protocol
NAFTA	North American Free Trade Agreement	**TRIPS**	trade-related aspects of intellectual property rights
NCSA	National Center for Supercomputer Application	**UNCTAD**	United Nations Committee on Trade, Aid and Development
NES	Nintendo Entertainment System	**WAN**	wide area network
NII	national information infrastructure	**WI-FI**	a trade name for wireless networking devices (often thought to stand for "wireless fidelity," although this is not the case)
NTIA	National Telecommunication and Information Administration		
P2P	peer to peer	**WIPO**	World Intellectual Property Organization
PBS	Public Broadcasting Service	**WSIS**	World Summit on the Information Society
PDA	personal digital assistant		
RFID	radio frequency identification	**WTO**	World Trade Organization
RPG	role-playing game	**WWW**	World Wide Web

1

Introduction to New Media

Questions to Consider

- How is communication mediated by technology? Why is this significant?

- Why is it important to think about nuanced understandings of what *new media* means?

- How can the "digital divide" be variously understood and what are the causes and consequences of such divides?

- In what ways is globalization significant when thinking about new media?

- Why do you think the Internet and Web 2.0 have become so popular? What are some benefits and drawbacks of this popularity?

Chapter Outline

In this chapter, we consider what society finds novel in new media and what role new media plays in wider social change, as it is already deeply embedded in the debates, processes, and practicalities of our society. We explore how new media is an outcome of the digitization of content, which has enabled **convergence**—the process by which media technologies, industries, and services merge—through changes in computing, communication networks, and content. Although convergence is important, we attempt to put these changes in perspective and recognize that long-standing social, cultural, political, and economic factors remain important and mitigate and filter the impact of technological change. This chapter explains the characteristics of digital information and how those characteristics result in a particular type of communication that can be summed up as **interactive.** We examine the Internet as one of the most important new media forms of the late twentieth and early twenty-first centuries, and review its history, social implications, and recent growth into **Web 2.0,** focusing on the role of search engines. We also look at the importance of online encyclopedias, status updates, friend lists, and online video, in the context of a growing and globalizing technology. The chapter concludes with a deeper examination of the implications of convergence on how we create and consume media content and the role of Web 2.0 in this process.

Why "New" Media?

In any discussion of new media, a question that needs to be addressed is why some media are considered "new." There is a temptation to simply list the latest developments in media technologies and call these new. Yet this approach is inadequate, partly because the rate of change in media technologies, services, and uses is so rapid that any list of this sort will quickly become dated. It also conflates what is new with what is novel. At one extreme, "newness" can simply refer to updates of long-established commodities, as when car manufacturers reveal their "new" line of vehicles for the coming year, television networks present the "newest" sitcom or reality show, or mobile-phone companies announce their latest model that is jewel-encrusted or has a relocated camera.

Such an approach is also problematic because media technologies now considered to be "old," such as film, radio, and television, were themselves once new (Gitelman and Pingree 2003; Marvin 1988). To many of those born after the 1980s, whom Marc Prensky (2001) terms "digital natives," even the idea of a world without the Internet, email, mobile phones, computer games, digital cameras, and instant text messaging is simply preposterous: only the folks on reality TV shows such as *Big Brother* and *Survivor* lack access to such devices, and that is their choice. Indeed, in developed countries, networked personal computers and other digital media technologies are now so common in our work, our home lives, and the many everyday interactions we have with each other, that they are ceasing to be "new" in any meaningful sense of the term. As a result, any approach to new media that simply catalogues the technologies themselves, and fails to ask broader questions about their contextual use and their social and cultural impacts, ignores the central question of why there is a need to look at new media in the first place.

There is a need, as Sonia Livingstone notes, to ask, "What's new for society about the new media?" rather than simply, "What are the new media?" (1999: 60) This takes us to the larger question of whether, and how, technologies can act as factors in wider social change while being already embedded in a social context (Cowan 1997; Flichy 2005a). In *Novum Organum*, first published in 1620, the English philosopher Francis Bacon proposed that three discoveries had been central to marking out the period in which he lived as one that was dramatically different from those preceding it:

> It is well to observe the force and effect and consequences of discoveries. These are to be seen nowhere more conspicuously than in those three that were unknown to the ancients, and of which the origin, though recent, is obscure: namely, printing, gunpowder, and the magnet. For these three have changed the whole face and state of things throughout the world; the first in literature, the second in warfare, the third in navigation; whence have followed innumerable changes. (Graham 1999: 26–7)

One way that *new media* has been defined—in previous editions of this book (Flew 2002, 2005a; Flew and Smith 2011) and elsewhere—has involved the combination of the three *C*s:

1. computing and information technology (IT);
2. communications networks; and
3. content and digitized media, arising out of another process, a fourth C, convergence (cf. Barr 2000; Miles 1997; Rice 1999).

Convergent media can be seen as combining computing, communications, and media content in the way shown in Figure 1.1.

Convergence

Convergence can mean many things. In one sense, it refers to the interlinking of computing and IT, communications networks, and media content that occurred with the development and popularization of the Internet. It also refers to the convergent products, services, and activities that have emerged in digital media space. So, for example, we not only have media companies that own Internet companies, but also television shows with complementary websites, all available on devices such as mobile

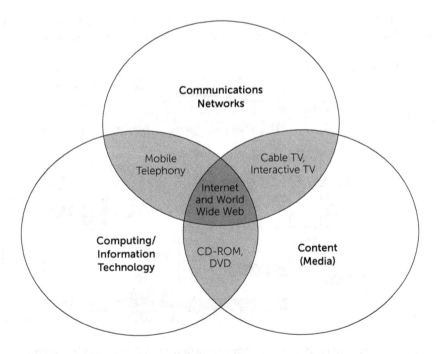

Figure 1.1 The Three Cs of Convergent Media

Source: Barr (2000).

phones and computers, which have historically been dedicated to conversations and calculations, respectively. Many see this as simply the tip of the iceberg, since all aspects of institutional activity and social life—from art to business, government to journalism, health to education—are increasingly conducted in an interactive digital media environment, across a plethora of networked information and communication technology (ICT) devices. This ubiquity, the possibility that one might speak of convergence from three quite different perspectives (technology, services, and industries) makes the term not only "slippery" but also prone to confusion among new media writers and students. The careful reader is wise to pay attention to which of the three (or which combinations of these aspects) is being referred to when reading about convergence.

A recent report by the Canadian Radio-television and Telecommunications Commission (CRTC) shows that "in 2008, over 80% of communications revenues were generated by converged companies offering both broadcasting and telecommunications services" (2009: i). In the fall of 2012, the CRTC considered an application for the merger of Bell and Astral, two giants of both conventional and digital media. Although the proposal was initially rejected by the CRTC, the merger was approved in June 2013, following some amendments. The proponents of this deal argued that it was necessary to merge their companies to compete in a globally converged industry.[1] Figure 1.2 illustrates how convergence is situated within a larger dynamic of telecommunications operating platforms. It should be noted, however, that interactivity and the complexity of convergence are not fully captured here; both of these are discussed later in the chapter.

For writers such as Thomas Friedman (2005), convergence is in turn generating a global "flat earth," where activities conducted through digital media can occur in any

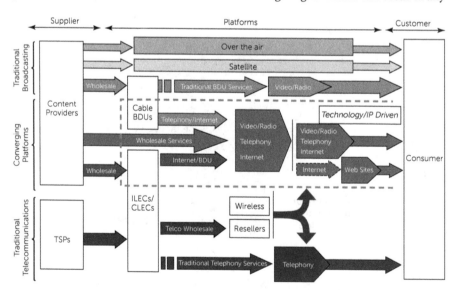

Figure 1.2 Broadcasting and Telecommunications Operating Platforms

Source: Communications Monitoring Report 2009, p. 100. Canadian Radio-television and Telecommunications Commission, 2009. Reproduced with the permission of the Minister of Public Works and Government Services Canada, 2013.

part of the world. We note in Chapters 8 and 9 that there are reasons to question this claim, and that culture, policy, and other variables remain critical to the geographical location of new media activities, particularly with the shift to a global knowledge economy. Nevertheless, convergence opens up the possibility of much broader geographic reach in the production and consumption of media.

The second element of convergence is the morphing of devices (computers, mobile phones, televisions, etc.) as they become multi-purpose conduits for a range of activities involving digital media (Zetie 2004). For example, computers become telephones via Skype, mobile phones like the iPhone are now major platforms for playing games, and new generations of Internet-enabled televisions have acquired multimedia capabilities through widgets that display online content.

New media can also be thought of as digital media. **Digital** media are forms of media content that combine and integrate data, text, sound, and images of all kinds; are stored in digital formats; and are increasingly distributed through networks such as those based on broadband fibre-optic cables, satellites, and microwave transmission systems. Such media, or forms of digital information, have the characteristics of being

- manipulable: digital information is easily changeable and adaptable, at all stages of creation, storage, delivery, and use;
- networkable: digital information can be shared and exchanged between large numbers of users simultaneously, and across enormous distances;
- dense: very large amounts of digital information can be stored in small physical spaces (e.g., USB flash drives) or on network servers;
- compressible: the amount of capacity that digital information takes up on any network can be reduced dramatically through compression, and decompressed when needed; and,
- impartial: digital information carried across networks is indifferent to how it is represented, who owns or created it, or how it is used.[2]

This still leaves open, however, the question of what is new for society from the new media. In this text, we take a broad social focus toward new media and stress the need to be aware of the importance of how communication is mediated by technology. We follow Lievrouw and Livingstone (2005: 2) in their observation that any approach to thinking about new media needs to take account of three elements: (1) the artifacts or devices that enable and extend our ability to communicate; (2) the communication activities and practices we engage in to develop and use these devices; and (3) the social arrangements and organizations that form around these devices and practices.

Lievrouw and Livingstone also make the point that these three elements should not be thought of as linear or layered—technologies influencing communications practices, in turn shaping social arrangements and institutions—but rather as constituting an ensemble characterized by "dynamic links and interdependencies among artefacts, practices, and social arrangements that ... guide our analytic focus" (2005: 3). In this way, critical analysis of new media also has wider implications for how the media are studied more generally, since media studies as it emerged in the twentieth century understood media production, texts, and audiences as discrete forms, following a linear model of different moments in the media production-consumption cycle.

In practical terms, what differentiates old media from new media, when you take into account the five characteristics of digital media listed above and Lievrouw and Livingstone's "three elements," (artifacts, activities, and arrangements) is that new media are interactive in a way that previous media were not usually thought to be. Old and traditional media, however, are still the basis for much of the conceptual apparatus that we bring to the media both as audience and producers. We regularly see new media undertakings that reconceive, or **remediate** in Bolter and Grusin's language (Bolter and Grusin 2000), existing media forms.

Online and console-based games, websites, and instant-messaging services, for example, all extend our abilities, change our practices, and transform social arrangements through significant levels of interactivity. Media technologies that were previously dominated by a one-way flow of content (newspapers, film, radio, television) are giving way to media forms that are inherently and profoundly interactive and two-way.

While interactivity has been around a long time (telegraph, telephone, and point-to-point radio), its use was limited to individual, mostly one-to-one conversations. New media take the power of the mass media to aggregate large groups and take the ability of interactive media to involve participants and blend these as never before. It is this blend that makes new media distinctive from previous media forms; it is also why the power of new media is not simply a matter of newness or specific technologies.

Internet History

The concept of new media is integrally bound up with the history of the Internet and the Web. While convergence has now spread across a range of platforms and devices, it was the emergence and mass popularization of the Internet that heralded the rise of new media, bringing together computing and information technologies, communications networks, and media content. It should be noted here that the Internet refers both to

1. a technical infrastructure of computers and other digital devices (e.g., servers, routers) permanently connected through high-speed telecommunications networks; and
2. the forms of content, communication, and information sharing that occur through these networks.

In their analysis of the social implications of the Internet, sociologists DiMaggio, Hargittai, Neuman, and Robinson define the Internet as "the electronic network of networks that links people and information through computers and other digital devices allowing person-to-person communication and information retrieval" (DiMaggio et al. 2001: 307). In 1995, the Internet Society (ISOC) developed a more technical definition, which resolved that the Internet

> refers to the global information system that: (i) is logically linked together by a globally unique address space based on the Internet Protocol (IP) or its subsequent extensions/follow-ons; (ii) is able to support communications using the Transmission Control Protocol/Internet Protocol (TCP/IP) suite or its subsequent extensions/follow-ons,

and/or other IP-compatible protocols; and (iii) provides, uses or makes accessible, either publicly or privately, high level services layered on the communications and related infrastructure described herein. (Leiner et al. 2003)

A very key point about the history of the Internet is that it not only developed in parallel with the general development of personal computers and other devices for digital information processing and retrieval but its history is both a history of the common networking protocols for the transfer of digital information and a history of systems for the publication, organization, and distribution of this information.[3]

The technical history of the Internet has been well documented and will not be discussed in great detail here; however, it is worth reviewing several elements of this history. First, while the commitment to developing an integrated communications network arose in the United States as a consequence of the Cold War with the Soviet Union, the priorities of the Advanced Research Projects Agency (ARPA)—established in 1957 after the Soviets launched the Sputnik satellite—were arguably driven as much by the desire of the US scientific community to perfect mechanisms of communicating with one another as by the demands of the military.[4] The most significant development to come from ARPA in the 1960s was packet switching. **Packet switching** meant that long messages could be broken down into smaller "packets"; messages could be rerouted if there was a blockage at one message route or point of connection between two computers; and messages would be sent in an asynchronous mode, meaning that the message would not come to the receiver until some time after it was originally sent. Not only did packet switching overcome limitations of the telephone system, such as the possibility of blocked access because of heavy use by others, but it also established the principle of a decentralized network with no single point from which control can be exercised, which has been so central to the Internet's development (Gillies and Cailliau 2000: 18–25). With the establishment of ARPANET as a national long-distance computer network in the United States in 1969, packet switching became central to this network, with the transfer of electronic mail being perhaps the major communications innovation arising from this development. In 1972, ARPANET demonstrated to the public its capacity to send and receive data at the International Conference on Computer Communication in Washington, DC, where the world's first email was sent—although it wasn't called this at the time (Hassan 2004: 13).

Another landmark in Internet technical history was the development of a common set of networking protocols, which enabled researchers in the various local area networks (LANs) to communicate with one another, through the interconnection of these LANs within a wide area network (WAN). The major breakthrough came in 1974, when Robert Kahn and Vinton Cerf proposed a common switching protocol that could meet the needs of an open-architecture network; this came to be known as TCP/IP (transmission control protocol/Internet protocol). The quasi-privatization of ARPANET in 1983, which allowed universities and commercial interests to play a larger role on the network and which marked the birth of the Internet we know today, was premised on the adoption of TCP/IP as a common interconnection protocol. In sharp contrast to other media, the Internet would become both a public and a global communications medium, as all computers and computer networks could communicate with one another in a common language, whether they were Apples, PCs, or mainframes, regardless of the local or national computing network they were operating within. As Internet use spread in the 1980s from outside its core constituency of the US government and military, scientists, and defence contractors, the importance of TCP/IP being established as a common Internet protocol would be of increasing significance to more and more people worldwide.

The development of the Web in the 1990s, however, was a major advancement that made the Internet what it is today. While developments such as TCP/IP and packet switching provided the means by which networks could connect with networks, and computers could connect with computers, the question of how people could connect with other people through such electronic networks had not received as much attention. The conception of the Web by Tim Berners-Lee in 1989, and its development by Berners-Lee and colleagues at CERN (Conseil Européen pour la Recherche Nucléaire, or the European Organization for Nuclear Research) from 1991 onwards would dramatically change the communications capabilities of the Internet. The significance of developing the Web became even more apparent in 1992 when Marc Andreesen of the National Center for Supercomputer Applications (NCSA) developed Mosaic as the first popular web browser. Andreesen went on to become one of the founders of Netscape Communication, which developed Netscape, the first major commercial web browser, in 1994. Microsoft quickly followed suit in 1995 with the release of its Internet Explorer browser, as part of its Windows 95 software suite, to much fanfare and to the sounds of the Rolling Stones' "Start Me Up."

The ability to use web browsers such as Netscape and Internet Explorer to access online content through the Web saw the mass popularization of the Internet, with the number of Internet users worldwide growing by over 1300 per cent between 1994 and 1998 (see Table 1.1 on page 14). Several features of the Web were particularly important in this popularization. First, it allowed for the display of colourful pictures, music, and audio as well as data and text, and introduced multimedia capability to the Internet. Second, it was based on **hypertext** principles. Hypertext allows for the linking of information, where links from one information source provide simple point-and-click access to related information available from other sources. The concept of hypertext had circulated in various domains since the publication of Vannevar Bush's article "As We May Think" in 1945, which proposed the development of a computational machine (the "Memex") that not only could store vast amounts of information but also could allow users to create ancillary "thought trails" (Bush 1996). Ted Nelson's experimentations with hypertext through Project Xanadu in the 1960s and early '70s pointed to the possibilities of interconnected electronic writing, and both the French Minitel system (developed as a national teletext system in 1983) and the Hypercard storage system (available on all Apple computers from 1987 to well into the 1990s) drew on hypertext principles in different ways. The value of hypertext became even more apparent with the development not only of web browsers such as Netscape Navigator and Microsoft Explorer but also of directories and search engines such as Yahoo!, Alta Vista, and Google, which provided vast and simple-to-use databases that gave users easy access to information stored on the Internet. Third, the Web was associated with the development of both the common hypertext transfer protocol (HTTP), which provided a platform-independent means of interconnection between websites, and hypertext markup language (HTML) as a relatively straightforward means of writing source code for the Web. As a result, a much wider range of people could become producers, as well as consumers, of content on the Web. This trend would gain momentum as commercial software for developing web pages became increasingly available—such as Macromedia Dreamweaver and Microsoft Front Page—and this has been further accelerated by the development of programs associated with what is known as Web 2.0 (see pages 21–3 for more on the nature and impact of Web 2.0).

The People behind the Internet and the Applications Side of Internet History

It is tempting to think of the Internet in terms of its signature technologies (switches, fibre-optic cables) and software (TCP/IP, SMTP, DNS)—and certainly these played a key role in the making of the Internet, but there is more to the story. Internet technologies enabled information to move from place to place and paved the way for email and computer sharing, but these capabilities alone were not sufficiently attractive to the world at large to account for the mass popularization of the Internet.

The Internet graduated from being a computer network akin to a highway, to a "place" with attractions along the way, in part because key entrepreneurs and their companies helped create valuable online destinations for everyday users. Many of these destinations allowed people to consume and share new media. Some of these sites provided services—like the search engine Google (or, before it, Alta Vista and Yahoo!)—or hosted users' content, like Wikipedia and YouTube. To fully appreciate the history of the Internet, it is important to consider some of the remarkable people involved in its creation and their significant contributions.

Cataloguing and Searching

At first, the problem of finding things on the Internet was a non-issue because the only stuff on there was put there for one user by another one. Typically, one user would send a counterpart an Internet address—perhaps in the form of login information to a file transfer protocol (FTP) server—and then whatever had been placed at that Internet address could be retrieved via the expertise of both users. There was little content available or even of interest to anonymous and non-expert users.

This all changed with the arrival of the Web.[5] Very quickly, content proliferated and finding something online became an enormous challenge. People tried to keep up, at first by saving and sharing links to interesting Internet websites, but this was both overwhelming and inadequate. Some organizations—perhaps recalling the challenges that a profusion of new products meant for retailers at the beginning of the twentieth century—decided to set up catalogues of all these new websites. They would turn the catalogues into a business by selling advertising alongside the listings. One of the most successful of these, and still in business nearly 20 years later—a remarkable achievement in the dot-com era—is Yahoo! (with its signature exclamation mark).

Yahoo! was built by a couple of Internet entrepreneurs—the classic story of college students with a great idea (founders Jerry Yang and David Filo were engineering students at Stanford University when they started their Web project)—a site that would bring together all kinds of useful website links, categorize them, and let the user either flip through them by heading or search within the entire set. This latter feature quickly became the most popular feature and the company focused on it, while adding additional properties (email, picture sharing, and so on), either by building them on their own or buying promising young companies. For example, Yahoo! purchased the famous picture-sharing site Flickr in 2005, which was once a small start-up in Vancouver.[6] More recently, Facebook's purchase of Instagram for more than USD $1 billion in early 2012 is another example of the way in which companies grow through acquisition.[7]

Searching for things, as anyone who has lost their keys knows all too well, can be a tedious business at best. Until recently, humans coped with disorder by devising, implementing, and sticking to a plan of organization (Weinberger 2008)—or at least trying to. If you have not yet filed your latest bank statements or income tax forms, you are not alone. Once we leave the realm of physical objects, however, searching online proves to be remarkably efficient, even if things are not filed properly. After all, computers don't complain about the humdrum tasks assigned to them. Searching, though, is not a simple task and doing it well proved to be the making of another key Internet entrepreneurial duo: the founders of Google. Sergey Brin and Larry Page, also college students, sought to help computers arrive at better answers to people's search questions. Brin and Page did such a good job of it that Google became one of the most well-known companies in the world and it outperforms all other search engines.

Search engines are doubtlessly important from a technical and ease-of-use perspective, but they have profound social, political, and cultural implications as well. Alex Halavais's 2008 book, *Search Engine Society*, tackles these important questions and, in particular, examines how search engines affect politics and privacy. The search engine, as Halavais concludes, is an important tool in the exercise of power in an information-rich society. For example, it has become common practice that the first step to finding something online is to *google* it. For many people, online searching is now second nature and, rather than bookmarking or remembering where they have been, users search again and again ("re-finding," as Halavais puts it). In this way, users are allowing search engines to determine the best path to navigate, with profound implications for sites that do not rank highly in a search engine.

Encyclopedias

For more than a hundred years, average people have looked to an encyclopedia for answers to everyday topics. The multi-volume family encyclopedia set was a resource for young people doing homework assignments and helped settle many a kitchen table argument. Not many people, however, would have imagined that they would participate in the creation of an encyclopedia. Early on in the history of the Internet, it became evident that computers and networks would be a good way to distribute the type of knowledge that encyclopedias contained. In fact, even before the Internet was in widespread use, Microsoft founded a company devoted to selling encyclopedias on CD-ROM.

For Jimmy Wales, founder of Wikipedia, putting an encyclopedia online seemed like an obvious thing to do, but how to get started? His first attempt seemed promising from a technical point of view but it took too long to get the encyclopedia entries through the editorial process. In frustration, he decided to open up the submission and review system, using a new set of tools known as "wiki" technology. The rest, as they say, is history. People loved creating, editing, and, most of all, having access to the encyclopedia entries.

While there have been (and continue to be) controversies over the validity or reliability of Wikipedia, it has survived both serious scientific scrutiny and public acceptance and has become one of the most widely used sources of information on the Internet. Thousands of Wikipedia entries are created each day and tens of thousands undergo constant revision. Although Wikipedia's very popularity has also made it a target for pranks and attacks, the "many editors" approach of the wiki software mitigates such problems. When necessary, the managers of the site lock down a Wikipedia entry, but for the most part, the site is maintained by the goodwill of many hundreds of thousands of amateur experts who strive for a neutral point of view.

(Amateur) Filmmaking

While the amateur bird watcher or automobile enthusiast might be inclined to write an online article about their favourite raptor or roadster, the Internet also has drawn the attention of those working with audiovisual content. Although the Internet was launched and initially functioned as a largely text-based medium, images and videos began to appear online in the twenty-first century. Much of that content came from home users who created so-called **user-generated content.**

Posting video online was difficult for amateurs until the arrival of video-clip sharing on YouTube. Now owned by Google, YouTube was also started by a small team of enthusiasts who famously uploaded a video of a trip to the zoo to start their Web-based service.[8] The team of three former PayPal employees (Steve Chen, Chad Hurley, and Jawed Karim) launched the service in February 2005 and sold it, less than two years later, for USD$1.65 billion. The videos on YouTube (as with the textual contributions on Wikipedia, although mainly less serious, and frequently silly or inane) can be enormously popular, becoming in some instances among the most viewed images in history. Justin Bieber's "Baby," for example, had more than 880 million views[9] by August 2013.[10]

Sites like YouTube make the circulation of amateur video much easier, but the creation of such video in the first place is the outcome of a downward spiral in the cost of recording, editing, and compressing audiovisual material. As recently as the mid-1990s, creating video content was expensive and cumbersome, and, once created, it was confined to tape or film archives, difficult and expensive to duplicate and distribute. The rise of low-cost digital video recorders, coupled with staggering leaps in the processing power of personal computers, particularly in the area of graphic processing capabilities, has made the raw material of sites like YouTube something that can be accomplished by just about every Internet citizen. In recent years, the addition of video recording capabilities to mobile telephones has resulted in a second explosion of videos uploaded and circulated online, often with explosive (literally) content. In fact, the distribution of videos from the July 2005 bombing in the London Underground (a.k.a. the Tube) is considered a turning point in both the awareness and acceptance of amateur video as a record of serious events, and not just the results of frat parties and pet tricks.[11]

Status/Friends

There was a time when the word *friend* was not used as a verb and *following* someone had a very different connotation from what it does today. Social media sites such as Facebook and Twitter—not to mention Instagram, Pinterest, and LinkedIn—have not only redefined the language used in communicating with others online, but they have also become hubs for socializing, political organizing, and commercial promotions. With more than a billion members by the fall of 2012,[12] Facebook was by far the largest online community, and it continues to grow rapidly. Although controversies have flared up from time to time over photographs or comments inadvertently shared, or inadequate or ill-understood privacy policies, the site that founder Mark Zuckerberg envisioned as a place to help people "understand the world around them" remains relevant and integral to a broad spectrum of users, from students to senior citizens.[13]

Facebook's assertion that its mission is to serve its customers first is not uncommon on the Internet. A claim of working for the public good is typical of Internet companies, including Google's famous claim that they will 'not be evil.' Along the way to "aiding understanding" or doing an Internet search, however, companies such as Facebook have spawned an entire industry of add-ons, applications, and linkages to other online software that generates considerable revenue. On Facebook, people can play Scrabble, work a farm, send each other (virtual) gifts, and spend a great deal of money. The tractor sales in the Facebook application FarmVille, according to *Fortune* magazine, exceed annual tractor sales—in numbers, if not revenue—in the United States by a large margin (purportedly 500,000 a day versus 5000 a year for John Deere, one of the largest manufacturers).[14] Selling virtual tractors for USD $20 each is a good business to be in, and Zynga, the creator of FarmVille and other similar games, reportedly made more than USD $500 million in 2010.

Zynga's challenges since 2011—its stock has tumbled lately, and FarmVille in particular is not as popular as it was back then—form an interesting footnote and highlight several key differences between real-world and online businesses. Online businesses change much more rapidly, and they are subject to upheavals and transformations (or even disappearances). While farming is an industry that has changed greatly over the last 200 years, it remains a huge part of the Canadian economy. It is not a fad, and it is too complicated for any one player to eliminate. Zynga's FarmVille, on the other hand, faced dwindling popularity with some people calling it, and the social games category it epitomized, a kind of fad. More importantly, Zynga's business relationship with Facebook changed dramatically. The terms of how they interacted with the Facebook user base and the Facebook "credits" system evolved over time, often as a result of unilateral decisions made by Facebook, with the result being that investors saw Zynga's stock price tumble in 2012. Questions were raised about the viability of Zynga. Then, in late 2012, the stock price rose again on news that the company was branching out from Facebook and entering the business of real-world gambling. The company that Zynga was in 2010 is being rapidly transformed.

Twitter was founded by Jack Dorsey, Biz Stone, and Evan Williams in March 2006 as a side project or spinoff from a company called Odeo. As with the YouTube pioneers, some of the principals had experience in previous social media sites, including Blogger (sold to Google). They used their expertise to create Twitter, one of the first popular sites in North America to have an explicitly mobile focus (the limitation to 140 characters was designed for messages to be sent and received as text messages—or SMS—on mobile phones), although it has since morphed into much more of an online service.

Facebook and Twitter each emphasize sharing brief updates, also known as "microblogging." Facebook currently gives you a small box with "What's on your mind?" (the question changes from time to time), while Twitter's Web interface has retained its simple look but eliminated any question/prompt and instead has a blank box with a countdown of how many characters are left as users enter text. Both services encourage the user to create, maintain, and build a social network. While they could be used to leave messages for the general public, those actively using them soon acquire friends (Facebook) or followers (Twitter) to share pithy remarks about life, the universe, and lunch ideas.

Each of these examples (Yahoo!, Wikipedia, YouTube, Facebook, Twitter) uses a different kind of sharing. People share their words to create knowledge (Wikipedia), their videos to entertain/enlighten (YouTube), and their statuses to create/maintain social networks (Facebook and Twitter). And while it may not be immediately obvious, people using Yahoo!'s or Google's search engines also contribute to the value of the search engine, with every search they do. You may not realize it, but every Google search (and the choices you make as a result of the search) provides a list of options, which are fed back into the Google search engine to enhance and refine the search performance. This "implicit work" is as much a form of user-generated content as that found with the other sites, if somewhat less obvious to the uninitiated.

The fact that we are working to create the very things we consume is not lost on critics of online services such as Google, Facebook, and Twitter. As with earlier criticism of how television viewers were "working" by watching advertisements and thereby learning to consume, Internet critics charge that not only are we working by viewing online ads, but we are also actually providing all of the content. Imagine if viewers had been compelled to produce their own television programs in the heyday of TV. In particular, critics such as José van Dijck note that this activity is "immaterial labour"—unpaid work that is captured and capitalized by the owners of the websites (van Dijck 2009: 50). Others, such as danah boyd and Oscar Gandy, have remarked on the considerable potential for privacy invasion by tools that encourage users to over-share through the use of default settings that are too wide open and the creation of a false sense of community and privacy through the requirement that users log in with a username and password (boyd 2008). Despite such criticisms, these sites continue to be enormously popular, in large part because they serve what seems to be a real need. Or, at least, people find them useful and entertaining.

The Growth of the Internet

The Internet has become the world's second-fastest growing medium, after mobile phones. It is estimated that as of 31 December 2011, there were 2.26 billion Internet users worldwide, having grown from 360 million users in 2000 (and 30.6 million users in 1995), or by almost 400 per cent over a 10-year period (Internet World Stats 2012). Table 1.1 indicates the number of Internet hosts worldwide, or the number of sites from which the Internet is accessed, as well as the rate of growth of Internet use over time.[15]

The incredible penetration rates and growth for mobile telephones and the Internet are blending in many countries, as more and more mobile phones are Internet enabled. Depending on how you define access (since many Internet services such as Twitter and Facebook are accessible in some fashion through SMS), one could use the mobile subscriber numbers in place of the Internet numbers. In this case, the number of people with some access to the Internet is approaching two-thirds of the world's population (ITU 2010).

Table 1.1 Estimated Internet Hosts Worldwide

Year	Estimated Number of Internet Hosts Worldwide	Annual Rate of Growth (%)
1991	376,000	—
1992	727,000	96.4
1993	1,313,000	80.6
1994	2,217,000	68.8
1995	4,852,000	188.5
1996	9,472,000	95.2
1997	16,416,000	73.3
1998	29,670,000	80.7
1999	43,230,000	45.7
2000	72,398,092	67.5
2001	109,574,429	51.3
2002	147,344,723	34.4
2003	171,638,297	16.5
2004	233,101,481	35.8
2005	317,646,084	36.2
2006	394,991,609	24.3
2007	433,193,199	9.7
2008	541,677,360	25.0
2009	625,226,456	15.4
2010	732,740,444	17.2
2011	818,374,269	11.7
2012	888,239,420	8.5

Note: Yearly figures are for January.
Source: Internet Systems Consortium, www.isc.org/services/survey/. Used with permission.

The Global Internet

In the 2000 US presidential election campaign, the Democratic Party candidate Al Gore (now a leader in raising awareness about global warming) made the claim that as vice-president during the Clinton Administration, he had "invented the Internet." Gore was roundly criticized for his hubris, particularly as the collaborative nature of the Internet meant that no single person could claim to have invented it, let alone a high-profile politician. Yet there is a subtext to Gore's claim that cannot be ignored. At the time of its mass popularization in the mid-1990s, the bulk of the major initiatives that led to the Internet's emergence came from the United States, its user base was predominantly North American, and the policies of the Clinton Administration—such as its promotion of the National Information Infrastructure (NII) and the Global Information Infrastructure (GII, modelled on the US NII)—played a key formative role in the way in which the Internet evolved globally.

Table 1.2 World Internet Usage and Population Statistics, 30 June 2012

World Regions	Population (2012 Est.)	Internet Users 31 Dec. 2000	Internet Users Latest Data	Penetration (% Population)	% Growth 2000–2012	Users % of Table
Africa	1,073,380,925	4,514,400	167,335,676	15.6	3,606.7	7.0
Asia	3,922,066,987	114,304,000	1,076,681,059	27.5	841.9	44.8
Europe	820,918,446	105,096,093	518,512,109	63.2	393.4	21.5
Middle East	223,608,203	3,284,800	90,000,455	40.2	2,639.9	3.7
North America	348,280,154	108,096,800	273,785,413	78.6	153.3	11.4
Latin America / Caribbean	593,688,638	18,068,919	254,915,745	42.9	1,310.8	10.6
Oceania / Australia	35,903,569	7,620,480	24,287,919	67.6	218.7	1.0
WORLD TOTAL	7,017,846,922	360,985,492	2,405,518,376	34.3	566.4	100.0

By contrast, the Internet today has a far more globally diverse user base (see Table 1.2). Of the estimated 2.267 billion Internet users in January 2012, the majority were from Asia and Europe, and the fastest growing regions for Internet take-up are the Middle East, Africa, and Latin America.

North America, with just 13.5 per cent of Internet users, is no longer the dominant player that it once was. This diversification has been growing for more than a decade, as the regional Internet populations have come to more closely resemble their absolute numbers in the world population figures. Although current statistics haven't taken the impact of mobile phones into account, the rise of the mobile Internet, accompanied by high and growing penetration rates for mobile phones in the developing world, suggests that mobile phones will be a factor in growing access to the Internet around the world. As the use of the Internet spreads beyond its origins in North America and Europe, two key issues have been highlighted: (1) the "digital divide" separating rich and poor; and (2) the importance of globalization as an economic and political force.

Digital Divide

During the late 1990s in the United States, the National Telecommunication and Information Administration (NTIA) used the term **digital divide** in its "Falling through the Net" reports on the differential access to networked personal computers. *Digital divide* has been defined as "the differential access to and use of the Internet according to gender, income, race, and location" (Rice 2002: 106). The term has also been important in the context of globalization, in clarifying the extent to which, as the United Nations observed in 1995, "more than half of the world's population lived more than two hours away from a telephone" (Couldry 2002: 186). Recent figures (2011) from the International Telecommunications Union (ITU) suggest that access to a phone is much more widespread in the twenty-first century than in the twentieth century. In fact, more than 85 per cent of the world's population (5.9 billion of the

7 billion people) subscribe to mobile cellular services (see www.itu.int/ITU-D/ict/ statistics). The developing world is not far behind the global figures, at 79 per cent. (see www.itu.int/ITU-D/ict/facts/2011/material/ICTFactsFigures2011.pdf).

In an overview of digital divide research, Norris (2001) proposes that it is important to distinguish between: (1) the "global divide," or differential Internet access between nations based on access to networked ICT infrastructures, computers, information transmission capacity, local website hosts etc.; and (2) the "social divide," or the gaps within nations in terms of access to the Internet as a means of social engagement. Critics of the digital divide concept argue that inequalities related to new media involve far more than access, but also include opportunities to participate effect-ively in online environments (Gandy 2002). Murdock and Golding (2004) argue that because the computing hardware, software, and skills required change so quickly, and opportunities to learn these new skills are unequally distributed, inequalities in the digital environment continue to reflect other sources of social inequality, such as those arising from income, occupation, or geographical location.

While these data provide considerable evidence of a global digital divide, they nonetheless also highlight how the world's Internet-using population is becoming more globally diverse. A good indicator of this is the change in the top 10 languages used on the Web. While English remains the dominant language, accounting for 26.8 per cent of languages used globally in 2011, Chinese has almost caught up (24.2 per cent in 2011). In terms of growth, the most rapid adoption is among Arabic and Russian speakers. There is also a **long tail** of languages, with more than 30 of them used by at least a million people on the Internet (see Figure 1.3).

Globalization and New Media

New media are often studied as part of one of the most widely discussed concepts in social theory today: **globalization**. *Globalization* is a term used to both describe and make sense of a series of interrelated processes, such as the rise of multinational cor-porations (MNCs); international production, trade, and financial systems; international communications flows; global movements of people and the increasingly multicul-tural nature of societies; developments in international law; global social movements (e.g., environmental activism); the development of international governmental organ-izations, regional trading blocs, and international non-governmental organizations; and global conflicts, such as the widespread war on terror after the 11 September 2001 attacks on the World Trade Center and the Pentagon. While many of these develop-ments are not new—trade and empire have been features of the world for millen-nia, and evident in North America since Columbus crossed the Atlantic in 1492—the speed, intensity, and interconnectedness of these developments are seen by many as marking a new stage in human social development. New media are central to debates about globalization and its impacts because they enable borderless communication.

Globalization has turned out to be a key issue for social justice activists and scholars, in particular since the infamous 1999 Battle in Seattle, which was a water-shed moment for both new media and activism in the sense that new media tools were widely used to both organize and document those resistance movements. From that day in 1999—a protest outside the World Trade Organization meetings in Seattle—right through to the 2010 G20 protests in Toronto and the Idle No More First Nations

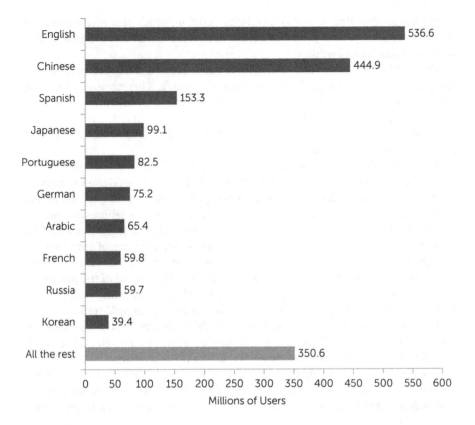

Figure 1.3   Top 10 Languages on the Internet, 2010 (in millions of users)

Source: Internet World Stats (2012), www.internetworldstats.com/stats7.htm. Copyright © 2000–2014, Miniwatts Marketing Group. All rights reserved.

movement that took off in December 2012, the role of new media has been front and centre for social justice activists. In fact, a whole cadre of tech activists has sprung up in the years since Seattle, creating sites such as Indymedia to share alternative news and tools like Crabgrass to enable anonymous and easy facilitation of group discussions in private (Milberry 2009).[16]

In the spring of 2011, we were reminded of this power when popular movements for change in both Egypt and Libya were closely linked to the use of social and mobile new media forms. The rise of the so-called Arab Spring was not solely due to texting and tweeting, but it gained power and agility via these tools. While some commentators, notably Malcolm Gladwell, have been dismissive of the link between social media and revolution, others, such as Clay Shirky, have argued persuasively that its potential should not be ignored. Both sides of this issue were debated by Shirky and Gladwell in back-to-back issues of *Foreign Affairs* from January/February and March/April 2011.[17]

When Canadians look back on the social movements that mattered in social (and regular) media in the winter of 2012–13, the Idle No More phenomenon will likely be one of the best remembered. In many ways, Idle No More captures the character and power of new social media–driven social movements and also illustrates an interesting dividing line between older digital activism, which depended a great deal on savvy tech activists, and newer forms built almost exclusively on existing platforms such as Facebook and Twitter.

Idle No More (or #IdleNoMore on Twitter) emerged as a call to action by a small group of First Nations organizers from western Canada. They created a Facebook page and called for rallies, protests, and "flash mobs"—impromptu gatherings coordinated by text message, email, Facebook messages, and/or tweets—to protest, at first, what they regarded as attacks on First Nations sovereignty in a variety of bills proposed by the federal government.

As with the Occupy Wall Street (OWS, #OccupyWallStreet) protests, these initial Idle No More events sparked attention and participation and quickly spread to other cities in and outside of Canada. In addition, the grievances that prompted the protest movement broadened to include a number of other issues—sometimes on purpose, sometimes by accident, sometimes against the wishes of the original organizers. This broadening of intent was a source of criticism and also seen as a sign of a more diverse support base. New constituencies of people, including non–First Nations people, added their voices to the online and offline activities. The spread of the movement was rapid and far-reaching, eventually hitting Brazil and connecting with the concerns of indigenous people there (e.g., www.facebook.com/IdleNoMoreBrazil).

The existence of easy-to-use and broadly available services such as Facebook and Twitter allowed the organizers, largely social media–savvy but non-technical people, to quickly launch a national movement, and facilitated the participation of affiliated and interested parties from around the globe. This reliance on external third-party services does bear some risk, however, as services like as Facebook and Twitter have been known to shut down sites or accounts that they deem in contravention of their terms of use.

The Conduit and the Content

The development and popularization of the Internet was a catalyst in the process of convergence. Through the Web, a rapidly growing number of Internet users were able to access a dramatically increased range of forms of digitized content (text, images, sound, video), delivered across telecommunications networks, via their personal computers, which increasingly became a single media platform able to deal with multiple media forms. This process of technological convergence, or the bringing together of computing, communications networks, and media content, was matched by the development of convergent products and services, and processes of industry convergence, or the range of takeovers, mergers, and strategic alliances that strengthened links between the computing and IT industries, the large telecommunications companies, and media corporations (Barr 2000; Flew 2005a: 11–2).

At the same time, early Internet content was frequently quite impoverished in terms of the capabilities of the new media form. Indeed, the imperative to provide content was often the problem, as it frequently led to the dumping of already existing text online with little consideration of how such material was viewed and used differently from its print-based variants. The much-publicized early initiatives to digitize the entire contents of the US Library of Congress envisaged not only a veritable army of minimum-wage information workers undertaking endless document scanning, but also an Internet where content was largely composed of straight liftings from print media. One problem was, of course, download speeds: with most domestic users reliant on 28.8-kilobyte-per-second modems for much of the 1990s, access to audio and video was bound to be slow for many.

The development of the Web gave a renewed focus to the nature of the **interface**, or the "front page" from which users accessed websites, typically through a web browser and search engine. The quality of interface design draws attention to the nature of human–computer interaction, which is fundamentally a consequence of technical design and the computer programming aspects of the interface, but which can operate effectively only when, as Anne Cranny-Francis observes, it recognizes "the cultural practices that enable users to engage with the technology," since it constitutes the "hidden engine of the user's interaction with the text" (2005: 120). The importance of interfaces to the usability and, hence, the popularity of computers was apparent well before the advent of the Web. The success of Apple Computers in the 1980s was strongly related to its development of a graphical user interface (GUI) that, in simulating the environment of a desktop (with files, folders, in-trays, trash cans, etc.), was intuitively more usable when compared with the PC-DOS system that was the leading personal computer interface at the time. Indeed, Apple fought a long, bitter, and ultimately unsuccessful legal case against Microsoft between 1994 and 1998 over its claim that Microsoft had infringed Apple's copyright when it incorporated the desktop metaphor into its Windows software, raising the question of whether or not the look and feel of a GUI—and software generally—is protected by copyright.

The question of the technical conduit, or the means by which online content is distributed, delivered, and accessed by the user, has become considerably more complex in the age of new media. With broadcast media, access to a suitable reception device (a television set or radio) gave its audiences content that looked and/or sounded more or less the same, regardless of the device being used to access it (except in instances such as the transition from black-and-white to colour televisions). With the Internet, by contrast, a variety of factors come into play in terms of both the accessibility and the quality of the user experience in accessing online content, including

- the age of the computer being used and the software installed on that computer;
- whether the user is accessing the content from a dial-up or broadband connection and the speed of downloads available from that connection;
- the overall quality of service and the available modes of delivery (dial-up, broadband, wireless broadband, etc.) in the physical location from which the content is being accessed;
- the type of computer being used (e.g., some material is not available for PCs or Mac computers);
- the software being used to access the content (e.g., the web browser); and
- the nature of the users themselves—for example, they may have a physical or mental condition that makes certain types of Web design inappropriate.

Sites such as Vincent Flanders's Web Pages That Suck (www.webpagesthatsuck.com) delight in demonstrating the principles of good Web design by drawing attention to examples of bad Web design in a highly amusing manner. In response to the often baroque features of many early websites, where the designers seemed to forget about both their users and the means by which they would access such sites, there was a turn toward usability in Web design, led by writers such as Donald Norman (1998) and Jakob Nielsen (2000).

The paradox of convergence and the reason why the concept becomes more problematic over time is this: as the computing, communications, and media industries are brought closer together by technological and industry changes, the disparities between and across content forms become more significant. For example, if we simply consider computer-based media, interactive online games require content that is sufficiently rich and compelling to provide an immersive experience for the gamer. Does this then make gamers who are used to the rich cinematics, surround sound, and complex gameplay found on consoles and in PC games impatient with online media that is, generally, considerably less complex because of narrower bandwidth, storage, and graphic capabilities of online and mobile media? While online and mobile games long had a reputation as "child's play" or insufficiently challenging for the hardcore gamer, some gamers report that they enjoy a casual or social game as an alternative to the so-called AAA games found on a console. And social, casual, and mobile games offer something the console—so far—cannot: the ability to play anytime, anywhere. And with new technologies such as "multi-core" graphics processors embedded in the latest tablets and smartphones, even the mobile experience can be remarkably immersive and rich. New technologies, such as eyeglass technologies and augmented reality (see Chapter 10) promise even further blurring of the distinctions by blending the real world with computer-generated worlds.

While the discussion of new media has thus far tended to focus on the Internet and computer-based digital media, a range of wireless technologies and applications have been developed that are shifting the locus of ICTs from the desktop to a range of portable, hand-held devices. At the forefront of this has, of course, been the mobile phone. As we have noted, the majority of the world's population subscribe to mobile cellular services. There have also been important transformations in how the mobile phone is used, with devices being increasingly used for short message services (SMS) or text messages, taking and sending pictures, viewing video, playing games, listening to music, and accessing email and the Internet. With these developments, the content that users seek to access from mobile devices has added to the complexity of issues of convergence: with the proliferation of interconnected digital media technologies and devices, the question of developing content that works across multiple media—in both a technical and a consumer-demand sense— becomes more and more complex.

Given the importance of mobile devices for our understanding of new media in the years to come, we will return to this topic in a later chapter for a more thorough examination of what is different—and what is the same—about the mobile Internet and mobile new media in general. While mobile technologies are clearly the emerging face of new media, the current face is what is known as *Web 2.0*. This development has transformed the Internet and the way it is used (leading one site to call itself "ReadWriteWeb"), from a passive consumption and selection process (surfing), to active production of new media content on sites such as YouTube and Flickr. The remainder of this chapter considers the Web 2.0 phenomenon in more detail.

Web 2.0

The concept of **Web 2.0** is central to understanding new media in the twenty-first century. The term was first circulated in 2003 and the first conferences were held on Web 2.0 through O'Reilly Media (formerly O'Reilly & Associates) in 2004. Tim O'Reilly (2006), who has been a key thinker and promoter of Web 2.0, defines it as "the business revolution in the computer industry caused by the move to the Internet as platform, and an attempt to understand the rules for success on that new platform. Chief among those rules is this: *'Build applications that harness network effects to get better the more people use them ... [or] harness collective intelligence'*" [italics added for emphasis].

There are both Web 2.0 evangelists and skeptics—as seems to be the case with most new media concepts. *Time* magazine drew particular attention to the Web 2.0 phenomenon when it declared that its Person of the Year for 2006 was "You," for each person's collective contribution to Web 2.0 (Grossman 2006). Not surprisingly, such prognoses generate equal doses of skepticism about both the sustainability of the phenomenon and the extent to which it is really marketing hype and what Steve Woolgar (2002) calls "cyberbole."

Nonetheless, the concept of Web 2.0 has caught on for two main reasons. First, it has embedded within it a range of features that have long been seen as central to the Web as a communications infrastructure, such as the scope for participation, interactivity, collaborative learning, and **social networking** (*social networking media* or just *social software* are commonly used alternative terms), as well as positive networking effects from harnessing collective intelligence. In other words, the quality of participation increases as the number of participating users increases, and this in turn attracts more new users to the sites. Second, some of the fastest-growing websites of the 2000s have been based on Web 2.0 principles. These include sites such as the photography service Flickr; the encyclopedia Wikipedia; the user-generated-content video site YouTube; aggregated weblog (blog) sites such as Blogger, Livejournal, and Technorati; and the various personalized Web space sites such as Tumblr, Facebook, Instagram, and Pinterest.

Software programs and Internet sites that conform to Web 2.0 principles have core principles, in that they are

- many-to-many in their connectivity;
- decentralized in terms of control;
- user-focused and easy for new users to use;
- open in terms of their technology standards and their applications programming interface (API);
- relatively simple and lightweight in their design, their administrative requirements, and their start-up and ongoing development costs; and
- expected to evolve and change over time as users make new modifications to the sites.

In their overview of design and application principles that underpin and drive Web 2.0, Musser and O'Reilly (2007) identify the following principles (see also Table 1.3).

Table 1.3   Principles of Web 2.0

Principle	Examples
Harnessing collective intelligence—deriving the benefits of large-scale ongoing participation and user co-creations and peer review of content to continuously improve the quality of the service	Google Wikipedia Flickr Amazon Delicious
Data as the next "Intel inside"—new wealth from online enterprises to be derived from database management	Amazon eBay Craigslist
Innovation in assembly—open APIs that allow for online remixing of content (mash-ups) and the use of RSS (really simple syndication)	Google Maps Yahoo! Flickr
Rich user experiences that promote user interaction and immersive engagement with the available online content	Google Maps Gmail Netflix
Software above the level of a single device—services that can span across media devices, particularly mobile media such as smart phones and PDAs	iTunes TiVo
Perpetual beta testing—software is incrementally released and understood as a service rather than as a final product	Google Flickr Open-source software more generally
Leveraging the long tail—recognizing that there is a move from mass markets to niche markets, but that niche markets can be sustainable over a long period of time (cf. Anderson 2006)	Amazon eBay Google
Lightweight models and cost-effective flexibility—Web 2.0 marketing works off word of mouth rather than high up-front costs in business set-up and marketing	Digg (allegedly established with an up-front investment of USD $2800) Flickr

Source: Musser and O'Reilly (2007).

The concept of Web 2.0 clearly implies a relationship to an earlier form of the Internet (Web 1.0). O'Reilly (2005) identifies some of the differences between 1.0 and 2.0 as related to a move from personal websites to blogs and blog-site aggregation; from publishing to participation; from Web content as the outcome of a large up-front investment to an ongoing and interactive process; and from content-management systems to links based on **tagging** or what is known as **folksonomy**. The dot-com crash of 2000 has been a significant factor in the way Web 2.0 emerged. In that crash, a large number of investors lost money when unrealistic business models resulted in the failure of many Internet start-ups that had high initial costs in infrastructure, personnel, and marketing strategies. The infamous marketing budgets and high-roller lifestyles of that era have now been largely removed from the start-up scene, with a growing focus on "lean" start-ups that "pivot" to new products and services using "agile" project-management methods. This sounds like a great deal of business lingo, but it is in fact a return to a practical and pragmatic approach to building companies.

Importantly, many of the hard-won lessons of the first Internet explosion have resulted in tools and technologies that make it much easier to bring a product or service to market than in the previous decade. So, for example, a team of two or three is usually sufficient to develop a mobile or social game or Web service. The software can be distributed to an audience of hundreds of millions of people, and at no cost (aside from sharing revenues) by mounting that service on an existing platform, such as Apple's or Google's online mobile app stores. Web products no longer require an investment in networks and servers and can be launched on Web service technologies such as Amazon Web Services (AWS) and scaled up quickly if they prove popular. Even massively popular services such as Twitter were able to launch with small teams and minimal technical infrastructure. From a business perspective, this means that the founders no longer have to give away a large portion of their company to investors but instead can start their company from savings or small loans. The result is a profusion of offerings, exploring many possible permutations and combinations of entertainment, socializing, not to mention all of the practical uses of mobile and online technologies.

Bloggers such as Carr (2005) and Shaw (2005) have expressed skepticism about Web 2.0, arguing that such a term is simply marketing bait that will promote overinvestment in a new Internet capital-raising bubble (Bubble 2.0) on the basis of poor understanding of the Internet as a social technology.

Nevertheless, second-generation Web content continues to dominate Internet usage. One of the interesting outcomes of this is the way that traditional media and new media have created hybrid forms. The CBC, Canada's national public broadcaster, has pioneered in this area (see the following case study) and has continued to support new media elements in its existing services.

One of the key benefits of new media is that it is endlessly adaptable. This is changing from something to be feared by old media to something to embrace. Old media—newspapers, radio, television—may not be as threatened by new media as was originally thought, once they begin to adopt and adapt to the new possibilities that digital distribution presents. Some recent Canadian examples include the expansion of the CBC into digital multimedia broadcasting, the adoption of user forums by the *Globe and Mail*, and the extensive use of streaming video by Global Television.

CBC Radio was one of the early adopters of new media, making extensive use of rich media websites from an early stage. There are several ways in which new media can provide an interesting and compelling companion to the old medium of radio. New music is one of these, as is radio drama. In the case of new music, the core of the experience is the music itself. That is what draws people in, and music has to be listened to. But if you are not familiar with a piece of music, how can you find it again? What if you forgot the band or artist's name after the announcer moved on to the next song? What if you want to know other songs that the band has recorded? Or perhaps you want to buy their CD or downloadable song. Here is where new media excels. The music can be accompanied by links to other songs by the band, photos of the band members, links to the online sales of their album, and histories and stories about the band. It can provide information about upcoming live shows as well. Importantly, you can branch out to other music similar to the song you've just listened to, make comments and tag the music, and follow the recommendations of others.

CASE STUDY

CBC Radio 3

Before reading this case study, perhaps take a minute to visit the Waterlife website (http://waterlife.nfb.ca). It is a wonderful example of new media at its best. The production is slick, the visual elements are artfully combined with facts and data, and there is lovely music. The producer of that piece, Rob McLaughlin, is based at the National Film Board, but he started at CBC Radio 3,[18] which began its life in Vancouver in January 2000. Radio 3 still exists (music.cbc.ca/#/radio3), but the earlier version was quite different, more like Waterlife than the present version.

When Radio 3 was conceived, the CBC already had some experience with the Internet, via a program on CBC radio called *Real Time*. That program incorporated the Internet to some extent, making early experiments with streaming and trying out live chat lines (IRC) during the show.

In 1998, Robert Ouimet, one of the members of the *Real Time* team, worked on a proposal for a third radio network in Canada, one targeted at younger people and adding elements of what was then still a new Internet. The CBC decided not to proceed with the conventional radio broadcast network but decided instead to launch it online. Ouimet started putting a team together in late 1999 and they were live on the Internet—as well as producing about 40 hours of traditional radio material a week for use on the existing Radio 1 and Radio 2 networks—by June 2000.

Some of their early challenges were technical. In 2000, streaming was just beginning. Most people connected to the Internet by modem, and the idea of a live stream—where there is no intervening stage in which the files are prepared for streaming, but rather, are pumped directly to the net—was a very new thing. They had to work closely with one of the pioneering firms in the field, Real Networks, Inc., of Seattle, to get beta versions of software to run on their servers. They had much the same story with Macromedia, the creators of Flash, the software used to create their web pages. They were pushing the envelope in those days and many people looked at what they were doing as state of the art, or indeed as cause for inspiration.

Much of the content on the three websites came from the public. But it wasn't user-generated content as we know it today. The notion of user-generated content, the driving force behind sites like Flickr and YouTube, scarcely existed when the CBC Radio 3 team started. The idea that you could build a successful website with material from the public was initially greeted with some skepticism. The Radio 3 team worked hard to support their contributors, which they called pro-consumers, and created a model in which their story ideas

All of these things are available on the excellent website for CBC Radio: www.cbc.ca/radio. In addition to live streams of national and regional content of the broadcast network, there are multiple Internet streams, including live—with a host and in real time—as well as pre-recorded (podcast) concerts and themed stations that run without a host. Listeners can tune in via their web browser or a mobile Internet device, such as an iPhone. New media increase the CBC's ability to present more original material as well as the quality and richness of that material, by providing the ability to make available multiple, parallel streams in contrast to the single stream provided by a radio broadcast. Textual and visual additions were extremely limited prior to the Internet, with the possible costly exception of printing and distributing a program guide or magazine.

Another radio feature that benefits from a new media complementary website is drama. At first, this wouldn't seem obvious, but there are some types of radio drama that are very difficult to carry off successfully without some sort of supplement, at least in the present style of listening. These days, people rarely schedule their lives around were nurtured and shaped, sometimes by helping them form partnerships with other people that had complementary skills.

Musicians were well along in creating digital versions of their work, at this point. A site called MP3.com already had 15,000 Canadian artists by 1999, at a time when Canadian radio stations in aggregate were playing perhaps 400 musicians. Graphic artists, animators, and photographers also had begun to work in digital formats but translating that to an online experience did not always come easily. Unlike sites such as Flickr or YouTube, which do not get involved in the things users upload, the Radio 3 team worked hard to support their contributors in order to keep up the quality of the Web content. They also made sure that the material featured on the site (e.g., the front page, profiles) was the best of what was received, even though they accepted almost everything.

These efforts were widely recognized, in the form of continuing financial support from the company and various awards, both in regular media and the emerging new media categories. CBC Radio 3 won awards in California and New York—at a time when Vancouver was far from the epicentre of new media—bringing attention and recognition to the new media scene in Canada. They also had local admirers who drew inspiration from their work and even tried to outdo them.

This sort of friendly competition led to a very high level of web capability (including Flash programming and audio streaming) in the Vancouver area. Although Radio 3 has moved on to a more generic site now, integrated with the rest of CBC's Web presence, the people responsible for the initial efforts continue to have an impact. Some of the team moved into local advertising and graphic production houses, gaming companies and, of course, Rob McLaughlin has moved to the NFB.

Case Study Questions

1. Reflect on your use of streaming media over the Internet, especially streaming audio. Does it replace your use of stand-alone devices such as a portable radio? Do you "tune in" via your computer rather than radio? Where do you *not* listen to streaming audio but instead prefer a special device? Why?

2. CBC Radio 3's website featured a great deal of additional interactive content: images, video, and text. Do you think that those sorts of "augmentation" are a distraction from the core value of the site (presumably music) or do they add to it? Many people listen to music via YouTube these days, but when you do that, do you pay attention to the video? Do you look for lyrics? Do you seek out the band's web page? Do you read and respond to the comments?

broadcast times. Gone are the days when a family might set aside Saturday afternoons to listen to a regular broadcast. As a result, modern listeners may find it difficult to keep track of the complex plot or diverse array of characters required for many dramatic forms. Some dramas would likely not succeed on the air without the interesting solution of an accompanying website. Such a website was created for a multi-part CBC drama about farm life in Saskatchewan that aired in 2006. The plot was complex and there were many characters. It was broadcast every day, but if you missed an episode, you risked losing the thread of the plot and then might have decided to stop listening. With the website, not only were you able to catch up by listening to archived recordings but you could also click through to biographies of the main characters, read plot summaries of past episodes, and even get additional background information and images that were not accessible in an audio-only medium. The result was a winning combination of sound and story. The website, and all locally produced radio drama from CBC in Saskatchewan, was cut in 2009 because of funding concerns (McWilliams, 2013).

As we have seen, new media is a rapidly evolving and complex assemblage of technology, social uses, and business models. While much remains up in the air, and the future is far from certain even for popular services such as Facebook, the pathways that new media are following have, in many ways, been laid down by previous generations of "new media," such as the telegraph and television. In the next chapter, we will examine the roots of new media in previous media forms and the influence that these developments continue to exert.

Useful Websites

Internet Society—History of the Internet
www.internetsociety.org/internet/what-internet/history-internet

This is an excellent collection of papers on the early development of the Internet and the Web. It includes Vinton Cerf's "Brief History of the Internet," Tim Berners-Lee on the past, present, and future of the Web, and the website for the series *Nerds 2.0.1*, produced by the US Public Broadcasting Service (PBS) in 1998.

Internet World Stats—Usage and Population History
www.internetworldstats.com

This site has the most up-to-date information on how many Internet users there are worldwide and where they are geographically located.

Alexa—The Web's Top 500
www.alexa.com/topsites

Alexa, a service that monitors websites, publishes a live list of the most popular sites on the Web. It is available in a number of formats and provides in-depth information about each site that it has ranked. As of January 2014, the list starts with these in the top 10:

1. google.com
2. facebook.com
3. youtube.com
4. yahoo.com
5. baidu.com (Chinese search engine)
6. wikipedia.org
7. qq.com (China's largest instant-messaging site)
8. taobao.com
9. amazon.com
10. live.com

Further Reading

New New Media, 2nd Edition, Paul Levinson (2012). Levinson's slim volume, coyly titled with a double "new," provides students and lay readers with an elegant and accessible introduction to new media, one that doesn't focus on technological features or business models so much as it speaks to the new capabilities and affordances that social and interactive media provide. Freshly updated, *New New Media* provides useful information on the latest new media trends.

Handbook of New Media, Leah A. Lievrouw and Sonia Livingstone, eds. (2006)
This handbook provides an excellent and broad perspective on new media. First published in 2001, it was updated in 2006, and while it misses some of the latest developments, this is more than compensated for by its rich treatment of new media from a theoretical point of view and its firm grounding in the social shaping method. This focus on method gives students a perspective and a tool kit on new media that can be adapted and

extended to more recent developments. Lievrouw and Livingstone also provide useful introductions to the way in which networks form an essential metaphor for understanding new media. The book also helps the student with historical, economic, social, and political background and context for new media.

New Media Reader, Noah Wardrip-Fruin and Nick Montfort (2003)

This reader provides an excellent collection of original texts, articles, and book excerpts that sets the new media revolution in context for the student reader. If a reader would like to find a comprehensive collection of scholarship, from a wide array of sources, this is a helpful companion.

Remediation: Understanding New Media, Jay David Bolter and Richard Grusin (2000)

A welcome reassessment of what it means to be new media, and in particular the borrowing that goes on when web pages, streaming video, and podcasts emulate, modulate, and simulate previous media forms by remediating them. As Bolter and Grusin remind us, it isn't just the media who are altered in this process but ourselves (especially when we are participating in Web 2.0, a term that was not in circulation at the time they wrote the book).

Discussion Questions

1. What are some key differences between what we would today refer to as *new media* and the media that preceded it?
2. How is *convergence* a term that is prone to confusion? In what ways are the current trends in convergence perhaps only the tip of the iceberg?
3. In what ways do new media devices affect our communication activities and practices, as well as larger social arrangements and organizations?
4. Comment on the following: "The quality of participation increases as the number of participating users increases, and this in turn attracts more new users to the sites."
5. What does it mean to describe the Internet as having graduated from being a computer network akin to a highway to a "place" that can allow people to "understand the world around them"?
6. What are some of "the cultural practices that enable users to engage with the technology" and what best describes the "hidden engine of the user's interaction with the text"?
7. Give the following a close reading: "Media studies as it emerged in the twentieth century understood media production, texts, and audiences as discrete forms, following a linear model of different 'moments' in the media production–consumption cycle." What does this mean and what are the implications?
8. In what ways do trends in new media reflect trends in globalization?

Class Activities

1. In groups of five with your classmates, discuss which websites you spend the most time at per day and the activities you engage in with those sites. Consider if those activities were the same a year ago, what changes have occurred, and why. Discuss with your group what you think about the growing use of social media.
2. Visit a website, such as Alexa, that provides a list of the top-10 sites in the world. Take a look at the sites you might not be familiar with and classify these sites into different types.
3. Given the global nature of much new media, compile a list of local, or regional, websites that you are aware of or use for news, information,

entertainment, and so on. Compare these with some national or multinational sites. What are the key differentiators?

4. Almost anything related to new media is subject to rapid change. Firms come and go; technologies change; and numbers of users, viewers, and creators for new media content and memes change every day. Using online sources, look up a fact or figure in this chapter and verify whether it remains true today. Identify corroborating or supporting sources for your findings.

Not only will you have the new facts but you'll also have an appreciation for how quickly things change and, most importantly, a visceral sense of the way in which the Internet and new media are self-revealing to the diligent and inquisitive scholar. If you discover a fact that needs updating, you can even submit your update (with page reference and new citation) in the form of a rewritten paragraph, to the author: Richard Smith (smith@sfu.ca). He promises to reply.

Debate Questions

1. Some people argue that the form of media dramatically changes the content. Debate the merits of listening to music via the Web, as opposed to a CD or radio station.

2. Social media provide opportunities to bring people together, as in a Facebook "event," or comments on your birthday, but it can also result in bad feelings and malicious or even criminal behaviours. What should parents do—if anything—about their children's use of social media? Give free rein? Set age limits? Keep them off social media altogether?

3. The role of comments in news and social media sites is one of the interesting aspects of the Idle

No More phenomenon that occurred during 2012–13. Whenever a news site, such as CBC.ca, or a social media site, such as YouTube, featured the protest, it attracted a large number of comments, many of which were hurtful or harmful and could not be remotely described as constructive criticism or useful debate. Argue for and against the proposition that this sort of behaviour is inherent in news and social media and we should either get used to it or ignore/eliminate open comments in online media. Is online trolling an inherent or solvable problem?

2

The History of New Media

Questions to Consider

- What are some challenges of human communication in terms of sending and receiving messages across distances? How have these changed over time?

- In what ways have advances in communications and connectivity been historically linked to key enabling technologies, institutional configurations, business models, and products and services? How are these links still evident today?

- In what ways was privacy a concern in media technology of the past? How does it remain a concern today?

- What ideological or political implications are there to consider in regard to policies, practices, and changes/advances in communications and new media?

Chapter Outline

In this chapter, we set new media in its historical context, drawing connections between current network technologies, convergence trends, and prior inventions such as the telegraph, radio, and television. Although the path has been circuitous, ever since we have been able to send messages without moving physical objects (the first telegraph), the immediacy factor has forever changed our expectations about communication media. With new capabilities came new institutions and social arrangements and these have proven to be foundational and influential for subsequent generations of media.

Journalism, politics, and business were all transformed by the use of the telegraph and the telephone. Radio, and later television, provided a testing ground for key elements of new media and, in particular, the business model in which content could be accessed for free, if one was willing to accept a little bit of advertising with that content. We conclude the chapter with a brief discussion of the educational potential of earlier new media.

Early Traces of New Media

Although some online accounts suggest otherwise, new media did not spring, wholly formed, from the minds of computer and network engineers. Just as Newton famously claimed that he was able to see further and do more than his contemporaries because he was able to "stand on the shoulders of giants," advances in new media have their roots in technologies that predate the Internet by at least 50 if not 100, years. The pioneers of new media also built on foundations laid long before, and sometimes in unexpected places. As we discussed in the first chapter, although new media are profoundly different from old media in many ways, there are some aspects of old media and old telecommunications technologies that set the pattern for things to come. In this chapter, we look at some of these antecedent technologies to better understand how they have shaped present-day understanding of media.[1]

Institutionalized, Instantaneous, Worldwide Communication: The Telegraph

One of the challenges of human communication has always been that to send a message any further than you can see, you have to send some sort of physical object to carry the message. Various attempts to overcome this limitation—with towers, balloons, or smoke signals—ultimately proved unwieldy, and most people settled down to writing letters and sending them by post. In the 1700s, there was some experimentation in sending messages by relay stations, using towers with semaphores or other signalling apparatuses. Although this worked reasonably well, it could still take hours for a message to go a long distance. These early attempts to overcome the problem of sending messages across distances did get people thinking about the possibilities of these kinds of technologies, however, especially for military applications.

In the 1800s, with a better understanding of the properties of electricity, attention turned to the potential of wires to send messages. Samuel Morse, an American, is widely credited with bringing the **telegraph** into popular use, even if he did not invent it. His name is still attached to the coding system—which is digital and formed of dots and dashes—that was used on the telegraph, that is, Morse code (see Figure 2.1).[2]

Morse code, the system of dots and dashes used to represent the alphabet, has had a remarkable conceptual impact. While no one (or almost no one) uses this system to encode messages anymore, the idea of using a digital coding scheme to break a message down into smaller components was both revolutionary and incredibly prescient. The system of dots and dashes at one end of the telegraph line corresponding to long and short pulses of electricity that triggered a buzzer at the other end of the telegraph line can be seen as an antecedent to the contemporary binary system used by computers, with dots as 0s and dashes as 1s. Telegraph encoding was first done by telegraph operators who converted words into letters by hand and each letter into code. Later, encoding became automated by the teletype machine, which sped up the process.

1. A dash is equal to three dots.
2. The space between parts of the same letter is equal to one dot.
3. The space between two letters is equal to three dots.
4. The space between two words is equal to seven dots.

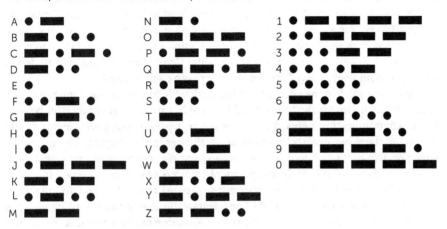

Figure 2.1 International Morse Code

Source: http://en.wikipedia.org/wiki/File:International_Morse_Code.svg.

Postal Tweeting?

An article by Sarah Milstein asks the question, "What Would Jane Austen Have Twittered?"

It turns out that in Jane Austen's lifetime (1775–1815), the post was delivered up to six times a day in London. After watching a show about Austen's life and letters, Milstein reflects that, "The speed of mail at the time and the content of the Austen sisters' letters suggest that the desires to communicate instantly and to let other people know what you ate for breakfast aren't [just a] modern phenomenon. . . . The Jane Austen show . . . suggests just the opposite: our human patterns are surprisingly consistent, and technology evolves to meet us."

Source: Milstein (2009).

Morse code was a practical method of sending information since it was simple, reliable, and easy to implement. More importantly, it established an approach to the digitization of information that has persisted into the present day.

When the telegraph was launched in the 1840s, it soon became enormously popular. Telegraph offices were built in cities and towns and within a few decades the world was overlaid by a network of wires and cables on land and under sea. You could visit any telegraph office in the world and send a message instantly to a receiving office. As antiquated and limited as the telegraph may seem now, at the time, it provided a new and relatively immediate level of connectivity, as people were able to send messages to each other across the globe. It should be noted that global communication did not come easily, especially across oceans. The first transatlantic telegraph took many attempts, finally reaching land at Heart's Content in Newfoundland. Canada served as the nearest land to Britain several decades later, when Guglielmo Marconi first sent a radio signal across the Atlantic to the nearest land in North America: Signal Hill in Saint John's. For a long time, the crucial geographic position of Eastern Canada vis-à-vis New York and London was economically and strategically important to many small Canadian communities along the Atlantic Coast. Later advances in undersea telegraph technology allowed for signals to bypass Newfoundland.

If the telegraph had the effect of making worldwide instantaneous communication seem normal, it also set the tone for the kinds of businesses that would later be built to run communication networks and for the regulations that governments would impose on them (we discuss this in more detail later in the chapter). The use of the telegraph also prompted cooperation [per s/s] and collaboration among global institutions for technical standards and payment transfers that were necessary to ensure that a message could pass seamlessly from one network to another, and that all parties would be reimbursed for carrying it.[3] The telegraph brought attitudes, awareness, and an appreciation of immediacy to the general population but behind the scenes, it also fostered key enabling technologies, institutional configurations, regulatory schemes, and business models that would also be foundational for future new media products and services. For example, telegraphs pioneered input devices, storage devices, and underlying technological methods such as "multiplexing" (sending more than one message at a time to make the most of the limited amount of capacity available on wires). Telegraph companies grew into large monopolies that attracted regulation and configured themselves as cooperative networks, sharing revenues and carrying each other's traffic. These product, service, and business innovations had repercussions that are evident today.

The telegraph, however, is not just a technological and business achievement and antecedent for the Web. It also served as a pivotal technology in terms of its ability to overcome the limitation of moving information by moving things. As we've noted, the telegraph broke this link and allowed instantaneous communication over long distances for the first time (Carey 1992). Canadian theorist Harold Innis explains, however, that bridging this gap inevitably had its costs in terms of how people used the media. Specifically, the content of new "space-binding" media forms such as the telegraph were biased toward more ephemeral topics, like news from afar (Innis 1951).[4] (See a profile on Innis in the accompanying New Media and Theory box.)

The Telegraph as Scanner

While an appreciation for worldwide, instantaneous communication was surely one of the most important contributions of the telegraph, some other more technical aspects were important as well. One of these is the concept of "scanning."

Morse code, as we have noted, was a breakthrough in transmitting content. The process of encoding information—in effect digitizing it—allowed for the movement of complex ideas using simple "on-and-off" electrical impulses. Yet, this was still limited to text, not pictures. Sending pictures through the telegraph required an additional leap forward. Telegraphs were eventually adapted to send photographs (wire photos)

Harold Innis

Harold Innis was an economist at the University of Toronto, interested in the evolution of economies and the impact of dominant local products on the livelihood of a community, region, or nation. He is well known among Canadian economists for his "staples" theory, which sought to explain economic life in terms of the basic (staple) trading goods in an economy (e.g., fish, wheat, or furs). His focus on these basic commodities required that he pay attention to how they were traded and moved, and he came to see the importance of transportation and communications technologies and systems. As communications scholar Paul Heyer has pointed out, when Innis began looking at another staple product, pulp and paper, his attention to detail and meticulous research led him to examine the uses of paper more closely and he also began to scrutinize not only commodities but also culture (Heyer 2003, p. 30).

Innis's focus on media forms and their impact on culture and community resulted in a novel approach and, eventually, a theory of communication media as being either "time binding" or "space binding." A time-binding medium is something with great durability, such as clay or stone tablets, monuments, or statuary. These types were media of communication with great power to carry messages across long periods of time. They were, of course, incredibly difficult to move and as such their "bias" was to move information across time. Other media—for example, paper, or, later on, the telegraph—were more ephemeral and easily destroyed but could be moved without difficulty. As such, they were biased to moving information across space. In his renowned book, *The Bias of Communication*, Innis argues for greater attention to the ways that a culture uses communication media and explains how those media affect the ability of a culture to have stability over time (via time-binding media) or powers over space (via space-binding media). In another book, *Empire and Communications*, Innis explores how the ability of the British Empire to manage vast holdings around the globe was—in Innis's view—directly linked to its capacity to control and use a space-binding medium such as the telegraph.

For Innis, the Internet would have presented an interesting challenge. The Net is obviously a space-binding medium in the sense that it is global, immediate, and provides similar powers of control at a distance that the telegraph gave to empires. It becomes more complex, however, because there are some interesting time-binding elements to the Internet. These range from the way in which old websites are being saved—and made instantly available by the Internet Archive library—to simple tools like genealogy databases. Even seemingly frivolous sites, such as Flickr and Youtube, may appear to be ephemeral but are, in fact, preserving our culture in a minute-to-minute and exquisitely searchable way.

by having a light-sensitive sensor scan for light and dark parts of a picture. A white area would be a dot and a dark area would be a dash. The picture was wrapped on a drum that was slowly rotated while the sensor moved back and forth in front of it. In this way, the whole picture was eventually scanned and represented as a string of dots and dashes. The telegraph operator would send this content down the line to a remote printer, which was equipped with light-sensitive paper wrapped around another drum. The paper would be exposed to a bit of light for each dash and the result would be a dark spot. The process eventually produced a facsimile of the original.

Scanning like this was crude, but seemed miraculous at first. Today, computer scanners, digital cameras, camcorders, and just about anything else that works with images uses a similar system of breaking a picture into "bits" (binary digits) of black and white (and now shades of grey and millions of colours) to encode media for transmission on networks and for further processing by software.

Telegraphs as Storage and Pricing Pioneers

The torrent of telegraph messages being sent from large cities all over the world meant that the system could become overwhelmed and messages lost. Telegraph operators worked out a system of "punching"—using a small device to create holes in a **paper tape** to represent the code—and then running those tapes through another machine that read those holes and generated Morse code. This allowed the company to send the telegram later, when the system was less busy. The same could be done at the other end, where messages would be received en masse and then printed out later, to distribute to homes and businesses. This helped to balance the load on the system and increase overall capacity.

These and many other innovations helped to solve the technical problem of capacity in the system, and telegraph companies used these to identify new business opportunities. Given the ability to store and forward messages, they were able to offer pricing options based on how quickly a message needed to be delivered (similar to the "evening and weekends" pricing that is familiar to today's users of cell phones). Modern computer networks carry on this same storage and forwarding model with email, making copies and letting messages pile up wherever necessary, resending if required.

Telegraphs as Network Pioneers

Telegraph systems extended all over the world and there were literally hundreds of telegraph companies in the United States by the 1850s. Bringing them all under one umbrella company, as Western Union did in the 1860s and '70s, was a shrewd business move that illustrated the value of networks, now known as **Metcalfe's Law**. First described by Robert Metcalfe in the 1980s and popularized by George Gilder in a 1993 *Forbes* article, Metcalfe's "law" is more of an observation, describing the increasing value of a network according to the number of connections it has.[5] According to Metcalfe's Law, "the value of the network increases at the square of the number of connections," which can be mathematically represented as $O(n^2)$, where O is the value and n is the number of connections (see Figure 2.2).

Metcalfe's Law has driven the business side of communications networks for over 100 years and famously incited serious economic hysteria during the dot-com boom. As such, it is worth exploring further and is perhaps best explained with an example:

> The foundation of his eponymous law is the observation that in a communications network with n members, each can make $(n-1)$ connections with other participants. If all those connections are equally valuable—and this is the big if as far as we are concerned—the total value of the network is proportional to $n(n-1)$, that is, roughly, n^2. So if, for example, a network has 10 members, there are 90 different possible connections that one member can make to another. If the network doubles in size, to 20, the number of connections doesn't merely double, to 180, it grows to 380—it roughly quadruples, in other words. (Briscoe, Odlyzko, and Tilly 2006)

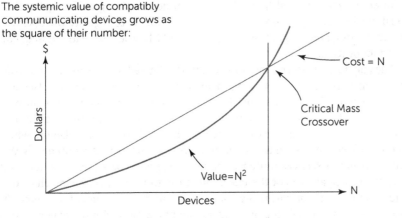

The systemic value of compatibly commununicating devices grows as the square of their number:

Figure 2.2   Metcalfe's Law

Source: Adapted from Metcalfe's original slide, reproduced by S. Simeonov (2006), http://blog.simeonov.com/2006/07/26/metcalfes-law-more-misunderstood-than-wrong.

To illustrate this in a different way, consider this: If there are two networks, both with 50 nodes and thus 50(50–1) or 2450 connections each, if they were joined, then there would suddenly be 9900 possible connections (100[100–1]), simply by putting a link between the two networks. In other words, one link almost quadruples the value of the two networks. Western Union quickly understood the value of linking networks and began to acquire hundreds of small telegraph companies over a very short time.

Metcalfe's Law also explains why at some point, most people do end up getting a telephone, or signing up for email, because (1) the value of the network grows enormously as more and more people join and (2) *not* being part of the network means not having access to something that is increasingly valuable. The exploding growth of Twitter, Instagram, and Pinterest are examples of how this value proposition manifests itself in new Internet products and services. It isn't just the direct users of those tools who experience dramatic change: these days, a small company that gets "pinned" in Pinterest by a popular user can experience an explosion in demand for its product(s).

There is some skepticism that the math of Metcalfe's Law continues to work in the same way throughout the life of the network (at some point, you run out of people to call or do not care to call everyone). Nevertheless, it is a powerful economic force for network owners and subscribers.

The Telegraph and Early Signs of Communications Media Monopolies

The telegraph proved to be the impetus for many successful enterprises, but it also carried with it the risk that these newly consolidated companies would start to behave as monopolies and raise prices beyond what the market would bear. At first, telegraph messages were considered luxury items, and could be priced accordingly (early prices for transatlantic telegrams were several dollars per word and this was in an era of 25-cent meals!). As the telegram became integrated into business and social life, however, pressure was put on governments to regulate the operations of telegraph companies (as we will see, this would be the case with subsequent new media innovations).

The telegraph spread rapidly and became dominated by large monopolies, often by combining with the railways, using their rights of way as a convenient place to string wires and poles. Their importance for other businesses and their monopoly practices eventually led to calls for regulation.[6] In the 1870s, control of the telegraph system in the United States was almost entirely in the hands of Western Union, which had an exclusive contract with the Associated Press, ensuring that AP used only Western Union telegraph services (rather than rival telegraph companies). As news services were the principal users of the telegraph at the time and paid for much of the tele-graph traffic, it is not surprising that this business arrangement was lucrative for Western Union. Capitalizing on their dominant position with the major users of the telegraph system, Western Union continued to buy up rival companies—it eventually became synonymous with telegraphy in the United States, carrying over 90 per cent of telegraph traffic in the country (Nonnenmacher 2001).

Despite repeated calls for regulation of the telegraph business in the United States—and bills to that effect being introduced in Congress in practically every sitting of the House from 1850 to 1900—the Western Union lobbyists were able to fend off almost any serious control of their industry (Nonnenmacher 2001). Those following the debates on "Net neutrality" in the United States today will remark that the role of lobbying by the telecommunication industry is a continuing story.

Telegraphy arrived in Canada in 1846 with a public demonstration of the tech-nology at Toronto's City Hall and followed soon after with the creation of the Toronto, Hamilton, Niagara and St. Catharines Electromagnetic Telegraph Company. Railways, both the Canadian National Railway and Canadian Pacific Railway, were the primary operators of telegraph systems in Canada (Burnet 1996) and, because railways were already regulated in Canada, their operations were at first governed by the regu-lation system in place for transportation systems.

The Telegraph and Newspapers—Dire End or Happy Marriage?

As the Internet has spread to more and more corners of the world, and home and mobile access to the Web has converted so many people to online reading, news-papers are suffering from a decline in print readership and advertising dollars. Many from the newspaper industry—most notably, outspoken publisher Rupert Murdoch—have accused Google and other Internet search engines of being the cause of their woes. While this may seem to be a thoroughly Internet-age problem, the telegraph was implicated in a similar "death of newspapers" scare more than 150 years ago, when James G. Bennett, founder and publisher of the *New York Herald*, predicted in 1845 that some newspapers must "submit to destiny, and go out of business."

The telegraph was able to shake up the newspaper industry because, prior to the early 1800s, newspapers operated on a casual sharing of old news, with relatively little attention to timeliness. Toward the middle of the nineteenth century, particularly in the rising commercial centres on the east coast of the United States, some news-papers sought to distinguish themselves by being "first with the news." By the 1830s,

Early "Text-Speak" on Telegraphs

The costliness of telegrams led a variety of strategies—individual and social—to keep costs down. At the individual level, those sending telegrams began using abbreviations to save money. The practice of abbreviating telegram messages—where every letter, every space between words, was precious—created a convention that continues to this day: the text-speak of today and the codes and abbreviations in the telegraph age, in this sense, are surprisingly alike.

Abbreviations only work, of course, if they are understood. Code books for telegraph abbreviations were therefore published and circulated widely. In 1879, one of the most popular codes, the Phillips code, was first published as a book by Walter P. Phillips in New York.[7] It contained thousands of abbreviations, even for relatively short words. In addition to economy of space, abbreviations permitted an economy of time: using these abbreviations, Walter Phillips was able to copy 2731 words in a single hour. This was not typing as we know it, but tapping out letters using dots and dashes in Morse code. For this, Phillips won a gold pen from Samuel Morse himself![8] The speed of entering messages was particularly important to court reporting and so, too, for news agencies, which competed with each other to get the scoop on breaking stories. The practice of doing telegraphy with abbreviations even had a word: *stenotelegraphy*, meaning a type of shorthand with dots and dashes.

newspapers were employing a wide range of techniques to beat their competitors to publish the latest international news—these included semaphores, carrier pigeons, even rowing out to meet ships arriving from Europe and elsewhere, then racing back to port faster than the cumbersome ocean-going vessels.[9] To the press barons of the day, the arrival of the telegraph seemed to make competing on the basis of being first with the facts a losing proposition, as newspaper operators, business people, and just about anyone else would all have access to the news at the same time. In hindsight, this concern may seem ridiculous and, in fact, it quickly proved to be so. While the telegraph could effectively move the news from one city to another, it had a terrible "last mile" problem: the news would arrive by telegraph to offices across the globe, but how to get it from those offices to thousands of people at once? People were not going to stand in line to wait for the news and they were not likely to pay for it, unless it could be delivered to them, in one way or another.

As it happened, newspapers provided their own solution: As the biggest customers of telegraph services, they quickly became outlets for a steady stream of wire clippings. Indeed, journalist W.J. Stillman, writing in *The Atlantic Monthly* in 1891, complained that "America has in fact transformed journalism from what it once was, the periodical expression of the thought of the time, the opportune record of the questions and answers of contemporary life, into an agency for collecting, condensing and assimilating the trivialities of the entire human existence."[10] Others, like Stillman, also wondered if the telegraph (and, thus, newspapers) would convey nothing but inanities. Henry David Thoreau, upon hearing of the plans to build a telegraph line across the United States, wrote in his journal, "We are in great haste to construct a magnetic telegraph from Maine to Texas; but Maine and Texas, it may be, have nothing important to communicate."[11] Both of these comments recall Innis's observation of the bias of communication toward the ephemeral in space-binding media such as the telegraph.

Neil Postman

As much as Thoreau was unsure of the value of immediacy in news, in the century and a half since he first wondered about the use in knowing about trivia from afar, others have gone much further in their criticism. Media theorist Neil Postman (1931–2003), best known for his withering analysis of television in the book *Amusing Ourselves to Death* (1985), wrote about the perils of depending on a form of communication that was principally about entertaining people, rather than informing them. He argued that a society that cannot take the time to verify or trust their sources of information because they are overly sensationalized, abbreviated, and simplified will be unable to operate successfully as a democracy. Postman argued that in this regard our modern era was not so much in danger of thought control (as in Orwell's *1984*) but thoughtlessness brought on by distraction (as in Huxley's *Brave New World*). Postman's approach to media is related to both Innis and McLuhan, in that he argues strongly that the form of the medium affects what can be said. Print, he argues, provides a strong basis for rational argument, allowing people to reflect, rebut, and (re)consider a logical and fact-based line of thought. Electronic media, and in particular the television, are—in Postman's view—inherently biased toward the trivial, the sensational, and the emotional and, therefore, unsuited to rational thinking.

Yet, the changes in journalistic writing style brought on by the telegraph were not entirely without benefit. The market and the technology led to the kind of newspaper content that is now expected: dependence on facts and (the appearance, at least) of a neutral point of view. The ability of the telegraph to transmit news instantly also meant that politicians could be held more accountable; for example, they could not take a particular position on an issue in one city and then take a different position in another city. They had to be more consistent in their messages.

This kind of "control at a distance" didn't just affect politicians, of course. The telegraph introduced—or sped up—the use of data for the trading of commodities, the movement of goods, and the pricing of products. Railways were able to operate their lines more efficiently by optimizing the timing and speed of trains, for example. Shippers could deliver goods to the market where demand and prices were highest. And bosses were able to control the work of their labourers from vast distances. This ability to control things to a finer degree and from a remote location often resulted in a diminution in the degree to which people had local control over their activities. Fewer decisions were made locally, and there were fewer breaks and gaps while information was sent and less waiting until answers were received.

This kind of control and feedback system—when it is adapted to use sensors and computers that can make split-second decisions—is what Norbert Weiner called a "cybernetic" system. A household thermostat is a very simple automated feedback system, as it is configured to switch on the furnace when the temperature drops below a certain level. Weiner, a pioneer of information theory and information science, worked at the Massachusetts Institute of Technology (MIT) as a mathematician and helped shape our understanding of how humans and computers could work together. Targeting guns from a moving platform—a ship at sea—another early example of an automated feedback and control system illustrated to Weiner the importance of maintaining an ethical stance toward research outcomes.

Weiner wrote of the issues that scientists should consider when doing research and famously refused to take government money for his own research.

As we will see in greater detail in the concluding chapter, cybernetic systems have advanced significantly in recent years. The way in which we have started to integrate those systems into our daily lives, complete with embedded knowledge and decision-making power that is startlingly "human-like," will come to transform the twenty-first century the way that electronic networks transformed the twentieth.

Newspapers thrived under the telegraph and eventually the business adapted to take advantage of the features that it offered, including ready access to foreign news, easy sharing of stories via telegraph-connected news agencies, and the wire photo.

> What lessons does the telegraph hold for newspapers now grappling with the internet? The telegraph was first seen as a threat to papers, but was then co-opted and turned to their advantage. "The telegraph helped contribute to the emergence of the modern newspaper," says Ford Risley, head of the journalism department at Penn State University. "People began to expect the latest news, and a newspaper could not succeed if it was not timely."[12]

In the twenty-first century, a similar revolution is at work as the proliferation of handheld reading devices (the Apple iPad or Amazon's Kindle, for example) is leading to changes in how we experience newspapers and magazines. Some believe these new technologies will spell the end of newspapers and magazines; others point out that the content—journalism—is what is important to a democracy and, while the look and feel may be completely different (e.g., the *Globe and Mail* **app** on a hand-held/mobile device), the social and political impact remains.

One of the defining features of new media in the twenty-first century is how it has been turned to commercial ends and, in particular, to advertising. Everything from animated television commercials to advertisements that pop into the background of an iPhone app are evidence of the ways in which new media are integrated with the advertising industry. The telegraph was similarly entangled with advertising—in fact, is implicated in the development of the advertising industry (specifically, the advertising agency). Just as the telegraph made it possible for trains to better coordinate their activities on single tracks, the insertion of advertising copy in multiple newspapers—and all the billing and coordination that entailed—made it possible for agencies to use the telegraph to move into this "coordination business" by becoming adept at buying and then reselling blocks of space (and later, time on radio and television) in newspapers. Canadian advertising experts Terry O'Reilly and Mike Tennant, the co-creators of popular radio programs on advertising (*O'Reilly on Advertising, The Age of Persuasion, Under the Influence*), draw attention the role of the telegraph:

> [It] revolutionized marketing. The telegraph followed on the heels of the European industrial revolution, and in North America, manufacturing had mechanized and expanded. Rural families had gravitated to cities to work in the fast-growing factories, which in turn churned out products for burgeoning urban populations. With the rise of railways through the nineteenth century, goods could be transported over land, en masse, to

distant markets, resulting in more product choices in stores. And how did the telegraph fit into the picture? It allowed manufacturers to communicate instantly with newspapers in distant cities and towns, buying advertisements to attract thousands of potential new customers. (O'Reilly and Tennant 2010: xvi)

While this helps explain the importance of the telegraph to the development of advertising, O'Reilly and Tennant go on to discuss the meeting point between manufacturers and newspapers—the advertising agency as technology-enabled middleman—in this way:

Barely a year after Morse dotted, dashed, and dotted his way into history, Philadelphia businessman Volney Palmer opined, quite rightly, that many manufacturers had neither the time nor the inclination to place ads in dozens—even hundreds—of newspapers on a regular basis. Palmer offered his services as a sort of middleman, buying large amounts of advertising space in several newspapers and parceling and selling it to businesses, who would have to create their own messages. And so ... the advertising agency was born. (O'Reilly and Tennant 2010: xvi)

In all, the telegraph contributed significantly to a multitude of innovations in long-distance, instantaneous communication as well as in technology, business, and regulatory changes.[13] Through the rest of this chapter, we present examples of both clear and less obvious links between the telegraph and other new media technologies.

From Telegraph to Telephone: A Revolution in Sound

Visiting a telegraph office and speaking to someone who would write down a message and then send it through the wire was simply the way things were done in the early days of the telegraph—there was no system for home telegraph terminals. Morse code, while relatively simple, still had to be learned and remained out of reach for most people. It was clear that taking the encoding out of the equation would make the ability to transmit messages more useful for people.[14]

Several inventors set to work on the problem of sending voice across wires and Alexander Graham Bell's telephone emerged as the winner (after some trouble in the patent office).[15] Bell, a Scottish-Canadian, worked in his lab in Boston, as well as at home in Brantford, Ontario, throughout the years and months leading up to his successful first call. The obvious benefit of the telephone was that it gave people the ability to speak directly to others, with their own voices, without reducing everything to code. Understandably, the telephone very quickly became popular, for both workplace and household. In fact, once people started installing telephones in their homes, it was so difficult for the telephone companies to keep up with demand that they started running promotions urging people to reserve phones for emergency or important use. It is a testament to our collective human curiosity, our shared interest in communication technology, that overuse of new communication media is a recurring problem. Most recently, it has affected the telephone company AT&T. In 2009,

AT&T struggled to keep up with the data usage of all the new iPhone users, who loved their apps so much that they drove mobile data use up by as much as 4000 per cent. The AT&T response has been to urge customers not to use the service so much.[16] More recently, Twitter's Fail Whale—which appeared with great regularity during the rapid growth phase of the service—became emblematic of a new media form that was expanding too quickly for those running the service.

Telephone use became a widely adopted form of communication in the early twentieth century because as soon as a telephone connection was set up, it was ready for use. That said, the telephone was also a new tool and people had to learn how to use it properly. Knowing to pick up the earpiece (the microphone was typically built into the device itself) and saying hello had to be learned, as has been the case with other communication tools. In fact, in the early days of the telephone, companies mounted advertising campaigns, in print and at the opening of movie reels, introducing people to the telephone and urging them to "pick it up and say hello."

It may seem comical now to think that instructions were needed on how to use a telephone. Most new communication technologies, however, not only have an adoption curve (in which people acquire the devices) but also a learning curve (in which people learn how to use the devices properly and work out appropriate etiquette). The mobile telephone experienced a similar curve: at first, people did not know how to put them on silent mode or they spoke loudly in classrooms and restaurants. Again, both private and public campaigns were launched to encourage people to use their communication devices responsibly as we continue to see to this day at plays, movies, and concerts.

Although it was relatively easy to use the telephone and a standard way of greeting was adopted, another problem arose: with so many people using the telephone, the process of connecting everyone—a manual process in the early days—began to put a strain on the system's resources. There were not enough telephone operators to handle the volume and an automated means had to be found. The answer was the mechanical telephone switch, which replaced local operators first and, later, long-distance operators.

Changing Telephone Connections—The Telephone Switch and "Network Neutrality"

The telephone switch or telephone exchange was a wonderful invention in terms of saving labour, but it also gave users the freedom to make calls without involving other people.[17] The secret call, the late-night call, calls between teenagers without their parents' knowledge . . . all these were enabled by putting a machine instead of another human being in the middle of the call. Although telephone operators were trained to uphold professional standards and were not supposed listen in on calls or judge who was calling whom (and when), callers could not be sure of the privacy of their conversations. In fact, the inventor of the mechanical telephone switch was supposedly motivated by his suspicions that an industry rival's girlfriend was diverting business to her sweetheart.

Human beings have generally preferred making contact directly rather than through an intermediary. At the time of the invention of the automated telephone switch in 1891, people were well acquainted with the postal system approach: those doing the mailing put addresses on letters and did not concern themselves with how the items got to their destinations. Similarly, the telephone switch allowed people to dial a phone number directly and make their own calls.[18] In a way, the mechanical telephone switch made **network neutrality** a reality. Although *network neutrality* is a term used today for Internet technologies, in the early days of the telephone, a similar principle applied: *common carriage* law, which is a reference to the regulation of railroads. These regulations were originally put in place to keep railroads from charging different rates to different companies (for example, subsidiaries) and giving unfair advantage to some at the expense of others. In telephone terms, the common carriage laws meant that everyone paid according to a common fee/charge structure and—more importantly—telephone companies could not discriminate on the basis of what callers were saying. This separated carriage from content and it remains a cornerstone of telecommunications law to this day. Common carriage law protected the telephone companies, too, since they could (and did) argue that they could not be held responsible if someone used the telephone to plan a crime, for example.

Network neutrality has emerged as a key issue in the debates about control of and payment for Internet services. In principle it means that the network is unbiased in relation to the content that is transmitted, but this has been under stress in recent years by both user behaviour and competition between telecommunication carriers. User behaviour became an issue as data-heavy new media forms such as music and movies began to move onto the Internet. These activities (mainly downloading of content) threatened to swamp services that were deemed both more important for business and lighter in terms of data load (e.g., email). In response, some Internet service providers sought to charge differential rates or to limit the amount of bandwidth available for these activities. Users, as might be expected, protested. The issue became more complicated as telecommunications and media companies merged and it became possible to imagine a world in which a broadband network owned by a media giant (as is the case for several Internet service providers in Canada) might provide preferential access to their network for services that come from their corporate family. We present more about network neutrality and common carriage agreements later in the text, in the discussion of Internet service providers and data services (see Chapter 9).

The Cost of Communicating—Early Regulatory Frameworks for Products and Services

Early telephones were expensive. People leased their telephone service and did not own any part of the system, not even the phone itself, which was the property of the telephone company. This arrangement lasted until well into the 1960s and only slowly eroded as customers gradually won the right to purchase "terminal equipment" of their own choosing. For a long time, telephone companies argued that the system was so finely tuned and complicated that they could not keep it operating unless they had complete control of all parts. This argument gradually became untenable in both practical terms and from a legal point of view. Most telephone companies no longer even try to rent telephones, although in one recent case in Vancouver, a person discovered that the elderly woman next door had been paying $4.95 a month for telephone rentals going back decades. After being contacted by a local newspaper, the telephone company offered a $600 refund (Shaw 2012).

In practical terms, telephone companies wanted to take advantage of the reliability and cost advantages of using standardized products and had long set rigorous standards for all aspects of their system. At first, these companies owned their own manufacturing arms. Northern Electric, later Northern Telecom, was once a wholly owned subsidiary of Bell Canada (itself a subsidiary of Bell Telephone, the US parent company). As other manufacturers began to prove that they could also make telephone equipment, the telephone network gradually evolved into one with competitive provision of components from a multitude of suppliers and, eventually, consumers were able to purchase and install their own telephones and businesses were able to buy (or lease) small office switches (a "private branch exchange" or PBX). This evolution in the industry was brought about for business reasons, spurred on by legal challenges and regulatory changes. As a result, telephone companies were closely regulated, almost from the outset.

As with the telegraph companies, the economics of operating a network meant that consolidation happened early and quickly in the telephone industry. The bigger the network (and getting bigger by buying others was a fast way to grow), the more money the network could make. Consolidation of networks also made sense in the way that consolidated electricity distribution makes sense: having one company provide the service prevented wires from blocking the pathways and ensured that the system was reliable and well maintained. In exchange for permission to operate as a monopoly, telephone companies were either nationalized (owned by the provincial/state or national government) or regulated, or both. This kept companies that had no competitors from charging excessive rates, limiting them to a regulated rate of return, and it ensured that they met certain performance standards, including coverage of all the homes in a service area. Telephone service, in North America especially, gradually came to be seen as a basic service for everyday life. In fact, in many rural areas, telephones were more common than electricity, and arrived decades before. Treating telephones as a universal service was a foundation of government intervention into telecommunications in Canada, either through public sector monopolies (in the Prairie provinces) or regulation of private companies (Mussio 2001: 3–4).

In Canada, with the vast distances and extreme climate, telephone service was regarded as a lifeline. Doctors (and veterinarians) were summoned via the telephone service, as were fire trucks and ambulances, so, as a result, telephone service has been deemed an essential service.[19] For example, in Canada, monthly telephone costs are included alongside housing costs and utilities in calculating social assistance income levels. Other countries have recently taken the essential service argument much further into the arena of new media, making access to high-speed Internet a human right (as we discuss in more detail in Chapter 9).

Jeremy Shtern

Jeremy Shtern is professor in the Department of Communication at University of Ottawa. With a Ph.D. from the Université de Montréal, Shtern focuses his work on communication governance (national and international), globalization and communication, the political economy of the Internet, and creative labour and media industries. He has been a key player in pulling together a policy working group within the Canadian communications research community. He is active on Twitter: @jshtern.

What are the key policy questions relating to new media and communication in Canada?

Canada has a legacy system of social and cultural policy for one form of electronic mass communication: broadcasting. And we have an emerging regime for the governance of another form of electronic communication: digital media and Internet-based communication. Most of the key policy challenges involve the integration of these two sets of policy frameworks. Recent policy debates over new media broadcasting, over set-top boxes and even over the renewal of the CBC's mandate, underline this tension between the past and future of mass communication in Canada. It is clear that some harmonization will be required to avoid a situation in which Canadians can access content over screens delivered through a regulated system and, in parallel, the same content on the same screen that could be equally delivered through an unregulated system. In the process, we will be forced to make decisions about the principles that have shaped Canada's approach to regulating mass communication since at least the development of radio in the early part of the twentieth century, including. . . . Do we want to ensure a place for Canadian-produced media content? Do we want Canadian media to be owned exclusively by Canadians? Will public service obligations that have defined the CBC and the structure of Canada's media system endure? Each of these questions and others are at least partially at stake in the present and near-future regulatory debates around the Canadian media.

By the Flickering Light, We Will Conjure Movement: Film

While the telegraph managed to transmit a still image from one part of the world to another (almost) instantly, such transmission was not possible with moving images, as this required another innovation. Photography was developing at the same time as the telegraph and people were enchanted by the realistic images that it produced. Although photographs are not altogether different from paintings, photographic images are considered a nineteenth-century new media form because many images, presented in rapid order and with slight variations between them, give the illusion of movement. This illusion is derived from what is known as "persistence" in human vision: what the human eye sees will remain in the mind's eye for a brief period of time and so, if one image is quickly replaced with another image that differs only slightly from the preceding one, the human brain interprets the change as movement. This effect can be exploited in a number of ways (such as flip books), but to make the illusion of movement realistic, very accurate images—such as photographs—are needed.

It took enormous initiative and invention by a wide range of people, including Thomas Edison in the United States and the Lumière brothers in France, but

You have written about how Canada's response to developments in new media are resulting in unequal access. What could be done about that?

Certain communities have access to more robust broadband access than others. New generations of technologies make older devices obsolete and create new literacy challenges. Uneven rollout of new networks—for example, in the switchover from analogue to digital over-the-air television signals—can effectively disconnect Canadians where access had previously been close to universal. Achieving universal access to mass communication is not a problem that can be eradicated but rather a dynamic and perpetual policy challenge that requires constant monitoring and vigilance. Equality of access to new media requires social policy solutions: capacity building, training and literacy, alongside economic stimuli designed to increase the penetration of networks and the reach of systems. Canadians need to ask themselves what access means in this new media environment and then develop our capacity to not just receive new media, but also to participate in its creation and make meaningful use of these tools in our social, economic and political lives.

What are some key emerging concepts or challenges or ideas?

To me, it is less about emerging ideas and more about re-emerging ideas: What does public service communication mean in this environment? What does it means to have "Canadian" media in an ever more multicultural country and globally interconnected media marketplace? How do we continue to develop and support professional storytellers and where and in what format does their work reach the public? The most key idea, the one that would tie this all together, is probably the one that has yet to come: "Canada's New Media System." In place of the series of often unconnected discussions that are all, to degrees, discussing this big idea implicitly, it is probably time to have a serious, coordinated discussion about the future of mass communication in Canada and start planning for it.

eventually the "moving picture" was perfected. In moving-picture systems, which have only recently been largely replaced by digital projection systems, small frames of film with a still image are projected with a strong light behind them onto a screen at the front of a viewing room. Then, a small shutter very briefly—and imperceptibly to the human eye—blacks out the image while the next frame is moved into position. This process of projection—blackout, movement, and then a stop and projection again—is responsible for the characteristic clatter of a movie projector as the film moves, stops, moves, and stops again, at 24 frames per second.

The effect, to the audience, is the "magic of movies," and much of what digital technologies have been seeking to perfect over the past half century is to recreate what was achieved, mechanically, at the turn of the twentieth century. This is another example of what Lev Manovich might have been referring to when he said, "We will see that many of the principles [of new media] are not unique to new media, but can be found in older media as well."[20] The many-frames approach, however, remains the way of achieving the illusion of movement even now. Today, the frames are no longer whole images but instead are painted pixel by pixel by computers. In fact, the images built on computer screens are assembled much in the same way that the telegraph assembled photographic images: line by line. Computers perform essentially the same function as telegraphs did, just in more detail and very, very quickly! These same early traces of new media can also be found with the television, but to connect the new media dots, so to speak, some attention must first be given to further innovations in sound.

Speaking without Wires: Radio

As magical as the telephone was, it was nothing compared to the mystery and magnitude of radio. How could sounds, created in one place, be heard at once in so many other places, so far away? Radio technology brought forth a number of developments that proved extremely important for the Internet and new media. Key among these are (1) the importance of hobbyists (radio amateurs or "hams"); (2) the identification of new business models, including advertising and sponsorship; and (3) the regulation of content.

Unlike the telephone and the telegraph, which required knowing other subscribers in a network in order for it to be useful, the radio was useful to listeners as soon as they turned it on—once there was something to listen to. Moreover, the basic elements of a radio transmitter-receiver, once the technology was well understood, were relatively inexpensive and the parts needed to build a radio were available in kit form. Indeed, before the First World War, radio was primarily a hobby activity, particularly popular with young men and boys. Prior to the 1920s, radio was not a **broadcasting** undertaking.

Radio pioneer Guglielmo Marconi and a few companies operated radio telegraph stations as a point-to-point communication technology for ships at sea or as an alternative to wired telegraphs in difficult terrain. Since only Morse code was being used at the time, radio telegraphy did not have much widespread appeal, beyond use among trained operators for commercial messages. Nevertheless, there was a dedicated group of amateurs who liked experimenting with radio and, in fact, it was among these hobbyists that many of the early technical advances were made. Plans circulated in special hobby magazines and an important industry of radio parts/kits suppliers grew, providing the parts for both the entry-level and more advanced radios that could be built at home. Marconi himself owned and operated radio stations in Canada through a subsidiary, Marconi Canada. One of these—CFCF—went on to become a pioneer in the soon-to-emerge world of radio broadcasting (Godfrey 1982: 56–71).

A Canadian living in the United States, Reginald Fessenden, is credited with sending the first spoken words over the radio.[21] In one of his early experiments, Fessenden played his violin and some Christmas carols from a record player and, much to the surprise of radio operators who had been encouraged to listen in on their headphones, it turned out that the airwaves were entirely suitable for voice, once Fessenden figured out how to get the signal from a microphone on to the channel. One thing that spurred hobbyist creativity was the growing commercial importance of radio after the First World War (all non-military use of the radio waves was curtailed during the war). With business taking over the airwaves, amateur radio operators found themselves banished to higher and higher frequencies (up where AM radio is now) and they had to be creative about how they could make use of the radio spectrum there.

In many ways, these developments paralleled and anticipated how early computer users would meet in user groups to discover how to program and build their own computers and connect them to bulletin boards and later, to the Internet. These early, informal social connections were both enabled by the medium and by the topic that members of a group were interested in, so it was a felicitous match. Where telegraph operators had developed some camaraderie, it was constrained by the need to get work done and by the limited number of people connected through the telegraph. Radio amateurs could connect with a seemingly limitless group of people and without restrictions on the time they spent on the air. They used that time to socialize, to compare notes on equipment, and to learn more about their hobby. The early radio universe was not without conflict, of course. There were some people who hogged the airwaves, while there were others who voiced extreme opinions and annoyed others, much like chat rooms and discussion forums have trolls and flamers today. But the fact remains that hobbyists helped advance radio technology in significant ways. Early web-page design also had similar hobby roots, with HTML code being shared and many people *using* the technology *to learn about* the technology.

Hobbyists can also be credited with finding the business model that would take radio from being more than a military or point-to-point communication medium (as it was used by telegraph companies that wanted to reach beyond their wires, for example). It was Frank Conrad, a radio amateur from Pennsylvania, who is widely credited with transmitting the first commercial radio broadcast in 1919, playing records provided by a local record store.[22] When Conrad saw a store that was advertising receivers capable of bringing in these radio signals and broadcasts, he convinced the executives where he worked (Westinghouse) that there might be a market in selling radio receivers. Up until that time, radio technology had been considered only a business tool or the domain of the hobbyist. Canadians living in Montreal in 1919 would have been surprised to hear that a Pittsburgh station claimed to have the first commercial broadcasts, however, as they had been listening to CFCF—a privately owned station—since late 1918 (Godfrey 1982).

More important than making claim to having conducted the first radio broadcast or owning the oldest broadcasting station is how the commercial content of radio broadcasts changed the way governments regulated the medium, which up until that time—and well into the 1920s in Canada—was very light-handed.[23] As commercially sponsored radio grew quickly through the 1920s and '30s to become big business, the content changed: in particular, soap operas—named because of the many soap commercials they carried—and comedies began to displace high-culture content such as symphonies or radio plays.

In the United Kingdom, radio broadcasting was assigned to a public agency, the British Broadcasting Commission (BBC), while in the United States, private interests were behind almost all of the broadcast activity. A Canadian model emerged in which there was a role for both private and public broadcasters (Dewar 1982). In all instances, however, much of the impetus for regulation was the content of the broadcasts and—in the case of Canada—the need for a national voice distinct from the stateside voices pouring over the border via radio waves. Canadians were particularly concerned about having a national radio system, so, because of the unique Canadian situation, the federal government set up a royal commission to look into the specifics of broadcasting in Canada. Led by John Aird, a prominent banker from Toronto, the Royal Commission on Radio Broadcasting issued a report in 1929, which recommended the

CASE STUDY

Canadian Radio Pioneer Edward Rogers—Making Radio Easier and Better

Today, the latest in new media arrives smoothly on your computer screen courtesy of high-speed Internet technologies. The new media of an earlier era—radio programs of the 1920s—were also enjoyed around the world, but people struggled with the heavy, dangerous, and expensive batteries required to power a radio set in those days (IEEE n.d.). Although household electricity was widely available in cities, there was no way to connect a radio to the alternating current that reached households. The solution to this—a vacuum tube design that took alternating current (AC) and converted it to the direct current (DC) that radios required—was provided by Edward Samuel Rogers of Toronto.

Rogers did not invent the AC tube itself, but he purchased the Canadian patent rights for the design and improved it dramatically. The new tubes not only allowed radios to be powered by household electricity—eliminating trips to the battery store with large, heavy batteries—but they also didn't cause the stains and damage to floors and carpets from the inevitable acid spills of those early wet cell batteries. Radios powered by these tubes—ingeniously—also made use of the wires in the house as an antenna for the radio set, eliminating the need for an external antenna. Rogers not only designed radios with internal tubes, he also created an external power supply that could be hooked into a household socket and then subsequently to a radio from another manufacturer (Anthony 2000).

Rogers was born in 1900 and began his radio career as a precocious child, operating radio sets from his home and winning international contests from the age of 13. He appeared in both Toronto newspapers (for hearing about a shipwreck off the coast of Ireland, via a radio alert sent from Massachusetts) and US magazines (QST, the American Radio Relay League's monthly magazine, noting his achievement of contacting Scotland in 1922) (Anthony 2000).

Rogers was a radio operator on Great Lakes ships through his teen years and helped build

establishment of publicly funded radio broadcasting in Canada. This resulted in the creation of a national broadcaster, the Canadian Radio Broadcasting Commission (CRBC) in 1932. The CRBC had the task of being both a national radio broadcaster and a regulating force for the emerging industry. Parliament subsequently split these roles and created the Canadian Broadcasting Corporation (CBC) to focus on broadcasting while the CRBC continued with the regulatory aspect, eventually becoming the Canadian Radio-television and Telecommunications Commission, or the CRTC. As with radio, modern new media have also stirred calls for regulation and raised concerns related to material unsuitable to national audiences (in some countries); influence on children (in most countries); and impacts on politics, business, and the family.

From Early Radio Broadcasts to Commercial Radio

Both Westinghouse (Conrad's KDKA station in Pittsburgh, Pennsylvania) and Marconi (the CFCF station in Montreal) were originally interested in broadcasting because they thought it would be a great way to sell radio receivers. They would soon discover, however, that the profit and power were elsewhere. The large corporations that came after Westinghouse and Marconi—including companies that remain important today, such as NBC, CBS, and ABC—brought a new approach to the radio business, and advertising has been a mainstay of commercial radio ever since.

a radio station (called 9HA) for the *Toronto Star* newspaper in the early 1920s. He also built a "radio car" to help publicize the newspaper and its radio station. His AC tube was perfected in 1924 and Rogers founded the Rogers Radio Company to manufacture and build the "batteryless radio" (Foundation Radiomuseum Luzern n.d.). Rogers first thought he could sell the tubes for the power supply to other radio manufacturers, but he found little interest and ended up building the whole radio himself (Murray 2003: 196). He went on to build a whole line of radios and later merged with a US company to produce radios for that country under the name Rogers-Majestic (Foundation Radiomuseum Luzern n.d.).

In 1927, Rogers founded the radio station CFRB ("Canada's First Rogers Batteryless"), which continues to this day at 1010 AM in Toronto. Although Rogers died quite young (at age 39), his son Ted went on to turn this single radio station into a media empire, Rogers Communications, which is now one of the largest media companies in Canada, owning cell phone, cable, Internet, and sports franchises. Interestingly, it all started with getting the batteries out of radios.

Case Study Questions

1. The nuisance of charging a home radio, especially one that used large, heavy batteries that had to be returned to a store or depot for charging, was clearly an impediment to widespread adoption of the radio. How has the battery life in your cell phone affected what you use it for, and how often?

2. Rogers made his fortune by improving on a known technology, adding power circuitry to radios. These days, the *add-on* world is made up of *apps*. What is the most useful add-on to your computer or cell phone? Who makes it?

3. Rogers Communications is now a large, complex company with many lines of business. Using a Web search, try to identify the extent and reach of the organization. See if you can find all of the subsidiaries and minor holdings. Once you are done, consider this question: would Edward Rogers still recognize the company that bears his name?

If the telegraph helped set in motion the *mechanics* of advertising (moving advertising *copy* from headquarters to the market, creating a demand for advertising *agencies*), radio (re)created these conditions and went even further. Newspapers had for a long time charged a nominal price for the paper itself, making most of their money selling print space to advertisers. But radio didn't have that option. How could you broadcast and charge a subscription fee?[24]

The answer, it seemed, was to embed ads, either before/after radio programs, as we are familiar with these days, or right in the middle of the program, with actors taking time out of their story to shill, or even working the product itself into the story (what we would call *product placement* today). This form of embedded advertising persists to this day: in the advertising that lines Google search pages and in many commercial blogs and news sites; in the advertisements that appear within video games; and in the pop-ups that appear at the foot of email. Thanks to the precedent set by radio, it has been incredibly difficult to get people to shift back to a subscription model, which would, in theory, work with the new Internet technologies because online content can be encrypted to a single machine or user and can be delivered without broadcasting it to the entire world. But, media consumers had come to expect free content (though not content free of advertising), something the new media pioneers had to inherit.

Radio also achieved something unprecedented by a mass medium: it took hold of people's attention in the privacy of their homes and during their daily routines.

Shortly thereafter, with transistor and automobile radios, the medium also accompanied people on their travels. Terry O'Reilly and Mike Tennant capture this well in their book *The Age of Persuasion*: "Print ads could be skipped, set aside, or noticed at the reader's pleasure. In contrast, radio ads reverberated through people's homes on the broadcaster's own schedule, adding the evocative nuances of voice and personality, and the subconscious power of music, to the language of persuasion" (2010: xvi). The influence of radio, however, would soon be eclipsed by something even more powerful: television.

Pictures and Sound, Educational Potential: Television

We have discussed the telegraph's capability to send a single-frame image over long distances (by scanning and reprinting the scan) and film's creation of the illusion of movement by showing a series of images at high speed, but how to combine these two innovations? The idea was obvious to many people and was widely predicted, even in the 1920s, but it was a devilishly difficult problem to solve. Both telegraphic scanning and filmmaking were difficult. Combining them made for a long series of frustrating experiments and the challenges involved were not overcome until just before the Second World War. The eventual solution—after ill-fated attempts at using mechanical scanning systems—involved television receivers that contained an electron beam yoked between powerful magnets at the end of a vacuum tube. The other end was painted with material that would glow when struck by the beam. By moving the beam from side to side and top to bottom very quickly (much faster than the human eye can perceive), an image is "painted" on to the screen.

Although the war put the advent of television (and much else) on hold, by the late 1940s, television burst onto the airwaves and was in widespread use by the 1950s, coming to Canada on a commercial basis with the start of Montreal's CBFT station in 1952 (the first experimental broadcasts were in 1932, also in Montreal).[25] Not long afterwards, the CBC cemented popular interest in television by arranging to have footage of Queen Elizabeth II's coronation flown across the Atlantic on a jet bomber and thereby made available to Canadians on the same day it took place.[26]

Many of the hopes and dreams that people had for television mirrored the early aspirations held for radio: that it would be a civilizing force for society. Although commercial radio had largely degenerated into an endless stream of advertisements, proponents of television thought that the educational aspects of the medium would prove extremely powerful. Some of the CBC's first broadcasts were of political events (e.g., the opening of Parliament) and educational programs. In the twenty-first century, however, the allure of television appears to be fading. Audience sizes are shrinking (especially in key demographics) and the power of the TV schedule (once the stronghold of the big networks) has been slipping away. Television networks with set schedules based on target demographics, requiring viewers to watch the programs they provide and the advertisements that fill those programs, now face the challenge of audience time-shifting: with personal video recorders or the option of downloading shows from the Internet, people can now watch when and where they want, and they're able to strip annoying ads from the shows. This shift seems almost inevitable today, but in the 1950s and '60s, television was all-powerful, dominating the media landscape in ways that now seem ensconced in the distant past.

Television—and the satellite transmission of broadcast signals that arrived in the 1960s—brought together the key features of all preceding new media up to that point: it had the global reach of the telegraph and telephone (and even extraterrestrial reach, with the coverage of the moon landings), the movement of film, and the sound and private consumption aspects of radio. In 1972, Canada led the world in the use of broadcast satellites for national television when its Anik AI came into service, responding to the need to deliver service to the Far North and other remote areas of the country.

With the advent of television, concerns arose that both film and radio would disappear in the face of this new medium—and, certainly, both film and radio had to evolve (they found new niches over the years). Radio has since become more of a subordinate technology in cars, at work, and around the house, providing a kind of background companion to people in their workaday lives. Film has adapted and advanced with widescreen product, elaborate sound, special effects, and 3D technology. From a new media perspective, the arrival of the small screen in the living rooms of North America made TV the multimedia of its day; the later introduction of the TV remote control brought a form of interactivity, albeit one restricted to the user flipping channels and pressing "pause" on the VCR/ DVD player. Still, television was a remarkable achievement, both technically and culturally. No longer were people required to go out for their entertainment, as they had done with the movies. Television allowed for personal and private interaction with the medium, and multimedia began to establish itself. The early television networks worked to successfully elicit a willingness among people to sit in front of a small screen for significant chunks of time, and this is carried forward to today as people spend so many hours a day in front their computer monitors, both at home and at work.

The educational, children's, and documentary features of television were among the first areas of focus for early multimedia developers. Similarly, when the CD-ROM format emerged in the 1980s, much of that early, non-networked, content was educational, including dictionaries, encyclopedias, and science and nature material. As with the media that had come before it, however, television quickly succumbed to commercial pressures. It was simply too powerful a tool (for advertising, in particular) to be left in the hands of educators and news organizations. In order to attract as wide an audience as possible, television gradually became the "vast wasteland" or "idiot box" that prompted writers such as Neil Postman (*Amusing Ourselves to Death*) and Noam Chomsky (*Manufacturing Consent: The Political Economy of the Mass Media*) to decry its very existence.

Although the television as an electronic device can hardly be blamed for all the ills of society, "TV" has become a shorthand for a larger *media ecology* that includes the pieces and all of the players of today's media landscape.[27]

One of the lessons that can be learned from the advent and dominance of television is that new media entering society do not entirely displace old media forms, new media and theory

Noam Chomsky

Noam Chomsky introduced the *propaganda model* of media theory in which he—along with co-author Edward S. Herman—spelled out the five filters that distort messages coming from commercial media, and are epitomized by television. The five filters are

1. Size, ownership, and profit orientation—the interests of the owners of media firms align with those who advertise in the media, resulting in a consistent bias toward commercial interests.
2. The advertising licence to do business—the advertising that is required to sustain an expensive business such as a television station makes the broadcaster beholden to the advertisers, who would jeopardize the viability of the firm if they withdrew their support.
3. Sourcing media news—large organizations such as government bureaucracies and corporations provide inexpensive, prepared versions of the news in the form of briefings and press releases. These are cheaper to include and distribute and, as a result, get added to the news mix without sufficient scrutiny. In addition, alternative news sources are often not included in the distribution of these items, raising the relative cost of including them, since the reporters would have to go and dig them up, taking time and effort that wasn't required when distributors provided a feed.
4. Flak—if a media outlet were to break ranks and report critical information, their owners would be subject to expensive and time-consuming litigation. It is sometimes easier to just keep quiet about certain news items.
5. Anti-communism—Chomsky has since suggested that this major bias in Western media has lately been replaced by the "War on Terror." Regardless, a dominating political ethos can bias established media outlets, who do not wish to be seen to be "at one with the enemy."

Chomsky's criticism of the media is largely connected to what we would call traditional or big media. It would be a useful classroom exercise to take a new media form, perhaps one that is reliant on advertising, as Facebook is, and run it through Chomsky's five filters. How would it deal with anti-communism/the war on terror, for example? We certainly saw a number of media companies distance themselves from WikiLeaks, when the US government deemed their actions "anti-government." On the other hand, the very existence of WikiLeaks itself—and the Wikimedia platform that it uses and the networks and servers that it lives on—could be considered a very strong counter-argument to the susceptibility of new media to the same criticism.

New media forms also offer many examples of resisting flak—they often break rank with the traditional media, even going so far as to create entirely new media outlets, in the form of blogs or wikis, when the attacks shut one down.

In terms of sourcing news, bloggers have shown incredible resourcefulness and ability not only on their own (think of Nate Silver, the person who single-handedly predicted the outcome of several US presidential elections and became famous for his "538" blog (http://fivethirtyeight.blogs.nytimes.com/author/nate-silver), but also sites such as Twitter have proven incredibly effective at aggregating the inputs of thousands of people. Certainly inaccuracies can creep in when filtering isn't professionally managed, but the sum of all those writers is a contribution to discussion and debate and, thus, can be said to enhance democracy.

Advertising—and the threat of withdrawing it when sponsors are displeased—can be a problem for any media form, including social media, but there are some interesting mitigating features. One is the ability to target ads to specific audiences, which can almost eliminate the "offended reader" problem. Lower costs and lower values are another mitigating feature about advertising in new media; quite simply, there is less at stake from a single ad.

The large size of an organization or media conglomerate, and the inclination that it will "side" with the establishment, is almost inherent in big media like newspapers and television stations that have high capital costs. Media companies simply can't even be in the game without having a lot of money and, so, are more likely to be aligned with other deep-pocketed organizations. Social and new media do not have that filter. Certainly, rich people operate new media sites, but so do many, many others.

but, rather, they rearrange relationships (in some ways, significantly so). Although movie studios and radio station owners were disrupted by the arrival of television, both found new niches and mutually compatible roles and reconfigured their offerings to fit the new reality. In exploring the newer new media, it is important to keep in mind that there will always be a balancing act between old and new forms, without a complete displacement (or not for some time, at least). Further, although media forms and uses have precursors or antecedents, new media (such as Twitter or Facebook, today) do bring with them fresh behaviours and effects that shape society in new ways.

Useful Websites

YouTube
www.youtube.com

The idea of turning to YouTube for historical information might seem a little odd at first, but once you have searched for "semaphore telegraph" or "telegraph" or "how does radio work," you will be convinced. This video-sharing site is full of interesting and explanatory videos that help the layperson understand information and communication technologies. Many of these videos are professionally produced and added to the site from the BBC and other reputable sources.

About.com
www.about.com

This site has explanations for and history behind most media and communications technologies. A search on the history of radio, for example, will turn up many entries, including "The Invention of Radio," "Radio History," and so on.

Canadian Broadcasting Corporation Digital Archives
www.cbc.ca/archives/index.html

The CBC Digital Archives are a treasure trove of media history from the earliest days of the

corporation to recent days. For media history, look in the Arts and Entertainment/Media category (www.cbc.ca/archives/categories/arts-entertainment/media); for the history of technologies, look in the Science and Technology/Technology or Science and Technology/Computers categories. A special radio broadcast, commemorating the centenary of Alexander Graham Bell's first phone calls, is a good example of what's available.

The Secret Life of Machines
www.secretlifeofmachines.com

This series of British television programs, available online, had its early inspiration from a series of newspaper comic strips depicting the workings of machinery from the sewing machine and internal combustion engines to the elevator and video camera. The series captures the early days of radio and television, including easy-to-understand explanations of how the technology works.

Radio Waves (Online Engineer), 2012
www.youtube.com/watch?v=sRX2EY5Ubto

A good introduction to the principles of radio waves and how they work, created by TheOnlineEngineer (theOLE.org). Covers basic principles as well as applications and underlying technologies.

Further Reading

The Master Switch, Tim Wu (2010)
Wu's history of telecommunication networks and mass media in the twentieth century not only

provides a wealth of detail and insight but it very also adeptly unpacks the repeated efforts by those who have just unseated a previous dominant media form to then protect their own turf with special legal and financial privileges. The book provides excellent background to current debates about copyright infringement and the situation of the music and movie businesses.

Spirit of the Web, Wade Rowland (1999 and 2006)

This text offers a historical approach to the Internet, generally, with chapters on major inventors and technologies from the semaphore telegraph to search engines. In the 2006 revised edition, Rowland's attention to the people and the players at each stage, including fascinating accounts of those who laid the first undersea telegraph cable, for example, makes for a marvellous read.

The Victorian Internet, Tom Standage (2007)

This book provides a detailed look at the telegraph and how it predicts the modern Internet in many ways. Standage offers many examples of modern media use and communication that have their roots in behaviours and techniques first worked out at the end of the nineteenth century. It is a fascinating chronicle.

"History of the US Telegraph Industry," Thomas Nonnenmacher (2001)

A concise history of the telegraph told from an economic perspective. This article contains a timeline and key technological features of the telegraph as well as useful explanations of the business drivers and uses of the telegraph, including interesting facts about the benefit of the telegraph for the railroad industry and how it allowed them to better coordinate trains and thereby avoid double-tracking their system, saving enormous capital costs. Available at http://eh.net/ encyclopedia/article/nonnenmacher.industry. telegraphic.us.

Lev Manovich's Introduction to New Media Reader, Noah Wardrip-Fruin and Nick Montfort (2003)

In addition to his Language of New Media, Manovich has provided a useful historical perspective to new media in his Introduction to Wardrip-Fruin and Montfort's New Media Reader, titled, "New Media from Borges to HTML." The original text for that introduction is available on the Web at www.intelligentagent.com/CNM200/ manovich_new_media.doc..

Canadian Railway Telegraph History, Robert Burnet (1996)

Burnet's history of the telegraph in Canada is packed with historical anecdotes and interesting features, with a focus on the people and technology that helped make telegraph communication—especially that which was carried out by the railways—possible in Canada.

"Sandford Fleming and the Pacific Cable: The Institutional Politics of Nineteenth-Century Imperial Communications," Graham Thompson (1990)

In this article, Thompson makes the case for seeing Canadian investment in telegraphy as part of a larger project of integration into the (British) imperial project and becoming a key link in a global network. Thompson's view is that we are too quick to see the national aspects of our early telecommunications (and transportation) systems and fail to realize how they were viewed at the time of construction as part of Canada's contribution to the successful running of a global empire.

Discussion Questions

1. In what ways has connectivity changed over time? What are some examples of communication technologies that were soon taken for granted? Why might that be the case?
2. In your view, is there a problem with overuse of communications technology and new media and, if so, with which technologies and what are the consequences?
3. To what extent is privacy a concern for you as a user of communications technology and new media? How has privacy as a concern changed over time?
4. What are some changes in how news has historically been moved from one location to another and what effects have these changes had on how news is captured, presented, and shared? What are the corollary effects on society?

5. In what ways does the value of a network increase as more people make use of it? Or could the argument be made that the opposite is true in some cases? What are some other consequences of increased network activity, in terms of points of contact as well as content?
6. How has telecommunications technology historically been used for connectivity between

and among people with shared interests (whether personal, professional, political, etc.)?
7. What are some of the implications of user expectations of free content, whether for creators of content, copyright owners, vetting of content, quality of content, access to content, searching content, etc.? Do such considerations change depending on genre and medium?

Class Activities

1. Locate a "how does it work" video or website for a technology from the history of new media—using a search strategy such as "how does the telegraph work?"—and then explain the process in your own words or make a storyboard for your own video.
2. Choose an historical antecedent technology, such as the telegraph or the telephone, and trace the linkages between that technology and present-day new media. Consider economic linkages, technological linkages, and socio-cultural linkages (usage).
3. We've described in this chapter several examples of "prior art" for everyday new media activities (e.g., abbreviations and text-speak found in telegrams, tweeting via the postal system). Can you find examples of these from your own family, either memories of grandparents or historical artifacts (e.g., old postcards)?
4. Locate a piece of very early "new media" (the CBC Archives on the Web are good for this) and

review it in class. What makes it similar to and different from new media today?
5. Almost anything related to new media is subject to rapid change. Firms come and go; technologies change; and numbers of users, viewers, and creators for new media content and memes change every day. Look up a fact or figure in this chapter and verify whether it remains true today, using online sources. Identify corroborating or supporting sources for your findings. Not only will you have the new facts, but you'll also have an appreciation for how quickly things change and, most importantly, a visceral sense of the way in which the Internet and new media are self-revealing to the diligent and inquisitive scholar. If you discover a fact that needs updating, you can even submit your update (with page reference and new citation) in the form of a rewritten paragraph, to the author: Richard Smith (smith@sfu.ca). He promises to reply.

Debate Questions

1. Does a historical perspective on digital media or new media help with your understanding of today's technology, or are they too remote in time to be useful?
2. While old media content have found new life online (e.g., old episodes of television programs can be downloaded), these do not advance the form or take advantage of the capabilities for which digital media are recognized—such as interactivity. What is more important to you, in

your use of the Internet, interactive experiences (gaming, commenting, blogging/tweeting/emailing) or consumption experiences (listening to music, playing YouTube videos)?
3. Are you convinced that new media are able to resist Chomsky's five criticisms, as described in the New Media and Theory box? What are some counter-criticisms, with examples of new media and social media that seem to have succumbed to these or similar pressures?

3

Approaches to New Media

Questions to Consider

- In what ways do different approaches to new media bring with them different perspectives?

- What hype and counter-hype has accompanied the evolution and discussion of new media?

- What is meant by McLuhan's phrase, "The medium is the message"? Why do you think it has become so widely known?

- In what ways can the term *technoculture* invite you to consider both technology and culture as multi-faceted and complex?

Chapter Outline

A well-rounded view of the role and effects of new media in society can be achieved only by taking a number of perspectives. For this reason, we look at several theoretical approaches to new media while providing insight into their strengths and weaknesses. Particular emphasis is placed on a "social shaping" perspective, in which groups and individuals are understood as able to influence how media is used and how it evolves. We explore some of the excitement that surrounds new media and we try to understand why science-driven messages are so compelling, while critically examining both the overly positive and the unnecessarily negative portrayals of the effects of new media. Both cultural context and media forms are explored as ways of understanding new media, along with social, psychological, and economic explanations.

Getting Perspective

We examine in this chapter different approaches to new media and we explain how different perspectives contribute to an understanding of new media. In some ways, learning about a new topic is like going to a new city. If you were new to a city, how would you approach it? Would you stand on a hill nearby and look down, or walk the streets? Would you buy a map, look at it using Google Earth, or read a travel book? Looking down or looking up, with a book, a map, or Google Earth, each of these different approaches offers a unique view. Once you have chosen an approach, you might then consider an appropriate tool to inform your perspective. A telescope would help with the view from a hill. A computer would be required for Google Earth. You can use your own eyes for reading a book or you could listen to an audiobook. Different tools or methods for looking at a topic and different perspectives on that topic are part of your approach to it and together shape your understanding. In the case of new media, there is a wide range of approaches ranging from the technical, artistic, social, political, economic, and historical.

This multidisciplinary interest reflects both the importance of new media for society and the special place that communications media occupy as both a technological form and a cultural form. A wide variety of theorists have developed many approaches to account for both the form and content of media. These are further complicated by how the content of media is affected by the form. Media technologies, especially new media technologies, are part of the social world, and as such their influences are felt through the people who develop them and are heavily affected by how people interpret the messages they contain. This is especially true in how people adapt and modify the intended use of new media. The mash-up, scratch music, the "response" video on YouTube—these are all examples of people making something new out of the content of others' messages.

For a student of new media, familiarity with multiple theories not only helps with your own investigations but also proves invaluable when you encounter commentary from others: you will know what the strengths and weaknesses of an approach might be and when one perspective might be more appropriate or useful than another. Such an understanding can also give you an appreciation of how multiple perspectives are helpful—as with the many ways of exploring a new city, each offers a different vantage point.

As you read the remainder of this book and in your own encounters with new media, we encourage you to try to deploy multiple views, to think about how your perspective influences what you find and your understanding. We particularly encourage you to see human beings as creative actors in the media world they live in—not simply reacting to or being affected by the new media world but using independent thinking with agency, with free will.

What to Believe: The Hype or the Counter-Hype?

Writing in 1998, Kitchin (1998: ix) described **cyberspace** as "probably one of the most universally over-hyped terms of the latter part of the twentieth century." Fifteen years later, this has not changed. Indeed, a recurring feature of the development of the

Internet and the popularization of digital media technologies has been their capacity to generate excitement about how they are expected to change everything, typically for the better.

Lister and colleagues (2003: 11) suggest that this tendency is linked to the modernist belief in technology as socially progressive: new is the "cutting edge" or the "avant-garde" and the place for "forward-thinking people" to be. This attitude characterized many analyses of the Internet in the 1990s (e.g. Dyson 1999; Dyson et al. 1994; Kelly 1997; Negroponte 1995; Rheingold 1994), which also tended to debunk criticism of the new technologies (Postman 1993; Robins and Webster 1999; Sale 1995; Stoll 1995). This early "polarization between narrow suspicion and uncritical enthusiasm" (Woolgar 2002: 3–4) that characterized new media studies in the 1990s has to some extent given way to more empirically grounded research into new media, its uses, and impacts (Flew 2001; Livingstone 2005; Silver 2000; Wellman 2004).

The **dot-com crash** of 2001 was a harsh lesson in the dangers of investing in new media companies that had fatally flawed business plans. At the same time, the buzz around new media remains pervasive, partly because it helps to boost share prices, persuade politicians, and sell product, but also because it taps into what

---

new media and theory

Vincent Mosco

Canadian social scientist Vincent Mosco has been long identified with an approach to media and technology known as political economy. A political economist strives to understand our society by better exposing the ownership structure and money flow that surrounds an event, a technology, a media form, or political movement. The basis of these types of argument is that if you can find out where the money goes, you will find out where the power flows and with that you will have a better insight into how things occur and why.

Currently an emeritus professor at Queen's University in Kingston, and before that at Carleton University in Ottawa, Mosco's examination of traditional media businesses helped scholars better understand a changing landscape for radio, television, newspapers, and magazines throughout the 1980s and '90s. His 2004 book, *The Digital Sublime: Myth, Power and Cyberspace*, extended that analysis to digital media and helped us better appreciate the power of the stories that surrounded the rise of the Internet era and also gave students and scholars a better appreciation of how many of these stories are similar to, and hearken back to, tales told about earlier technologies, such as the telegraph.

The mystique of technology may have been somewhat tarnished following the dot-com boom and bust in the early twenty-first century, but each year a new technology or new media pioneer seems to appear on the scene and assert itself. Whether it be Facebook or Twitter or Pinterest or Ingress, the student of Mosco's work will seek to step back from the hyperbole and ask a few hard questions about how money is being made, who owns this service, and what is the role of the audience/user/creator?

Mosco also makes a key observation when he states that the moment a media form achieves the height of its power is when we are so used to it that we no longer even notice its existence. He looks at something as everyday as electricity and shows how it is when we never even notice it that it is having the greatest impact on our lives: we are taking it for granted and, in so doing, becoming dependent.

These days, the Internet is gradually falling into the background, and it probably won't be long before the cell phone is also so common that we don't even notice it. The importance of Mosco's work is that it helps us appreciate that moment for what it is: the moment when a technology has us most in its grasp (Mosco 2004).

Vincent Mosco (2004) refers to as the "digital sublime." Mosco describes the extent to which cyberspace possesses not only technical, political, and economic properties, but also how it is a form of cultural myth and, as such, offers possibilities of transcending the limits of contemporary society and the material world.

Popular writing about the Internet and cyberspace in the mid-1990s had no shortage of pronouncements regarding the utopian, almost transcendent nature of the implications surrounding new media. Nicholas Negroponte's *Being Digital* (1995) was one of the most influential texts promoting this view. As founding director of the Media Lab at MIT and a founder and columnist for *Wired* magazine, Negroponte championed the idea that digitization had reached a point where the transition from an economy and society based on "atoms" (tangible physical assets) and the production of goods, to one based on "bits" (intangible wealth based on knowledge) meant that "computing is not about computers any more. It is about living" (1995: 6). Negroponte concluded *Being Digital* by proclaiming that "the empowering nature of being digital" meant that "like a force of nature, the digital age cannot be denied or stopped and that it has four very powerful qualities that will result in its ultimate triumph: decentralizing, globalizing, harmonizing and empowering" (1995: 229, 231). Despite the obvious technological determinism in Negroponte's claim, his observations relating to the ways in which digital media have an effect on society remain useful. It is important to examine each of these four forces. Digital media provides a decentralizing and globalizing force when it decouples production and removes or reduces the necessity of being co-present in order to coordinate our activities. A simple example is the ease with which a Vancouver-based fashion designer might work with a Montreal factory and a Toronto ad agency to deliver her dresses to markets in Asia and Europe, using Skype, email, and file sharing. We all experience the harmonization aspect of digital media when an Internet meme such as a viral video ("Gangnam Style," anyone?) becomes a phenomenon in multiple countries and cultures and across ages and genders. Whether new media will be as empowering as Negroponte hoped is yet to be seen, but elsewhere in this book we look at examples of political action initiated and coordinated through computers and cell phones.

Incredible optimism and predictions of transformation are widespread in discussions of new media. Electronic Frontier Foundation (EFF) co-founder John Perry Barlow argued that "with the development of the Internet, and with the increasing pervasiveness of communication between networked computers, we are in the middle of the most transforming technological event since the capture of fire" (1995: 36). George Gilder (1994: 49) predicted that the Internet would mean the death of television, which he saw as being "a tool for tyrants . . . [whose] overthrow will be a major force for freedom and individualism, culture and morality." (1994: 49) In 1994, through the Progress and Freedom Foundation (www.pff.org), Esther Dyson, George Gilder, George Keyworth, and pioneering new media thinker Alvin Toffler (1970, 1980) published *Cyberspace and the American Dream: A Magna Carta for the Knowledge Age*, which claimed that the Internet was a concrete expression of uniquely American values of entrepreneurship and rugged individualism, and identified cyberspace as "the land of knowledge . . . civilization's truest, highest calling" and the basis for the "creation of a new civilization, founded in the eternal truths of the American Idea" (Dyson et al. 1994).

This optimism wasn't confined to academics and industry players. In 1994, then US vice-president Al Gore's speech to the International Telecommunications

Union, for example, proclaimed that the US-led Global Information Infrastructure initiative would promote "robust and sustainable economic progress, strong democracies, better solutions to global and local environmental challenges, improved health care, and—ultimately—a greater sense of shared stewardship of our small planet" (Gore 1994). John Brockman's anthology of interviews with and short pieces authored by the "digerati"—defined as those who "evangelize, connect people, adapt quickly . . . [and] give each other permission to be great" (1996: xxvi)—is an excellent primer on mid-1990s "cyberbole" for readers who did not experience the adventure first-hand.

Not surprisingly, such enthusiasm faced counter-analyses and debunking. Knights and colleagues (2002) refer to this as the "'emperor's-new-clothes' story," in which inflated claims were pierced by skeptics. Former cyberspace advocate Clifford Stoll (1995: 13) also had second thoughts about cyberspace, warning that "life in the real world is far more interesting, far more important, far richer, than anything you'll ever find on a computer screen." Critics of the digital age such as Brook and Boal (1995) and Sale (1995) reinvoked the spirit of the **Luddite** opposition to industrial technologies of early nineteenth-century Britain to warn of the need to "resist the virtual life," with Sale going so far as to smash a computer on stage while promoting his book (Silver 2000: 20). Barbrook and Cameron (1995: 1) argued that the new media discourse fostered by *Wired* magazine was part of a Californian ideology that constituted "a bizarre fusion of the cultural bohemianism of San Francisco with the hi-tech industries of Silicon Valley," combining political **libertarianism** with a belief in free markets in a world where "everybody can be both hip and rich." Postman critiqued the entire relationship of culture to technology in modern societies as one of technopoly, defined as "the deification of technology, which means that the culture seeks its authorization in technology, finds its satisfactions in technology, and takes its orders from technology" (1993: 71). When the sharp decline of the NASDAQ index in April 2000 led to the collapse of many of the dot-com enterprises that had started up in the late 1990s, a veritable cottage industry of corporate *mea culpas* was generated over the dangers of believing in the buzz (Kuo 2001; cf. Lovink 2002; Malmstein 2001).

Interpreting Hype and Counter-Hype: Methodological Considerations

In their review of the social implications of the Internet, DiMaggio et al. (2001) present a fivefold typology of Internet impacts that identifies positive and negative assessments (see Table 3.1).

Overly optimistic or pessimistic accounts of the impact of new media—cyberbole—have been countered by approaches that seek to identify a middle ground between extreme positions. Some have called for a "new empiricism" in Internet studies that goes beyond utopianism and critiques and engages with new media users and the environments, both technological and socio-cultural, in which they make use of networked ICTs (Flew 2001; Silver 2000). In other words, the new empiricism—which is not that new any more, being over a decade old—tries to ground new media studies in real data and the real experiences of those who use media. As such, it is a both a break from the earlier utopian and dystopian approaches and also an implicit

Table 3.1 Social Implications of the Internet

Internet Impact	Positive	Negative
1. Inequality	New access to information based on computer use and availability (digital opportunity)	Patterns of access, availability, and use of ICTs reflect other social inequalities (digital divide)
2. Community	New forms of social interaction and community formation through virtual communities that are not space-bound	Online activities become an obstacle to real-life interactions; declining commitment to locality-based social capital formation
3. Politics	New opportunities for online political engagement, information exchange, and deliberation; a virtual public sphere	Isolation from others in politically effective geographical locales; management of participation by political and economic elites
4. Organizations	Flexible organizations; networked interaction among those within and outside of the organization; more "horizontal" channels of online communication	New forms of internal surveillance; online communication remains hierarchical; online as a low-trust communications environment
5. Culture	"Demassification" of access to and use of media content; new opportunities for users to become media producers ("produsers" [Bruns 2005])	Hyper-segmentation and "I media" as a barrier to communication with others; fragmentation and dilution of a common culture

Source: DiMaggio et al. (2001).

acknowledgment that what we are talking about is not a separate sphere (cyberspace) but rather the online aspects of regular life.

At the same time, there are limitations to the new empiricism approach. We will return to current themes in new media research later in the chapter, however, it is worth noting here three implications of a new empiricism for new media studies.

First, any approach lends itself more readily to some research and theoretical traditions than to others. Empiricism lends itself to statistically based sociology and quantitative, survey-based methodologies that are intended to generate advice for government policy-makers on managing technological change. It is important to remember, however, that these empirical approaches exist alongside others, such as (1) speculative media theory, which has tended to approach the interaction between technology and culture in more future-oriented terms; (2) critical political economy, which has questioned whether policy-making organizations possess sufficient distance from the most powerful private interests to be able to act in the public interest; and (3) online ethnography, which looks at the use of new media and the Internet in everyday life (Bakardjieva 2005). These alternative approaches can provide insight into the meaning of changes—changes that the empirical approach can identify but not always explain. For example, we might observe by counting Internet connections that there are more connections in homes, but what are those connections being used for? Porn? Home-based businesses? Education? These types of questions are sometimes better answered by spending time with people and seeing what they do with their new media tools and technology.

Second, an empirical approach to new media tends to have an "after-the-event" element; it seeks to manage change rather than to make change. This in itself may be a legacy of ways of thinking associated with earlier one-to-many broadcast media systems, such as television. Kress (1997: 78), for example, makes the observation that, just as the binary opposition between producers and consumers of media is challenged by new media technologies, so, too, is the distinction between design and critique, where "some individuals set the agenda and others either follow or object." One of the recurring themes of new media developments is the extent to which critique of existing systems happens through design—such as open-source software, open publishing, citizen journalism, and participatory media systems—so that the politics of new media is as often enacted through the relationships between large-scale corporate media and those who pursue alternative forms of digital creativity, as it is between those who analyze the power relations of new media from an academic or research perspective.

In Canada, there is a design-based new media form that through its very existence is questioning and reducing the power of the private publishers of academic journals. This project, the Public Knowledge Project (PKP), and the software created by it, Open Journal Systems (OJS), is spawning a renaissance of scholarly publishing around the world. Not only are more journals springing up because the tools are freely available and easy to use, but also many of them are providing their articles free of charge. The PKP, led by John Willinsky, got its start at the University of British Columbia and is currently hosted by the Simon Fraser University Library, where a hub has been established to coordinate and support the efforts of dozens of open-source programmers around the world. The project has since led to the creation of companion tools to make it easier to host an academic conference (Open Conference System, or OCS) or publish an academic monograph (Open Monograph Press, or OMP). You can learn more about PKP and OJS at their website: http://pkp.sfu.ca.

Third, it is important to consider the recurring significance of optimism about new media as a form of *myth* that is historically grounded. In his discussion of the "cyberspace myth," Mosco notes that his interest in this topic stemmed in part from his experience as a graduate student in 1973 when he looked at claims that multi-channel cable television would "usher in a Wired Society governed by Electronic Democracy" (2004: 1; cf. Streeter 1987). Mosco points out not only how claims about the democratizing potential of cable television now look silly (30 years after the advent of cable), but also that such claims bear a striking resemblance to those made about the transformative impact of the Internet (now roughly 20 years later). He also draws attention to the pioneering analysis by Carey and Quirk (1992) of the parallels between recent prophecies about the "electronic revolution" of new ICTs and the late nineteenth-century utopian idea that industrial machinery and electrical technology could be harnessed in harmony with nature to provide both material prosperity and social peace.

Approaches to Technological Change: Divergent Perspectives

Many of the utopian propositions noted above (and elsewhere in this book) can be seen as marked by **technological determinism**. While technological determinism is not a theory of technological change, it is a pervasive way—especially in popular media—of thinking (or perhaps not thinking) about the relationship between new technologies and society. A technological determinist, whether optimistically or pessimistically, sees people as being forged in a crucible of technological forms. The way in which those technologies arrived among us, or how they work, is generally left unexamined in a rush to see the "impact" of the technology.

Technological determinism sees social change as driven by technological change. Williams defines technological determinism as a view that "research and development have been assumed as self-generating. The new technologies are invented . . . in an independent sphere, and then create new societies or new human conditions" (1974: 13). The literature on the impact of the Internet is rich with examples of this type of thinking. In relation to new media, Buckingham (2000: 45) observes that in such arguments, "the computer is predominantly seen as an autonomous force that is somehow independent of human society, and acts on it from the outside."

Historical analysts of technology such as Winner (1986a, b), Cowan (1997), and MacKenzie and Wacjman (1999) demonstrate the flawed logic of technological determinists—who would have technology advancing of its own accord, propelled by innovation, free of outside influence. These flaws have been highlighted by several real-world new media developments:

- the VHS–Beta wars of the 1980s, where the adoption of a common standard for video recorders had less to do with the inherent superiority of one format over another (many suggested that Beta was a superior format) than with the capacity of other video recorder hardware manufacturers to squeeze Sony (the principal promoter of Beta) out of the crucial US market;
- the legal battles between Apple and Microsoft in the late 1990s over ownership of the "desktop" graphical user interface, which indicated that GUIs did not simply evolve from earlier to newer versions but that they might constitute highly lucrative forms of intellectual property;
- the more recent battle between Apple and Samsung, in which designs for new smartphones, which Apple claims were copied, resulted in a fine of more than $1 billion against Samsung;
- the excitement around Facebook's initial public offering (IPO) of stock and subsequent decline in value to less than half of what it originally sold for;
- the over-investment of telecommunications companies in 3G wireless broadband spectrum in the early 2000s, driven by an assumption—largely untested—that users sought to access Internet content through their mobile phones; and
- the continued difficulties in developing digital television in many parts of the world, as the implications of a more economical use of spectrum come up against the resistance of incumbent broadcasters to the possible development of new television services (Galperin 2004).

We question the argument that the relationship between new media technologies and society is technologically determinist. In doing so, there are two important caveats to be noted. The first is related to the question of whether a cluster of technologies will, in fact, shape historical development over the long term. Heilbroner (2003), for example, has argued that a particular technological form contains within it implicit forms of social organization that are difficult to reverse. Once it is created and adopted, it is hard to go back. A good example of this is the household washing machine, which carries with it the implicit assumption that clothes will be washed by homeowners, and no longer by servants—otherwise, why make it so fancy? And once you have one, why hire someone to wash your clothes? (Rowland 2006) The second caveat to keep in mind is to observe the partial truth of technological determinism, in that once particular technologies are widely adopted and used, they acquire a degree of "lock-in" that shapes society and culture in a wider sense. Winner (1986a,b) makes this point in relation to what he terms "inherently political technologies" such as nuclear power, whose very existence requires hierarchical, command-and-control forms of internal organization and high levels of external surveillance. In a different but related vein, Arthur's (1999) example is the QWERTY typewriter keyboard and how it achieved dominance in the early twentieth century, with adoption by large organizations and training among prospective workers, leading to technological lock-in because the costs of change for individuals and organizations became too great to contemplate.

Though these are valid points, we will focus on the **social shaping of technology** approach, the major alternative to technological determinism. This theory argues that social, institutional, economic, and cultural factors shape the choices made about the forms of technological innovation, the content of technological artifacts and practices, and the outcomes and impacts of technological change for different groups in society. This approach stresses the need to analyze "the socio-economic patterns embedded in both the content of technologies and the processes of innovation" (Williams and Edge 1996: 866). This, in turn, requires a broader understanding of technology than simply its most basic application as tools and artifacts used by humans. Rather, a definition of technology as simply "hardware" needs to be extended to consider the uses of such technologies, their contexts of use, and the systems of knowledge and social meaning that accompany their development and use (MacKenzie and Wacjman 1999). This multi-dimensional understanding of technology is apparent in the origin of the word *technology* in ancient Greek, combining *techne* ("practical or applied arts and skills") and *logos* ("systematic reason, knowledge, or discourse") as well as in French and German, where the words *la technique* and *die Technik* convey a meaning of technology that involves the tools, their uses, and associated forms of knowledge (MacKenzie and Wacjman 1999: 7).

The broad framework of social shaping of technology theories has within it three distinctive strands: (1) the diffusion of innovations model; (2) the political economy model; and (3) theories of culture and technology. The **diffusion of innovations model** is associated with communications theorist Everett Rogers (2003), who sought to model the rate of adoption and eventual spread of an innovation in the social system through communication via particular channels—influential individuals, related businesses, social networks—over time. Rogers's model identifies different categories of user (including early adopters) and the adoption threshold at which an innovation becomes a mature technology. In *The Invisible Computer*, Norman (1998) draws on Rogers's earlier work to argue that there is a shift in market focus from the attributes of the technology to its ease of use and ability to solve problems as it evolves through a given diffusion cycle (see Figure 3.1). The "innovator's dilemma" (discussed in Chapter 8) draws upon this framework, allowing the expert to observe the risks of

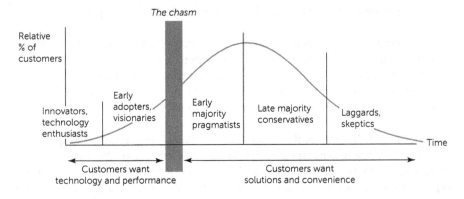

Figure 3.1 Consumer Demand and the Diffusion Cycle

Source: Norman (1998: 30).

developing more complex technological solutions at the stage where a technological product is becoming a mass-market commodity.

Where the diffusion of innovations approach tends to focus on social uptake of new technologies and has what Rogers acknowledges is a "pro-innovation bias" (2003: 106), the **political economy approach** focuses much more specifically on the politics and power relations embedded in technological development. MacKenzie and Wacjman (1999) argue that an understanding of how technologies developed both historically and in the present era requires that close attention be paid to dominant economic relations, social relations of production, military priorities, the role of the state, and gender relations.

Critical theories of technology, one of which is the political economy approach, see technology as part of the interplay of power and domination in society. So, for example, Sholle points out that "technologies are . . . processes that structure the world in particular ways. . . . We should not see technology and the social as separate domains" (2002: 6).

The political economy approach and critical theories of technology, more generally, draw attention to the ways in which politics, power, and economic relations are embedded in the process of scientific and technological research itself. This can occur directly, through the capacity of large corporations, government agencies, and the military to shape the research and training priorities of academic institutions through large-scale funding at a time when government funding and other traditional sources are being cut back. Indeed, Schiller (2000) argues that this has become increasingly central to Internet and other new media research.

Less directly, but perhaps more profoundly, it is argued by Feenberg (2003) and others that "technological development is constrained by cultural norms originating in economics, ideology, religion, and tradition." These kinds of constraints are often obscured by an underlying technological rationality, or what Feenberg terms a "technical code." Technical code—often in the form of software for programmable machines—is "not merely a belief, an ideology, but is effectively incorporated into the structure of machines" (2003: 657, 658). Thus, the computer that has Windows software presents the user with a vast array of established user–computer relationships that are mainly commercial.

Picking up on Feenberg's **critical theory of technology**, Sholle argues that

> A technology such as the computer is a product of social processes from the beginning. The particular construction of knowledge in institutions of science and engineering, the economic interests of companies, the cultural patterns of consumption, the spatial arrangements of communities and nations, the political motifs of government policies are inscribed into the technology from the very beginning. (2002: 7)

This technical code does not always constrain freedom. More recently, Flanagin et al., building on Feenberg's concept of the technical code, argue that "the Internet's technical design supports interoperability and open access, while suggesting an enormous capacity for personalization and innovation" (2010: 179). A key feature of the design and a factor in much of the recent excitement about new media and Web 2.0 is the way in which Web users are able to take control over their configuration, use, and reuse of the Internet, which results in "a sense of individual empowerment achieved through enhanced agency" (Flanagin et al. 2010: 179).

When we think of media studies—apart from those examinations that are purely about a specific media form, such as film or television, as a technology—we often think about audiences. What is the audience for this medium? What is the effect of this medium or this content on the audience? As media have become social and interactive, the notion of "audience"—with the assumed passivity and implications of being a "couch potato" (the lean-back experience, it is sometimes called)—has become less important.

Even before the current age, a growing number of scholars pointed out that the audience is far from being a passive recipient of media messages. Anything that is sent out on television or in film is read through a lens of culture, of habit, of interpretation both personal and social. The audience has always been more active than has been assumed by many people.

New media accentuate this effect and require that we think carefully about what we say in terms of audiences and how they are "affected by" media. In many cases, the media message—and even the media form itself—is greatly influenced, if not wholly created by the users of that medium. Blogging is a good example of this. While many people simply read a blog and could be said to be an "audience," the typical blog post (or status update on Facebook, or tweet on Twitter, or snap on Pinterest) is more of a conversation than a final product. The audience is at least sharing what they see around them, if not creating entirely new things. And everything that is created or shared is subject to reinterpretation, reposting, and revision. Web 2.0 marks a major shift in what we think is most important: the consuming audience or the (creative) user of a service.

Technology and Cultural Studies

Feenberg's (2003) observation that technology and culture are interdependent has also been developed in work from a cultural studies perspective. Cultural studies theorists view new media as "cultural technologies." In other words, they are interwoven collections (sometimes called "assemblages") of technology, content, context, power relations, and social knowledge.

Berland proposes that media as cultural technologies produce not only content (media texts), but also spatial arrangements and modes of consumption that "are material practices with their own structural effects and tensions" (1992: 40). The concept of "technocultures" has been used by Penley and Ross (1991), Menser and Aronowitz (1996), and Green to refer to "tools of mediated communication through which cultural material is created and circulated" (Green 2002: xxx–xxxi). Green makes the important point that, while all technologies have cultural impacts (think, for instance, of the myriad cultural implications of the automobile), media technologies have a particular significance in this regard because they carry both explicit and implicit messages. A website, for example, delivers its explicit content (the words and images on the screen) as well as a message about its creator (and the society in which it was created), delivered implicitly through elements including design choices such as colour and font styles, set-up and configuration, and the level of language used. Via these implicit messages, media technologies enable the circulation of what Thompson (1991: 132) terms "symbolic forms . . . by virtue of which individuals communicate with one another and share their experiences, conceptions and beliefs."

The significance of this conception of culture as communication mediated through technologies becomes apparent when recognizing that, just as the concept of technology has multiple levels of meaning, so, too, does culture. On one level, culture can be understood in terms of *aesthetics*, which equates culture with the arts. Cultural studies, however, have drawn attention to a more *anthropological* definition of culture as the whole way of life, or forms of lived experience, of people, communities, and social groups. Such an expanded definition of culture draws attention to the significance of forms of communication, social relations, and practices of everyday life. As Raymond Williams observes in *The Long Revolution*,

> Culture is the description of a particular way of life, which expresses certain meanings and values not only in art and learning but also in institutions and ordinary behaviour. . . . Such analysis will . . . include analysis of elements in the way of life that to followers of the other definitions are not "culture" at all; the organization of production, the structure of the family, the structure of institutions which express or govern social relationships, the characteristic forms through which members of the society communicate. (1965: 57–8)

In addition to artistic and intellectual activity and the habits communities or groups, culture can also be understood as derived from what Thompson (1991: 136) refers to as the *structural conception* of culture. This conception of culture "emphasizes both the symbolic character of cultural phenomena and the fact that such phenomena are always embedded in structured social contexts." Noting the observation of the renowned semiotician Umberto Eco (1976: 9) that "every act of communication . . . presupposes a signification system as its necessary condition," this structuralist approach to culture draws attention to the ways in which individuals are "produced" as social beings within a given system of social, cultural, linguistic, and psychological relationships, which possess an underlying structural "code" not necessarily accessible to outsiders. Drawing out the implications of this for new media studies, Poster (2005: 136) observes that "computer-mediated communication fundamentally shifts the registers of human experience as we have known them in modern society. . . . Time and space, body and mind, subject and object, human and machine are each dramatically transformed by practices carried out on networked computers." It is clear that, from a cultural studies perspective, these different ways of looking at culture can be extended to technology. Table 3.2 provides a summary of these perspectives.

Table 3.2 Defining Technology and Culture: A Three-Level Approach

	Definition of technology	Definition of culture
First level: "common-sense" definitions	Technology as physical objects, tools, artifacts	Culture as "the arts" and aesthetic excellence
Second level: contextual or user-based definitions	Technology as content or "software," defined by how it is used	Culture as "ways of life" or the lived experience of peoples, communities, or groups
Third level: communicative or structural definitions	Technology as systems of knowledge and social meaning	Culture as an underlying structural system

Political Economy and Cultural Studies

Cultural studies, while important for understanding new media, benefit from being considered alongside the political economy of new media (Flew 2007). New media, after all, are a business, and their economic implications are important factors in whether or not and how widely they are deployed. Political economy approaches tend to start from the perspective of economic and industrial dynamics. They focus on the extent to which access to resources at various levels influences the directions that new media developments can take (or may not take, because those proposing them lack sufficient resources). These resources include access to investment capital to participate in new media ventures, access to political influence on the basis of economic power and significance as a decision-maker, and access to the technologies themselves on the part of potential users, with the focus on inequalities of access across all of these levels. These are seen as relating to various indicators of social inequality, such as class, gender, race, ethnicity, and other markers of disadvantage.

Theorists such as McChesney (1999, 2000, 2003), Schiller (2000; cf. McChesney and Schiller 2003), Mosco (1996, 1997, 2000, 2004), Gandy (2002), and Murdock and Golding (2004) are among the most influential contributors to the development of a political economy approach to new media. Their work is mostly skeptical about claims that new media have led to fundamental changes in the socio-economic structures in which they are embedded. In an essay refuting claims that the rise of the Internet promises new forms of democratic media politics, McChesney (2000: 33–4) observes that "despite its much-ballyhooed 'openness' . . . [the Internet] will likely be dominated by the usual corporate suspects. Certainly a few new commercial players will emerge, but the evidence suggests that the content of the digital communications world will appear quite similar to that of the pre-digital commercial media world." Similarly, Kumar argues that developments associated with new media and the knowledge economy have not produced a radical shift in the dynamics of capitalist societies since "the imperatives of profit, power and control seem as predominant now as they have ever been in the history of capitalist industrialism. The difference lies in the greater range and intensity of their applications . . . not in any change in the principles themselves" (2005: 154).

While political economy theories start from the perspective of economic power, cultural theories start from the perspective of communications and culture, and they examine the complexities and power dynamics that emerge in the relationship between the production, reception, interpretation, and use of messages arising from technologically mediated forms of communication like new media. While cultural approaches have a common lineage with political economy in their historical relationship to neo-Marxism and critical theory, the tradition within this field to regard audiences as *active* (having minds of their own and able to make decisions about the worth of those messages) has seen advocates tend to make more positive assessments of the transformative potential of new media. Jenkins (2006a) captures the extent to which, from a cultural studies perspective, the relationship between producers and users of new media constitutes a contested space where positive outcomes *can* occur. This is akin to earlier work in cultural studies on the relationship between popular culture and power relations in society (cf. Flew 2007: 39–43; Hartley 2003):

> We are entering an era of prolonged transition and transformation in the way media operates. Convergence describes the process by which we will sort through these options.... Media producers will only find their way through these current problems by renegotiating their relationship with their consumers. Audiences, empowered by these new technologies, occupying a space at the intersection between old and new media, are demanding the right to participate within the culture.... The resulting struggles and compromises will define the public culture of the future. (Jenkins 2006a: 24)

Those working from a cultural studies–oriented perspective have tended to be more optimistic about the potential of new media. By contrast, political economy acolytes are often skeptical about the transformative capacities of new media, and they take pains to stress the continuities between old and new media. At the same time, this correlation is complicated at several points.

From a perspective grounded in Marxist political economy, Graham (2006: 16) argues that the current phase of what he calls "hypercapitalism" has transformed the dynamics of capitalist economies so fundamentally that "use-values and exchange-values are not necessarily separable in a knowledge economy." In other words, the traditional categories for understanding capital—labour, capital, and exchange—get blurred in a **knowledge economy**, making analysis difficult and traditional assumptions about workers and bosses either irrelevant or at least worth reconsidering. When you work at home, using your own computer, and do some blogging on the side as a hobby, are you a labourer?

Similarly, Tiziana Terranova describes the "cultural politics of information"—which breaks with conceptions of information as mere communications content that requires subsequent critical decoding—as "immaterial" and of lesser importance than the dynamics of industrial production (2004: 3). In Terranova's view, information is important *because* it is not all-powerful, convincing people to make decisions they would not otherwise make, nor is it entirely subject to interpretation by the receiver. Instead, there is a dynamic at work that must consider both the material force of information (who owns it, who buys it, who controls the sale) and the messages contained therein, including the potential for creativity and change.

At the same time, there has been debate within cultural studies over its relationship to new media. Bassett (2007) examines how a focus on both the politics of signification (acknowledging that the encoding of messages cannot be value-free) and the focus on the sender in the text message–receiver relationship often diminishes the significance of the media technologies as drivers of systems of meaning in their own right. Bassett proposes that a cultural studies practice oriented toward new media needs to consider the forms of political engagement that are specific to digitally networked media, such as "tactical media" (Cubitt 2006) and "hacktivism" (Dyer-Witheford 2002; O'Neil 2006), while also requiring the "(re)incorporation of the political economy of new media into cultural studies" (Bassett 2007: 234).

One such scholarly project, by researcher Kate Milberry, examined the work of activists who contributed to political and social causes through the development and management of software for political groups. This form of contributing to a cause, the aforementioned hacktivism, gained prominence around the time of the 1999 Battle in Seattle (tumultuous protests surrounding a meeting of the World Trade Organization). Milberry's 2009 dissertation, *Geeks and Global Justice: Another (Cyber) World Is Possible*, examined the ways in which the technology is developed so that it "embodies values of equality, freedom, and justice" (iii).

Pioneer Media Theorists: Marshall McLuhan and Raymond Williams

The relationship between new media technologies and media content raises a series of complex issues about the social and cultural impacts of media themselves. While the new media discussed in this book have largely been developed and popularized since the 1990s, it is important to consider the long-standing provenance of whether media technologies have the power to transform society and culture (cf. Lister et al. 2003: 72–92). Two of the key thinkers from the 1960s and '70s were the Canadian communications theorist Marshall McLuhan and the Welsh cultural theorist Raymond Williams. In many ways, their respective approaches to the question of how media technologies relate to the wider society and culture have constituted the two competing poles of thought about new media that we have been discussing—technological determinism and social shaping theory.

Marshall McLuhan was a controversial and eclectic theorist, whose work stressed the extent to which cultural content was embedded within specific technological forms, meaning that media influence not only *what* people think but *how* people think. His work, developed in key texts such as *The Gutenberg Galaxy: The Making of Typographic Man* (McLuhan 1962), *Understanding Media* (McLuhan 1964), and *The Medium is the Massage* (McLuhan and Fiore 1967), has always polarized opinions, with his advocates arguing that "his was the first coherent interpretation of the electric world" (McLuhan and Zingrone 1997: 6) and his critics maintaining that his writings assumed "an importance which has nothing to do with their worth" (Ricks 1968: 59). McLuhan's ideas became unfashionable during the 1970s and '80s, particularly in light of the critique of technological determinism levelled by Raymond Williams and others (see below), but the rise of the Internet saw McLuhan championed as a visionary (for example, see de Kerckhove 1998; Levinson 1997; Wolf 1996).

Central to McLuhan's theory of communications media is his well-known aphorism that "the medium is the message." What this means is that technologies are first and foremost extensions of human selves and human capacities: "The personal and social consequences of any medium—that is, of any extension of ourselves—result from the new scale that is introduced into our affairs by each extension of ourselves, or by any new technology" (McLuhan 1964: 23). At the same time, the impact of any medium on the conduct of human affairs is neither transparent nor obvious. For McLuhan, the key to understanding electronic culture is not in the technologies themselves, such as machines or computers, nor in the uses of their content or alleged effects, but rather in the ways in which they subtly alter the environment in which humans act and interact. He proposed that the logic of the electric age can be found in electric light, since it is pure information, "a medium without a message," which can have content only when it is used in conjunction with another medium—for example, the use of electric light to spell out a neon sign:

> The electric light escapes attention as a communication medium just because it has no "content." And this makes it an invaluable instance of how people fail to study media at all. . . . The message of the electric light is like the message of electric power in industry, totally radical, pervasive and decentralized. For electric light and power are separate from their uses, yet they eliminate time and space factors in human association exactly as do radio, telegraph, telephone and TV, creating involvement in depth. (McLuhan 1964: 24–5)

One implication of McLuhan's analysis is that "the impact of the communication media on sensory perception influences not only what we think but how we think" (McPhail and McPhail 1990: 69). For McLuhan, the "grammar" of a medium structures human sensory responses to it, fundamentally altering perceptions of social reality:

> All media work us over completely. They are so persuasive in their personal, political, economic, aesthetic, psychological, moral, ethical and social consequences that they leave no part of us untouched, unaffected, unaltered. . . . Any understanding of social and cultural change is impossible without a knowledge of the way media work as environments. (McLuhan and Fiore 1967: 26)

In contrast to McLuhan's focus on how media technologies reshape society and culture, Raymond Williams was primarily interested in the question of how technologies *are shaped by* social, cultural, political, and economic forces. This stress on the social shaping of technology meant that Williams focused on the social forces, power relations, and conflicts between competing interests that lead to some (technological) options being pursued while others are not developed or are actively foreclosed upon. For Williams, a failure to focus on the social dimensions of how technologies are developed and how they are used is an example of technological determinism, which he accused McLuhan of and which Williams believed was an ideology used by the powerful to support their own interests:

> If the effect of the medium is the same, whoever controls and uses it, and whatever apparent content he may try to insert, then we can forget ordinary political and cultural argument, and let the technology run itself. It is hardly surprising that this conclusion has been welcomed by the "media-men" of the existing institutions. (Williams 1974: 131)

Using the historical development of television as his principal case study, Williams argued that the medium's development needed to be understood as arising from a series of primarily commercial investment decisions in the technologies of mass broadcast communication, which had been shaped by the development of radio and which promoted a relationship between technology and the wider society based on "centralized transmission and privatized reception" (1974: 24). Media both shaped and was shaped by a wider set of developments in industrial capitalist societies, such as mass production, the rise of consumer society, large-scale commercial investments in communications technologies, and the development of suburban housing, which saw a spatial separation of home from places of work. Williams also noted the significance of different institutional forms for the broadcast television content that emerged and placed particular emphasis on the contrast between the US commercial broadcasting system and the role played by the BBC as a public service broadcaster in the United Kingdom.

In the context of new media, the frameworks developed by Williams and McLuhan generate important differences in focus. The social shaping of technology approach that Williams championed draws attention to how people, groups, and social institutions have the power to make decisions about the development and adoption of new media technologies and the possible alternative uses of these technologies (cf. Winston 1998 for an extension of such themes). It draws attention to the political economy of communications media and technology. By contrast, McLuhan's approach stresses the extent to which societies and cultures become so immersed in modes of being and behaving (that are shaped by their wider technological environment) that the very ways of being human are inherently linked to the technological forms through which people extend their capacities and senses. Such an approach, therefore, questions the extent to which culture can be understood independently from the technological forms through which it is always already mediated.

Social Psychology: Identity and Interpersonal Relations Online

There has always been a strong interest in the social psychology of new media use, or what is also termed **computer-mediated communication (CMC)**. Reasons for this range from the well-established corporate interest in how best to target marketing activities to new consumers, to government interests in managing concerns about access to new media, to those who see CMC generating new forms of community, sociality, and identity. A curious feature of debates about new media and CMC is the tension between ensuring that children, in particular, have access to new media while also navigating moral panics about the dangers of online pornography, violent video games, cyberstalkers, and so on. While concerns about the adverse impacts of a new medium on children have been common (see Critcher 2006 for an overview of this literature), new media debates have also been marked by a visionary utopianism (Buckingham 2000: 46), whereby the young, variously termed the "N-Gen" (Tapscott 1998), the "screenagers" (Rushkoff 1996), and the "digital natives" (Prensky 2001), are seen as already immersed in a digital environment that promises a better world—more interactive, democratic, and communicative—than that of one-way broadcast media. This highly positive spin on the social psychology of the Internet has deep roots in the literature of the 1990s.

Two of the most influential books of the 1990s on the social psychology of Internet use were Howard Rheingold's *The Virtual Community: Finding Connection in a Computerized World* (1994) and Sherry Turkle's *Life on the Screen: Identity in the*

CASE STUDY

The Tetrad

Marshall McLuhan did not use explicit or easy-to-follow methods in his analysis of media in our society, and even when he did propose a method, it was as quirky and challenging as everything else he did. Nevertheless, the **tetrad** has become a useful lens through which to view new media and, if nothing else, it is a good place to start asking questions.

The concept of a tetrad first appeared in a book compiled with Bruce R. Powers before Mcluhan's death in 1980 (but not released until 1989), *The Global Village: Transformations in World Life and Media in the 21st Century*, and reappears in McLuhan and McLuhan's *Laws of Media: The New Science* (1988). Both books are an attempt to make sense of a world increasingly linked by instantaneous video communication (mainly, in that era, via satellite television).

McLuhan was dissatisfied with traditional media analyses, which did not provide sufficient dynamism, in his view. He proposed an alternative method—which he called "tetradic analysis"—that did not rely on causal relations but instead offered a way to perceive the "resonances" between effects (see Figure 3.2). The approach called for creating a "tetrad" (four sides) composed of explorations of four questions:

- What does the medium enhance or enlarge?
- What does it erode or obsolesce?
- What does it retrieve from the past?
- What does it reverse or flip into when pushed to the limits?

It is important to note that McLuhan believed that these effects were not sequential but simultaneous, in a "resonant relationship."[1] In McLuhan's view, media forms are extensions of human sensory and expressive capabilities, similar to the way that machines enhance our physical abilities. He described these questions

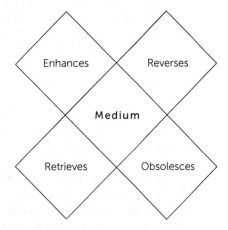

Figure 3.2 McLuhan's Tetrad

Source: McLuhan and McLuhan, 1988.

as a tetrad rather than a simple list of "media effects" to highlight the extent to which they were interrelated and did not have a simple cause-and-effect relationship.

For McLuhan, there were no right answers to the tetrad inquiries. Rather, the concept and its questions were provocations, things to get a discussion going. One of the class activities for this section suggests doing a tetrad analysis on new media (e.g., the Internet, mobile phones, or instant messaging). In keeping with McLuhan's view of the usefulness of tetrads, the objective should be to come up with as many possible interpretations for the questions as possible, and then discuss the implications of each, rather than to seek closure in arriving at a common interpretation.

Case Study Questions

1. When you have completed the tetrad exercise, compare it to one of your neighbours. Did you find similar things were enhanced, retrieved, eroded, and reversed?
2. If you chose a media technology that was pervasive in your grandparents' youth, do you think they would have answered the questions in the same way?

Age of the Internet (1997). For many people, one or both of these books were their introduction to thinking about the world of CMC in a systematic way. Previously, communications specialists had viewed CMC with skepticism, concerned that the absence of visual and other non-verbal cues in online communication when compared to face-to-face interaction would make CMC a risky business (Baym 2005). What both Rheingold and Turkle brought to bear was a perspective that saw CMC as playful, fun, interactive, socially progressive, and very possibly a better world than that of real or offline social experience. Moreover, both developed their arguments from intellectually well-grounded and theoretically sophisticated positions that were, nonetheless, readily accessible to the lay reader.

In perhaps the most famous early account of CMC-based online cultures, Rheingold defined virtual communities as "social aggregations that emerge from the Net when enough people carry on those public discussions [using the Internet] long enough, with sufficient human feeling, to form webs of personal relationships in cyberspace" (1994: 5). While recognizing that the origins of the Internet lay in the US military-industrial-governmental complex, Rheingold observed that the democratic potential of CMC lay in the decentralized nature of such networked communications. They present, in a way very different from one-to-many mass media, the possibility to "piggyback alternative networks on the mainstream infrastructure" and to "use CMC to create alternative planetary information networks" (1994: 14). Rheingold was enthusiastic about the development of virtual communities, seeing in them the possibility of a reinvigorated sense of community-building and citizen participation in public life. This potential arose from three interrelated attributes of CMC: (1) the building of social networks and social capital; (2) the sharing of knowledge and information; and (3) the enabling of new modes of democratic participation in public life. With an optimism that was drawn from experiments in virtual community, Rheingold emphasized the elements of social choice and political activism that would be involved in the achievement of such outcomes:

> The technology that makes virtual communities possible has the potential to bring enormous leverage to ordinary citizens at relatively little cost—intellectual leverage, social leverage, commercial leverage and, most importantly, political leverage. But the technology will not in itself fulfill this potential—this latent technical power must be used intelligently and deliberately by an informed population. More people must learn about that leverage and learn to use it, while we still have the freedom to do so, if it is to live up to its potential. (1994: 4–5)

Turkle (1997) identified virtual communities as sites of play and performativity through the creation of online identities that were indicative of the transition from modernity to postmodernity. Turkle presented a detailed argument about how participants in various forms of online communications—most notably MUDs (Multi-User Dungeons) and MOOs (Multi-User Object-Oriented Domain)—were engaged in forms of performativity online that differed significantly from their personas in real life. Drawing on psychoanalysis, Turkle found that participants in virtual communities increasingly came to view real life as simply one "window" through which a personality is developed and expressed, and that CMC constitutes a constructive and potentially liberating space through which "the obese can become slender, the plain beautiful, the 'nerdy' sophisticated" (1997: 12). Turkle found in this multiplicity and performativity of identities in online environments a parallel to (1) postmodernist and post-structuralist arguments about the fluidity and fragmented nature of contemporary personal identity; and (2) developments in human–computer interface interaction that promote "surface" interaction over deep engagement with the technology. Turkle argued that through both identity play within CMC and the simplification of GUIs seen with Apple and Microsoft Windows, "we are moving toward a culture of simulation in which people are increasingly comfortable with substituting representations of reality for the real" (1997: 23).

Like many of the prophetic enthusiasms of early Internet culture, the passage of time has seen the puncturing of some of these speculative balloons in favour of more empirically nuanced accounts of the nature of community and identity in CMC. It must be noted that CMC has also had its critics. To take one example, Lockard (1997: 225) argued that "cyberspace is to community what Rubber Rita [an inflatable sex toy] is to human companionship." The novelty of CMC has also decreased over time, Herring (2004: 33) observes, in that many current students "do not relate to the utopian and dystopian speculations of earlier decades, and find the debates of the 1990s about online democracy, identity and virtuality hyped and vaguely silly." This point is not simply technological or generational. It also reflects a strong tendency in the 1990s Internet literature to counterpose the virtual to the real, understanding the two as almost parallel universes into which people entered and left with varying degrees of personal commitment and intensity. In the present age, this distinction is blurred, with many younger people not even comprehending how the two could be seen as distinct. Life proceeds, with both its online and offline aspects.

Wellman and Haythornthwaite (2002) argue that speculative accounts of the Internet in terms of "hype" and "counter-hype," as compared to more everyday forms of communication and interaction, were both poorly grounded empirically and deeply unhelpful in terms of understanding how users integrate communication media of any type into their everyday lives. Slater (2002: 544) argues that this dichotomy emerged at a transitional stage of new media research and it is not surprising, given that a medium like the Internet evolves based on change in technologies, user behaviours, questions of access, and legal and commercial environments. As a result, it is important that we engage in a "process of disaggregating 'the Internet' into its diversity of technologies and uses, generating a media landscape in which virtuality is clearly not a feature of the media but one social practice of media use among many others." This is not to reject the importance of research into the social psychology of Internet use and CMC. It is, rather, to make the more modest claim that forms of community formation, civic engagement, and social interaction through CMC are likely to be diverse and contradictory and that "it is better to ground this understanding of the complexity . . . in research than in speculation and assertion" (Rice and Haythornthwaite 2005: 108).

Useful Websites

H2O Playlist: Political Economy of New Media
http://h2obeta.law.harvard.edu/78774

Compiled by Vincent Reynauld of Carleton University, this is a blog site housed with the Berkman Center for Internet & Society at the Harvard Law School. It has an extensive list of websites, blogs, and other electronic resources relating to political economy and new media.

McLuhan Program in Culture and Technology
mcluhan.ischool.utoronto.ca

The online hub for McLuhan studies at the University of Toronto, this link provides useful resources, and contemporary applications of the work of Marshall McLuhan.

MIT Communications Forum
http://web.mit.edu/comm-forum

This website captures many of the leading international contributions on new media, particularly through the papers from MIT's annual media-in-transition conferences.

Further Reading

The Net Delusion: How Not to Liberate the World, Evgeny Morozov (2011)
Morozov tackles the uncritical belief in the benefits of new technologies, and especially the Internet, with an unblinking examination of many of the flaws and failures of our overly optimistic (and ultimately technologically deterministic) views about the impact of networks. In particular, he is harshly sceptical of the so-called Google Doctrine, that the open Internet is somehow uniformly and in all ways good for democracy, freedom, and liberal thinking.

Extraordinary Canadians: Marshall McLuhan, Douglas Coupland (2009)
This recent biography of McLuhan manages to convey much about his theories in an accessible fashion while fusing a writing style that McLuhan scholars might appreciate. The book is a helpful supplement that can be used to better understand the man and his theories, which have been enjoying a renaissance.

Internet Society: The Internet in Everyday Life, Maria Bakardjieva (2005)
This book provides a comprehensive look at the Internet from a strong social shaping of technology perspective—it's influenced by critical theory and critical constructivism, and makes a careful nod to other theories and perspectives. It gives an interesting look into the small details of research and a view on an era (the early days of home Internet use) that has been almost forgotten.

Under Technology's Thumb, William Leiss (1990)
In this wide-ranging exploration of technology and its role in society, Leiss probes the power relations behind, implications of, and potential of a technological society. See especially Leiss's critique of the information society in Chapter 9, and consider his words in the context of emerging phenomena such as social software and user-generated content like Wikipedia.

1. What has been some of the hype about new media, in terms of the expectation that they are able to change everything, typically for the better? What has some of the counter-hype been?

2. In what ways can identifying the strengths and weaknesses of different approaches to and perspectives on new media bring an understanding of how multiple perspectives/ approaches are helpful and when one might, in some cases, be more appropriate or useful than another?

3. What is meant by the term, *technological determinism* and how is this different from a *social shaping of technology* approach?

4. Discuss the three-level approach to technology and culture as presented in Table 3.2 on page 68 and the ways in which such an approach can inform your understanding of new media in society and how people engage with new media (or *less* new media, for that matter).

5. In *Being Digital*, Negroponte proclaimed that "like a force of nature, the digital age cannot be denied or stopped and that it has four very powerful qualities that will result in its ultimate triumph: decentralizing, globalizing, harmonizing and empowering." What is meant by these four qualities? What are your thoughts on the likening of the digital age to a force of nature that cannot be stopped?

6. Flanagan describes "a sense of individual empowerment achieved through enhanced agency" derived from recent developments in new media (such as the way in which Web 2.0 users are able to take control over their configuration, use, and reuse of the Internet). Consider both empowerment and agency in this context and discuss.

7. In what ways does the work of Marshall McLuhan and Raymond Williams inform new media studies? Why is it useful to consider the differences between the two?

8. Consider Mosco's description of the "digital sublime" and discuss how cyberspace possesses not only technical, political, and economic properties, but also how it is a form of cultural myth.

9. What is meant by a "new empiricism" for new media studies? What are some of the reasons such an approach has been called for?

1. Marshall McLuhan's tetrad of media effects (see the case study in this chapter) is a fun way to "unpack" a new media form. Divide into four groups with your fellow students—one each for *obsolesce, retrieve, reverse,* and *enhance*—and come up with an example and/or insight for a series of new media forms. Mobile rich-media cell phones, or smartphones, are good examples with which to start.

2. How do you see the Internet today? Discuss how your vision relates to the following quote from Marshall McLuhan (1962): "The next medium, whatever it is—it may be the extension of consciousness—will include television as its content, not as its environment, and will transform television into an art form. A computer as a research and communication instrument could enhance retrieval, obsolesce mass library organization, retrieve the individual's encyclopaedic function and flip into a private line to speedily tailored data of a saleable kind."

3. Almost anything related to new media is subject to rapid change. Firms come and go; technologies change; and numbers of users, viewers, and creators for new media content and memes change every day. Look up a fact or figure in this chapter and verify whether it remains true today, using online sources.

Identify corroborating or supporting sources for your findings. Not only will you have the new facts but you'll also have an appreciation for how quickly things change and, most importantly, a visceral sense of the way in which the Internet and new media are self-revealing to the diligent and inquisitive scholar. If you discover a fact that needs updating, you can even submit your update (with page reference and new citation) in the form of a rewritten paragraph, to the author: Richard Smith (smith@sfu.ca). He promises to reply.

Debate Questions

1. Are cell phones nearly invisible, in the way that electricity is these days, or are they still prominent and obvious?
2. Internet "hacktivists" have provided support for social and politically progressive groups, enabling them to coordinate and organize in difficult situations. What if these tools fell into the hands of criminals or terrorists?
3. Taking the stance of a technological determinist, argue for or against the proposition that the Internet is good for democracy.

4

Mobile New Media

Questions to Consider

- In what ways can mobile devices be seen as evolving along the path of earlier technological developments?

- How does the proliferation of mobile devices affect your personal, academic, and/or professional life?

- What are your thoughts on the debate about whether or not dependence on mobile devices (and other new media technologies) has resulted in an unhealthy relationship to these technologies (as suggested by the term "crackberry")?

- Are you aware of ways in which mobile phones and networks, like many telecommunication undertakings, are seen as part of the national interest of a country, taking on a national character or receiving special treatment within a home country?

Chapter Outline

Mobile technologies, including but not limited to cell phones, are a vital and important part of new media today. In this chapter, we explore the mobile phone and related technologies, such as the tablet computer and netbook, from an historical, technological, and economic basis. Some of the key features of mobile phones are explained and examined with an eye to making this sometimes mysterious technology more accessible to the reader. We also look in-depth at the mobile Internet, including how social software such as Facebook or Twitter is deployed on mobile devices, and how people are using the Internet differently on a smartphone than they do on a home computer. Another focus in this chapter is the implications of the user's location—which is revealed by smartphone technology—to the evolution and business models for advertising-based services such as Google and Facebook. Later, we examine some of mobile new media's significant cultural impacts (e.g., effects on children) as well as social, health, and environmental issues—plus current surveillance implications.

Many Kinds of Mobile

If this chapter were being written even a few years ago, it would have focused on the mobile phone, perhaps with special emphasis on the **smartphone** (a type of mobile phone that reads email, takes pictures, and surfs the Internet in addition to making and receiving calls). There are now, however, many new media devices that either are not a phone at all—e-book readers (e.g., the Kindle)—or are so multi-faceted, it is difficult to consider them solely as phones. With the addition of the tablet computer, what has become increasingly significant is not a particular type of device, but rather, the ways of interacting that are now possible while people are away from their homes and offices.

In earlier work on mobile and wireless communication (see, for example, Gow and Smith: 2006), the distinction between "mobile" and "portable" seemed important. A phone was mobile because it could be used while the user was moving, in contrast to a laptop, which was portable, since the user could not be mobile when connecting to a network (even a wireless network). This distinction is eroding, as more and more laptops offer 3G (and beyond) connectivity, which works while the user is moving. In fact, a growing number of automobile companies provide the ability for cars to be a mobile "hot spot," specifically to enable the use of computers while driving (presumably by the passengers!).

For these reasons, we focus in this chapter on *mobile new media* and not mobile phones or even smartphones. It is useful, however, to first consider the origins of the mobile phone in order to better understand where this technology has been and where it may be in the future. As with all aspects of technology in society, with mobile new media, there is a surprising amount of path dependence at work whenever things change. That is, technological developments that occur and the social uses of media that arise from those technologies are influenced and constrained by the path along which they evolved and were used in the past.

The Origins of Mobile Phones

Wireless communication has a significant advantage over wired communication because of the fact that—in principle—the people connecting to each other do not need to be anchored to a particular place and, further, they do not even need to know the precise location of each other. In the early days of radio telegraphy, as Marconi was building his business and finding it difficult to compete with wired telegraphy on land, he took advantage of the limitations of the technology by targeting the cargo ships at sea. Ships at sea certainly could not be reached by wire and they were large enough to carry the heavy equipment needed to generate the power for a radio signal by the spark method used in the day. Also, because ships carried large quantities of valuable cargo (people and goods), ship owners were inclined to pay Marconi's fees for a radio and radio operator. The safety benefits of having a radio on board a ship became clearly evident when the *Titanic* struck an iceberg and the radio operator was able to call for help.

As we discussed in Chapter 2 on the history of new media, radio communication advanced over the course of several decades, including voice communication and better sound quality from less expensive and smaller receivers. Most radio development focused on the broadcasting business model, in which there is one powerful transmitter and many inexpensive receivers. Few people, aside from hobbyists and the military, engaged in transmission and receiving. Gradually, however, the benefits of a mobile two-way communication method expanded from the early niche communities into the business sector. Size and expense remained problems, so the initial portable radio systems were built into vehicles, but by the time of the Second World War, a hand-held two-way radio—the walkie talkie—was on the market (Agar 2004; Gow and Smith 2006).

This type of radio had a significant disadvantage for business users, however: it was severely constrained by limited capacity in the system and it was unreliable for calls that went beyond the local area. Capacity problems had plagued radio systems since the earliest days, as the **electromagnetic spectrum** is very much a shared resource. One way to understand the shared electromagnetic spectrum is to imagine it like the water in a lake: radio waves are like waves in the lake and excessive use makes it difficult to know which waves belong to whom; they can become confused or even cancel each other out.

In order to cope with radio interference problems, governments around the world agreed to certain standards relating to the power and frequency of transmissions. These agreements were settled in the early part of the twentieth century (and have been revised every few years at World Radio Congress meetings). As a result, in a typical city, the likely place where a business user might want a two-way radio connection, it has always been extremely difficult to get a licence. In New York City in the 1950s and '60s, the waiting list to have a mobile radio-telephone numbered in the thousands; and this was for a service that was very limited by today's standards, as it worked only in a vehicle and in the city where the licence was purchased.[1] The service did have one significant advantage, however: it was connected to the regular phone system, so it could be used to make a call to a telephone.

The solution to the problem of too many people and not enough capacity lay in a **cellular** radio system design, so named because the service is divided into small hexagonal units that look like cells, or perhaps a honeycomb, with a radio tower at the intersections pointing in three directions (see Figure 4.1).

The design of the cellular system was deliberately low powered. Earlier radio telephones had been built on the same model as the radio broadcasters: a single tall tower was built, reaching the whole city, and every radio would transmit back to the tower. This kept tower-building expenses down, but it also drastically limited the number of two-way connections, since each call required a channel or a bit of the radio spectrum that was licensed from the government.

The cellular system was different. Instead of there being a radio system that could reach people no matter where they were in the city, the cellular system was deliberately low-powered so that radio frequencies could be reused over and over again. Instead of one large tower, the cellular system used many little towers that would

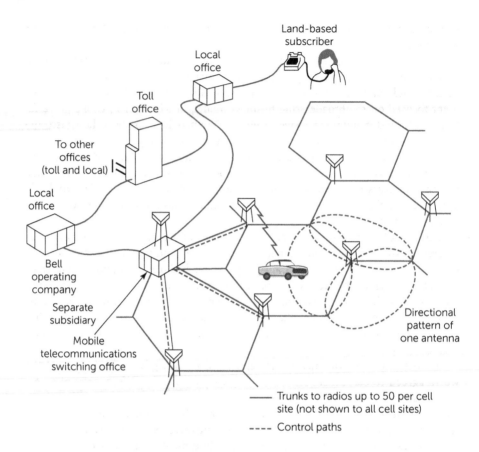

Figure 4.1 Advanced Mobile Phone System Service Plan

Source: Adapted from Private Line, www.privateline.com/Cellbasics/AMPSsystemplan.gif.

cover very small areas. The design of the cellular radio system was developed in the 1940s by an engineer at Bell Telephone Laboratories,[2] but the first cellular telephones did not arrive until the 1980s. This development may seem to have taken a long time, but while cellular telephony is elegantly simple in theory, it is very complicated in practice. As it turned out, creating a telephone that could listen to one tower and ignore the others (and especially one that could switch from one tower to another when the phone was mobile)[3] was a much larger and more complicated task than first anticipated. It was, as it turned out, a task that required very fast computers. In the 1940s, those computers did not exist. Even in the 1960s and '70s, the computers with sufficient capacity were much too large to consider putting in a vehicle let alone giving to people to carry in their hands.

Gradually, however, the miniaturization of computers resulted in the first cellular telephones (still mounted in cars) and a first boom in sales. Cellular telephone companies soon could be found all over the world, building the devices for both users and operators of cellular telephone networks. These networks got a second boost when hand-held cellular telephones—fondly referred to as "the brick" in some circles—were made available. These phones were based on an analogue transmission and reception technology and, as a result, were expensive, heavy, and consumed batteries at an alarming rate. The third boost came from digital cell phones, which accomplished the same thing as earlier phones but with far less power and hence smaller size and lower cost. The era of the pocket-sized cell phone, which almost anybody could afford, had arrived.

New Services

With the digital cell phone—called "personal communication services" or PCs when they were launched in Canada in the mid-1990s—came a number of additional features. At first, these features were modest (such as caller identification) and they did not change the user experience in any fundamental way. People still used a mobile phone for the primary purpose of making phone calls. One feature, however, would have an enormous impact from both a business perspective and a social perspective: the short message service (SMS) that is now referred to as **text messaging** or texting (Agar 2004).

The story of how texting came to be added as a feature of mobile phones is an interesting one. According to one of the engineers on the team that worked on the technical specifications of the mobile phone, the initial idea for text messaging was to give the service provider a way to send a message to users, to tell them that they had a new voice-mail message, for example (Wray 2002). The decision to allow *users* to initiate messages and send those messages to any other subscriber was (as the story goes) almost an afterthought. What began as an afterthought has become the common practice of texting, as billions of messages are now sent every day (not to mention the billions of dollars they generate for mobile operators) (Katz 2008).

Text messaging (SMS) was possible because the terminal device, the telephone, was a kind of special-purpose computer. It had memory, processing power, an input device, and a display. That computing power was needed in order to cope with the challenges of being a mobile device, but once the phone had that computer power, it was reasonable to look at other ways the phone could be used. The phone business then, as now, was intensely competitive and phone manufacturers were always looking for additional ways to attract attention.

The popularity of SMS grew because it was, at first, free to use (or at least very inexpensive). Indeed, it seemed economical compared to a high-priced voice call, but in point of fact, text messages are very expensive when you compare the price of data in a text to the price of data in a data plan on a home Internet service, or even on a mobile phone, when cost per byte is the deciding factor.[4] Whatever the pricing model, the fact remains that SMS proved to be incredibly popular, especially with young people. We return later in this chapter to further discussion about the way in which young people adopted mobile phone technology—first in Northern Europe and then around the world—and how that has changed youth culture, but first we look at some of the other "things that are not voice" in a mobile device.

SMS proved not only to be incredibly lucrative in its own right but it also opened the doors to thinking about the mobile phone as a platform for other things. As using text became more popular, people grew to appreciate a larger display, for example.

With a larger graphical display came the possibility of non-ASCII (American Standard Code for Information Interchange) text and the opening up of markets outside of Northern Europe and North America. The larger display also enabled games and the phone-game era began.

The first game on a mobile phone is widely thought to be "snake" on a Nokia handset from the early 1990s. According to one industry legend, the designers showed the possible game to their manager who decreed that it would not be included in the phone, but the engineers liked it so much that they added it anyway. While this story may well be apocryphal, it illustrates the extent to which the mobile phone business was driven not only by engineering but also by people (mainly in the Nordic countries of Finland and Sweden) who loved their phones (Ling 2004). The latest features and capabilities were a source of constant discussion among young people, especially people in their twenties who were employed and could afford new phones—and they would upgrade their phones frequently. A feature like a game also appealed to those who were texting often, since they had their phone in their hand and were looking at it, rather than keeping it in their pocket except when talking (Ito et al. 2005).

From the game that came with a phone when it was purchased to games that could be installed on a purchased phone (a challenging undertaking, at first), these add-ons were a growing source of revenue for phone companies. In a similar way, competitiveness and a desire to distinguish one phone from another—not to mention the newfound capabilities of memory, computing power, and tone generation to make a game work—led to the practice of building phones with multiple ringtones. The ability to buy and install new ringtones became immensely popular.

For many of these kinds of additional features, SMS was a kind of backbone or enabling technology. A ringtone could be purchased by sending a message. A game could be installed by receiving a special kind of SMS called an MMS (multimedia message) or EMS (enhanced message service). The mobile phone was quickly becoming a multi-purpose technology and SMS was acting as the computer network linking phones to each other and to the many businesses trying to reach this market and sell things.

The Internet on Your Phone

The mobile phone industry grew explosively through the 1990s, just as the Internet was extending beyond government offices and universities and into wider public consciousness. It was clear that these two technologies were going to intersect, but how that was going to happen was not clear at first. Despite the advances in phones made since the early days of analogue cell phones, or even the first digital cell phones, mobile devices did not connect to data networks at a very high rate and still had very limited ability to display or process data.

A Slight Detour: Wireless Speeds

The simplest radio connection—as Hertz demonstrated more than 150 years ago—is made by creating a spark in one place and detecting that spark in another. The spark creates a disruption across the entire electromagnetic spectrum and contains very little information (other than that a spark occurred and lasted a certain amount of time). This was good enough to get dots and dashes across the Atlantic and to ships at sea, but it required a long, slow process of encoding and decoding messages and further, due to interference, was an inadequate way to communicate when there were multiple users needing the airwaves.

One of the key breakthroughs for wireless communication was to create a carrier wave—which is like a single tone in music—and then to encode differences from that wave. There was a double benefit to the carrier wave: (1) it went out on a single frequency (or, more precisely, within a narrow band of frequencies) and others could tune out or tune in; and following from this, (2) there was an added commercial benefit in that it became possible to have many more radio stations. Of course, the spectrum is not unlimited and not all of it is equally usable, so carrier waves could not solve all capacity problems because it eventually becomes infeasible to use additional frequencies. What then?

Radio operators learned from both the telegraph and telephone operators, who faced similar challenges of fitting a growing number of calls into a single wire: the solution was something called **multiplexing**. For the purposes of this chapter, rather than focus on engineering details, consider a simple analogy of a plot of land (from which the goal is to get the greatest possible value). One simple way to increase the capacity of the land is to build many lots on top of each other by building a multistory building. Each floor can be further subdivided into offices, and so on. This is a rough equivalent of the multiplexing process. In the electromagnetic spectrum, the techniques of creating these subdivisions are based in software and codes, but the outcome is similar: more useable space/capacity from the same resource. The methods to achieve this are myriad and are growing in complexity and sophistication all the time. All of these things are being done to put more capacity into the airwaves: first to allow additional callers, then to provide a better experience for each caller, and then to add more data for each person with a phone.

Each of these refinements is typically given a technical name and a specification and all of the equipment that is used has to abide by those specifications so that everyone can connect and be understood. When there is a major change in the way that mobile phones work, it is called a "generation." The first analogue cell phones were the first generation, the first digital cell phones the second generation (or 2G). The current generation is the fourth and this is why phones of today are described as 4G phones. Within each generation, there will be refinements and enhancements, especially as one generation approaches the next. The latest enhancement in 4G service in Canada is called "long-term evolution" (LTE).[5] LTE is in operation in many cell phone markets in the world, including Canada, where it is the standard used to bring the fourth generation (4G) of mobile communication, a fully Internet protocol–based network.[6] Although the term 5G is not yet in widespread use, engineers and scientists are starting to speculate on the applications that could be possible, using advanced capabilities such as spread spectrum, cognitive, or "smart" radio technology (in which the functions of the radio are defined by software) and "mesh" networking implementations, where the radio receiver helps neighbouring users by handing off and relaying data.

Although the quality of voice calls has not changed very much in years (or even decades), there have been some recent attempts by cell phone operators and device manufacturers to take advantage of new high-speed data networking to deliver so-called HD voice calls. This feature may become more important in years to come, but most of the recent enhancement efforts have involved software—apps—that take advantage of the high-speed data connections between mobile devices and the global Internet. The mobile broadband experience, when using the newest LTE networks and compatible devices, results in web pages that load quickly, music that arrives in seconds, and video that looks like it does at home or at the office. Prior to the 3G revolution, one of the ways that mobile phone network operators, Internet entrepreneurs, and phone designers tried to bring the Internet to phones was to recreate miniature versions of web pages that were programmed in special languages, with limited amounts of text and graphics (or no graphics at all). These and almost every other attempt to create a simplified, separate Internet for phones proved to be spectacularly unsuccessful and many people wondered if the Internet would ever be available on a mobile phone.

There has been an interesting turn of events, however, spearheaded in part by SMS (of all things). As unlikely as it may seem, the short message service, with its 140 characters and no underline, italics, or bold (let alone graphics), has become one of the dominant ways that people interact with the Internet on their mobile phones. This interaction occurs through intermediaries, however, because the Internet— and the operators of large Internet sites such as Facebook and Twitter—realized the potential of adapting their services to the sending and receiving of SMS, of reaching out to text-message users, rather than asking users to reach out to the Internet. So, for example, status updates on Facebook can be made with a text and alerts from Facebook can be received as simple texts. The **microblogging** service Twitter is premised on SMS and offers only 140 characters per update, regardless of how the characters are entered. Visitors to the Twitter website get no more space than someone sending a tweet by phone.

From Multifunction Phones to Smartphones

We have already mentioned the beginnings of the multifunction or "feature" phone, with games, ringtones, caller ID, and text messages. Phone manufacturers did not rest, however, because once they had a device with processor, memory, storage, and user interface, they essentially had the ingredients for a computer and, therefore, all of the potential of a computer. Phones have gained the ability to do calculations, maintain address books and calendars, and perform many small organizational tasks.

A parallel technology, called the personal digital assistant (PDA), appeared for a short time as though it might take on these sorts of roles, but people quickly tired of yet another gadget in their pockets and purses, and as soon as phones were able to offer those organizational capabilities, interest in PDAs dropped. Small portable game machines mounted a stronger resistance to encroachment by phones. With bright colour displays, graphics processors dedicated to games, and important development resources tied to specific platforms, the Nintendo DS and similar gadgets have continued to do well. That said, mobile phones such as the iPhone have increasingly targeted the gamer with their offerings, their user interface, and their pricing.

As phone usage grows toward unity with population (that is, the point at which every person has a phone) in country after country, the ability of mobile phones to colonize product categories continues unabated. Consider one example: a simple feature that phone designers added very early—time display on the front of the phone—proved to be the death knell for the makers of inexpensive watches. Although watches continue to be sold as a fashion accessory, many young people have stopped purchasing watches because their phone is their watch, their timer, their alarm clock, and their calendar. It is also, as we will see, their music and video player. One interesting exception to this trend is the remarkable success of Canadian inventor Eric Migicovsky, the developer of the Pebble "watch," which isn't really a watch at all but a Bluetooth-connected display for a smartphone. This gadget raised more than $10 million in presales at Kickstarter.com.

In the past five years, mobile phones have moved into the camera and video-recorder markets—these are useful examples of how the mobile phone is able to displace better products because it is (1) always in the consumer's pocket; and (2) much more integrated into the consumer's life. Phone cameras have been steadily improving, and they have begun to approach the features of a dedicated camera, but they remain limited. Yet, as the maker of an iPhone app designed to help people with the phone's admittedly limited camera, says, "The best camera is the one you have with you." His product, called The Best Camera, makes some modest improvements to the built-in camera software on the iPhone, but, more importantly, it connects the user with a community of photographers who exchange tips and upload pictures into a common space for sharing with others. Instagram is the most popular of these services that offer photo-sharing via smartphone and Internet applications. Developed by two graduates of Stanford University, Instagram was recently purchased by Facebook for more than $1 billion.

These twin capabilities—being both ever-present and also a link to the social use of the technology—are what give mobile phones a key advantage over specific-purpose technologies. These twin capabilities are helping mobiles become popular devices for recording video, and they are even leading users to watch television on their phones. This is not so much because phones perform these functions particularly well, but because phones are present and they make it possible for users to share—immediately—what they create, experience, and think.

When Is a Phone No Longer a Phone?

By 2005, a new category of phone was emerging: the phone that included calendar and address-book functions, a capable email program, and possibly a camera and a web browser. The smartphone was not for everyone, as it was expensive both to purchase and to maintain, and it depended on a data connection to get onto the Internet and get email, which was very expensive. The larger screen meant that smartphones were bigger and heavier, and they drained their batteries more quickly. Nevertheless, they were popular with business people and politicians. Access to email, in particular, was seen to be essential and a growing number of people became very active users of mobile email, particularly with the ubiquitous BlackBerry devices made by the Canadian firm, Research In Motion.

The BlackBerry and similar devices (the Nokia Communicator and E-series phones in Europe, for example) enabled a kind of "always-on" approach to phone messaging, which led to the colloquial term "crackberry" coming into circulation, drawing a parallel between dependence on drugs and dependence on sending and receiving email at all times of the day or night and in inappropriate times and places. Whether such use constitutes an addiction remains open to debate; however, the growth in non-phone uses of phones, when coupled with the use of a mobile phone as a planner and calendar, as an address and phone book, as a game platform, and as a camera, seemed to herald a transition of the phone from being just a phone to something more like a computer and as a result a "general purpose technology" (Lipsey et al. 2006).

By 2007, the smartphone had become familiar to most people. It may have been associated with business executives or high-ranking politicians, but people commonly knew what it was. Those following the technology industry at the time knew that Apple was widely thought to be developing a phone. What Apple would release, however, was not really a phone. Apple had hinted at what they might do with a phone a couple of years earlier when they put a version of iTunes onto a Motorola phone. Apple's iTunes is a software program that runs on personal computers and enables the purchase of music online for playback on computers or Apple's own MP3 player, the iPod. Although the Motorola ROCKR (as it was called) was not much of a commercial success, with it, Apple gave indication of an interest in mobile phones.

As the largest-selling gadget on the planet, the mobile phone was both an obvious market for Apple and a threat, since it seemed likely that mobile phones could repeat their colonization of music players, the way they had with cameras and watches. If Apple were to make no attempt to enter the phone market, they would be vulnerable to dwindling returns in the music player market as people began listening to music on their phones. What Apple developed was the iPhone and the iPod Touch, devices similar to each other—especially now that the iPod Touch has a microphone—with a large screen and no keys. Both devices integrate completely with iTunes and all of their features are implemented in software. There are virtually no buttons, aside from a "home" button, volume control, and on/off, with everything else done by tapping on the screen. These Apple devices have been very successful commercially and—for people who can afford a high-end phone—they have been sought-after items for reading email, browsing the Web, and talking to people (it is a phone, after all) while moving around.

The key difference between previous smartphones and the iPhone (and iPod Touch), however, is the way that they are integrated into iTunes; in particular, the section of iTunes called, the App Store. Making a clever link to both "Apple" and "application," the App Store is the place to go for new iPhone software. Apple recruited and supported—with free development software—an army of software developers in the months leading up to the launch of the iPhone. Further (and perhaps more importantly), Apple agreed to take a fee (currently 30 per cent) for retailing the applications created by developers.

Although the App Store and Apple's relationships with its developers have not been without problems since the launch, the overall environment has been spectacularly successful. During Christmas 2009, Apple announced that more than 3 billion copies of the 120,000 applications available at the time[7] had been downloaded since the launch on 10 July 2008. That number had grown to over 300,000 by October 2010 and more than 7 billion downloads. The number of downloads grows every day and has been such a success that Apple's sales slogan, "There's an app for that," is widely recognized and poised to enter popular culture.

What Apple has done is redefine the relationship between people and their phone and between people and their phone company. By emphasizing—and delivering on—all the *other* things the phone can do, Apple has created the first example of hand-held general-purpose technology. Others have quickly followed suit (in particular, Google's Android, and the many companies building Android phones), so it is by no means a guarantee that Apple can continue to occupy the position of premier designer and manufacturer of these mobile new media devices. The highly successful launch of the iPhone 5 in September 2012, however, saw Apple maintain its dominance in people's minds of what a desirable smartphone looks like. What they have done, in a way that previous phone developers and network operators were unable to do, is establish a hand-held device equivalent to the personal computer. It is a device that takes on a character based on the programs that are loaded into it and is valuable because of that malleability and mutability.

"New" New Media on Phones?

The phrase *new new media* is courtesy of Paul Levinson, who has written a book by the same name. He is against calling things Web 2.0 (or 3.0) in favour of the awkward but definitely evocative term *new new*. In his view, new new media are distinguished from the old media, and even new media, by the ease with which regular folks can participate in the creation of content. Some of these elements are discussed, above, as they relate to mobile phones, particularly the ability of phones to capture sound and video and post updates to sites like Twitter. But what about moving beyond that to something really new, something that could not be done on a regular desktop or laptop computer? What is *really* new media on mobile devices?

One of the most promising—and perhaps overhyped—technologies to emerge on mobile devices recently is something called **augmented reality**. Augmented reality works by creating an overlay of data on top of what is already visible to the user. Users may be somewhat familiar with this in the form of the "heads up display" that is featured in movies about fighter pilots or is even now available in some high-end cars, pinpointing the location of pedestrians and wildlife through infrared cameras, for example, and projecting them onto the windscreen of the car. (We will return to a more detailed discussion of augmented reality in Chapter 10.)

Video- and computer-game players are familiar with this feature as well, as games commonly have multiple "gauges" or "readouts" with important information about what is happening on screen, layered over the action. Sometimes these appear in the lower half of the screen, but in many games they float "above" the screen, augmenting the players' ability by giving instantaneous feedback on the scores and the health and status of the various bits of equipment, monsters, or players that they are controlling, depending on the type of game.

These sorts of augmentations are helpful; however, they do not quite capture the full capability of an augmented reality application on a smartphone. Consider the following example: Imagine that you are walking in an unfamiliar city, unsure of the directions to the nearest coffee shop, or perhaps you'd like to know which of two coffee shops is best. You can, with the appropriate application on your phone (and restaurant recommendations are one of the first places this has been used, as it turns out), turn on your device, launch the application, and then look at the places you were considering through the lens of your camera. As the coffee shop comes into focus, comments about it float into view. You can also receive coupons from the shop itself or even access a database that reveals its last health inspection report. More importantly—and this is particularly "new new" for phones—you can add your own comments if you choose to do so. Your comments "stick" to that place, courtesy of geographic encoding, image recognition, computer databases, and the wireless networks linking them together. A free application, called Wikitude, is available for iPhones and enables this type of interaction with locations and information.

This augmentation of reality is particularly attractive not only to retailers but also for municipalities that might use it for a "report a pothole" application, or to museums that might use it for guides—indeed, any number of still-unthought-of public service uses. The key aspect of this is people's interest in—and willingness to create—content and desire to share it online. YouTube and similar sites have shown that user-generated content is enormously popular. Augmented reality applications on mobile phones provide a way to anchor those contributions in space and time and to do so in a way that creates value for people at the moment in which they need information or have some information to share.

The benefits of location information extend far beyond public service. In a mobile device with an Internet connection, a Web search takes on a new meaning as the results from Google, for example, can be customized to take into account your location. A simple query, such as "pizza" on a mobile device that reports its location to the search engine, will result in links to nearby pizza restaurants. As you can imagine, the accompanying advertising and value of a sponsored link (those links at the top of the page) is commensurately higher as well. Advertisers and ad agencies know that a question asked on the street has a much higher click-through and purchase probability, and these ads are therefore much more expensive and profitable for the search-engine company. Taking control of those queries is the reason for Google's enormous investment in mapping technology and data (Reed, 2012). It also helps explain why Apple would risk the initial bad publicity of their maps product in the new iPhone 5. They were willing to annoy a few customers in order to regain control over all of their mobile search queries.

Spime, Anyone?

Anchoring things in space and time is the responsibility of a whole new range of devices, which science fiction writer Bruce Sterling terms **spime** (Sterling 2005). The term is a blend of *space* and *time* and, thus, devices which exhibit the ability to locate themselves in space and time are spime. These devices seem like the furthest thing from new media since they are often just a "dumb sensor" or even just a radio frequency identification (RFID) chip that responds with a unique number when it receives a specific radio frequency signal (much like a bell rings in a specific tone when struck).

Rather than dismissing spime as dumb objects, however, it is better to see them as a component of a much larger network that—when working together with all the other components—enables considerable elegance and elaboration (just as the cells in the human body combine to create each unique person). Spime in a user's shoes might connect to spime in their music player to allow the user to run with an inspiring soundtrack that is responsive to his or her running pace or location (accelerating up a long hill or easing off before returning home, for example). Upon returning home, spime could help in logging a user's runs or to compare statistics, set goals, or track progress in a global database of runners. All of this is not achieved solely by any one component part, and many of them operate completely without a user interface, but the combination offers a richer, more elaborate, increasingly interactive experience. Already, we are seeing examples of this type of system design, both at the level of manufacturing and distribution as well as in consumer goods. Many running shoes, for example, come equipped with the Nike+ system, which works with your iPod to enable the running scenario described above. Representatives from Ericsson, a designer of mobile telephone infrastructure, noted that machine-to-machine communication driven by devices such as spime would be the leading driver of mobile connections by 2020, with 50 billion devices connected according to their estimates.

> Machine-to-machine communications, or M2M, will be a key component in the future growth of the mobile industry. For energy companies it could be smart meters that read themselves, increase business efficiency and cut operational expenses. In transportation—tracking solutions improve route optimization and safety for vehicles on the road. Digital signs that can be updated remotely, cameras that can send pictures halfway around the world and even a soda machine that requests restocking when needed are other examples that machine-to-machine technology make possible. (Ericsson 2010)

Kids on Phones

Back in the 1980s and '90s, mobile phones—expensive, unwieldy, and restricted to workmanlike tasks—were associated almost exclusively with business and government. This changed in the twenty-first century (and even earlier in Asia and Europe) as mobile phones evolved and became more affordable. As a result, they have reached a very high level of popularity with young people. Such a shift is unsurprising: as a group, young people value privacy and independence and are very likely, if given a new device with unexpected capabilities (such as text messaging), to quickly figure out how to use that capability to maximum advantage.

North Americans (and especially Canadians) have seen broad adoption of mobile phones by young people in the last two decades. Adoption was slow at first compared to elsewhere in the world, perhaps related to high prices in Canada, incompatibility between the text-messaging systems of the major providers prior to 2002, and ready availability of land lines—with many homes having a "teen line" as a second phone line. Young people in other parts of the world, in contrast, were early adopters of the technology. Telephone companies facilitated this process with pay-as-you-go plans, inexpensive basic phones, and low prices for text messages. Young people quickly adopted this technology as a way for getting in touch and staying in touch, arranging social events and romantic contact, and even sharing homework (and sometimes cheating) via their mobile phones. Although Canada continues to lag behind other developed (and even many developing) countries in mobile phone adoption, in the last five years, Canadians, especially young people, have begun to emulate mobile phone users in the rest of the world, adopting the mobile as their only telephone and sending billions of text messages.

Children in some cultures, such as Korea and Japan, found in the mobile phone a tool for liberation from their parents (Ito et al. 2005), and several writers have gone so far as to consider mobile phone use as part of a revolution in youth culture (Ling 2004). The phone has brought mobility to young people, and it has contributed to a last-minute-arrangements orientation while also fostering entire linguistic sub-genres and shorthand. Youth slang—or slang among any demographic group, for that matter—is nothing new, but some of the abbreviations adopted in text-speak have migrated into the wider culture and have spread around the world.

Slang is not just a way of keeping messages private from parents, but it also facili-tates a form of ad hoc compression, allowing more information to fit into the limited space of a text message. Text slang also aids speed of composition, since messages were often composed on the traditional telephone keypad—this was very import-ant to users at the outset of the messaging era. Early mobile phones did not even have QWERTY-style keyboards, or a touchscreen, or even text-expansion capability as is now common on phones (for example, the T-9 system), and, as a result, some of the best phone typists still do not use **predictive text**, preferring the old-fashioned method.

Although there have been periodic alarms raised that typing short messages full of abbreviations would lead to the downfall of the English language and the inability of today's youth to make themselves understood, research on the topic has not been definitive and several studies report exactly the opposite: that texting is writing, at least, and encourages people to both read and write. Nearly all students understand the difference between texting and term papers.[8]

The impacts flow both ways, of course. Youth adoption of mobile phones may have been unanticipated at first, but both system operators and manufacturers were quick to act upon the perceived needs and interests of young people and provided plans and handsets that suited these new consumers. In this sense, the role of youth in the evolution of mobile phones and mobile carriers can be seen as a signal example of the social shaping of technology that we discussed in Chapter 3. As you may recall, a social-shaping approach considers technological change and development from the perspective of the users' impact on the development of a new technology. The inter-ests and activities of mobile users have been enormously important in the way in which mobile phones evolved, especially the case of text messaging. When the first SMS was implemented, the developers thought that it would be a modest ancillary feature to help people be aware of system outages or get notifications that there was a voice message waiting for them (Agar 2004). The ability to send a message from one terminal (phone) to another was added, almost as an afterthought (Haddon and Green 2010). The incredible popularity of this feature, which shouldn't have been a surprise given previous experience with short messages and bulletin posting inside the French Minitel service (Veak 2006; again, added as an afterthought to a service that was primarily a directory), gave rise to amazing fortunes and many new busi-nesses, such as ring tones purchased over the network, not to mention user innova-tions such as "sexting."

Other concerns related to texting include health effects ("texter's thumb"), disruption of sleep patterns (staying up late, being interrupted while sleeping by a phone buzzing or beeping with a new text), contact with inappropriate or undesirable friends, cheating on tests, and the expense, especially when young people who are on a plan that is paid for by their parents go over the limit and incur large mobile bills. As the trend continues for younger and younger children to have a cell phone, inevitably there are some times when children do not fully comprehend the implications and power of the device in their hands (indeed, the same could be said for some adults).

While parents are concerned about how the phone might harm their children, the parents are also the ones who are making the purchasing decisions and paying the bills (especially for younger children). It gives parents peace of mind to know that their child could call them whenever required, especially given the declining number of pay phones. Texting also provides a way for children and parents to break through the voice-mail wall when parents (or teens) are at work. Parents find that texting, something they might rarely do with friends and colleagues, is an easy way to stay in touch with children. While it is difficult to tell if the technology is feeding on or fuelling the need that parents have to hover over their children, cell phones are definitely implicated in the "helicopter-parents" phenomenon. It is of little surprise, then, that an entire category of kids' phones and corresponding plans for those devices have been developed by telephone companies eager to serve every niche in the market.

The Business of Mobility

Mobile phones and networks (and other mobile devices, discussed later in the chapter) are big business by any measure. Recent data suggest there are more than 5.6 billion lines in operation worldwide, with some countries approaching a 130 per cent penetration rate.[9] In other words, many people have multiple mobile phone lines. With an increasing use of mobile devices for security services, car safety systems, and the like (see the discussion about spime above), it is not hard to imagine the numbers going even higher.

Mobile networks are considered—like many telecommunication undertakings—part of the national interest of a country and often take on a national character or receive special treatment within their home country. Mobile networks are inevitably involved in multiple aspects of public safety and even national defence, from the 911 phone call to the construction of regional and national data networks managing the operations of police and security forces. These networks, therefore, are often regulated, employing large unionized workforces, with close ties to other strategically important industries, such as microelectronics, electronics, software, and computing.

If considering Canada, for example, the mobile device in the pockets of many Canadians at one time would have been made by a Canadian company, Research In Motion (RIM). Now simply BlackBerry, RIM was at one time a leading manufacturer of smartphones in the world. Based in Waterloo, Ontario, RIM made the famous phones so well loved by Barack Obama that he had special steps taken to ensure that he could still use his while serving as president of the United States. The future of RIM is uncertain at this time, and there are no other Canadian manufacturers of cell phones (Novotel, of Alberta, closed many years ago). Other North American players in the industry include Apple (of California) and Motorola (of Illinois, now owned by Google). Additional large players are Nokia (Finland, recently sold to Microsoft); Sony Mobile Communications, formerly Sony/Ericsson (Sweden/Japan); LG and Samsung (from South Korea); and HTC from Taiwan.

Of these, Nokia was by far the largest in terms of total units shipped worldwide, employees, and revenue prior to 2009. Nokia may have been the largest but after the iPhone came out it had difficulty competing in the smartphone category—the fastest growing and most prestigious—and this is remarkable because Nokia more or less defined the category with its Communicator and N-Series phones. It is unlikely that Nokia will disappear in the near future and their importance on a global level, given the number of people who cannot afford a loaded smartphone, can be expected to remain for some time yet.

The smartphone has unleashed another aspect of the mobile business. Prior to smartphones, there were few things you could add to a mobile phone. Some people were willing to pay for a non-standard (and perhaps commercial) ring tone, and a lively business existed for a few years, selling ring tones—often directly to the handset using SMS codes—for a dollar or more, but recently this has waned. The new hot addition, aside from phone cases and Netsuke/Sagamono (phone "charms," mainly popular in Japan), is the application, commonly called an **app.** Previous smartphones had apps that users could install, but Apple's (belated) embrace of apps—they were not included in the launch version of the iPhone—launched an industry of spectacular diversity and stunning growth. The Apple, Android, BlackBerry, and Windows Mobile app stores, combined, have more than a billion different types of apps available for download—most are free, many are inexpensive, and everyone is trying them. They are not only providing income to the operators of the app stores, who typically take a percentage of the fees charged, but also their additional functionality is driving people to use their phones more often, for more things, and hence are more likely to spring for a data package. These data packages are a new source of revenue for mobile network operators.

Mobile phones would be of little use without a **network operator**, however. Just as a home telephone does not work unless it is plugged into a phone jack in the wall, the modern mobile phone is dependent on a network. Until 2009, there were the Big Three in the Canadian cell-service landscape: Telus, Rogers, and Bell. Each also has a subsidiary discount brand that it uses to give itself increased access to the market. So, for example, Telus owns Koodo, Rogers owns Fido, and Bell operates the Virgin brand under licence from Virgin in the United Kingdom. Those living in Manitoba or Saskatchewan may also have access to MTS Mobility or SaskTel Mobility.

These large companies have recently been joined by a group of newcomer outfits, the most well-known of which is Wind Mobile. Another, Mobilicity, launched in 2010. These companies are part of a group operating on new electromagnetic (radio) spectrum licences that were auctioned off in 2008 with regulatory preference given to new entrants, virtually ensuring that some of the spectrum would go to new companies. This strategy of encouraging new entrants has been pursued in the past by the Canadian regulators: when the first digital cell-phone licences (PCS) were allocated, preference was also given to new companies. Of the two that actually launched a service, Clearnet was purchased by Telus and folded into its existing service, and

CASE STUDY

Canada's Smartphone: The BlackBerry

The BlackBerry—a smartphone made by Research In Motion (RIM), based in Waterloo, Ontario—was for many years a major player in the global market for advanced wireless devices. Having a long association with the University of Waterloo, the company expanded its offerings and capabilities from its first products—digital sync devices for film and then two-way pagers—back in the late 1980s.[10] Since then, RIM at first held its ground in the face of considerable competition from Apple's iPhone, myriad Android devices (powered by Google's Android operating system), and then industry leader Nokia's line of smartphones. More recently, BlackBerry (which replaced RIM as the official name of the company) has seen its market share—and even more importantly, its status as a "cool" device—drop dramatically along with Nokia, leaving Apple and Android-based phones from Samsung and LG and others in control of the market. In the fall of 2013, Blackberry released BlackBerry Messenger (BBM) for iOS and Android, providing both a migration path for former users hoping to keep in touch with their friends who still had a Blackberry, and a new possible line of business for Blackberry. The release was a success with millions of downloads in the first few weeks.

The BlackBerry was in many ways the quintessential smartphone. First, it combined a number of functions (such as a camera, a PDA, and a GPS) that once required additional devices. The result was not just convenience for individuals but also a significant socio-cultural impact as more and more people became accustomed to having BlackBerry features with them all the time. As well, BlackBerrys are connected to the Internet via a data network and so connect the user to a global network in a way that less advanced phones—even those with text messaging—did not ever achieve because of the high cost

of international calls and texts. BlackBerry Messenger, which is included for free with the phone, also includes free picture messaging, an added cost feature on a regular cell phone. Although its app store BlackBerry World, previously known as App World, is not nearly as popular as the Apple or even Android app stores, it contains a broad range of solutions and coverage in all major categories.

Overall, the BlackBerry offers the three features—capabilities, connectivity, and extensibility—that combine in smartphones to make them a key player in the social media revolution of the twenty-first century. Applications for social media tools such as Facebook, Twitter, Foursquare, and Flickr provide the means for rapid creation and sharing of content from the hand-held device.[11] This capability is proving to be enormously popular and smartphone sales are growing rapidly: 51.8 per cent of all mobile devices in the second quarter of 2013, up 46 per cent over the previous year (Gartner 2013). For BlackBerry, technical capabilities alone do not seem to be sufficient, as their market share has dropped to less than 2 per cent of mobile devices sold and have fallen below phones with Microsoft Mobile OS (Gartner 2013). Some of this decline can be attributed to a product that is not as capable as the competing Apple products, but there is no denying the effect—which has also overtaken Nokia—of the company being no longer "hip" and "cool" in the eyes of the ever-important youth demographic. Mobile devices, which have moved from being a business tool to a fashion accessory, are now subject to this sort of rapid change in popularity, it seems.

That a Canadian company was a major player in this realm is perhaps a surprise, but we might remember that the largest manufacturer of mobile phones also came from a northern country with a small population: Finland, home of Nokia; as well, the largest manufacturer, Samsung, is from Korea. Also, despite the fact that Nortel has all but disappeared in the wake of its 2009 filing for bankruptcy, Canada does have a long tradition of excellence in tele-communications, and wireless technologies

continued

in particular. In fact, in the early days of RIM, when they made wireless two-way pagers, one of their major competitors was Glenayre Electronics, of Vancouver. Proximity to and connections with the University of Waterloo[12]—both founders are alumni—has no doubt also led to some of the strength of their technology offerings.

Research In Motion did not start out in the mobile telephone business. In fact, RIM's first unit with voice capabilities did not hit the marketplace until 2002 (the breakthrough 5810 model). Their email device—the first BlackBerry—was tightly integrated to corporate email systems (it arrived in 1999, around the time widespread use of email was taking hold in the general population) and offered the speed and security that big corporations demanded. It became so popular in government, industry, and business circles that it garnered the nick name "crackberry" in reference to its purportedly addictive properties. Sweeny describes the extensive use of the BlackBerry in the corporate and government world:

> Today the BlackBerry monopolizes the world of work—nobody else comes close. An astounding 85 percent of public corporations are supplying staff with the devices, and more than 175,000 BlackBerry Enterprise Servers are installed worldwide. The US Congress was MRI's first big client, and Uncle Sam is still the biggest consumer of BlackBerrys. Today, more than 500,000 devices are installed in every department of the US government and throughout the US Senate and House of Representatives. (2009:2)

Although RIM became embroiled in some high-profile patent litigation—most notably a suit with patent-holding corporation NTP, which resulted in a judgment against RIM of USD $23.7 million that was then appealed, only to be settled years later for more than USD $670 million—RIM continued to expand its offerings and market share, even as Apple's iPhone started to take over the role of being the "cutting-edge" smartphone. Perhaps most

surprising of all, the BlackBerry's image as a business phone morphed over time and it became increasingly popular among young people, who appreciated the new-found possibility of creating and consuming large numbers of text messages. In this regard, BlackBerry had an advantage over other mobile-device manufacturers, as these competitors did not typically supply any infrastructure software. As with the integration tool for corporate email systems (BlackBerry Exchange Server), there was a separate—and free to the user—messaging platform, called BlackBerry Messenger (BBM). The software came pre-installed on BlackBerry phones and was a surprise hit among certain groups of young people, who are sometimes burdened by expensive text-messaging bills. Another feature—anonymity—proved popular in countries where premarital conversations between men and women is discouraged. BlackBerry Messenger provided a safe and untraceable way of connecting with others, as BBM messages were constructed so as to not be easily linked to your phone number.

The privacy provisions went even further than that, and with even more serious national security and crime implications. BlackBerry's Enterprise Services provided for user-created encryption keys, making it much more difficult to snoop on email passed through the system, even with the cooperation of BlackBerry or the telecommunications provider. The Indian government, in 2008, delayed approval of sales of BlackBerry services by the telecommunications company Tata on the basis that the government would not be able to monitor email sent through the BlackBerry Exchange Server. In 2010, the Indian government threatened BlackBerry, as well as Skype and Google, with exclusion from the Indian market if some sort of back door to their encrypted services was not provided to the security authorities in that country.[13]

RIM was the fastest-growing company in the world in 2009 (according to *Fortune Magazine*[14]), but its stock slumped in early 2010 in the face of fierce competition from Android devices—especially on the Verizon network in the United States—as well as the iPhone (Poletti

2010). Still, sales of BlackBerrys remained strong (more than 11 million handsets in first quarter of 2010, compared to 8.75 million iPhones) and the company continued to push forward into touch-enabled devices as well as their signature device with a separate QWERTY-style keyboard. Recent layoffs have markedly reduced the number of employees, and some retailers reported disappointing sales in mid-2012, with the result that the future of the company is in doubt, even after the seemingly successful launch of their new Z10 and Q10 products along with the new operating system (from QNX, a Canadian software company with deep roots in *real-time* software, especially for automobiles). With more than 12,000 employees worldwide and revenues of almost $15 billion, BlackBerry was briefly in 2007 the most valuable company in Canada[15] and should it shrink or fold, it would be a significant loss to the Canadian technology landscape.

Case Study Questions

1. If fashion is the driver of cell-phone sales, should a company like BlackBerry employ fashion experts? What else could the company try?
2. Do you know anyone who is a fanatical user of the BlackBerry? Why are they so dedicated to it?

Fido was purchased by Rogers and kept alive as a parallel and complementary brand. It is too early to tell if a similar fate awaits Wind, Mobilicity, and the other upstarts.

A cell-phone company provides service to end consumers both through monthly and prepaid (pay-as-you-go) options and to business customers (typically, large accounts, who pay on a monthly basis). Phone costs may be subsidized in order to entice users into signing longer contracts (typically two or three years), during which time the phone will be locked to the carrier from which it was purchased. Until recently, there were some fundamental technical differences between the network operated by Telus and Bell (which used a CDMA network, referring to the kind of division scheme used for handling multiple calls within a single frequency; see page 85 for our description of multiplexing) and that of Rogers/Fido (which used GSM). At present, all three of the big companies in Canada use a GSM-based system, and even the new entrants are using something compatible. In theory, users can roam from one network to another, although agreements are not in place in all cases.

Service from a mobile carrier typically includes the purchase of a service bundle with a certain number of minutes of voice calls, some text messages, and (perhaps) some Internet/data access. A bundle, before taxes, can range from $15 to $50 per month for a typical consumer. Another $30 or more would include added data features such as email and web browsing. If users exceed the amount they have paid for, extra charges are applied, by the minute, by the message, or by the megabyte. These overage charges can be quite high.

Mobile companies in Canada build their own radio towers and maintain their own links back to switching, interconnection (to phones from other companies), and billing operations. There is some tower sharing and the regulator has mandated that, in future, towers be shared equitably in order to lessen the proliferation of towers and to ensure that the newcomers are able to build their networks in a reasonable length of time. Roaming agreements are similarly mandated to ensure that a new company does not have to build a whole countrywide network just to get started. Any use of a competitor's

The Mobile Phone Industry in Canada—Facts and Figures

- Wireless communications generate a total economic value of some $43 billion for the Canadian economy.
- Canada's wireless carriers have invested more than $30 billion in communications infrastructure.
- The members of the CWTA pay licence fees in excess of $150 million each year—more than two-thirds of the total fees collected by Industry Canada from all spectrum users.
- More than 261,000 people are employed in Canada as a result of the wireless industry. The wireless sector offers high-value employment—it has an average salary level of $64,000, compared to a Canadian average salary of $44,000.
- The demand for highly skilled wireless-communications specialists is so great that Canadian post-secondary institutions are creating programs specifically geared to the wireless industry.

- Canada's wireless carriers now offer coverage to more than 99% of Canadians.
- Advanced wireless networks that support handsets such as smartphones and Internet sticks are available to 98% of Canadians.
- At the end of March 2012, Canadian wireless phone subscribers numbered 26 million.
- Half of all phone connections in Canada are now wireless.
- Seventy-five per cent of Canadian households have access to a wireless phone.
- Canadians send 254 million text messages per day.
- More than half of all calls to 911 come from mobile phones.
- Wireless revenues in Canada totalled $18 billion in 2010.
- Wireless market sector revenues are the largest component (43%) of total telecommunications revenues.

Source: The Canadian Wireless Telecommunications Association, http://cwta.ca/facts-figures.

tower or network, of course, has to be paid for by the newcomer. In other countries, towers are actually a separate business and mobile operators typically just lease space on the towers. There is some concern that this practice has been limited in Canada in part to make it harder for new entrants in the Canadian market (Townsend 2004).

The mobile phone industry is represented by the Canadian Wireless Telecommunications Association (CWTA). The CWTA publishes industry statistics regularly, as does Statistics Canada. The accompanying box offers some details on the size of the industry in Canada.

Mobile Phone—Usage Patterns

Mobile phones are just one of the many screens that people interact with each day. Others include the television, the tablet, and the computer or laptop. Not surprisingly, we use these devices for different purposes and in different places. The television is predominantly a "lean back" type of media consumption, in which viewers are watching broadcast or pre-recorded material. The mobile phone, however, is tied into the television experience in a number of ways. For example, people often chat with their friends via text message while watching a TV program. They may even be encouraged to provide feedback—as with shows such as *American Idol* and *So You Think You Can*

Dance—where audience members are allowed to vote on the best singer or dancer. More elaborate television and cell-phone interaction is possible with the smartphone, as service providers and app developers have made it possible for users to start and stop a personal video recorder (PVR) remotely from their phone or pick a show to watch using a schedule guide distributed through an app. Owners of an iPhone can use Airplay and an AppleTV to send video from their phone to a connected television.

Mobile devices are the tool of choice for people out and about. Even if you happen to have a laptop with you, the bother of locating a wireless zone, sitting down, and opening your laptop does not compare with the ease of doing a search on your smartphone. Search requests outside of the home or office are predominantly via mobile device.

Interestingly, many people are now starting to "sequentially screen" media content. In other words, they start on one device (for example Netflix on a smart television) and then continue watching on another (for example a smartphone or tablet). The interaction and "hand-off" from one device to another has been identified as a key growth area for mobile software and hardware makers, and features such as bookmark sharing across platforms are becoming more common via services such as iCloud (Apple's offering).

A recent study by Google Research revealed that 57 per cent of the time, when people are using a smartphone they are also using another device (either a PC or a television). The top activities while watching TV were composing email, Web browsing, updating social networks, and playing games. Many consumers (22 per cent), particularly the youth demographic, regard multi-device use as complementary rather than competitive: they are looking up more information on a movie star on IMDB, or trying to find a definition of a word, or seeing if they can find a pair of boots just like the ones worn by their favourite celebrity (Google Research 2012).

What Matters with Mobile?

Although the mobile phone industry is large, it is changing rapidly and with these changes there are also significant challenges ahead. In the remainder of this chapter, we examine some of those changes, issues, and why mobile is important to society.

Probably the most notable shift in mobile phones from a new media perspective is that just as the mobile phone is becoming a full player in the new media space, by virtue of its user interface and ability to display and record full motion video and audio, it is also being joined by an army of other mobile devices. One group of these new devices includes a crop of special-purpose products that are wirelessly enabled, such as game players and e-book readers. In another category are laptops and netbooks that have either built-in or plug-in cellular data connections, which make them not only portable, but also truly mobile. Some of the devices that appeared to be under threat by the popularity of mobile phones—cameras, in particular—are getting wireless capability either built in or through memory cards with WI-FI capability. The tablet computer is even more flexible and appears poised to compete significantly with the smartphone, the laptop, and e-book readers. The distinguishing feature of phones—the ability to make high-quality voice calls—is being usurped by many of these other devices that are now able to make voice and video calls through services such as MSN and Skype.

The former dividing line between mobile and portable—a mobile being something you could use as you move around and a portable being something you can move around and then use—is being broken down by ever-spreading wireless local area networking (LAN) via WI-FI and the growing availability of mobile hot spots on planes, trains, and even automobiles. These hot spots gain Internet access through another technology, such as satellite or wide area wireless (for example, WiMAX) or just the local 3G telephone data networks, then redistribute it via a LAN that is wireless and mobile.

The result to date is an interesting combination of blurred lines (increased mobility for previously generic and non-mobile computing devices and increased capabilities on mobile devices like iPhones and Androids) with sharp lines drawn by the addition of wireless Internet access to very specialized devices like home audio equipment, e-book readers,[16] cameras, bedside clocks, televisions, and a vast array of sensor devices.

Health Implications

In these turbulent market conditions, there are significant controversies related to the health, environmental, and social and cultural impacts of any new technology. Wireless and mobile devices such as smartphones are implicated in a variety of health concerns. Because of the nature of the electromagnetic energy used for almost all consumer technologies—it is very weak and non-ionizing—there is little in the way of a proven link to direct health impacts on humans. In other words, if there is harm being done (which is not at all clear), the mechanism of that harm is unknown.

On the other hand, because so many people use wireless mobile devices and use them so heavily and from such an early age, the companies that manufacture and regulate these devices would be sensible to take a prudent approach. Concerns about the health impacts of mobile devices have prompted numerous studies and a review of those studies was completed by the Royal Society of Canada in 1999. Their conclusion reflected the findings of most of the science that has been done on mobile technologies over the past couple of decades: there is minimal risk.[17] Nevertheless, health concerns persist and new studies may yet support a more restrictive use of these technologies. For those who are concerned, the general advice is to limit use, to use a (wired) headset, and to consider texting instead of talking.

Surprisingly, the most significant vector of harm from the use of mobile devices is not the radiation, but rather the tendency of mobile devices to divert users' attention away from what they should be focusing on (e.g., texting while driving or walking). A recent US study linked mobile phones—texting or talking—to an astonishing 28 per cent of all traffic accidents. These findings include more than just vehicles: evidently people also bump into things or even walk into traffic or fall into holes when texting while walking. A growing number of jurisdictions now ban the use of mobile phones while driving or at least restrict use by requiring a headset.

A secondary area of concern—although not something about which any direct health linkage has been proven—is the impact of cell-phone towers on people living nearby. In Canada, as in many other countries, decisions about the sites of cell-phone towers is a nationally regulated and mandated undertaking, and when a tower is planned for a sensitive area—such as near a school—people in the area quite often object strongly. In most cases, these objections can be overcome through moving the tower, but there have been cases where issues related to cell-phone towers have caused considerable anxiety and threats of lawsuits due to perceived health risks.

Since a physiological link is difficult to identify at the low power that mobile devices use, it is challenging to find evidence of how harm may be occurring and so far the only way to study these sorts of issues has been through indirect means. These have typically been population health measures, which look for statistically significant increases in health concerns across a broad spectrum of people over a long period of time. The problem with evaluating these studies is there are so many other variables (work, home, diet) that can affect human health, that it is difficult to identify correlations if they are at low levels. It is not surprising that this is also an area for considerable amateur opinion and conjecture, which does not tend to include sound, scientific research.

Environmental Concerns

Mobile phones are also tied to an array of environmental concerns, many of which are linked to health issues. These span a considerable range and include direct and indirect impacts on people and the environment. At one level, mobile technologies factor in an ongoing erosion of the aesthetic aspects of the environment, both natural and human made. Despite the best efforts to disguise the towers that bristle from the top of almost every major building in an urban area, they can be seen as detracting from the horizon, the skyline, and even the building design envisioned by an architect. Yet, since many of the people who those towers hope to reach with their signals are on the ground, the antennae have to be visible, for the most part.[18] The towers are even more obtrusive outside of urban centres, despite some attempts to camouflage them as faux trees or church steeples.

Cell-phone and other radio towers also have an impact on wildlife, especially birds, which become entangled in wires or confused by blinking lights (or to a lesser extent, electrocuted in power-supply circuits). Cell-phone antennae are somewhat less prone to these things, as they are not as large as the old TV and AM/FM towers, but in rural areas cell antennae are typically affixed to tall towers (sometimes abandoned radio and television broadcast towers) and in these situations they are disruptive to the local and migrating bird populations.

While the harm done to natural and architectural beauty, as well as wildlife, should not be underestimated, by far the most serious impact of mobile phones comes from their impact on the soil, water, and air due to the manufacture and disposal of the devices. Mobile phones have a considerable environmental impact in this regard for a host of reasons. These include

- Mobile phones include electronic components manufactured from rare earth elements, which are sourced in so-called conflict zones and, as such, are subject to significant concerns regarding human-rights and environmental regulation in the mining process.
- Mobile phones are made in factories all over the world, so they have a very high carbon load in the form of transport energy that goes into moving parts to factories and finished products to customers.

- Manufacturers of mobile devices have moved increasingly toward a fashion mentality in which phones are an element of style and are replaced (sometimes more than once a year) for reasons that go well beyond functionality or features. And, of course, the features change regularly in a competitive marketplace. This means more phones, more components, and more transportation than would otherwise be necessary.
- The eventual disposal and (hopefully) recycling of mobile phones is not only at a very early stage in most countries, but it is also difficult, dangerous, and dirty work that is inevitably farmed out to people in developing countries, if it is done at all. If not properly disposed of, a phone enters the waste stream, where it has not (until recently) been well designed for biodegrading.
- Even during use, there are environmental implications. Mobile phones are typically plugged in at night and often sit all night in a charger when they probably need only an hour or two of charge at most. The charger itself is typically left in the wall, consuming power even when not charging the phone. The wasted energy is considerable and has prompted European governments to issue new regulations for the design of cell-phone chargers.

Almost all of the concerns linked to mobile phones or wireless devices should be viewed in light of the fact that these are devices that—in a very short time—virtually every person on the planet may well be carrying. Even though mobile devices are small, they do, in their ubiquity, have a significant impact on the environment.

Social and Cultural Impact

One further area of concern for those looking at the impact of mobile phones and other wireless technologies on society are the social and cultural impacts. Some of these are common to new media generally and apply to both wired and wireless activities in society, and others are specific to mobility.

The impact on young people has already been mentioned, but this bears repeating because the increased youth independence and autonomy accompanying mobile technologies has been linked, if only in the popular media, to numerous possibly anti-social trends, such as mobs of young people gathering for impromptu events; the spread of sexual communication (sending salacious text messages—the aforementioned sexting—or posting nude photos via cell-phone camera); or simply as a vehicle for bad manners, cheating, and escaping from school and other responsibilities. Certainly, the injuries and deaths resulting from texting while driving have had a disproportionate impact on youth as well.

Mobile phones are blamed for the erosion of customary separations between males and females in more traditional societies, which may be less of an issue in Canada than elsewhere, but it is a concern in cultures that have long kept the sexes apart prior to marriage. While increased freedom might be a concern for some people, the mobile phone is also implicated in some significant declines in freedom. We noted earlier the extent to which parents are able to use mobile phones to keep tabs on their children. The helicopter-parent phenomenon is eclipsed by the much more significant impact mobile phones have on a global basis because of the general surveillance capabilities that they enable (see Chapter 10 for more on surveillance and new media). In part, this is because of cell technology: cell phones are effectively miniature tracking devices, by design. In order to create a system that was manageable in terms of completing and charging for calls, the designers of cellular phone services have to know where the phone is and what it is doing. In fact, cell phones engage in a constant silent dialogue whenever they are powered up. They send out a short, silent pulse of code to the cellular network and receive back a code. That code contains the cell-phone number and it is duly entered into a database, along with the tower that received the best reply. When a call comes into the system for that phone—whether from another mobile phone or from a land line—the location is looked up in the database and the ring is sent out to the cell where the mobile phone last checked in. That incoming call is then completed (assuming it is answered) and another set of entries is posted in the database—the start of the call, the end of the call, and who called whom. This information is not specifically designed for surveillance, but, rather, it is part of a billing system. It is a very useful tool for both law-enforcement and government agencies that would like to keep track of people, where they are, and to whom they are talking.

Employees may also be subject to tracking from systems like this, as services exist—most notably in the United Kingdom—whereby the phone location can be determined based on a lookup system available through the Web. The phone has to have this feature enabled and there is a cost for lookups, but in a workplace scenario these options are readily turned into requirements of the job: to always have the phone with you and keep it turned on. The delivery person or travelling salesperson who diverges from a known route can be called to account or, in a less sinister use, would be dispatched as the nearest person who could provide service (e.g., for a taxi or repair).

Being constantly connected—even when location is not part of the reported information—affects a vast number of people who increasingly use a smartphone or laptop as a way of keeping in touch with things at the office. This can lead to the feeling that work is becoming too pervasive, invading personal lives, and vice-versa. This kind of impact, as Ladner notes, is not strictly an outcome of the technology but is also part of the social relations and expectations of the workplace (Ladner 2008).

Other uses of these tracking systems include locating people in emergencies. These situations may happen when individuals are away from home, making it difficult to dispatch emergency services to an unfamiliar location. Again, the cell-tower information (especially when combined with information from other towers that might be slightly further away, but can sense a signal) will allow for pinpointing a phone (and user's) location for fire, ambulance, or police. In Canada, this is called Enhanced 911 or E911.

Useful Websites

Centre for Mobilties Research (CeMoRe)
http://cemore.blogspot.com

Kingsley Dennis, at the University of Lancashire, keeps this blog up to date with the latest on mobilities, with lots of current events and

commentary from an academic perspective. The Centre for Mobilties Research (CeMoRe) studies and researches the newly emerging interdisciplinary field of mobilities: the large-scale movements of people, objects, capital, and information across the world.

SmartMobs

www.smartmobs.com
Howard Rheingold started this blog while writing his book of the same name (2002), but the blog continues on and includes both news and commentary about the mobile world, with a strong emphasis on the social aspects of mobile technologies. The website tag line is "The next social revolution: Mobile communication, pervasive computing, wireless networks, collective action."

Open Gardens

http://opengardensblog.futuretext.com
Open Gardens is more focused on the mobile and wireless industry than the other two sites listed above, but it provides excellent coverage on a global basis for everything relating to mobile, especially on how the Web is mobile and on movements toward a more open mobile environment (in contrast to the largely proprietary mobile landscape we have had up to now).

Further Reading

Mobile Communications: An Introduction to New Media, Leslie Haddon and Nicola Green. (2010)
Haddon and Green paint a lively and compelling picture of the mobile phone and the history of its use. Importantly, they engage with the question of how mobile phones are "new media" and not merely devices for making and taking calls.

Mobile and Wireless Communications: An Introduction, Gordon Gow and Richard Smith (2006)
The book provides a blend of technical and socio-cultural explanations of mobile technologies that tries to balance the questions "how does it work?" and "what does it mean?".

Smart Mobs: The Next Social Revolution, Howard Rheingold (2002)
Rheingold was not the first scholar to tackle the social implications of mobile technologies, but he brought much greater attention to the topic and provided both a wide-ranging and insightful look at trends and issues many years before they were well understood outside of Europe and Asia. The book remains useful more than a decade later (see also Rheingold's www.smartmobs.com site, mentioned above, for ongoing contributions).

Mobile Nation: Creating Methodologies for Mobile Platforms, Martha Ladly and Philip Beesley (eds.), (2008)
This is an edited collection from a conference that brought together Canadian social and technical researchers with designers, developers, and investors to imagine ways in which they could better connect sociological insight to the commercializers of mobile technologies. It includes contributions from a wide variety of participants and some very interesting and novel research projects.

Discussion Questions

1. In what ways is path dependence evident in the development and social uses of mobile technologies?

2. How did the cellular system present a solution to the capacity problem of earlier radio and telephone systems?

3. What capabilities give mobile phones or mobile general-purpose devices a key advantage over specific-purpose technologies?

4. Several aspects of telecommunications policy are discussed in this chapter. What are these and why are they significant?

5. In what sense was the advent of short messaging service (SMS) an important turn in the evolution of mobile communication?

6. What is the significance of the way(s) in which the operators of large web sites such as Facebook and Twitter seized the potential

of adapting their services to the sending and receiving of SMS, of reaching out to texters rather than asking users to reach out to the Internet?

7. What are some of the favourable and unfavourable implications of the "always on" capability of mobile devices? In what ways are these becoming almost default characteristics in personal and professional life, and what are the consequences?

8. Mobile phone use is considered by some as part of a revolution in youth culture. Discuss what this means and in what ways such changes are evident in varying degrees across generational (and/or other demographic) lines.

9. In this chapter, we note that there are significant controversies related to health, the environment, and the social and cultural impacts of mobile technologies. Discuss these (and any others) and what could be done to address the concerns raised.

Class Activities

1. In small groups with other students, take out your phone and hand it to the person beside you. Take some time to reflect on and share how you feel about giving someone else access to your phone. What is the significance of having such a device?

2. Explore the various price plans and services (minutes, texts, data, voice mail, features) both for the mobile device(s) you have and (perhaps) the one you wish you had. What sacrifices do you make, if any, to afford this plan?

3. Break into small groups and create a re-enactment or skit that portrays the many things that people do, both rightly and wrongly, while they are using their mobile device (e.g., consuming other media, eating dinner with family, visiting with friends, driving). Comment on the implications of this task switching or interruption.

4. Almost anything related to new media is subject to rapid change. Firms come and go; technologies change; and numbers of users, viewers, and creators for new media content and memes change every day. Look up a fact or figure in this chapter and verify whether it remains true today, using online sources. Identify corroborating or supporting sources for your findings. Not only will you have the new facts but you'll also have an appreciation for how quickly things change and, most importantly, a visceral sense of the way in which the Internet and new media are self-revealing to the diligent and inquisitive scholar. If you discover a fact that needs updating, you can even submit your update (with page reference and new citation) in the form of a rewritten paragraph, to the author: Richard Smith (smith@sfu.ca). He promises to reply.

Debate Questions

1. Using a cell phone while consuming other media might seem natural and efficient when you are at home, but what about texting while watching a movie in a theatre? Is that okay?

2. Location-based enhancements to a smartphone—it knows where you are and can adjust your search results based on that information—can be helpful, but are they an invasion of your privacy?

3. BlackBerry, floundering in the summer and fall of 2012, seemed poised for a rebound in January 2013. What happened? Based on what you know now, do you think BlackBerry's actions were the right ones? Is its status as an iconic Canadian company important to you?

Social Networks and Participatory Culture

Questions to Consider

- What does it mean to live in a network society?
- What kinds of issues and questions arise when considering participatory culture?
- In what ways are social capital and social media linked?

Chapter Outline

This chapter has two parts. In the first half of the chapter, we consider the concept of social networks and how these enable a culture of mass participation—a **participatory culture**. We also examine how these networks enable and enhance many other social processes. Although networks are not new phenomena, they are enhanced and extended by new media and we explore this process in more detail. Networks are economic and political as well as social phenomena. Given their importance, it is not surprising that new research methods have arisen to explore their features, their mechanisms, and their impact. We explore one of these methods, social network analysis, in detail from both a practical and a historical point of view. We will also discuss social network theories and criticism of these theories. In the second part of the chapter, we look at social production and the participatory culture that has emerged in social networks. Social production and participatory culture, often taking the form of a "gift economy" in which people contribute to sites such as Wikipedia and YouTube out of sense of pride and community and sharing, existed in earlier times but have been greatly enhanced by widespread availability of new forms of information and communications technology and the resulting ability to contribute at very low cost and with few barriers to entry.

Networking for Fun and Profit

The ability of electronic communication networks to foster collaboration in the production of media has been evident for more than a century. Our earlier discussion of the effects of the telegraph on newspaper chains and news associations illustrates how quickly businesses recognized and capitalized on the ability of networks to remix, reuse, and repurpose online and digital materials. Until fairly recently, however, the ability to create and take advantage of networks was limited to professional and commercial settings, due to the high cost and relatively complex nature of the required infrastructure. In the analogue media era, community media often meant a (heavily subsidized, typically by conditions of licence on new stations or cable companies) community cable channel or radio station, but bearing nearly the same weight of equipment and expertise to operate it as a commercial station. Similarly, printing presses were complicated and expensive to operate, reducing the number of people who might have had an interest in participating in zine (amateur magazine) culture.

The computer era has reduced those costs dramatically and in the process has enabled an enormous outpouring and sharing of media works by professional and non-professional users—for example, the uploading of millions of songs, photos, videos, and blogs every minute, thus using the physical, technical networking of modern computers to create intangible networks of shared experience.[1] Computers have also made it easier to study the social connections embedded in those networks (social networks) and easier to understand a network's power and capabilities. In other words, you can use computers to make it easier to see how computers are affecting social networks. In the next section, we look at some of the academic research that is focused on social networks and then talk about how networks are used in the production of participatory or user-generated media.

The Nature of Networks

Human beings are social creatures and we exist in a vast array of social networks, including kinship, friendship, neighbourhood, and community. The first electronic networks—the telegraph and the telephone—provided important enhancements to those social networks by speeding up and extending the reach of our connections to one another. As a result, communications networks are a central factor in social theories, and particularly social theories about new media. A key feature of networked electronic communication, in contrast with earlier forms of communication, is the ability to connect, directly, with almost any other person in your various social networks. You do not have to make an appointment or navigate an assistant or servant in order to send an email. In fact, the telephone was a bit of a shock to nineteenth- and early twentieth-century British culture because of the possibility that "just anyone" could call you (Rowland 2006: 127–8). Communications networks are central to the organization and operation of twenty-first-century society and culture. The speed and reach of these networks gives us the ability to connect directly into rules and systems, as we do when we, for example, arrange travel by directly accessing an airline database—this means that we start doing things without intermediaries, we do things in different ways, and we come to rely on a very tightly coordinated system of interconnected networks.

Computers have propelled networking—in both a communications sense and a social sense—further than might have been imagined in the early days of the telephone. Of course, social networks are not just a recent phenomenon. In their 2009 book, *Connected: The Surprising Power of Our Social Networks and How They Shape Our Lives*, Christakis and Fowler provide vivid and compelling examples of how social networks result in extraordinary outcomes—good and bad—in the real world, and have done for millennia (2009: 3–32). For example, social networks such as family, kinship, culture, ethnicity, and nationality have greatly affected human affairs since the dawn of civilization. The impact of those social networks, until relatively recently, was felt from people nearby, or with a considerable lag for interactions to spread across distance. Even with the rise of electronic media, beginning with the telegraph, connections sped up and greatly expanded the number of people one could connect with at the same time. But the power of those connections was mitigated by the lack of interactivity in broadcast media (so, while the number of connections could increase, the depth of engagement was moderated) or the lack of sociality in telecommunication networks (e.g., you could engage with only one person at a time on the telephone). Online networks have both sped up and expanded these existing social organizations to an unimaginable degree and breadth and created entirely new possibilities, such as the online support group or the massively multi-player online role playing game (Christakis and Fowler 2009: 253–86).

Elaborating on the link between the Internet and the network as a factor in the production and reproduction of social structure, Wellman (2001) argues that a computer network is part of our **social network**. Proposing that both individuals and organizations socialize into communities through networks rather than groups, Wellman identifies the many social advantages that the Internet and related ICTs provide for sustaining both geographically specific community ties and enabling new global networked ties. A key distinguishing feature between a network and a group, in this context, is that everyone knows everyone in a group, but you might "know someone who knows someone" in a network. In other words, there are indirect connections, which are seen as part of a general process of modernity "away from place-based inter-household ties [toward] individualized person-to-person inter-actions and specialized role-to-role interactions" (2001: 231). Finding that "cyberspace fights against physical place less than it complements it," Wellman observes that the relationship of new media to social networking shows that it "has increased the importance of network capital in the fund of desirable resources, along with financial capital, human capital, and cultural capital" (2001: 247, 248).

The growing importance of computer networks as a part of social networks can be understood from (at least) two angles. One emphasizes the growing significance attached to networks in areas of social, cultural, political, economic, and, indeed, military relations. The other considers how the Internet (which is a technological form that is fundamentally grounded in networks) has permeated all aspects of society in terms of the form and content of social relations.

Networking amid Politics and Terrorism

The growing political significance of networks is well documented. It has had clear manifestations since the 1960s in the forms of rapidly declining memberships in major political parties, waning participation in electoral politics, and a growing sense of popular alienation from formal political institutions and processes (e.g., see Castells 1998: 342–53). Paul Miller draws attention to the rise of network campaigns pursued by social movements through loosely organized representative agencies and coalitions, outside of traditional political channels, and how new media enables this:

> Network campaigns allow a diverse grouping of organizations and individuals to participate through commitment to a shared purpose, while remaining autonomous individual agents. In this way, it is possible to gain additional leverage over decision-making bodies through the "multiplier effect" of a coherent message and more efficient deployment of resources and effort, while maintaining the flexibility and energy that more bureaucratic forms of co-ordination tend to squander. (2004: 208)

Groups as diverse as Anonymous (a loose collection of online hackers), the Occupy movement (a global campaign to protest inequality and injustice) and the Tea Party (a US-based right-wing political group) have taken advantage of this new form of "organization without organization." The specific characteristics of network campaigns that generate such advantages include having a shared goal; being "structure-light"; mobilizing a diverse coalition of skills and resources around shared goals; making advanced use of new media technologies; embracing diversity and openness; cultivating the ability to draw upon and develop media celebrity; expoiting media spectacle around specific targets; using time-limited strategies; maintaining high levels of media visibility; and being ready to act quickly and cheaply (Miller 2004: 208–13).

Miller had in mind network movements conducted by peaceful means for noble ends, such as the Jubilee 2000 debt-reduction campaign for developing nations or the role played by environmental organizations like Earthwatch or Greenpeace. It is also the case, however, that network strategies are tactics used by terrorist organizations like al-Qaeda and its notorious late leader Osama bin Laden.

Al-Qaeda's stated goal of the elimination of Western power and influence from Muslim states would have had peripheral influence on world events had it been conducted solely from the mountains of Afghanistan and northern Pakistan. What has helped al-Qaeda make such an enormous impact on current world events is the alignment of such a goal with aspects of network politics. These include

- the capacity to use new media to disseminate messages widely to current and potential supporters;
- the high level of visibility attached to events such as the terrorist attacks on the World Trade Center and the Pentagon on 11 September 2001, as well as subsequent terrorist attacks in Bali in 2002, on the Madrid subway in 2004, and the London Underground rail network in 2005; and

- the inherently structure-light nature of this organization, which maintains itself through a dense and seemingly amorphous network of agents and activists.

Al-Qaeda has continued to operate in spite of the massive growth in surveillance in the aftermath of 9/11, the war in Afghanistan to depose the Taliban government, the assassination of bin Laden, and the war in Iraq. Friel (2002) observes the extent to which bin Laden exemplified the network logic of developing and running a global organization:

> He decentralized decision-making authority and created a flat management structure to quickly respond to changes in his operating environment. He overcame turf battles by creating an overarching sense of mission and doctrine. He used the Internet and the globalization of news and the revolution in telecommunications to advance his organization's goals worldwide. He developed a complex organizational network in which information gets only to the right people at the right times. In his network, connections between individuals and groups are activated at key times to get work done and severed when they are no longer necessary.[2]

While al-Qaeda may have used electronic networks, including distribution of messages via the Internet and cell-phone technology for coordinating attacks, it remained a relatively traditional guerrilla/terrorist group in the sense of focusing on physical world targets while having recognizable leaders, most famously bin Laden, and using conventional methods, such as bombs and hijackings. In recent years, however, the Internet has given rise to a form of protest and attack that is not just coordinated over the network, but it also takes action through the network and is often entirely focused on the network.

Anonymous, the hacker group known for its role in defacing government and corporate websites, for participating in the Occupy Wall Street movement (and other Occupy events), and even taking action against online pedophilia websites, is emblematic of this new form of online activism, or the aforementioned "hacktivism." For Anonymous, not just the mode of coordination but both the target and the means of attack are all online.

It is largely thought that Anonymous originated on the discussion board and image-sharing site www.4chan.org, probably in 2003. It would be straining the definition of the word *organization* to call it an organization, however. In a sense, it is more like an idea or an ideal. As one member (if one can even use such a term) of the group stated in a 2008 interview with Jesse Brown for the CBC program *Search Engine*,

> We [Anonymous] just happen to be a group of people on the Internet who need—just kind of an outlet to do as we wish, that we wouldn't be able to do in regular society. . . . That's more or less the point of it. Do as you wish. . . . There's a common phrase: "We are doing it for the lulz." (Brown 2008)

Despite their lack of organization, Anonymous has been remarkably successful in raising the profile of a broad range of issues, ranging from Ugandan government treatment of lesbians and gays to the protests over the Stop Online Piracy Act (SOPA) in the United States (a copyright-reform bill, eventually defeated by Congress in part because of awareness raising that resulted from Anonymous's actions).

Sometimes, when the perceived harm or activity is originating online, as in the case of Internet pedophilia websites, the actions taken by Anonymous have been directly responsible for the closure or disabling of those sites and (sometimes) the exposure of those responsible.

One of the favoured tools of Anonymous is the distributed denial of service (DDOS) attack on a target. In this scenario, computers across the world—typically, they're not owned by the activists, but instead they are other people's computers, which are engineered to participate in the attack via a type of virus or malware—are enlisted in a simultaneous request for files and information, thus overwhelming the organization's web server or the Internet service provider or both.

In Canada, we recently had an unfortunate situation in which social networks and Anonymous-style revenge were highlighted. Following the suicide of Vancouver-area teenager Amanda Todd, apparently related to cyberbullying (see the accompanying box), a number of avengers went online to "out" her tormenters. Todd's poignant YouTube video, which soon attracted 17 million views and thousands of tribute/response videos, was the trigger for an Anonymous-style attack on those deemed responsible—the attackers claimed to have found the perpetrator of the bullying and revealed his personal information to both the police and general public.

Cyberbullying: What Is It and What Can We Do about It?

Cyberbullying is understood to be any situation in which one person—typically with some sort of power over another, perhaps through age, size, or reputation—engages in repeated and unwelcome personal attacks via the Internet.

These days, social networks such as Facebook are common vehicles for such attacks, but they can also be launched in chat rooms and in text messages. Although mean-spirited comments and hurtful messages directed at a person are usually how it starts, cyberbullying often expands to include things like fake accounts and pages on Facebook or other social media. When information is gleaned about a person—or, in some cases, compromising or embarrassing photos—and then posted online, the sense of violation and victimization can be intense.

Although commonly associated with young people, adults are subject to cyberbullying as well. Although suicide following cyberbullying is what gets the headlines, most situations do not go that far, but the impact is nonetheless real, harmful, and more widespread than

people realize. Vicitms of cyberbullying, or any other form of bullying, typically suffer a loss of self-esteem and fall into an ensuing downward spiral in marks at school or productivity in the workplace.

Following a series of high-profile Canadian cyberbullying events in 2012, legislation was proposed Parliament to address the issue, designed mainly to focus on education but also to implementing effective tools for policing and punishing those who engage in the practice. Parents, counsellors, friends, and colleagues should all be alert to the possibility that someone is being bullied online and be prepared to intervene and help. If the bullying extends to threats, a criminal charge can be brought against the perpetrator. Police are becoming increasingly adept at pursuing these sorts of crimes and should be involved in serious cases as soon as possible. Copies of all materials in which bullying appears should be retained for investigative purposes. Because posts may be deleted later, it is important to secure them at the time they appear, using screen-capture tools if possible.

Social Network Analysis

Social network analysis is a methodology developed in the social and behavioural sciences to map interpersonal linkages using statistical and graphical techniques. Wasserman and Faust identify the distinctiveness of **social network analysis** in that "the social environment can be expressed as patterns or regularities in relationships among interacting units" (1994: 3). Understanding forms of self, activity, and behaviour as related is fundamental to this approach. Wasserman and Faust identify four key elements of social network analysis:

1. Actors and their actions are viewed as interdependent—that is, formed through relationships to others.
2. Relational ties, or what are referred to as linkages, are channels for the flow of resources, which may be material (capital, commodities, etc.) or immaterial (power, influence, information, etc.) in nature.
3. Network models view the network structural environment as providing opportunities for, or presenting constraints upon, individual behaviour.
4. Network models conceptualize structure (social, economic, political, etc.) as lasting patterns of relations among actors. (1994: 4)

Networks and Organizations

Podolny and Page (1998: 59) observe that "every form of organization is a network," since the nature of an organization—whether it be a business or a not-for-profit—requires ongoing exchange between more than two social actors. At the same time, one of the distinctive features of a social network is a set of ethical orientations around behaviours such as trust, reciprocity, goodwill, and mutual obligation that differ from the contractual nature of purely market-based transactions and the notion of authority that characterizes businesses. Moreover, the focus of network analysis is as much on relations between organizations as it is on relations within organizations. Benefits of social network forms of organization include

- the capacity for collective learning among agents across the network;
- the accrual of legitimacy or status for individual agents from being part of a larger network;
- greater adaptability to unanticipated changes in the wider socio-economic environment; and,

- minimizing forms of vulnerability arising from resource dependency upon others (Podolny and Page 1998: 62–6).

In considering why the reliance on networking as a basis for an organization's activities will vary, Podolny and Page note three key variables:

- the importance of power relations to the interactions between organizations—the more power is exercised to achieve organizational goals, the less significant network forms will be;
- the age of an organization—older organizations are typically less imbued with a networking culture than newer ones; and,
- national, cultural, and legal differences: network forms of organization tend to be associated more with collectivist cultures than with more individualistic ones—they are, for example, more characteristic of Asian countries than they are of the United States or the United Kingdom (Doremus et al. 1998; cf. Hofstede 1980; Podolny and Page 1998: 67–8; Scott 1986).

Social network analysis characteristically works from the bottom up, in that it aims to identify relationships that exist in a particular place and time, the mapping of which can contribute to wider hypotheses about social structure. Wasserman and Faust identify seven core concepts (1994: 17–21):

1. Actor: an actor is a discrete unit of decision-making and action, which may be an individual, but may also be a corporation, a government agency, or some other form of organization such as an association, a trade union, or a university.
2. Relational ties: this refers to the establishment of links between actors, which can include mutual admiration, shared membership of associations, regular meetings and other forms of communication, movement of actors between places, formal relationships of authority, and biological relationships based upon kinship.
3. Dyad: this is the information used to establish a relational tie between two actors, so that they can be seen to constitute a pair.
4. Triad: this identifies probabilities of relationships between three actors based on knowledge of dyadic relationships.
5. Subgroup: if identification of the existence of dyadic relationships can be established, and these can be triangulated to the potential for triadic relationships, then this will form the basis for the existence of a subgroup of actors.
6. Group: the group in social network analysis is "the collection of all actors on which ties are to be measured" (Wasserman and Faust 1994: 19). Such a group should be finite in its nature (i.e., the set of actors involved is already established) and there is a need to establish that these actors constitute a group as a bounded set.
7. Relation: this refers to the evidence of interaction and relationships among members of the group that indicate both durable ties and the capacity to act in response to a situation in the social environment.

Social network analysis has its origins in the development of the "sociogram" as a way of illustrating the nature of interpersonal relations within a group. Two of the core elements of what was termed "sociometry"—as a precursor to social network analysis—were the use of visual representations of group structure and a probability-based model of structural outcomes.

Another important approach to social networks is the **actor network theory** pioneered by Bruno Latour. This approach places not just people in a network, but also things. Both ideas and technologies, for example, can be seen as "actants." A social network analysis of something like Facebook would have to include not just the participants but also the software and servers that enable that network, as well as the concept of a "friend" as used in that context. Importantly for actor network theory, these relationships are in a state of constant evolution, being remade each time the actors interact (Latour 2005).

Many questions within the social sciences and, more recently, theories of the creative economy and creative industries, have prompted the use of social network analysis. It can be used to explore the existence and operation of the ruling class in capitalist societies (what C. Wright Mills [1956] referred to in the American context as a "power elite"). Identifying that rich people exist is only part of the story; what social network analysis can do is demonstrate that these people may be able to act cohesively and collectively in order to pursue shared interests. Social network research aims to provide this type of evidence by examining the effects of interlocking corporate directorships and their relationship to other ties, such as those based on corporate share ownership and investment financing. Research on these kinds of questions has been critical in clarifying some of these issues and in establishing points of difference among various capitalist models—for example, comparisons between the US, Japanese, British, and/or German models (Scott 1986, 1991; cf. Stokman et al. 1985).

Interpersonal networks are a second area of inquiry that uses social network analysis. Researchers who are interested in the linkages that the Internet creates between our various forms of personal or face-to-face social networking using the interconnections established through technology often draw on the tools and techniques provided by network analysis. Wellman's point that "we find community in networks, not in groups" (Wellman 2001: 227) draws attention to the way interactions that form the basis for social networks are increasingly developed through mediated communication (e.g., email correspondence) and provides clear points of intersection between the analytical concerns of social network analysis and the Internet's capacity to map "data transfers." A good example of this is the blogging process, as bloggers often provide a "blogroll" of other bloggers they consider to have opinions that are worth looking at.

A third question within the social sciences relates to the attention given to interpersonal networks or what is referred to as "soft infrastructure" in the literature on creative industries and creative cities. Charles Landry (2000: 133) defines soft infrastructure as "the system of associative structures and social networks, connections, and human interactions that underpins and encourages the flow of ideas between individuals and institutions." A club or association is a good example of soft infrastructure. The process of uncovering such interconnections is the basis of social network analysis and Wellman's (2001) work on the social networks at play in emerging online communities in Toronto's suburbs was a pioneering effort in this regard.

Social network analysis is rapidly moving from the academic world to the business world as the importance of social networks continues to grow. Facebook, with more than 1.15 billion members as of September 2013, is among the most compelling examples of this phenomenon. Facebook founder Mark Zuckerberg coined the term *social graph*[3] to describe "the global mapping of everybody and how they are related"[4] on Facebook. The term has been expanded to include all of the social networks and connections a person has on sites such as Facebook, Twitter, and Foursquare—anywhere that you have "friends" or "followers." The distinction between the social graph and social networks is that the social graph is strictly about online relationships. The problem with this distinction is that many of those online relationships have parallels in the real world. For businesses, the potential represented by the social graph is to take advantage of the value of those relationships—for example, by selling you things that your friends or followers are buying.

Networks and the Economics of Social Production

Much of the work on the socio-economic role of communications networks has focused on the ways in which they transform organizational relations, as seen in the literature on network enterprises (Barney 2004: 83–90; Castells 2001: 64–116; Thompson 2003: 111–48). In *The Wealth of Networks* (2006), Yochai Benkler argues that the impact of networks runs deeper than this. He says that the early twenty-first century has brought the rise of a networked information economy, whose core characteristic is that "decentralized individual action—specifically, new and important cooperative and coordinated action carried out through radically distributed, non-market mechanisms that do not depend upon proprietary strategies—plays a much greater role than it did, or could have, in the industrial information economy" (2006: 3). The key driver of such development is the generalization of the Internet and networked personal computing, whose degree of connectivity continues to grow as the cost of accessing ICTs continues to fall, and the capacity of each networked computer to produce, retrieve, and store data of all sorts continues to rise. For Benkler, this "removal of the physical constraints on effective information production has made human creativity and the economics of information . . . core structuring facts in the new networked information economy" (2006: 4).

The growth of the Internet and networked ICTs provides a necessary but insufficient explanation for the rise of the networked information economy. Benkler's work points to three subsidiary conditions. First, there is the rise of information, knowledge, and creative industries themselves, which even at their most industrialized—as they were in the second half of the twentieth century—needed to be more flexible and more reliant on non-market motives than traditional manufacturing industries. Second, the existence of the Internet itself has given a major boost to all non-market forms of production and distribution of information, knowledge, and culture. This is because the Internet provides coordination for the millions of individual actions that greatly enrich the networked information environment. For example, when you or I select a particular item from a list provided by a search engine, that selection is retained as a bit of information relating to those search terms and thereby increasing the quality of future searches by moving that selection up higher. When one superimposes the information retrieval capacity of an Internet search engine like Google on the billions of web pages that exist on the Internet, it is possible to see what Benkler terms the "'information good' that . . . is produced by the coordinate effects of the uncoordinated actions of a wide and diverse range of individuals and organizations acting on a wide range of motivations—both market and non-market, state and non-state" (Benkler 2006: 5). Third, there is increased "peer production" of information, knowledge, and culture through large-scale cooperative efforts. The conceptual and practical origins of this rest in the free and open-source software movement, but the rise of Web 2.0 and social software has seen effects across a range of domains. Peer production—or user-generated content as it is often called in the Web 2.0 world—is the basis for the business model used in notable sites such as Flickr, YouTube, and Facebook. No corporate media production department exists for these sites. Instead, they rely almost entirely on the productive efforts of their users (this phenomenon is explored in greater detail below).

This draws attention to the growth of **social production** and models of information, knowledge, and cultural production that are loosely collaborative, not necessarily driven by market criteria, and not directly proprietary in terms of who owns and controls the use of the final product. Observing that individuals have a variety of motives to act, to make information available to others, and to cooperate, Benkler argues that social production has gained prominence in the networked information economy from the confluence of two factors: (1) the fact that knowledge as a uniquely valued input to production is always possessed uniquely by individuals, and (2) that the majority of these individuals "have the threshold level of material capacity [i.e., networked computers] required to explore the information environment they occupy, to take from it, and to make their contributions to it" (2006: 99). Given that in any society an excess of useful human knowledge and creativity exists relative to what is required economically, Benkler identifies two features of those projects that can most successfully harness the human resources necessary for effective social production.

The first feature is **modularity**, or the properties of a project that determine "the extent to which it can be broken down into smaller components, or modules, that can be independently produced before they are assembled into a whole" (Benkler 2006: 100). At one extreme, development and management of a nuclear power plant is extremely difficult to modularize, as the centre needs to be sure not only of the quality of all work (in order to avoid nuclear accident) but of the loyalty and commitment of all staff (because of the dangers of trafficking nuclear products to third parties). By contrast, Wikipedia demonstrates successfully the degree to which the assembling of an online encyclopedia can occur through the agglomeration of a vast and diverse range of independent inputs.

The second feature identified by Benkler is that of **granularity**, or the size of the modules, in terms of the time and effort that an individual must invest in producing them, which sets "the smallest possible individual investment necessary to participate in a project" (2006: 101). Wikipedia is again a good example, as the investment of time and resources involved in making a single contribution is relatively small, or, in Benkler's terms, fine-grained. As an illustrative example, Table 5.1 indicates not only the growth in the number of contributors to Wikipedia between 2001 and 2005, but also the degree of granularity that exists between those who have been occasional contributors and those who maintain an ongoing relationship to the site and its contents. Two notable features of the table are that while the number of contributors of all types grew exponentially over the period, the fastest rates of growth were in the number of occasional contributors (reflecting granularity) and the number of non-English language contributions (reflecting the globalization of the Internet):

Table 5.1 Contributors to Wikipedia, January 2001 to June 2005

	Jan 2001	Jan 2002	Jan 2003	Jan 2004	July 2004	June 2005
Contributors[1]	10	477	2,188	9,653	25,011	48,721
Active contributors[2]	9	212	846	3,228	8,442	16,945
Very active contributors[3]	0	31	190	692	1,637	3,106
No. of English-language articles	25	16,000	101,000	190,000	320,000	630,000
No. of articles, all languages	25	19,000	138,000	409,000	862,000	1,600,000

[1] Contributed at least 10 times

[2] Contributed at least 5 times in last month

[3] Contributed more than 100 times in last month

Source: Benkler (2006: 72).

Recent research on Wikipedia (e.g., Suh et al. 2009) suggests that the period of exponential growth in the early 2000s may have slowed or plateaued. This is particularly pronounced among those who are not insiders to Wikipedia but instead make casual or infrequent contributions. Part of the problem—if it is a problem, as growth in contributors need not necessarily continue upward at such a rapid pace—may be that the governance mechanisms for Wikipedia sometimes have failed to keep pace with changes in the community. In fact, complaints about cliquish behaviour among Wikipedia's elite—and that there even is an elite—dogged the service during 2008 and 2009. Recent changes to a more decentralized governance structure (Forte et al. 2009) may address this, but the criticism of Wikipedia is ongoing. Wikipedia itself maintains a large page documenting these criticisms, including more than 130 references as of September 2013 (see http://en.wikipedia.org/wiki/Criticism_of_Wikipedia).

Benkler believes that the combination of the Internet and the network marks a seismic shift in the socio-economic order of the twenty-first century as compared to the twentieth. The title of his book, *The Wealth of Networks*, alludes to the foundational text of market economics, Adam Smith's *The Wealth of Nations*, published in 1776. Smith and other classical economists identified the expansion of markets and trade as being at the core of new forms of wealth creation (on Smith, see Dobb 1973). In the late nineteenth and early twentieth centuries, free-market economics was somewhat usurped by the rise of the large corporation—what James Beniger (1986) termed the "control revolution" and what Alfred Chandler (1977) referred to as the "visible hand"—where the combination of corporate control over resources on a large scale and scope, the capacity of planning to enable control over the external environment, and the combination of rewards and sanctions over individual employees that ensured loyalty and identification over time, made the corporation the superior form of economic organization. Benkler's argument is not that social production through networks will quickly supplant both markets and corporate hierarchies as the dominant form of economic organization. Indeed, he acknowledges that "the rise of social production does not entail a decline in market-based production" (2006: 122). For many businesses, the principal change is in "the relationship of firms to individuals outside of them . . . [as] consumers are changing into users—more active and productive than the consumers of the industrial information economy" (Benkler 2006: 126).

Social production will have the greatest effect on the areas of economic life that lend themselves most readily to its core characteristics, such as the industries connected to information, knowledge, communications, culture, and creativity. At the same time, as the size and significance of these sectors grows, particularly in advanced capitalist economies, the impact of social production will have a considerably wider resonance over time. As a general rule, the more important that non-contractual factors are to an economic relationship—such as gifts, reciprocity, and trust—the more significant social production will be. This will in turn generate conflicts and contradictions in the core sector of the networked information economy, as "social production in general and peer production in particular present new sources of competition to incumbents that produce information goods for which there are now socially produced substitutes" (Benkler 2006: 122). The prototypical example of this is the way in which Wikipedia has outcompeted traditional encylopedias, both in terms of volume and—according to a number of studies—quality and reliability of information. Copyright law has often been the flashpoint at which these conflicts have been played out.

In Chapter 9, we will explore in more depth the nature of these conflicts and the role of authors such as Benkler, Lawrence Lessig, and others associated with the Creative Commons as a socio-legal response to these debates.

Others dispute Benkler's claim that peer production (as in Wikipedia) will eventually supplant commercial production mechanisms. While acknowledging that commercial encyclopedias seem to have clearly been overtaken by peer production, writers such as Nick Carr are skeptical that this is somehow a death knell to all forms of media production. This debate led, famously, to the Carr–Benkler Wager of 2006 (see Nick Carr's account of the events, plus updates since then, here: www.roughtype.com/?p=1599), in which Benkler proposed a bet to see who would win on the question of the dominant form of media production in the year 2011. As of 2013, both writers are claiming victory, pointing to examples that support both of their perspectives. (Benkler clearly has the "win" in terms of Wikipedia, but blogging has turned commercial with the rise of sites such as *The Huffington Post*, providing support for Carr's position.)

As we now turn to a discussion of participatory media cultures, it is important to keep in mind that without the content and the culture that is embedded in media exchanges, social networks are little more than empty webs. In fact, when social networking is seen as empty of meaning, it often becomes the object of ironic criticism, such as the early, scathing critiques of Twitter. People network in order to accomplish something, and in doing so they add meaning to their messages—in this meaning, a culture is born. In the remainder of this chapter, we examine participatory culture in more detail.

Participatory Media Cultures

The creation of a participatory media culture has long been one of the great promises of new media. Early writers such as Rheingold (1994) envisaged the rise of a virtual public sphere, while Turkle (1997) saw identity as something that could become much more fluid and changeable in the virtual world of cyberspace. The discussion surrounding the participatory potential of new media arose from its apparent structural differences from the forms of mass communication that dominated twentieth-century society. Thompson (1995) and McQuail (2005) have identified some of the key features of these earlier models of mass communication:

- the use of media technologies which enable large-scale production and distribution of informational and symbolic content to reach the largest audience possible, who in turn possess technological devices for reception of such content;
- institutional separation of the producers/distributors and receivers of media content, arising from both the costs of access to technologies of production and distribution, and the role played by various media gatekeepers as determinants of what constituted professional media content;
- an asymmetrical power relationship between producers/distributors and receivers of media, with the latter having little scope to respond to a largely one-way communications flow;

- relations between producers/distributors and receivers/consumers of media that were largely impersonal, anonymous and, in most instances, commodified through the reliance of large-scale commercial media industries upon advertising revenue (i.e., the audience was viewed as a target market); and,
- tendencies toward standardization of content, as the desire to maximize aggregate audiences (market share) created dynamics that promoted media content with the broadest possible appeal (i.e., limited scope for market segmentation through product differentiation).

For each of these key features, there is a counterpoint or alternative provided by new media and participatory media in particular. We leave it as an exercise for the reader—or perhaps a classroom or tutorial activity—to delineate these and think of current examples.

The mass-communication paradigm rested on the transmission model of communication, which—allowing for factors such as feedback, noise, and signal failure—saw communication primarily in terms of a one-way flow of messages from senders (typically few) to receivers (typically many). While this model was being challenged conceptually from the 1970s by cultural studies and their focus on the complexities of decoding and the activity of audiences (Hall 1982; see Bassett 2007 for a recent evaluation), and was further eroded during the 1980s as a model for understanding media industries, it was the ascent of the Internet and networked ICTs in the 1990s that heralded claims of a decisive break from mass communications. This argument typically had two components, one relating to the capacity of new media to enable greater participation in politics and political communication, the other relating to new media's potential to enable more people to become media producers and distributors as well as consumers. Many have identified the possibility of new media and ICTs enabling greater democratic political participation, and fostering a new, more egalitarian form of citizenship and political engagement. The factors commonly cited as enabling ICTs as a force for broadening and deepening democracy have been identified by several authors (Blumler and Coleman 2001; Clift 2000; Hague and Loader 1999; Tsagarousianou et al. 1998) and include

1. the scope for horizontal or peer-to-peer communication, as distinct from vertical or top-down communication;
2. the capacity for users to access, share, and verify information from a wide range of global sources;
3. the lack of government controls over the Internet as a global communications medium, as compared to more territorially based media;
4. the ability to form virtual communities, or online communities of interest, that are unconstrained by geography;
5. the capacity to disseminate, debate, and deliberate on current issues, and to challenge professional and official positions; and,
6. the potential for political disintermediation, or communication that is not filtered by political organizations, spin doctors, or the established news media.

The second distinction between participatory media through the Internet and networked ICTs and earlier forms of mass communication is their capacity to promote "do-it-yourself" (DIY) media production. Blogs and other Web 2.0 technologies are substantive manifestations of what McKay (1998) terms—in the context of protest activities in 1990s Britain—"DIY culture." McKay defines DIY culture as "a combination of inspiring action, narcissism, youthful arrogance, principle, ahistoricism, idealism, indulgence, creativity, plagiarism, as well as the rejection and embracing alike of technical innovation" (1998: 2). Picking up on McKay's suggestive proposition, Hartley (1999a) developed the concept of DIY citizenship, which relates the decline of deference, and a growing reluctance to accept the authority of established institutions of the media as well as government, to a demand for speaking rights, meaningful interaction with authority figures, and what Hartley (1999a: 186–7) terms "semiotic self-determination" or the right to determine one's own identity. Although new media is not at the centre of either McKay's or Hartley's analysis of DIY culture and citizenship, it certainly is significant in relation to tendencies in the wider media and public culture where, as Deuze argues, "people not only have come to expect participation from the media [but] they increasingly have found ways to enact this participation in the multiple ways they use and make media. . . . [T]he Internet can be seen as an amplifier of this trend" (2006: 68).

Participatory Media

The concept of participatory media predates the Internet and networked ICTs. The Hutchins Commission on Freedom of the Press, launched in the United States in 1942, argued in its final report in 1947 that a responsible press needs not only to have full, truthful, and comprehensive reporting of events, but should also "serve as a forum for the exchange of comment and criticism" while providing "a representative picture of constituent groups in society" (McQuail 2005: 171). The sense that mainstream commercial media have failed to meet such objectives was a catalyst for the development of various forms of community or alternative media in the second half of the twentieth century. In some countries, these took the form of party-political or openly partisan forms of media (print media examples in Canada might include *Canadian Forum* [1920–2000], *Canadian Dimension*, *Alberta Report* [1973–2003], and the *National Post*), to locally based newspapers and monographs, and the community broadcasting sector.

In Canada, community broadcasting got a dramatic boost with the emergence of cable television in the 1960s. In order to gain permission to set up a cable television service, many operators promised—and eventually it became seen as a condition of licence—to set up and fund a community channel, complete with studios, cameras, and a few paid staff to support the volunteer-run community television activities. These stations were designed to promote access, participation, and openness to perspectives not covered in mainstream media, and such activity was at the cornerstone of PBS in the United States (see Rennie 2006 for an overview). Community radio, often in association with low-powered stations set up on university campuses across Canada and the United States in the 1970s and '80s, also provided other important alternative media voices in North America.

Atton (2001, 2002, 2004) draws attention to how confusion about what constitutes "community," "alternative," and "radical" media may have understated the significance of these forms of media to the contemporary media landscape. Atton defines alternative media using three measures relating to professionalism, institutionalism, and capitalization:

1. de-professionalization: the capacity to write; publish; and distribute news, ideas, and comment that is not contingent upon a set of professional skills, values, and norms that make a potential contributor "qualified" to disseminate such material;
2. de-institutionalization: the ability to get such material into the public domain, which is not contingent upon the decision-making practices of large-scale media institutions, whether in the commercial or public sectors; and,
3. de-capitalization: the willingness to distribute media in all forms through mechanisms that require low up-front investments and low recurrent costs, so that the capacity to disseminate media content is not thwarted by the prior need for market viability of the distributing venture. (2002: 25)

By adopting practices that minimize the need for capital, institutions, and professional training, alternative media have been able to more easily take advantage of the strengths of new media technologies. Traditional media, with sunken investments in all three domains, have not been able to react as quickly or as meaningfully.

Cultural studies provide a different way of understanding participatory media. This theoretical framework gives insight into the way in which the circuit of mass communication was never complete and always contested during the era of mass media. The personal, political, and emotional meanings and investments that audiences made in the mass-distributed products of popular culture were frequently at odds with the intended meanings of their producers.

Cultural studies theorists (e.g., Fiske 1987, 1992; Hall 1986; Turner 1990) questioned the claim that the dominant meanings of popular media reflected the class interests of those who owned and controlled the institutions that governed the means of production and distribution. They drew attention to the complex and contested nature of the politics of meaning through use of the Italian Marxist Antonio Gramsci's concept of "hegemony" (1971, published posthumously). This work discussed the extent to which readings of popular cultural texts rarely duplicate the preferred reading of their producers, but are instead commonly characterized by "negotiated" or even "oppositional" readings; and textual polysemy, or the ways in which the meaning of a text is never limited only to the intentions of its author, but instead is subject to a wider social negotiation and interpretation.

One important implication of such work, made most explicit in the work of John Fiske (1987, 1992), was that there were two economies in mass media: a financial economy, driven by the profit-maximization strategies of commercial media institutions, and a cultural economy, where the popularity of media texts is determined through "the exchange and circulation of . . . meanings, pleasures and social identities" (Fiske 1987: 311). Since success in the former is contingent upon success in the latter, it followed that popular media needed to be open to multiple interpretations by a socially diverse and mixed population in order to be both popular and commercially successful.

This brief detour through active audience theories in cultural studies is relevant to our discussion about participatory media in the new media context because it draws attention to arguments that have been central to what Jenkins (2006a) terms **convergence culture**. For Jenkins, contemporary phenomena associated with Web 2.0 activities like blogging, and sites such as YouTube, MySpace, Instagram, and Flickr, need to be understood in the historical context of fan cultures that have developed with popular media over a number of years. This pop culture includes fan interest as diverse as fanzine reinscriptions of the *Star Trek* series, engagement with scripts of the HBO series *True Blood* through virtual community fan fiction sites, and the engagement of game developers as well as the developers of reality TV programs such as *American Idol* and *Survivor* with their online user communities (Jenkins 2006a, 2006b). Following earlier insights from cultural studies, Jenkins proposes that convergence is a cultural as well as a technological phenomenon and both a top-down and a bottom-up process:

> Media companies are learning how to accelerate the flow of media content across delivery channels to expand revenue opportunities, broaden markets, and reinforce viewer commitments. Consumers are learning how to use these different media technologies to bring the flow of media more fully under their control and to interact with other consumers. The promises of this new media environment raise expectations of a freer flow of ideas and content. Inspired by those ideals, consumers are fighting for the right to participate more fully in their culture. Sometimes, corporate and grassroots convergence reinforce each other, creating closer, more rewarding relations between media producers and consumers. Sometimes, the two forces are at war and those struggles will redefine the face of . . . popular culture. (2006a: 18)

Jenkins refers to struggles that are both visible and invisible. The struggle over media content is visible when community members take video from popular films and mash it up with their own content. A good example of this is found in the numerous "Hitler has a meltdown" videos that can be found on YouTube. The use and reuse of professionally produced media sometimes stirs a backlash, however, and sites are forced to remove community-member submissions when they are found to contain copyrighted material. Other times, the reuse is permitted and even encouraged by savvy media companies that know it ultimately promotes their own product, at the risk of losing some control. This strategy does not always work, however. General Motors, who made an extensive library of clips available to remixers, hoping to promote a new model of sport utility vehicle, instead found itself mocked (Bosman, 2006).

The struggle over media content is less visible in other cases. Sometimes, the very popularity of completely amateur content more subtly undermines the broadcast model of popular culture. In other words, if people start to ignore the mainstream media and create their own media content and culture—think "Clark the talking dog," cat videos, even the many recreations of "Gangnam Style"—they are being just as subversive, and perhaps even more so, than when they repurpose existing content. In a way, every minute spent watching YouTube videos could be a minute away from regular television. The problem, these days, is that the advertising has followed the audience online and streaming video is just as ad-saturated as regular television programming. Below, we explore how participatory media work and how their widest expressions, these days, can be found in what is commonly described as Web 2.0.

Participatory Media and Web 2.0

One of the issues that has arisen with second-generation new media technologies, referred to under the general rubric of Web 2.0, is whether they have provided significantly more opportunities for people to produce and disseminate creative work and to demonstrate their creativity to a wider community. In noting the growing capacity of new media technologies to enable the capturing and sharing of digital content in its various forms, Lawrence Lessig observes,

> This digital "capturing and sharing" is in part an extension of the capturing and sharing that has always been integral to our culture, and in part it is something new. It is continuous with the Kodak model, but it explodes the boundaries of Kodak-like technologies. The technology of digital "capturing and sharing" promises a world of extraordinarily diverse creativity that can be easily and broadly shared. . . . Technology has thus given us an opportunity to do something with culture that has only ever been possible for individuals in small groups, isolated from others. Think about an old man telling a story to a collection of neighbours in a small town. Now imagine that same story-telling extended across the globe. (2004: 184–5)

In the context of Web 2.0 and the websites and technologies associated with it, this has, of course, become a reality. Lessig's example of photography draws attention to the shift away from what he refers to as the "Kodak model," where photos become easy for all to take, but where their processing remains reliant on specialists. The Kodak model also presumes that distribution is largely contingent on the ability of photo snappers to show friends their photos in face-to-face situations (e.g., the photo album or slide night). In contrast, a completely new model is emerging with sites such as Flickr, Pinterest, and Instagram. Here, users are not just "developing" their own photos, but they are sharing them—and even getting famous for them, in some cases—with a global audience. It is no longer necessarily just a friends and family phenomenon. An adept and diligent young person could accumulate a considerable Pinterest following just by sharing other people's photos. (One student, Andrew von Rosenbach, has acquired almost 300,000 followers on Pinterest—http://pinterest.com/andrewvr_ca— by being passionate about what he does and regularly adding more items.)

Digital cameras (including those embedded in mobile phones) and their link to computers make it easy for photographers of all levels of skill to take pictures and upload them, via computer or directly to the Internet. While the camera and computer remove the necessity of processing pictures, a website like Flickr changes the distribution process. If, for example, you have a series of baby photos that you would like to share with your extended family, but that family is geographically dispersed, you can use Flickr's site capabilities to share those photos. If, however, you are a budding professional photographer and wish to make your work available to a wider community of users (including potential clients and buyers), Flickr allows your work to be subject to peer ranking systems that provide ongoing feedback about your photographs—the site "distributes" your work to potentially wide communities of interest.

CASE STUDY

Digital Storytelling

Digital storytelling emerged in the mid-1990s, and has been an important use of new media technology since. It enables ordinary people to tell their own stories in a compelling format that is readily available to others, and it frequently involves short, autobiographical films (usually no more than eight minutes in length) with an interactive element that can be distributed through the Web or television. In Canada, the National Film Board—which in the 1960s pioneered storytelling through film in its Fogo Island project (www .nfb.ca/playlist/fogo-island)—undertook a major collaborative initiative of digital storytelling across the country as part of the lead-up to the 2010 Vancouver Winter Olympics (Matlin 2009).

Importantly, this form of new media is not simply about enabling access—as found with web pages, web cams, social networking sites, and so on—but, rather, it involves a facilitated process whereby those who have specialized knowledge in the use of these digital technologies provide training to relatively new users, not only in how to use the technologies but also in how to tell stories in ways that have strong underlying narratives and are emotionally compelling for an audience (Burgess et al. 2006; Lambert 2002). This commitment to community engagement and empowerment differentiates digital storytelling from related new media forms such as interactive journalism, narrative-based games, or personal blogs and home pages.

Two broad developments mark the conceptual as well as practical origins of digital storytelling. First, US artist and media producer Dana Atchley developed a production workshop in 1993 at the American Film Institute. This was a catalyst for Joe Lambert and others to develop training workshops in the San Francisco Bay Area, which formed the basis for the Center for Digital Storytelling (CDS), established in 1994. Inspired by a vision of cultural democracy and community arts activism, the CDS's focus is on grassroots initiatives, personal narratives, and the empowerment of those unfamiliar with the use of digital technologies. The CDS is a "non-profit training, project development, and research organization dedicated to assisting people in using digital media to tell meaningful stories from their lives," with a focus on personal voice, thoughtful and emotionally direct stories, and facilitative teaching methods that enable knowledge-sharing and knowledge transfer (CDS 2007).

The second major digital storytelling initiative has come from the BBC and its 2001 decision to commission the Capture Wales project, led by Daniel Meadows from Cardiff University's School of Journalism, Media, and Cultural Studies (Meadows 2003). In 2002, the BBC undertook an initiative called Telling Lives. Digital stories produced with the assistance of the BBC are now distributed across many of their sites, including dedicated websites through BBC Television and satellite TV, and BBC Radio in the case of audio stories. The BBC further developed its resources for online DIY storytelling and media participation through its Create site (sadly, no longer available), which offered a plethora of tools and sites from which to develop digital content in the form of films, stories, music, artworks, reviews,

The significance of these kinds of changes to models of media content production, distribution, and access is a growing research topic. For example, Couldry, building on Atton's (2002) work on media democratization, draws our attention to the capacity of "hybrid forms of media consumption-production . . . [to] challenge the entrenched division of labour . . . that is the essence of media power" (Couldry 2003: 45).

Leadbeater and Miller (2004) refer to this as the **pro-am revolution.** Defining *pro-ams* as "innovative, committed and networked amateurs working to professional standards" (2004: 9), they identify activities as diverse as rap music and music sampling;

journalism, and family histories. There is also the BBC Action Network (formerly iCan) which has promoted grassroots community political activism (www.bbc.co.uk/blogs/actionnetwork).

While the BBC initiative shares obvious features with CDS, it is distinguished by the BBC's goal of promoting citizenship and representing experiences from across the United Kingdom. In the BBC Charter Review process that commenced in 2004 and was completed in 2007, the six core principles for the BBC in the twenty-first century were identified as sustaining citizenship and civil society; promoting education and learning; stimulating creativity and cultural excellence; reflecting the United Kingdom's nations, regions, and communities; bringing the world to the United Kingdom and the United Kingdom to the world; and Building Digital Britain (DCMS 1998). Initiatives such as digital storytelling serve this new active citizenship agenda in the digital age by creating opportunities for people to become more active citizens, particularly at the local and regional levels, and stimulating the creativity of audiences by giving them a chance to tell their own stories and make their own programs (BBC 2005). Initiatives in digital storytelling and related manifestations of everyday creativity support the proposition of Burgess and colleagues that

> Communication policy around networked media should not only be concerned with ownership, content regulation and controls, but should also try to "do no harm" to, and even support, platforms, technologies and practices that enable the flowering of the unpredictable forms of everyday and ephemeral creativity and engagement that make up active participation in the networked cultural public sphere. (2006: 13)

More recently, digital storytelling has been expanded in new directions with the emergence of so-called transmedia storytelling. Taking a holistic approach to the environment for stories—acknowledging and even playing up the fact that viewers are, for example, likely to surf the Web while watching TV—these new generations of storytellers craft their productions keeping in mind from the very beginning uses such as multiple screens and real-life activities such as meet-ups (opportunities for people to connect online but meet in real life) and live-action role-playing (LARP) games, where people dress up and re-enact scenes and characters from their favourite show, comic book, or video game. This form of storytelling is finding its way into popular dramas (such as the new Canadian sci-fi television show *Continuum*), where the investors, producers, and even the actors and website producers are working from the outset on a collection of media forms that far transcends what we could ever imagine as a television program.

Case Study Questions

1. Do you participate in the transmedia aspects of any media productions?
2. Do you regard these aspects as gimmicks or add-ons, or are they seamless and enjoyable aspects?
3. Can you imagine a scenario in which a transmedia story is less appealing than a "pure" single-media story? Why or why not?

the Linux open-source software program; the Jubilee 2000 campaign around Global South debt; user modifications of *The Sims* online computer game; and the activities of Muhummad Yunnus in alleviating poverty in Bangladesh through micro-credit schemes, as examples of how, "when Pro-Ams are networked together, they can have a huge impact on politics and culture, economics and development" (2004: 12). Arguing that "pro-ams work at their leisure, regard consumption as a productive activity, and set professional standards to judge their amateur efforts," Leadbeater and Miller (2004: 23) distinguish the pro-am from both the casual leisure enthusiast and the accredited professional through the following typology:

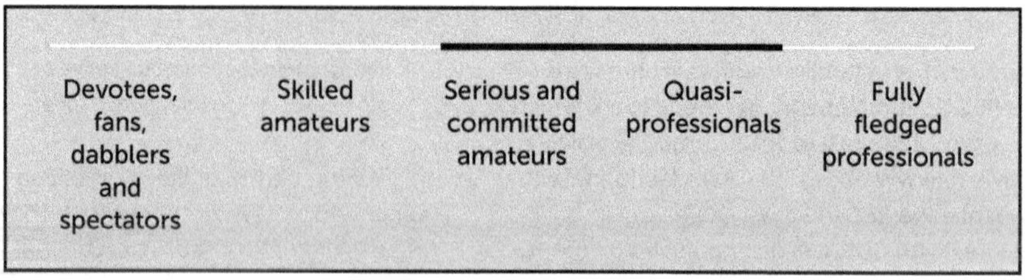

| Devotees, fans, dabblers and spectators | Skilled amateurs | Serious and committed amateurs | Quasi-professionals | Fully fledged professionals |

Figure 5.1 Pro-ams in the Wider Participatory Community

Source: Leadbeater and Miller (2004: 23).

Leadbeater (2007) proposes that modern capitalism is, as Benkler (2006) also argues, based on systems of social production that blur historical lines of demarcation between commercial production, public sector provision, and the community/non-profit sector. The rise of pro-am production models and the scope for mass distribution with continuous feedback through networked new media technologies, generate "a huge challenge to the established organizational order and the professionals who design, control and lead them":

> Consumers turn out to be producers. Demand breeds its own supply. Leisure becomes a form of work. A huge amount of creative work is done in spite, or perhaps because, of people not being paid. . . . They embody a new ethic of collaborative, shared effort, not often motivated by money. . . . The truth is that most traditional commercial organizations do not want their consumers to become collaborators. They quite like them passive and so dependent. . . . The idea that you might be able to lead more effectively in a far more open, transparent and conversational way ruins all the fun. *The irresistible force of collaborative mass innovation is about to meet the immovable force of entrenched corporate organization.* (Leadbeater 2007; italics added for emphasis)

Leadbeater seems skeptical of the ability of corporations to take advantage of social and participatory media; however, for those firms that do adapt, there can be advantages in collaborating with consumers. Many new businesses have been founded on these models and many existing businesses are adapting their practices to take advantage of the interactivity and creativity that working closely with a community offers. Sometimes, this creativity is contained within a site—as is the case with the reader reviews that make shopping on www.amazon.ca such a worthwhile process—and sometimes the creativity of the users is found beyond the confines of a site and extends across communities. A savvy media organization will participate in both and take note when, for example, a blogger is writing about its product or service.

Blogs as Participatory Media and Social Software

Blogs are user-generated websites where entries are made either by individuals or by groups, in an informal journal style, and are displayed in reverse chronological order. They are typically interactive and networked, and they solicit and respond to the commentary of others on the blog postings. Characteristically, blogs offer links to other blogs or websites with related fields of interest (the aforementioned blogroll), and—while some are mainly text-based—blogs often provide links to other media resources, such as video and photos (a video-based blog is called a "vlog," while a photo-based blog is a "photoblog").

The term *blog* refers to both the online artifact created and to the act of maintaining such an online resource, or blogging. The social network of blogs and bloggers is referred to as the blogosphere and it is through this network that "the social networking of blogs and the potential for collaboration . . . [provide] a decidedly human dimension to the publishing and publicizing of information" in ways that "represent for authors an opportunity to reach out and connect with an audience never before accessible to them, while maintaining control over their own personal expressive spaces" (Bruns and Jacobs 2006: 5). Blogs have been a vitally important component of social software, and Davies has argued that

> The principle of social software is to break down the distinction between our online computer-mediated experiences and our offline face-to-face experiences. It is software that . . . seeks to integrate the Internet further into our everyday lives, and our everyday lives further into the Internet. It is software that seeks to eradicate the gulf separating two such separate social networks. (2003: 7)

The significance of **blogging** as social software must also be considered in light of its popularity. In November 2006, there were 57 million active bloggers worldwide (BBC 2006). A 2006 survey of US bloggers conducted through the Pew Center's Internet and American Life project (Lenhart and Fox 2006) found that about 12 million Americans over the age of 18 (or 8 per cent of the Internet-using population stateside) kept a blog and that blogs were viewed by 57 million Americans over the age of 18 (or about 38 per cent of the Internet-using population stateside). The survey found that bloggers are considerably younger than the Internet population overall, with 54 per cent being under the age of 30, compared to 24 per cent of Internet users. Indeed, 19 per cent of Internet users 12 to 17 years of age kept a blog. In terms of general online media and communications practices and habits, bloggers overwhelmingly have a home broadband network connection, consume a large amount of other online media content (particularly news), are highly engaged with other forms of technology-based social interaction, and tend to source material more widely than other media users (Lenhart and Fox 2006: 4–6). In terms of what motivates people to establish and maintain a blog, the Pew Internet survey found that making money was the least important reason and that about one third of bloggers saw the content of their blog as a form of journalism, with creative expression, documenting of personal views and experiences, and keeping in touch with friends and family being the most important motives (see Table 5.2).

A recent study from the Pew Research Center indicates young people under age 30 (who were the largest contingent of bloggers in 2006) are blogging less and using social networking sites more, which makes sense since many of the described "reasons for blogging" listed in Table 5.2 are social, and can be achieved through Facebook, Instagram, and Twitter much more easily (Lenhart et al., 2010). In placing the rise of blogs in Internet history, Clay Shirky argues that they are part of a "third age" of social software (GBN 2002; Shirky 2003). The first age began with email and, particularly, the *cc* tag line, which allowed one-to-one or one-to-few communications. The second age came with the rise of virtual communities, as discussed by Rheingold (1994),

Table 5.2 Motives for Developing a Blog: Pew Internet Survey of US Bloggers

Reasons for developing a blog: US bloggers survey 2005–06	Major reason %	Minor reason %	Not a reason %
To express yourself creatively	52	25	23
To document your personal experiences or share them with others	50	26	24
To stay in touch with friends and family	37	22	40
To share practical knowledge or skills with others	34	30	35
To motivate other people to action	29	32	38
To entertain people	28	33	39
To store resources or information that is important to you	28	21	52
To influence the way other people think	27	24	49
To network or to meet new people	16	34	50
To make money	7	8	85

Source: Lenhart and Fox (2006: iii).

Turkle (1997), and others. For Shirky, one of the key limitations of the technology and how it was used in this period (the middle to late 1990s) is that both the software and the modes of Web content development tended to be static, had limited interactivity, possessed a centralized mechanism of content control, and operated on a largely "broadcast" model; whereas the participation in chat rooms, online discussion forums, and so on was not occurring through the Web, but, instead, through conduits such as email. As a result, there was a limited sense of community in the latter (which lent itself to flame wars, discontinuation of subscription, information overload, etc.) and a lack of interactivity in the development of web pages. By contrast, the third age of social software has evolved around the principles of Web 2.0, which place a particular emphasis on collaboration, community building, simplification of software and access points for users, "light touch" regulation of site content, and relative ease in producing, distributing, accessing, and responding to the full range of forms of digital media content. In cases where such principles have been extended to collaborative publishing models, such as Wikipedia, this also includes collaborative editing (Bruns 2005).

We are entering what may be a fourth age, with a form of blogging that is more about references to other material than it is about creating anything of substance in the first instance. In a way, this is the evolution of what was once a "sidebar" to a blog, known as the blogroll or linkroll. There, you would find links to other people's blogs, presumably with points of view or content in support or related to the blog you were reading. In the present era, we have whole sites and services dedicated to the act of seeing something interesting and capturing it, either as a photo (Pinterest, https://pinterest.com) or a link (e.g., Reddit, www.reddit.com). Sometimes, there is commentary (as on Reddit) but there is often simply a collection. Some might call this digital scrapbooking. Whatever the motivation, it is remarkably popular and both Reddit and Pinterest regularly rank among the top websites in the world.

Participatory Media, Social Software, and Social Capital

The growing use of social software may lead to an increase in social capital and virtual social capital. In his well-known work on the significance of **social capital**, Putnam (1995: 665) defines *social capital* as "features of social life—networks, norms, and trust—that enable participants to act together more effectively to pursue shared interests. . . . Social capital, in short, refers to social connections and the attendant norms and trust." Woolcock (2001: 13) defines the term as "the norms and networks that facilitate collective action," and Davies (2003: 11) defines it as the "value of social networks"; this is "a resource which we can invest time and money in, and which pays returns."

Promoting and maintaining social capital is critical to overall economic performance, to the avoidance of adverse social consequences (crime, drug abuse, public health concerns), and to the emergence of new forms of social entrepreneurship that fill gaps between market-led solutions and government-driven reform programs (Davies 2003; Leadbeater 2000; Putnam 1995; Woolcock 2001; World Bank 2003). Aldridge and colleagues (2002) distinguish between three main types of social capital:

1. bonding social capital, characterized by strong social bonds between individuals, for example members of a family, a local community, or an ethnic community;
2. bridging social capital, characterized by weaker, less dense but more cross-cutting ties, for example with business associates, links across ethnic groups, links between families and communities; and,
3. linking social capital, characterized by connections between those with differing levels of power or social status, for example between political elites and the general public, policy-makers and local communities, and individuals from different social classes.

Early commentaries on the relationship between the Internet and social capital identified a positive correlation between the decentralized and inclusive nature of the Internet and the revivification of civic engagement and a sense of community (e.g., Rheingold 1994; Schuler 1996; Sclove 1995).

Putnam, however, does not fully embrace the idea that Internet users would be more civically engaged and he expresses concerns about unequal access to new technology and "cyber-balkanisation" (2000: 177). There are related concerns about the adverse effects of Internet use on family life and on other offline activities (Nie and Erbring 2000), and the tendency toward group polarization and heightened political conflict among those with divergent points of view (Sunstein 2002). There was empirical work emerging during this period that showed the Internet acting as a positive stimulus for community engagement and civic and political participation; however, there was also a need to recognize that the Internet was changing such forms of engagement and participation and that new metrics were needed for new media (Wellman et al. 2001). In a similar vein, Aldridge and colleagues (2002: 48–9) concluded that the Internet was promoting a transformation of forms of civic engagement, particularly among younger users, where sustained engagement with globally networked organizations was becoming more important than traditional, locally based forms of participation in community organizations (such as sports teams, local churches, or Rotary Clubs).

An important question that remains is whether social software and its facilitation and promotion of large-scale, public, online participation is changing the nature of engagement and participation and their relationship to social capital. Keeping in mind the definitions of social capital provided here, it seems pretty clear that blogs' use of social software have developed new forms of social capital that are bridging and, to varying degrees, bonding and linking. For example, "permalinks" (which establish a permanent link to other blogs) indicate bloggers' desire to maintain an ongoing sense of kinship with their readers as well as the wider community of bloggers. It appears that the growth of blogging and other forms of social software are having positive effects on the development and maintenance of social capital, even if they may also represent to their critics (e.g., Keen 2007) a pandemic of narcissism.

Another key issue is whether blogging has peaked. While the number of daily blog posts grew from 500,000 at the time of the October 2004 US presidential election to 2.5 million at the time of the Israel–Hezbollah conflict in southern Lebanon (June 2006), there was subsequently a notable plateau (Doctorow 2006). The Gartner Group estimated that the number of blogs worldwide would level off at approximately 100 million. There are also an estimated 200 million abandoned blogs or blogs that were started, but whose creators have long since ceased to post on the site, including celebrities such as Lindsay Lohan, Melanie Griffith, and Barbra Streisand (*The Australian* 2007). It may well be that some former bloggers have moved on to other forms of social software and it is also the case—as often occurs in the age of the global Internet—that the fastest rates of growth are outside the English-speaking world. For example, as tensions escalated in the Middle East, the Farsi or Persian language—the majority language of Iran and Afghanistan and a significant language through Central Asia and the Middle East—became one of the top 10 languages of the blogosphere (Doctorow 2006). A more likely explanation is that blogging as an activity has spread across a number of platforms and technologies. Short entries are going onto Twitter and Facebook, longer entries are going into blogs but also into "blog-like" microsites hosted either online or via regular media outlets, such as *The Huffington Post*, and the whole new categories of repostings and pins is going into sites such as Pinterest, Reddit, Stumbleupon, and Tumblr.

Downsides of Networks, Social Media, and Participatory Media Culture

It is important to conclude this chapter—which has emphasized the beneficial and transformative capacities of networks for social, economic, cultural, and political relationships—with some consideration of the potential downsides to the network form, both in terms of its internal logic and its wider socio-economic impacts. The first is that, at a purely technical level, networks frequently fail. Servers crash, infrastructure systems fail, and website access becomes overloaded and, hence, unavailable. There are also concerns related to what contract lawyers term *force majeure*, which can range from a power blackout on a particular location because of an overloaded electricity grid, to an act of war or terrorism that decimates core communications infrastructures almost instantaneously, as happened in the Lower Manhattan district of New York in the immediate aftermath of 9/11.

Second, it is important to be conscious of the insider/outsider dimensions of networks. At a global level, Castells draws attention to the inclusion/exclusion dimensions of access, involvement, and participation that arise in a networked global economy and are based on geographical location and the geopolitical significance of that location in the global space of flows (e.g., Castells 2000a: 70–165). For example, while it would seem to be irrelevant where a blogger or online media site is located, many of these remain anchored in the traditional "home base" for such industries, such as New York in the case of news and fashion or Los Angeles in the case of gossip and movie information. Whatever "immaterial" aspects of online life exist, it remains that the people who run those sites have to live somewhere and they prefer to live in the centre of the action, among their peers.

In relation to the creative industries, McRobbie (2005) argues that a form of "network sociality" in these sectors has generated a form of "PR meritocracy" whereby familiar patterns of social exclusion on the basis of gender, race, ethnicity, social location, and other factors continue to occur, but they are based less upon overt discrimination than upon the question of who has the time and capacity for after-hours social networking. Gill's research (2002) on participation in project-based new media work and the very significant barriers confronting women and people with young children (again, mostly women) is pertinent in this context.

A third, notable concern is that some social networks have also historically been associated with corruption and crime. The Mafia is a case in point. The popular television program *The Sopranos* offered a useful fictional example of how bonding social capital can be used to serve anti-social purposes (Lavery 2002), and there are comparable cases in the (real-world) family-based and ethnically structured nature of criminal organizations such as the Sicilian mafia, the Colombian drug cartels, the Russian *mafiyas*, the Chinese Triads, and the Japanese Yakuza. As we have noted earlier, al-Qaeda and similar terrorist organizations used the innovative capabilities of networks and social media in ways that were massively damaging both in terms of wider geopolitical implications and in how they affect populations at a very local level (e.g., shopkeepers, tourism service operators, and restaurateurs in Bali seeking to maintain tourist-related trade after the 2002 and 2005 bombings).

In a different way, high levels of bonding social capital have been associated with racial intolerance and conflict between communities. One example includes the Catholic–Protestant divide in Northern Ireland, where there is a great deal of bonding social capital within the sectarian communities, but a lack of social capital that bridges these community divides. Whether or not the rise of the Internet, ICTs, and social networking media provide new forms of virtual social capital that can effectively work across social barriers remains to be seen.

Beyond these serious criticisms, participatory media is also vulnerable to the accusation that the "immaterial labour" (van Dijck 2009) of participants is being co-opted by owners of websites without any meaningful control over how it is being used. In part this is fostered by end-user licensing agreements (the notorious EULA) that assign blanket rights to the owner of the site. As well, user behaviour is meticulously tracked and, along with preferences and "likes," becomes data that can be sold to third parties for marketing purposes or other surveillance-related activities. We return to a discussion of these and other economic questions in Chapter 8 following an examination of games, the games industry, and creative industries in general in the next two chapters.

Useful Websites

Augmented Social Cognition
http://asc-parc.blogspot.ca/search/label/wikipedia

This website is a guide to "understanding how groups remember, think, and reason" from the Augmented Social Cognition Research Group at the Palo Alto Research Center (PARC). This group maintains a regular watch on Wikipedia, among other social media.

BoingBoing: A Directory of Wonderful Things
http://boingboing.net

This is a lively website committed to aggregating and publicizing the most interesting things to come from blogs and other forms of social networking software.

Center for Digital Storytelling
www.storycenter.org

Established in the San Francisco Bay Area in the mid-1990s, the Center for Digital Storytelling has been a pioneer in enabling people without digital media skills to develop online stories that reflect on their life experiences.

Confessions of an Aca-Fan: The Official Weblog of Henry Jenkins
www.henryjenkins.org

Professor Henry Jenkins practises what he preaches concerning participatory media in this lively blog where he posts daily with the aim of bridging the gap between academic media research and a general public trying to make sense of these emerging forms. Jenkins covers everything from computer games to censorship to professional wrestling.

International Network for Social Network Analysis
www.insna.org

This website is dedicated to gathering and distributing academic research on social networks. The INSNA was founded by Barry Wellman in 1978 and the professional society has over a thousand members worldwide.

Pew Internet
http://pewinternet.org

The Pew Research Center, based in Washington, DC, supports research across a number of fields. Calling itself a "fact tank" (to contrast with the usual *think tank*), the centre has been home to the Pew Internet & American Life Project since its first report was published in 2000. According to the project website, they produce "reports exploring the impact of the Internet on families, communities, work and home, daily life, education, health care, and civic and political life." When students are contemplating social changes relating to the Internet, the Pew Internet site is a fabulous resource for studies, surveys, and investigations of special topics or long term tracking of trends.

Technorati
http://technorati.com

This website aggregates blog contributions and provides data on hit rates for blogs and other forms of social software. It also provides analysis and commentary on developments in the blogosphere.

Digital Marketing Ramblings
http://expandedramblings.com

This is a very useful multi-contributor hub offering digital marketing news, numbers, and pointers. DMR also offers a great resource for those who want very up-to-date statistics on the digital world.

Further Reading

Internet Galaxy, Manuel Castells (2001)
Although Castells's *Information Age* trilogy may be too much material for an undergraduate reading list (volume 1, *The Rise of the Network Society*, is almost 600 pages), the smaller *Internet Galaxy* provides some of the same concepts as well as a condensed history of the Internet.

Convergence Culture, Henry Jenkins (2006a)
This book, along with Jenkins's other two books— *Fans, Bloggers, and Gamers: Exploring Participatory Culture* (2006) and *The Wow Complex* (2007)— reveals the breadth, depth, and complexity of a popular culture that is rapidly emerging from the top-down era of the twentieth century and both regaining its participatory elements as well as new digitally enabled versions of commodification and distribution.

Linked: How Everything Is Connected to Everything Else and What It Means, Albert-László Barabási (2003)
Studies of social capital are most commonly linked to Robert Putnam or Pierre Bourdieu but this text helps explain the science behind social capital in a lively and engaging way and makes it accessible to the general reader. The book is well worth reading for those who want to have a better sense of the underpinnings of social capital and social networks.

The Big Switch and *The Shallows*, by Nicholas Carr (2009 and 2011)
Science and technology writer Nicholas Carr has made a name for himself by scrutinizing Internet hyperbole and questioning the conclusions of a wide range of enthusiasts. His work has been subject to criticism but his analysis and his positions are well considered and well researched. *The Big Switch* tells the story of the transition from big telephone companies (e.g., AT&T) to big Internet companies (e.g., Google) and the implications of that. *The Shallows* asks us to consider the long-term implications of living in a hyper-connected world, especially when we can forget about memorizing things and instead rely on Web searches from our mobile phones.

Discussion Questions

1. What are the benefits of networked organizations as identified by Podolny and Page? What examples of these can you give in terms of your knowledge or experience with organizations in your personal, academic, or professional life?
2. Social network analysis is based on the understanding that forms of self, activity, and behaviour are relational. Discuss the four key elements and seven core concepts of social network analysis identified by Wasserman and Faust.
3. What is meant by the terms *social production* and *participatory media culture* and why are these significant in terms of understanding new media? Discuss not only the promise but also the peril of networks, social media, and participatory media culture.
4. Within the different kinds of networks that are central to globalization there are clear dynamics of inclusion and exclusion, as well as a diverse range of oppositional movements based on resistance identities and project identities. Why is this significant and what are some possible consequences?
5. Aldridge and colleagues (2002) distinguish between three main types of social capital. Discuss these, identify examples of these in your own work and life, and consider the implications for you (and others).

Class Activities

1. Do a degrees-of-separation experiment so see how many links connect you to your classmates, and from each of you to a famous person. Discuss how you use social media to enhance or take advantage of those links (e.g., Facebook friends or LinkedIn connections). Discuss the use of social media for professional (rather than personal) use. What are the differences?

2. As a class, compile a list of how you collectively both consume and produce participatory media (e.g., YouTube, Flickr, Facebook) using a show of hands or simple poll. Keep in mind the following statistics—that the general population typically includes 90 per cent who consume only, 9 per cent who contribute comments or stars or votes, and only 1 per cent who contribute content.[5] Compare your classes participation with participation more broadly.

3. Almost anything related to new media is subject to rapid change. Firms come and go; technologies change; and numbers of users, viewers, and creators for new media content and memes change every day. Look up a fact or figure in this chapter and verify whether it remains true today, using online sources. Identify corroborating or supporting sources for your findings. Not only will you have the new facts, but you'll also have an appreciation for how quickly things change and, most importantly, a visceral sense of the way in which the Internet and new media are self-revealing to the diligent and inquisitive scholar. If you discover a fact that needs updating, you can even submit your update (with page reference and new citation) in the form of a rewritten paragraph, to the author: Richard Smith (smith@sfu.ca). He promises to reply.

Debate Questions

1. Develop an argument for or against the use of Pinterest as an activity for a creative or socially concerned person. Is it a way to engage with or detach from the world? Is it an inspiration or a distraction?

2. When you think of your social media use over the course of a year, does it change depending on the seasons, or whether you are in school or not? Do you have distinct or overlapping circles of friends on the different services (Facebook, Pinterest, Instagram, Google+, etc.)?

3. Do employers have the right—moral, legal, or otherwise—to look at your Facebook profile prior to, or after, a job interview? Do you consider the future implications of something before posting it online? Is your Facebook profile open to view by non-friends?

6

Games: Technology, Industry, and Culture

Questions to Consider

- In what ways are technology, industry, and the culture of games linked?

- What is the significance of marketing and branding practices, immersive play, and interactive experiences in gaming?

- In what ways do the games industry and game culture have implications for issues such as privacy, identity, gender, modern concepts of childhood, and intellectual property?

- How do the values encoded into game cultures reflect offline cultural values? Conversely, how do mobile, social, computer, and video games offer a chance to emphasize alternative or subjugated values in the name of fantasy and play?

Chapter Outline

In this chapter, we offer a broad examination of games, gameplay, and the game industry as a prime example of new media in the twenty-first century. We examine games as a significant part of popular culture, extending beyond their economic impact. We also look at how the immersive nature and rapid pace of change places online and video games at the centre of debates relating to gender, cultural impact, childhood experiences, and intellectual property. We then consider how the performance of games has ramped up steadily over the past several decades as game platforms have evolved to deliver higher resolution, speed, and richer, more challenging and more social gameplay, including harder puzzles, more complex moves, more intricate storylines. We take a look at the economics of the game industry including its dependence on subcontractors and its rather diffuse economic model—the need for "smash hits" to finance the many "misses"—followed by a consideration of the value chain and the tension between the creative side of the business and the investment side, as well as the complex relationship between production and distribution. In the penultimate part of the chapter, we look at some of the most significant gaming developments in the past 10 years, including the rise of mobile and social games at the expense of so-called AAA console games, the movement toward downloaded games (e.g., from Steam, EA Online, or Microsoft), and behavioural changes such as the role of producer-consumers "modding" games, and the issues arising from that, including the question of who owns the subsequent content. We conclude the chapter with a discussion of the political economy of the game industry, as well as an examination of the game industry in Canada.

Game On

The global interactive games industry is large, growing, and at the forefront of many of the most significant innovations in new media. Global revenues in the games sector were projected to be at least USD $83 billion in 2016, and in the United States, the Entertainment Software Alliance (ESA), which represents the major players in the games industry, reported USD $24.75 billion in sales of video game hardware and software in 2011 (ESA 2011). Until recently, games were most commonly purchased as (1) a stand-alone package and played on consoles commonly attached to the television (video games); or (2) online **multiplayer games** (sometimes also called massive multiplayer online games, or MMOGs), which are played on personal computers that have broadband connectivity and are accessed on a subscription basis. Recently, the categories of online and mobile games—purchased directly online—have been outgrowing the former "packaged-goods" type of game. In 2005, video games accounted for over 85 per cent of the total games market (ESA 2006: 10), but in 2013, online and mobile sales revenue is expected to surpass console and PC games and be 36 percent larger by 2016 (PriceWaterhouseCoopers, 2012).

The significance of interactive games to new media development extends substantially beyond their economic role. As *The Economist* observed,

> Games are widely used as educational tools, not just for pilots, soldiers and surgeons, but also in schools and businesses. . . . Anyone who has learned to play a handful of games can generally figure out how to operate almost any high-tech device. Games require players to construct hypotheses, solve problems, develop strategies, and learn the rules of the in-game world through trial and error. Gamers must also be able to juggle several different tasks, evaluate risks and make quick decisions. . . . Playing games is, thus, an ideal form of preparation for the workplace of the 21st century, as some forward-thinking firms are already starting to realize. (2009)

Kline and colleagues identify interactive games as "the 'ideal commodity' of a post-Fordist/postmodern/promotional capitalism—an artifact within which converge a series of the most important production techniques, marketing strategies, and cultural practices of an era" (2003: 24). The games industry itself identifies direct spinoffs for technological innovation and consumer demand relating to computer processing, demand for broadband services, mobile telecommunications, and digital content, and indirect spinoffs and technology transfer to sectors as diverse as real estate and travel, military training, health care, intelligence testing, and corporate training (Crandall and Sidak 2006). The recently announced Titan supercomputer created for the US Department of Energy, for example, is powered not by custom processors but by graphics processing units (GPUs) developed for consumer gaming computers.

Another spinoff from computer and video games can be found in so-called serious games. A serious game is a blend of game technology and mechanics with educational, research, and training objectives. Although the topic has controversial aspects when taken to extremes (e.g., "games are everything"), the adoptions of the practices and methods of the game designer—the "gamification" of learning, sports, and even military recruiting—has found its way into many applications far outside the humble origins of computer games. Authors such as Ian Bogost and Jane McGonigal have highlighted the power of games for everyday and social impact. Both of these authors have also founded their own companies, making and distributing games that have social or health benefits as their objectives. Bogost's Persuasive Games (www.persuasivegames.com) and McGonigal's SuperBetter (www .superbetter.com) are striking examples of research-informed and socially conscious game-design studios. They are also examples of games as a way of life and the infiltration of a "reward culture" into our daily lives. A Vancouver studio, Ayogo, follows in this path as well, with "health gamification apps for chronic disease management" (see http://ayogo.com).

The convergence of continuous technological innovation, dynamic corporate marketing and branding practices, and the intensity of immersive play and interactive experiences place this sector at the leading edge of new media innovation—and central to debates associated with the cultural appropriateness of digital content, gender identities, the experience of childhood, and intellectual property. Moreover, the rise of games and gaming culture (and particularly the development of MMOGs), where players are increasingly the creators of the game's content and form themselves into online virtual communities, brings to the fore a series of debates about participatory media culture and user-led innovation, as users increasingly become the creators—and not simply the consumers—of their own media. At the same time, as critical work by authors such as Kline and colleagues (2003) and Terranova (2004) reminds us, there are significant disputes about issues ranging from the ownership and control of user-generated content in proprietary online games, to poor working conditions and burnout among those working in games production. More recently, Nicholas Carr has pointed out the disparities in who benefits from the millions of hours people spend uploading[1] content to sites such as Facebook or YouTube. Carr, in arguing that this is unpaid work, coined the term "digital sharecropping" as a way of pointing out the imbalance in the economic model (Carr 2012). As some commentators point out, if the service is free, then *you* are being sold. This same argument applies to many of the online and social games, which are built around a free-to-play-but-subject-to-advertising model. It isn't hard to imagine the way in which a reward-focused approach to life, built up over years of playing games and receiving immediate rewards in the form of loot, levelling, and bonus rounds could have an impact on our culture, leading to a form of "rewards culture," where everyone is motivated by the next shiny prize.

Games History

Early video games were developed by the military-industrial-academic complex, which also started the Internet, with researchers[2] involved in the US nuclear program at the MIT Artificial Intelligence unit creating games in their spare time, such as the joystick-based *Spacewar* (completed in 1962) and the paddle-and-ball game *Tennis for Two* (first created in 1958, but patented in 1968 by Ralph Baer).

These would be prototypes for the games that would find mass-market success in the 1970s, such as *Pong* (released by Atari in 1972) and *Space Invaders* (released by Midway in 1978). These games—and, later, games such as *Monaco GP* and *Pac-Man*—were primarily arcade-based games, played on coin-operated machines in public places, although console-based games systems, played at home through the television, were becoming increasingly significant. In 1982, worldwide home sales of video games were estimated at USD $3 billion and arcade games grossed USD $8 billion in revenue; this compared to international sales of popular music of USD $4 billion at the time (Kline et al. 2003: 103–4). The industry experienced a bust in the mid-1980s, however, partly triggered by the development of too many poor-quality games, and Atari (the giant of the industry at the time) incurred massive losses for its parent company, Time Warner.

The second half of the 1980s was dominated by Nintendo, as the crash of the North American video game market coincided with the launch of the Nintendo Entertainment System (NES) in 1985, accompanied by the remarkably successful *Super Mario Bros.* game, which had gross sales of USD $500 million by 1990. Learning from the Atari experience, that quality of games and not simply volume was the key to success, Nintendo games were marked by dramatically improved pacing, visuals, sound, and dynamism, thus greatly enhancing the experience of play. Nintendo also developed a way to outsource the development of games content to third parties while still retaining quality control over the games through strict licensing procedures, thereby starting the process of separating the game engine from the game content. Importantly, Nintendo developed a sophisticated marketing strategy, which gave information and support to players and consequently nurtured a gaming subculture, while also using this infrastructure to gain player feedback about the games. The Super Mario brand also provided the basis for spinoffs into other media, including a successful children's television cartoon and a less successful Hollywood film, as well as merchandizing in the form of T-shirts, comic books, removable tattoos, lunch boxes, and so on.[3]

The 1990s were marked by the entry of Sega into the games environment with the 16-bit Genesis console, which had micro-processing capability to generate bigger animated characters, more detailed backgrounds, faster play, and richer and more elaborate sound effects and music. While not initially successful against Nintendo, the Sega's strength was in its ability to attract game developers, in particular from the gaming company giant Electronic Arts (EA). Sega worked from the proposition, identified by economists Carl Shapiro and Hal Varian (1999: 196), that to develop new markets, "you need to offer performance 'ten times better' than the established technology" and, in 1991, Sega introduced *Sonic the Hedgehog* as its flagship game. Sega also developed riskier content, such as *Street Fighter* and *Mortal Kombat*, marketed strongly to teenage boys and criticized for being excessively violent (Kline et al. 2003: 132–5).

While Sega made significant market inroads, particularly in Europe, Nintendo responded by developing the GameBoy, a miniature, portable, hand-held console that would, among other things, transform the thumbs of a generation of users (it also prepared them for mobile phones!). The nature of the console wars changed again in 1994 when the giant media conglomerate, Sony, launched the PlayStation, which capitalized on both Sony's high-profile brand identity and the shift in storage devices from cartridges to CD-ROMs, which were much less costly to produce and distribute.

This period also saw computer-based gaming, which had long been the sleeping giant of the sector, rise in prominence with the development of such titles as *Wolfenstein* (1991), *Myst* (1993), *Doom* (1994), and *Quake* (1995), among many others. Building on new graphics capabilities in the personal computer, strengthened by the emergence of the dedicated graphics processing unit (GPU) in graphics cards, games on a PC started to rival the capabilities of dedicated console games. These games were less juvenile than standard gaming fare and, as importantly, exploited the possibilities presented by the Internet to generate player-developed content. The makers of *Doom*, id Software, released their source code online, thereby allowing players to develop their own levels of the game, and thus extend and modify the game itself.

By the early 2000s, the console-based games industry was organized as a large number of games creators, a smaller group of games distributors or publishers, and a very small group of games hardware producers. The games hardware industry was dominated by Sony, which released PlayStation 2 (PS2) in 1999 and Playstation 3 (PS3) in 2006; Nintendo, which produced GameCube in 2001 and followed up with the Wii, also in 2006, and the Wii U in 2012; and Microsoft, which launched its Xbox amid much fanfare in late 2001, and then the Xbox 360 in 2005. In a remarkable show of longevity, all three of these major platforms (PlayStation, Wii, and Xbox) continue to sell millions of units each year. New models of Xbox and PlayStation, widely anticipated, are both scheduled for release before Christmas 2013.

For companies such as Sony and Microsoft, involvement in the games industry was at the forefront of their efforts to establish their media-content platforms at the centre of the home-entertainment ecosystem and its growing Internet connectivity.[4]

Metacritic (metacritic.com), a key industry website, lists the top game publishers in the world, by popularity, score, and name. Surprisingly, the big publishers and developers, including Rockstar, Microsoft, Nintendo, Sony, Electronic Arts, Square Enix, Ubisoft, Sega, THQ, Namco Bandai, and Konami, are not the ones who rank in the top 10, at least in terms of user ratings. The top-ranking "big" publisher as of October 2013 was Rockstar Games, in no small part because of the success of its huge fall release of *Grand Theft Auto V*, which grossed over $1 billion in one day.

The dynamics of the games industry and games development reveal a sometimes bewildering number of small digital software production houses, which maintain a range of subcontracting, licensing, and fee-for-service arrangements with the small number of large games publishing houses. As an industry characterized by inherent risk, where 5 per cent of successful titles effectively subsidize the 95 per cent that do not break even in sales, the sector exhibits the classic risk profile of the creative industries, where misses greatly outnumber the hits (Cutler & Company 2002: 18).

Emerging Financial Models for Games

A number of new models for financing the development of, and extracting revenue from games have emerged in the last few years. On the financing side, collective or community financing is growing. As of July 2012, there have been more than 1300 game projects listed on Kickstarter, for example. While many of these are small projects, not all are. Independent developer Obsidian Games raised almost USD $4 million in the fall of 2012.

Increasingly used on the revenue side are new models such as "freemiums," in which games are free to acquire—usually by downloading—but then create a demand for additional in-game item purchases that cost money. These in-game purchases either remove annoying advertising or provide additional advantages, such as abilities or weapons or desirable attributes that are either unavailable or rarely available to the players who do not choose to make purchases. In-game purchases are a significant part of the revenue model for social games, as well as a growing number of mobile-phone games. The percentage of people who buy in-app items may be small, but the impact is very large. Some of the research on player habits—from academics as well as industry observers and game developers—has revealed the phenomenon of the "whale player." Named after a similar phenomenon in casino gambling, these are players who spend as much as $10,000 a month on games like *FarmVille* or *SimCity*. The casual and social game industry has come to depend on these players, but sometimes with disastrous consequences. If a small number of big-time players abandon your game, your entire business model could be thrown into jeopardy.

New distributions models, such as Xbox Live Marketplace and Steam, as well as the Apple App Store and Google Play, are filling in the gaps as retail distribution shrinks and the game industry sheds its "packaged-goods" roots. The days of buying a game at an independent game store or even a discount store are going away, just as the independent or chain video store has been replaced by digital distribution (e.g., Netflix). These online distribution networks are particularly important for independents because they increasingly provide access to a market—albeit at a price—that was previously unavailable or only available through the channel of a game publisher.

Games distributors nonetheless seek out a range of titles in order to ensure a diverse portfolio of creative product that is either in the market or under development, and games developers learn to live with chronic insecurity, high upfront costs, and the need to develop market savvy in dealing with games publishers and distributors. Although small in comparison, the so-called indie studios, who self-finance (or gather financing through crowdsourcing sites, such as http://indiegogo.com and http://kickstarter.com), are a growing force in the market, especially in online and mobile categories, which feature lower barriers to entry because of lower expectations from consumers.

The early 2000s saw a growing level of attention, and concern, over the growth of massively multiplayer online games, or MMOs (sometimes known as MMORPGs for massively multiplayer online role-playing games), epitomized in games such as *World of Warcraft*, *Skyrim*, and *Rift*. The origins of this format date back to games such as *Ultima Online*, which was launched in October 1997 and by early 2001 had almost 250,000 subscribers. Its success would in turn be overtaken by the striking popularity of the online role-playing game *EverQuest*, released in July 1999 by Verant Interactive, a division of Sony Entertainment Online. *EverQuest* is an online role-playing game, where players adopt avatars (online personas) and undertake a range of activities such as trading, exploring, producing items, and engaging in combat in the fantasy world of Norrath. Although it is no longer nearly as popular, *EverQuest* is still available at www.everquest.com. The growth in MMOs has been further stimulated by the emergence of games such as *Dark Age of Camelot*, *The Sims Online*, and *Star Wars: Galaxies*. In Asia, during the same period that saw *EverQuest* gain in popularity, the game *Lineage* had attracted more than 4 million subscribers by 2002, and it is estimated that 17 million South Koreans are regularly gaming in PC Bangs (Internet café–style online game rooms), where they are engaged in a wide variety of *eSports* (video game competitions), particularly involving games such as *StarCraft* (Cho 2006; Herz 2002; Rossignol 2006; Taylor 2012).

Florence Chee

interview with a new media expert

Dr Florence Chee has a Ph.D. in communication from Simon Fraser University. She is a recent research award recipient at the International Development Research Centre in Ottawa, where she worked on a project titled "Along Gender Lines, Online and Offline: The Challenges of Ethics and Accessibility in the Middle East and South Asia." In late 2013, she moved to a new position, teaching communication studies at Loyola University in Chicago. Dr Chee is active on Twitter as @cheeflo.

Dr Chee, much of your work has profiled the gamers of Korea, both in their native country and here in Canada, and their use of the PC Bang, a kind of gaming-focused Internet café. How did you happen to develop an interest in this topic?

Having been a gamer since the early 1980s, I have experienced first-hand the various contours and manifestations of online and offline digital games. I was wholly unsatisfied with the ways of understanding and portraying games and gamers that I came across in mass media and academic discussions. It seemed fitting that I marry my training in sociocultural anthropology and communication scholarship to contribute an investigation into the culture surrounding online games in different everyday-life contexts. The overall goal of my work has been to contribute a more nuanced

and grassroots perspective to the debates surrounding digital gaming and its place in society.

In my own pursuit of this research, as well as in everyday conversation, I have been frustrated by the disproportionate number of cliché memes—such as the "helpless addicted gamer," Asians as techno-fetishists, gamers as obese loners in their mothers' basements, and the like—upon which mainstream media has profited for years. Even more troubling is how these memes have been dominating the mainstream discussion and serving to sway public opinion and policy-makers toward more negative attitudes about gaming and what it means to be a gamer. Being interested in how society shapes technology and vice versa, I wanted to examine how people's lifestyles are in dialogue with gaming in international contexts.

I have heard that mobile games are proliferating in Korea. Will the PC Bang fall into disuse once everyone is playing on smartphones?

The number of PC Bangs has already decreased due to a variety of factors, including the emergence of ubiquitous WI-FI and the increase in mobile computing devices.

People still get together in person, but connectivity occurs in more varied spaces

continued

now, such as coffee shops, which have also increased in number. What hasn't changed is that people are using these games to facilitate their interactions. Even the Korean diaspora I observe here in Canada get together in coffee shops with WI-FI and sometimes gather around one mobile device to play a game, like *Anipang*.

Korean gamers have professionalized gaming to a degree that is not well known in North America. Is it just a matter of time until eSports are as popular here in Canada?

Video games as a spectator sport is not really popular in Canada, nor do I see it happening in the same way as Korea. The two countries are working with very different social histories, policies, and geopolitical circumstances. My fieldwork in Korea helped to really get an idea of how particular the media culture is there, grown in that particular cultural milieu.

A more productive mentality would be to examine the spectator sports that are popular here, and examine why that is. For example, in Canada we are much more geographically spread out and tend to socialize in different ways. Think of how we regard watching hockey games in Canada, and how that helps us socialize with one another. It is similar to how people get together and watch eSports in Korea.

Many people worry about the "addictive" properties of computer games. I know you have been critical of these interpretations in the past. Have your views changed? Does the popularity of "social" games, like *The Sims Online* or *FarmVille*, suggest a new kind of compulsion?

Addiction is still a contentious concept with which people continue to grapple, but so is the definition of *gamer*. The impact of social games has been especially visible because of the popular social networking platforms on which they occur, like Facebook. So, the phenomenon of playing games in this publicly visible way is new. I believe that is what surprises people the most—seeing people of such varied demographics playing games . . . like women! Who would have thought?

Blizzard's *World of Warcraft* (also known as WOW), which launched in 2004 and peaked at 12 million players, still claimed 7 million subscribers worldwide in the summer of 2013. Under the recently merged Activision Blizzard, WOW remains the single most popular game in the massively multiplayer genre (CBC 2010; Grey 2008). It successfully entered the Asian market with over 3.5 million subscribers in China and more than 2 million US subscribers. WOW has become something of a legend for surviving in an industry and category that had previously seen regular turnover and switching, as MMOG players shifted alliances to try the next big thing. Even as it drifted downward from 12 million to 10 million to 7 million subscribers, no other title seemed able to achieve those kinds of numbers.

China is both a source of enormous growth for Activision Blizzard and a continuing operational challenge, as China is home to many "gold farmers," a.k.a. large groups of players who are recruited and (poorly) paid to "play" by working in sweatshop conditions, grinding through levels and acquiring "gold," or game currency (Nardi, 2010). The gold is then sold to other players (who want to gain advantage or otherwise avoid the boring or difficult parts of the game) for real currency in unwelcome and unsanctioned but difficult-to-control online markets like eBay. Activision Blizzard also has a practical challenge in providing continuing service to its Chinese customers, as the game is distributed and managed in that country through a local partner company and there have been outages and shutdowns of the service by the Chinese government for both political and social (typically claims of combating "game addiction") reasons.

Consoles have moved to capitalize on online environments with Microsoft's Xbox Live and Sony's PlayStation 3 both having online connectivity and networked gameplay. Voicechat is also available, meaning that players in disparate locations can communicate with each other by talking rather than typing. This move away from keyboard controls is extended even further by Sony's PlayStation Portable (PSP), Nintendo's Wii, and Microsoft's Kinnect. The Wii has introduced game controllers that incorporate motion sensors and integrate players' movements with on-screen action. It is marketed especially to those outside of the traditional gaming community. Thanks to these developments, along with the many social/casual games such as Scrabble and Tetris, there is a game for almost everyone. Middle-aged women, for example, are now an increasingly important demographic for video games—especially when you count casual and web-based games.

The Games Industry: Integrating and Disintegrating the Value Chain

Over the past 30 years, the games industry has evolved a multi-layered structure in which games development, distribution, platforms, and users have found themselves in shifting and interconnected arrangements. Access to the gaming experience is important to users, but different players seek different experiences and often choose a platform (console vs computer vs Web vs mobile vs social) as part of that experience selection. One of the ways that both game developers and players have coped with the diversity of possible games is the creation of genres. Just as there are mystery and romance sections in the bookstore, so, too, have games evolved into categories that provide familiarity and predictability for producers and consumers. For example, there are the high-adrenaline games such as first-person shooters (FPS) or driving games, strategy games, social games, and casual games. And games frequently blend these genres, so you can easily find social strategy games, strategic first-person-shooter games, or multiplayer games with one-on-one aspects.

Industry profitability is typically tied to the software (i.e., the games), with hardware sold at minimal, sustainable costs and often at a loss. More recently, games development has been dominated by the rise of middleware, which straddles the hardware/software divide. Middleware involves the development of game engines, including physics engines that can be repurposed for different games, and also "renderware," which turns mathematical models of shapes (called "wire frames") into shapes with colour, shadow, texture, and even sweat. There are also other software tools that assist with the production of the game software. These bits of software, sometimes called "middleware," reduce the amount of time that developers need to spend on programming for each game and represent a move toward some standardization within the industry. One of the most popular of these tools, Unity and Unity 3D, reported over a million users of its development platform in the spring of 2012.

Open-World or Sandbox Games

When parents think of alternatives to video games for their children, they often turn to toys such as Lego, with their ability to spur imagination and enable creativity. Video games are often thought to be the antithesis of cerebral because they are closed and scripted and often contain violent imagery. A recent entry into the fray, *Minecraft*, throws over these stereotypes and presents players—young people, mainly—with a toolkit that is endlessly malleable within an open world. *Minecraft* is a so-called sandbox game, in which players are provided with basic elements in the form of building blocks (it even looks like Lego, with blocky graphics and bright colours[5]) that can be assembled, connected, and composed into elaborate creations limited only by the imagination of players.

Minecraft is composed of a core engine ("client") and servers that the player interacts with. The client is purchased on the *Minecraft* website, but then there are no further fees. Clients are available for Mac, PC, iOS, and Xbox. Interestingly, the server code is available for download, and users can create their own multiplayer servers for themselves and their friends, an activity that is sharply restricted by other server-oriented games such as *World of Warcraft*, which charge monthly fees to play.

Middleware has also been a major factor in the blurring of the lines between console and PC games, since it has allowed developers the luxury of creating for multiple platforms at the same time. Another reason for the increased blurring of lines and more multiplatform games is that the growing power of desktop graphic processing spilled over into the world of mobile devices in 2011. With the rising graphic processing power of tablets, we see games—often based on another middleware tool, Unreal Engine, that would have been unimaginable to create or play on a mobile device until recently. *Infinity Blade*, created by Chair Entertainment Group, is the epitome of this type.

What is most highly valued in the games industry is the creative abilities or intellectual capital of those involved in the development of games, in areas such as creative design and scripting, software programming, project management and production, and systems development. Yet, this can generate familiar tensions between those in creative roles, the technology developers, and the publishers, who are the ones responsible for the mass marketing of commercial games products. The crash of the video games industry in the mid-1980s and the meltdown of Atari, in particular, was said to have been triggered in part by the incompatibility of the creative ethos of game designers and the corporate environment, by expectations of traditional media giants such as Time Warner, as well as the pressure to rush poorly designed titles in to production in order to meet marketing and product deadlines. This in turn generated a consumer backlash against what Kline and colleagues (2003: 105) refer to as the "suck factor" or "software pumped out without quality control [which] failed because the experiences it offered were simply not worth the investment of time or money."

More recently, EA has been criticized for rushing products to market that still contained significant bugs and for overworking employees. In 2004, EA paid USD $30 million to settle class-action suits undertaken by both game artists and programmers for alleged non-payment of overtime and other benefits (Feldman and Thorsen 2004). Within the games industry, there is widespread criticism of reliance on "crunch time" in the period leading up to the launch of a game, when staff are expected to work in excess of 80 hours per week, leading to sleep deprivation, poor productivity, high levels of staff turnover (also known as "churn"), bugs and other errors in the games, employee burnout, and adverse effects not only on the employees themselves but also on their spouses and families (Robinson 2005). Chris Taylor, the founder and CEO of Gas Powered Games and lead designer of the PC-based real-time strategy (RTS) game *Supreme Commander*, drew attention to this when he argued at the 2007 Game Developers' Conference that employees in creative who worked regular hours produced considerably better games than those subject to crunch-time regimes:

> You make better games when you work regular hours. You're more creative—when you go home at night you're still thinking, because you're creative people. So when you get back at the computer, you have all these ideas and you get them down anyway. . . . We don't want people to live in the office at Gas Powered Games. (Ramsay 2007)

The long hours can also be linked to a kind of Silicon Valley machismo. Kline and colleagues (2003: 200) have argued that "management harnesses youthful technophilia to a compulsive-obsessive work ethic, one-dimensional character formation, and a high rate of burnout." The extent of this burnout and the impact it has had on family members was highlighted in the "EA Spouse" case, in which the partner of an overworked game-industry employee posted an open letter to a blog about the experience of living with someone who was suffering from the EA work environment:

> [The letter describes how] . . . initial enthusiasm for a job with a company listed as one of *Fortune*'s "100 Best Companies to Work For" had evaporated, as seven-day, 85-hour work weeks, uncompensated either by overtime pay or time off, became routine. It told of EA's "put up or shut up and leave . . . human resources policy"; of its dubious invocation of California labour-law exemptions on "specialty" employees to avoid paying overtime; and of creativity decomposing in a "money farm" churning out commercially safe game designs. Describing an industry pressing its workers "to individual physical health limits," EA Spouse wrote of how "the love of my life is coming home late at night complaining of a headache that will not go away and a chronically upset stomach, and my happy supportive smile is running out." (Dyer-Witheford and de Peuter 2006)

Notably, Dyer-Witheford and de Peuter do not simply paint the life of a video-game employee as that of an exploited worker. They give full acknowledgment to the agency and intent of those workers in choosing and continuing in their jobs. Using a formula that they call "enjoyment, exclusion, exploitation, and exodus," Dyer-Witheford and de Peuter describe a workplace that is a site of struggle and while people do enjoy working on video games and in the "game culture," they do not put up with anything and everything to remain there (2006).

It has been argued that the creative industries generally are an example of a **post-Fordist** business model, where the generation of creative content is structurally separated from its distribution and marketing (Aksoy and Robins 1992; Caves 2000; Christopherson and Storper 1986; Garnham 1987), and this certainly characterizes the games industry (Mosco and McKercher 2008). Just as the 1980s industry fallout marked the realization that games hardware should be developed separately from games software, the 1990s marked a further breakup between games development and games publishing or distribution. The games industry today is characterized by a complex and recursive game development value chain in which some companies are building tools; other companies are doing nothing but special effects; and still other companies specialize in motion capture, physics engines (the underlying algorithms that provide the effect of realistic gravity, inertia, and momentum), or faces. Sawyer (2002) argues that the games-industry value chain can be seen as having six distinct but connected layers:

1. capital and publishing layer, involved in investing in new titles, and seeking returns through licensing for those investments;
2. product and talent layer, which includes developers, designers, and artists, who may be working under individual contracts or as part of in-house development teams;
3. production and tools layer, which generates content production tools, game development middleware, customizable game engines, and production management tools;
4. distribution layer, or the publishing industry, involved in generating and marketing catalogues of games for retail and online distribution;
5. hardware layer, or the providers of the underlying platform, which may be console-based, personal computer–based, or accessed through new generation mobile devices; and,
6. end-user layer, or the users/players of the games.

Sawyer further identifies significant trends in the games industry in the early 2000s as follows:

- a shift from "shrink-wrap-based" distribution, in which games are marketed and sold as physical goods on cartridge or CD-ROM/DVD, to online distribution, which will make it much easier to upgrade games through online expansion packs;
- the simultaneous releases of games and associated products, such as music or movies, enabling greater marketing coordination in multiple markets;
- the global growth of pervasive gaming experiences, as games products increasingly span platforms (console, computer, television, hand-held device) and use mobile and wireless technologies to reach people wherever they are, and whenever they want; and,
- the rise of game players as fourth-party developers of game content, which will accompany more open-source models of game design, development, and engineering.

It is the last of these that is of particular interest, since it places the games industry at the centre of the shift from mass-media models based on producer-defined content where users are consumers of a defined product, to a new media model, in which there is the possibility of an endlessly recursive loop between producers and consumers. Sawyer (2002) observes that this loop has existed in the modification of game content by online user communities—known as **modding**—and has been a characteristic of computer-based games since the mid-1990s. Games such as *Counter-Strike*, for instance, are a user modification or "mod" of an earlier computer-based game, *Half-Life*. While this community of modifiers may make up only about 1 per cent of a particular game's user base, the number of those involved will clearly grow as both the international community of gamers grows and more games offer modifying opportunities. Sawyer, writing in 2002, estimates that this could generate as many as 600,000 established online game community developers by 2012 and that "for the industry value chain, this foretells the rise of an entirely new component to the gaming industry." As user-led development continues to mature, it will begin to integrate itself into the overall industry, but it will also seek tools and services specific to its role in the development process. Since Sawyer wrote this over 10 years ago, the community of developers and modders has grown steadily, with some commercial games (like *Minecraft*) launching that are platforms for modding, thus empowering developer communities, and publishing platforms, like Steam, that reach out to the community of modders, sometimes incorporating their mods.

The growing use of analytics—keeping track of every aspect of an online player's behaviour—could also be seen as an indirect form of user-led development. For game developers who have the capability, monitoring game-play, either in real time or through the examination of logs, can be a rich vein of insight into what works and what does not work in a game and reveal surprising opportunities to fine-tune the experience of players, based on their own behaviour and habits. It is not uncommon for games such as *World of Warcraft* to have monthly or biweekly updates based on these observations. In some cases, especially with games that are delivered in real time through the Web (e.g., *FarmVille*), the game itself is considered an active experiment, with sizes of objects, colours, placement of user interface elements in constant flux as the developers continuously try to enhance the experience, prolong playing time, and in the process extract even more revenue from players. This is especially the case where in-game purchases are involved.

Two additional recent trends are worth mentioning: mobile games and freemium games. Mobile took off in 2007 with the iPhone and freemium is an even more recent phenomenon, which was spurred by the popularity of Facebook and its platform for easy distribution of these games to hundreds of millions of people.

In the online-games environment, the emergence of user-led games development has been associated with a new dialogue between the games industry and game players. Total conversion of an existing game—as in the case of *Counter-Strike*—is uncommon and is often in breach of the original developer's copyright. More common are what are known as partial conversions or the addition of new items like weapons, characters, enemies, models, modes, textures, levels, and storylines by the players themselves (Wikipedia contributors 2007). Very popular games, such as *World of Warcraft*, the Star Wars games, the Doom series, *Command & Conquer*, and *Battlefield 1942*, are often experienced through a high degree of end-user modification. Lively online user communities exist to develop, distribute, and refine tools and software. This, of course, begs the question of who owns the subsequently modified content, as most games also have end-user licensing agreements (EULAs) that forbid modifications and assign the ownership of in-game content to the game's creators.

Control over intellectual property has become a key issue when game players take on an increasing role as content co-creators. Linden Labs, the creators of the popular online world/game called *Second Life*, is one of the few developers that honour player-created intellectual property to the extent that players are said to "own" their avatars and can buy and sell objects they create. Other sites are much more restrictive, and even go so far as to ban the trade of game objects (although, not always successfully, as we saw in the discussion about gold farming in China). The challenge of finding the right developer–player balance goes well beyond the actual game—it extends to associated fan-based media such as websites, blogs, and other community interfaces for users. These relationships and appropriations and repurposing practices are all subject to periodic upheavals as game developers and publishers wax and wane in their strategies around asserting rights to the characters and art associated with their games. Nevertheless, fan-created content is a powerful way to retain fans, and game companies know that they have to keep a respectful attitude toward their efforts and desire to deepen their connection to the game.

The Game Industry in Canada

Canada is home to numerous game companies, including branch offices of major players such as Electronic Arts (EA) and Ubisoft. Studios exist in the larger urban centres, with concentrations in Vancouver, Toronto, and Montreal (Smith 2004, 2006). Canada also has its share of superstar game developers, the most famous of whom is probably Don Mattrick, associated with a variety of games, including *Evolution* and *Test Drive*. He became a legend in the Vancouver game scene when his company was absorbed into EA in 1991, making him an instant millionaire.[6]

Many of the EA sports titles continue to be produced in their Burnaby, British Columbia, studios—these games have become well known for their use of cutting-edge technologies developed in the EA research and development labs, also based in Burnaby. Soccer, baseball, and football are all realistically recreated on computer screens using motion-capture technology. Star athletes come to the studios and wear special suits equipped with sensors, acting out their key moves, which are then embedded in the game for a greater sense of realism.

Three Canadian provinces, British Columbia, Ontario, and Quebec, have all implemented policies to encourage employment in the games industry. Various incentives are put in place to encourage companies to locate their studios in those provinces, including tax breaks and other programs for game employers. Ontario's Interactive Digital Media Tax Credit, for example, provides up to 40 per cent of wage expenses as a tax credit to eligible companies. British Columbia has a similar program, providing a 17.5 per cent tax credit for labour expenses on interactive media.

Some analysts have been critical of some games-industry power brokers for developing a type of sharecropper environment in which game developers are saddled with the task of creating games from licensed assets (typically spinoffs from Hollywood films and television programs), using standardized tools, leaving them with no intellectual property and only a fee for their service (Smith 2006). Small game companies sometimes turn to these contracts as a way to build revenues while they're starting out, but, unfortunately, are unable to break out and develop their own games.

They often end up folding or being bought by larger game companies. A Vancouver firm, Radical Entertainment—ironically developed as a breakaway boutique firm from the EA mothership—now develops games exclusively for its new media conglomerate owner, Vivendi (Smith 2006). The perils of corporate ownership were further clarified for Radical in the summer of 2012 when the studio was radically downsized following disappointing sales for their main game product, *Prototype 2*.

The Ontario tax credit system recognizes the dangers of this approach and provides those game studios that are developing their own intellectual property (as opposed to doing work for hire) a higher rate of tax credit.[7]

Game Cultures

Playing games can be a solitary pastime but it is more often done with other people, or as Sutton-Smith puts it, "primarily to be with others" (Sutton-Smith 1997). Digital games are increasingly social—a trend that works against the mainstream media's portrayal of players as isolated (usually adolescent) boys hidden away in darkened bedrooms and failing to engage with the outside world. Recent statistics show that between 40 and 50 per cent of computer-game players are women and that the average age of players is increasing and is now between the late twenties and early thirties (Brand 2007; ESA 2011). Digital games are played in many different settings, and they are often very social and public. Consoles and computers may be located in the living areas of domestic homes, where people play with friends and family. Local area network (LAN) parties, where people get together in larger public spaces and create networks of computers to play with each other have been held for many years now. Large gatherings of dedicated game fans have assembled at events like the Blizzcon, where several thousand players of *World of Warcraft* come together for a festival of game showcases, socializing and playing. In these ways, people create communities around their game-playing activities, much as they have done around sports, hobbies, and other pastimes.

In South Korea, the phenomenon of PC Bangs online game rooms is widespread.[8] South Korea has one of the highest rates of broadband penetration in the world, which has connected domestic spaces and enabled people to play online games together. The most popular offering is the strategy game, *StarCraft*, which is "not just a game in South Korea, it is a national sport. . . . Five million people . . . play. And three cable stations broadcast competitive gaming full-time to a TV audience" (Herz 2002). South Korea also had the largest online role-playing game for many years, *Lineage*, which had at one time more than 4 million subscribers (*World of Warcraft* exceeded this figure recently). Players of *Lineage* often played together in PC Bangs, talking to each other across the room as they play together in the virtual space.

The PC Bangs are a particularly illustrative example of the ways in which online and offline spaces can be seen as merged rather than separate. The high rate of broadband connectivity and the specific cultural mores of Korean society may mean that other countries do not develop public game cultures in the same way, but the potential is there (Rossignol 2006). Even when players are not physically located in the same space, they are often involved in socializing together. This is particularly true for the online gaming communities. In many of the online games, whether they are FPS (first-person shooter) games like *Quake*, action games like *Counter-Strike*, or role-playing games (RPG) such as *World of Warcraft* and *EverQuest*, play is organized around clans or guilds. Players will form or join groups that persist over many sessions of play, sometimes for years. Clans and guilds can be made up of people who know each other offline (friends and families often play together), people who have never met in person, or a combination of these. Clans and guilds vary in their styles and functions. Some exist in order to fight or raid together, while others exist for more social purposes, providing an online family for players. Like sports teams, clans and guilds can create an experience of belonging and of cooperative teamwork, as well as competition. People learn to carry out particular roles within groups and organize themselves into joint projects (slaying dragons, completing quests, fighting other clans, raiding, building cities or empires, or whatever else the game environment enables).

Like any other social formation, these groups are both self-regulating, creating their own social norms, and subject to outside regulation through the game code, and sometimes through the policing of the game by owners, administrators, and publishers. Many of the values encoded into game cultures reflect offline cultural values, but games also offer a chance to emphasize alternative or subjugated values in the name of fantasy and play. Real-world law also comes into play in the regulation of game spaces. Players and publishers enter into EULAs or terms of service agreements and this is where some of the terms of game play are encoded.

It is often argued, particularly in the mainstream media, that digital games can incite players to commit acts of violence. Research that is based on a "media effects" tradition, and which gives rise to the "video games cause violence" discourse, is often linked to moral panics, particularly after horrific events.[9] However, cause-and-effect models of the relationship between gameplay and real-world violence have encountered criticism and the evidence that games cause violent behaviour has been challenged (Vastag 2004). Cause-and-effect models often take insufficient account of cultural contexts and the ways in which media such as games are just one part of the flow and creation of meaning in a culture. Also, differing outcomes from media consumption must be taken into account, which include the particularities of players, their interpretation of what they see, and how and why they play. As games have taken on a greater and greater social element, this, too, adds complexity to the equation. What can we say definitively about the "effect" of a game in which most of the players' time is spent in a chat room or playing with a live conversation among other gamers running in their headphones?

Games are also frequently cited as a source of anti-social behaviour among (mainly) young people, and especially boys, because of their supposedly addictive properties. These addictive properties are most often ascribed to role-playing games, but all video games have been tarred with this brush from time to time. As with debates linking gaming to violence, the argument rages back and forth between those who dismiss concerns and those who describe games as sharing certain properties with drug addiction. Chee and Smith have argued that rather than seeing games as akin to an addictive substance, it is more useful to look closely at the role of the community of gamers in the players' lives.[10]

Questions of identity often arise in relation to digital games. Key concerns related to issues of identity and games have focused on the representations offered to players (in the forms of avatars), the question of how players identify with or relate to

Violence in Video Games

As with violence in movies and television, violence in video games has a long history of controversy, including celebrated "incidents" in which violence has been linked to video games, and the ensuing regulation of violence, along with sexual content. Ratings systems, similar to movie ratings, have been developed and applied to the sales of video games, as a response to parental and legislative concerns about games.

Attempts by regulatory bodies to control the content of video games, and the assumption that the content of a particular game is affecting people's attitudes, beliefs, and cognition, is part of a much larger trend showing observers' approach media forms largely from the perspective of effects. Symptoms can be quite broad, ranging from health concerns over kids spending too much time indoors, playing a game that requires nothing more than twiddling thumbs or moving a mouse, to assumptions about people's inability to distinguish death on a screen from death in the real world.

Generations of researchers, from psychologists to social scientists to humanities scholars studying changes to culture, have all weighed in on these debates. Tragic situations, such as the Columbine High School shootings in Colorado, or suicides, have been linked to excessive video-game immersion or gameplay dominated by products with strongly violent themes. As games have become more "realistic" in their rendering of players, terrain, and situations, concerns have also been raised that this further blurs the lines between reality and simulation.

Despite these seemingly commonsensical concerns, real data on media effects remain elusive or contested. The fact that human beings are not simply lumps of clay, ready to be manipulated or unable to make critical judgments, continues to confound the results of studies on the impact of violence in video games. While the health impact of spending too much time on the couch and in front of the screen is undeniable, game players retain their "agency" while playing and stubbornly persist in their ability to distinguish between the streets of their own city and the streets of *Grand Theft Auto*. And, while violence and theft might gain you points in a game, it is still a bad idea in real life.

their avatars, and the styles of play suggested and enabled by games and whether they are gender-biased. Representations of gender in digital games are often sexist, with hard-bodied musclemen and soft-bodied, nearly naked women being the norm. Bryce and Rutter (2002: 246) found that "female game characters are routinely represented . . . as princesses or wise old women in fantasy games, as objects waiting on male rescue, or as fetishized subjects of male gaze in first-person shooters." These roles emphasize female passivity and highlight the dominance of masculine themes. Not all games are like this, but enough are to make it notable as a general characteristic. Access to the machines to play games may also be gendered; for example, studies have shown that male members of the family often displace girls from the family game console (McNamee, 1998). A further argument on gender and games is that people of different genders have their own unique gaming styles or preferences and that these differences are not catered to in the marketplace (Cassell and Jenkins 1998); however, this is much disputed.[11]

The context of play is a significant factor for identity in games. It is important to recognize that the game world, rather than being completely separate from the real world, is embedded in a real-world context that determines game experience (Chee et al. 2006). Issues of identity also need to be considered in terms of the choices that

CASE STUDY

Club Penguin

If you thought a simple web-based game (using Adobe Flash technology) about penguins living in igloos (never mind the North Pole–South Pole confusion) and aimed at preteens seemed like an unlikely success, you would have been wrong. *Club Penguin*, launched in October 2005 by an independent game company based in Kelowna, British Columbia, grew to almost 700,000 members before being purchased by the Disney Company in 2007 for USD $350 million (Barnes 2007). The game company has remained in Kelowna, with its 130 employees, and has continued to flourish under the new management. With more than 6 million members from 190 countries worldwide in 2010, it is the largest online computer game for children in the world. The runner-up, Webkinz, has garnered 3.8 million members (Barnes 2010). The *Club Penguin* site carries no advertising, relying on subscriptions for revenues. A free trial version is also available.

Club Penguin was created by three fathers who wanted to create a safe online space for children. The game emphasizes fun, through mini-games and modifications you can make to your penguin character (avatar) and his or her home (typically an igloo). Participants can also chat with each other, but with a high degree of control on what can be said and to whom, something that parents are concerned about. Players can play on a computer, but a Wii game console also became an option by June 2010 (BusinessWire 2010).

The founders have been very careful with the tone and style of the game, sometimes to the chagrin of Disney executives who hoped for more tie-ins to other Disney brands and theme parks (Barnes 2010). There is a strong focus on global awareness, and the founders have devoted 10 per cent of their initial purchase price to a foundation dedicated to child-centric charitable work (Stueck 2007). Game members can also donate their virtual money to the Coins for Change program found on the website. The patterns of donations helped shape the fund's operations into three categories: kids who are sick, kids who are poor, and the environment.

Designing games for children is a potentially controversial topic, despite *Club Penguin*'s best intentions. Critics worry about children spending too much time indoors playing in virtual worlds rather than partaking in face-to-face play (Levitt 2008); the possibility of stalkers or others who prey on children; and the commodification of children's play (Grimes 2008b).

Case Study Questions

1. *Club Penguin*'s founders were passionate about creating a game that was not just safe but also a place apart from the unrelenting commercialization of so much of children's media (e.g., the breakfast cereal and toys that seem to be the primary motivator of Saturday-morning television). Do you think that this altruism will persist as the company continues its relationship with Disney?
2. It could be argued that children's television and games were the real pioneers of transmedia storytelling, by blending real-world artifacts with media stories. Are there other elements of children's use of media and games that could find their way into teen or adult markets?
3. What games did you play as a child? Would they still interest you today? Why do you think you grew out of those games?

gamers make. Players use games and their enabling representations in many ways. For instance, a player may choose (or not choose) to play a stereotypical female avatar for different reasons: some women enjoy adopting what they feel to be an image of femininity more acceptable or desirable than their real-world body, while other women may feel completely alienated by what they see as an offensive or unreal representation of femininity. Some women may choose to play as a male character instead. Men may choose to play as female characters because they expect that they will be given more gifts by the male characters. Some men will play using a female avatar for quite instrumental reasons: if the female character has different abilities than the male, what the avatar looks like does not matter—what matters is what it can do (Newman 2002). Some people like to experiment with cross-gendered play out of their own curiosity. Identity tourism, as Nakamura (2000) notes, tends to perpetuate and accentuate existing stereotypes, as people adopt alternative identities based on understandings gleaned from other media representations. As Sherry Turkle notes, there is considerable "plasticity" when it comes to identity and the role that games play in both enabling and shaping our identity remains an important area for social research (Turkle 1997).

Games are also a serious issue for those who have concerns about the increasing commercialization of childhood and the role that video games, and online games in particular, play in this process. There is a growing trend to link games to television programs and children's toys, such as Webkinz (www.webkinz.com), for example (Grimes 2008b). This connection has, as one might imagine, stirred up a considerable controversy both in the academic world and in public policy circles. *Club Penguin*— one of the most successful independent online games for children—was developed in Kelowna, British Columbia, and is a remarkable Canadian financial success story. The Disney Company recently purchased *Club Penguin* with the intent to link the game to Disney movies, theme parks, and merchandising (see the accompanying case study).

Games and the Academy: Game Cultures and Game Studies

While the video-games industry has grown exponentially as both an employer and as an influence on the lives of millions of players, game studies have become a significant area of academic research. The Canadian Game Studies Association (http://gamestudies.ca) with its companion journal, *Loading: A Journal of the Canadian Game Studies Association* (http://journals.sfu.ca/loading), was an early entrant in the field, as was DiGRA, the Digital Games Research Association (www.digra.org). Other academic journals include *Game Studies* (www.gamestudies.org) and *Games and Culture* (http://gac.sagepub.com). Games research is conducted at sites such as the Experimental Game Lab at Georgia Tech in the United States (http://egl.gatech.edu) and the Center for Computer Games Research at the IT University of Copenhagen in Denmark (http://game.itu.dk). Some of the key texts in the field include *Digital Play: The Interaction of Technology, Culture and Marketing* (Kline et al. 2003) and *Game Cultures: Computer Games as New Media* (Dovey and Kennedy 2006). Video games have been studied from computer science perspectives, and their impact on players from medical and psychological perspectives, but the game studies literature is distinctive because it aims to bring insights from critical humanities traditions to the study of video games without subsuming their distinctive forms and properties into existing film, media, or cultural studies paradigms.

Some of the distinctive features of digital games that have drawn the attention of the research community are user interactivity, immersion in a virtual environment, social interaction within the game, and the players' capacity to become co-creators of content, especially in multiplayer games. While none of these are unique to games, they suggest an interesting and more productive relationship between the players and the game text than is expected from other media. This relationship involves more than active interpretation of the text or identity construction through consumption: it is a form of engagement that serves to *create* the text each time a person engages with the game.

Early game-studies debates were concerned with the ways game texts work, and a particularly intense debate arose between those who thought that narrative was the key organizing structure of a game (the "narratologists") and those who subscribed to play theory (the "ludologists"). Murray (1997) and Bolter and Grusin (2000), for example, discussed how video games employ aspects of narrative and they identified games as emergent forms of storytelling or "cyber-dramas," in which greater narrative complexity would evolve over time. By contrast, ludologists Aarseth (2001) and Juul (2003) argued that there was a quite different relationship of the player to the game, since the goal-driven nature of games brings an emotional engagement with the text derived not from appreciation of characters and events (such as occurs in conventional narratives) but, rather, because the players are actors themselves, seeking an outcome. The engagement is derived from the player being a performer and the game evaluates the performance and adapts to it. As a result, some ludologists argued there is a need to incorporate elements of play theory as an alternative to traditional models of literary theory and the applied humanities (Juul 2003; Liestøl 2003) in game-studies research.

Two further developments are notable in this rapidly changing field. One has been the growing awareness that games need to be taken seriously as big business. Political economists of media and game studies need to engage more systematically with the unique political economy of the games industry. There has been some movement in this direction in recent years. Kline and colleagues (2003) and Kerr (2006) give close attention to the changing economic dynamics of the global games industry, a concern that is also discussed in detail by Dovey and Kennedy (2006). Four features of the political economy of games are prominent in this literature. First, the games industry sector is subject to strong dynamics of concentration and consolidation, despite the large number of game titles available. This is most apparent in the console-based games market, where the big three console providers—Sony, Microsoft, and Nintendo—can exert substantial control over game publishers and developers, but it is also a characteristic of the PC-based and multiplayer online games markets (Kerr 2006: 54–61). Second, games production increasingly occurs through global production networks, although production in emergent countries remains very much tied to the distributional relations controlled by the big console and publishing companies based in the United States, Japan, and, to a lesser extent, Europe (Kerr 2006: 76–9). Third, as we noted above with the case of EA Spouse, workplace relations in the games industry are notoriously harsh, with long hours, extended crunch times, job insecurity, and a sense of forced workaholism leading to high rates of labour turnover and burnout among those employed in the sector (IGDA 2004). Gill (2002, 2006) also identifies how this work environment is particularly incompatible with family or parental responsibilities and how many women in new media sectors intensely dislike this combination of a boys'-club-type culture and a lack of interest in social skills or self-care; employment rates for women in the games industry are well below those of most other sectors (Dovey and Kennedy 2006: 61–2). Fourth, as the sector seems to clone a certain type of worker—young, male, and with limited responsibilities outside of work—and since males aged 13 to 25 represent the market best understood in the sector, it is highly likely that "the prospects for widespread innovation become very limited . . . [as] a minority of gamers with a particular set of tastes command a large cultural space which is disproportionate to their actual numbers" (Dovey and Kennedy 2006: 62).

Dyer-Witheford and Sharman's review of the political economy of Canada's game industry (2005), provides an excellent introduction to research on firms, labour relations, and government interventions in the game industry.

The growing presence and popularity of so-called emergent games is the second major development. Rather than dictating the direction of play, emergent games offer environments and sets of rules, but not a hard-and-fast direction in which play must proceed. Sandbox or open-world games take this phenomenon even further, with the players creating the entire world, based on a few basic elements and rules (see the box about *Minecraft* on page 144 in this chapter). What results is an endless variety of unexpected play directions emerging from players' own decisions about what to do within that environment. Many multiplayer online games take this form, to a greater or lesser extent. A role-playing game like *EverQuest* or *World of Warcraft* provides a world for players to log into and they play with each other within that world. There is a system of "levelling up" that gives players a sense of progress, but the particular ways in which they achieve that progress are not set and some players may choose not to progress and to do other things instead, such as focusing on more social aspects of the game. Structurally, the text is added to and changed by the player, rather than being finished by the developer. In this model, publishers rely on players to continue the development cycle. So, a game can be seen as the result of a combination of paid and unpaid labour, whose features arise in a variety of new media contexts, but are particularly marked in relation to games. It is clear that player creativity is part of the game-production cycle in a number of ways. Emergent games are based on a recursive model of production whereby players create various iterations of the text. Players can also become part of the production cycle as modders or people who make new objects for games, new levels or artificial intelligence for games, or even whole new games (like *Counter-Strike*, as we mentioned earlier).[12]

The Future of the Video-Games Industry

The games industry is currently faced with choices about how much it will embrace the player-creators or modder communities as part of its structure. Some industry leaders are openly encouraging these communities by releasing the source code and tools for creating content. Others have chosen to enclose their games in heavily policed copyright or intellectual property regimes, which precludes the creation of derivative works by fans. As business and intellectual property rights strategies, the former seeks to leverage the R&D capacities of player communities and harness the creativity of players, while the latter holds to more conventional production and intellectual property rights (IPR) management. Open-access licensing and the new crowd-sourced production models have given rise to opportunities for innovative industry structures—ones that fully embrace the recursive and fluid features of networked, interactive technology and the passion of the gamers. A recent Kickstarter campaign, which appeared to go off the rails when the funds raised were exhausted and the game seemed about to close up, was revived when the developers decided to release the code to the prospective game's community via an open-source model. This quickly attracted a flock of interested developers (where it had been reduced to one) and the project took on a new life.

It is here, too, that work must be done to determine what the rights of this passionate and productive community might be. Who should own the intellectual property rights of player-created content? How can IPR be managed so these practices do not become exploitative? Is intellectual property even the most appropriate model to be using? Intellectual property is much better suited to conventional texts that are fixed or finished rather than to ongoing collaborative creations like games made through a joint effort between developers and players.

Games are exemplary and illustrative of the possibilities and challenges presented by interactive online environments. The networked nature of the game production cycle is one that will become more prevalent with time. Some of the key issues arising in the games industry and game studies are not restricted to games but rather are indicators of structural changes that raise broad concerns about the way new media are managed and regulated.

Online social environments like multiplayer online games present the challenges of resolving issues of IPR management as well as community management. Players of social games must consider the ways in which governance regimes, instituted by media corporations that have as their main goal the generation of profit rather than social equity, have an impact on their community. Should there be any checks and balances on corporate behaviour in this respect or should it be left to the marketplace to regulate? These are questions will become more important as more people live parts of their lives inside proprietary spaces and thereby contribute to the economic success of media corporations. Although media publishers may not have financial obligations to the player-creators, they may have social obligations. Issues such as the terms of access to environments, freedom of speech, and privacy are all currently determined through EULAs or terms of service agreements, which in most cases are heavily weighted in favour of the publishers. Such imbalances may come to be a site of struggle and negotiation in the same way as is already the case with player-created intellectual property ownership.

Video games were successful interactive entertainment environments long before other applications. They have shown the way forward with structural design and technological innovation generating engaging and often profitable outcomes. The position of video games at the forefront of innovation in the digital world has meant that they often indicate where change, negotiation, and controversy will arise in much broader arenas. It is well worth attending to the issues that arise from video games: the structural changes to the nature of the text; the reorganization of production relations and the impacts on industry; the reshaping of the role of consumers and the effects on social relations; and the new configurations of authorship and the consequences for intellectual property are just some of the areas that have wide significance and justify academic attention.

Gamasutra
www.gamasutra.com

Gamasutra covers—as their subhead makes clear—the "art and business of making games." Whether they are online, mobile, console or PC, games are a big business but also an art form. Gamasutra follows the business side of games very well, with news, analysis, and features, but it also is a go-to site for many commentators and even academics because of its wide range of coverage and large audiences.

Game Studies
www.gamestudies.org

This is an online academic journal dedicated to developing cross-disciplinary research into games. It has been a leader in developing the play-based approach to studying games.

Canadian Game Studies Association (CGSA)
http://gamestudies.ca

The CGSA is an association supporting the work of Canadian researchers, graduate students, artists, game designers, programmers, theorists, and others working in the interdisciplinary study of digital games. It also has a journal: *Loading: A Journal of the Canadian Game Studies Association*.

International Game Developers Association
www.igda.org

This is the website of the premier international game developers' association. It includes particularly interesting resources on quality-of-life issues for those working in the games industry.

WomenGamers.com
www.womengamers.com

This website is for women who play video games, who work in the games industry, and for anyone interested in questions around gender and gaming.

Terra Nova
http://terranova.blogs.com

This is a must-read site for both academic and industry observers of the virtual worlds' aspect of games and for those working in the game industry. Founded by four prominent game scholars, it contains well-written and insightful commentary by a rotating group of practitioners and academics.

Gamine Expedition
http://gamineexpedition.blogspot.ca

Sara M. Grimes's frequently updated and insightful blog covers the world of games for children from the perspective of an active researcher and an avid gamer. Dr Grimes, based at University of Toronto, conducts research on a wide range of childrens' cultural activities, not just games. She is an associate director of Semaphore (http://semaphore.utoronto.ca), a research group that looks at "inclusive design in the area of mobile and pervasive computing."

How to Do Things with Video Games, Ian Bogost (2011)
Carnegie Mellon professor and game developer Ian Bogost is a prolific writer and creator of video games, and his books are entertaining and informative for those who are interested in a behind-the-scenes look into how games are made, and why. In this book, he looks at the ways in which games serve as a platform for education, music, history, art, and even pornography. He makes several of his books available online, and tweets regularly under the handle @ibogost.

Critical Play: Radical Game Design Mary Flanagan (2009)
Flanagan looks into unusual places, folk culture, experimental media, and art, and finds a world of different and interesting games. Her 2009 book for

MIT Press helps reveal the world of games as more complex—and inspirational—than many people, who tend to see only the first-person-shooter genre, would imagine.

For The Win, Cory Doctorow (2010)

Doctorow's novel about unrest in the "gold-farmer" ranks in a near-future world presents an eloquent portrayal of game culture and the issues and the economics of virtual economies. Available as a Creative Commons download or as a printed book, this would make an excellent supplement for those who are interested in knowing more about life for non-Western gamers as well as people who play games but are not familiar with the backroom decisions that go into the economic aspects of games with virtual currencies.

Learning with Digital Games: A Practical Guide to Engaging Students in Higher Education, Nicola Whitton (2010)

One of the interesting developments in the past few years has been the use of games for learning, premised on the notion that people are both used to learning through games (of course, they are learning game-related concepts), and that games, being fun and engaging, will help people with the repetition or exploration that is required to learn new material. Games can also bring in a competitive aspect that motivates some players/learners. Whitton's book examines this phenomenon in the context of higher education and discusses both using existing games and developing new games.

From Barbie to Mortal Kombat: Gender and Computer Games, edited by Justine Cassell and Henry Jenkins (1998)

Although this collection is a bit dated now, it lays the groundwork for what has become a considerable scholarship on games and gender. The book is worth a read, if only to dispel some of the old stereotypes of games being something that boys play only, or that girls do not play action games.

Additional games titles include *The Business and Culture of Digital Games: Gamework and Gameplay* (Kerr 2006), *Computer Games: Text, Narrative and Play* (Carr et al. 2006), *Understanding Digital Games* (Rutter and Bryce 2006), and *Worlds in Play: International Perspectives on Digital Games Research* (de Castell and Jenson, eds. 2007). Each of these provides additional insights into games and gaming from an industry-insider perspective (Kerr), semiotic analysis (Carr et al.), and game-research overview (Rutter and Bryce, as well as De Castell and Jenson's edited collection).

Discussion Questions

1. What are the different roles (and their corresponding communities of professionals) in the games industry and what are some ways of describing the dynamics among them?
2. What are some of the shifts in the games industry described in this chapter?
3. There is an ongoing debate about whether or not digital games cause people to commit acts of violence. Discuss both the legitimate concerns and justifiable objections in this debate.
4. What is meant by the term *game culture*, and in what ways are people creating communities around their game-playing activities, much as they have done around sports, hobbies, and other pastimes?
5. In this chapter, we draw attention to how the values encoded into game cultures reflect offline cultural values but also how games offer a chance to emphasize alternative or subjugated values in the name of fantasy and play. What are the implications of this and why are they significant?
6. Discuss the concerns related to issues of identity and gender bias in the games world as they are related to the following: the representations offered to players (in the forms of avatars), how players identify with or relate to their avatars, and the styles of play suggested and enabled by games.
7. Why do you think that the following distinctive features of digital games have drawn the attention of the research community: social interaction within the game, the capacity of players to become co-creators of content, and the relationship between the players and the game text?

1. Building on the notion of games in education (see the Nicola Whitton book mentioned on page 158), create a game version of this course. How would points be awarded? Would the assignments be like "quests" or "kills," or something else? Do you think you would be more engaged by this experience? Create a paper version of the game, or discuss the rules, and then debate the expected outcome. You might take a look at the article from the *Chronicle of Higher Education* about Lee Sheldon's course, in which the course itself is a game: http://chronicle.com/blogPost/At-Indiana-U-a-Class-on-Game/21981.

2. Online games/worlds, such as *Second Life*, frequently provide a free trial account that can be used by anyone. Hold a class discussion inside the game, with fellow students either logging in from their own laptops, from home, or from terminals at your school. Test the requirements (sometimes a game requires that software be downloaded, making it difficult to do on public computers), and if necessary, adjust to a virtual tour or demonstration by students who already have accounts. Consider a virtual tour of a particular type of game (e.g., a children's game such as *Club Penguin*). See the case study in this chapter for more on *Club Penguin*.

3. Almost anything related to new media is subject to rapid change. Firms come and go, technologies change, and numbers of users, viewers, and creators for new media content and memes change every day. Look up a fact or figure in this chapter and verify whether it remains true today, using online sources. Identify corroborating or supporting sources for your findings. Not only will you have the new facts, but you'll also have an appreciation for how quickly things change and, most importantly, a visceral sense of the way in which the Internet and new media are self-revealing to the diligent and inquisitive scholar. If you discover a fact that needs updating, you can even submit your update (with page reference and new citation) in the form of a rewritten paragraph, to the author: Richard Smith (smith@sfu.ca). He promises to reply.

1. Console games are sometimes seen as "serious" games, meriting the attention of serious gamers. They have been in decline lately, with fewer produced each year. Is this a regrettable outcome or something to be celebrated? Why or why not?

2. Transmedia games, role-playing games, and social games all cast the player in a stronger role relative to the story and the outcome. To what extent does this reduce the role of the storyteller, the "auteur" who creates the game? Are you more comfortable in a game environment that you control?

3. Some people who play a lot of video games claim that traditional linear plots of movies are no longer satisfying, and, in particular, the inability to move the camera (as you can in games, to alter your point of view) has become a limitation on their ability to enjoy a film. Do you find that you are trying to look "around" things on the screen, or inadvertently moving your mouse hand to adjust the camera? What do you think this might do to the future of moviemaking?

7

Creative Industries

Questions to Consider

- What has been the significance of creative cities, historically? How do cities today work to remain part of this tradition of creative industry?

- What are the creative industries? How can the dynamics of these industries be characterized?

- In what ways are knowledge and information different from each other? Why is this relevant to understanding both the knowledge economy and creative industries?

- In what ways do policy initiatives undertaken in Canada and different parts of the world affect cultural industries?

Chapter Outline

In this chapter, we consider the industrialization of creativity, something that was not initiated by new digital media—mechanical reproduction of works of art famously preoccupied Frankfurt School member Walter Benjamin in the first half of the twentieth century—but the process has accelerated, broadened, and deepened alongside digital media. We begin with an examination of creativity as a concept and especially the question of under what circumstances it can flourish. Next, we consider the notion of a creative industry and how and why this has become a policy objective of cities, provinces/states, and countries around the world. We discuss and debate the reasons for the rise of creative economies, creative cities, and a creative class, either as realities or as visions or ideals.

Creativity in Question

In the early 2000s, we have seen a surge of interest in creativity that shows few signs of abating. Popular business literature exhorts corporate managers to unlock the creative potential of their staff, while there is also an extensive self-help literature on how to realize personal creativity (see de Bono 1995; Flew 2004a; Gary 1999; Nussbaum 2005; cf. Osborne 2003). Tim Berners-Lee (2000), a key figure in the development of the Web, notes a critical flaw in the way in which the Web's evolution has been heavily commercially driven since the mid-1990s—that interactivity is promoted ahead of intercreativity—while the legal scholar Lawrence Lessig (2004) identifies the suppression of creativity as a critical flaw of current intellectual property regimes. In his highly influential book, *The Rise of the Creative Class*, Richard Florida (2002: 5) describes creativity as "the decisive source of competitive advantage" in the twenty-first century global economy. Leadbeater (2007) proposes that the twenty-first century socio-economic system is one that will be based on mass creativity.

Creativity, however, is a famously slippery concept. In one highly influential understanding, which has its origins in both Plato and nineteenth-century Romanticism, any harnessing of creativity to organizations or to policy agendas is anathema, as creativity arises from the "free, wakeful play of the imagination" (Negus and Pickering 2004: 7). In this tradition, creative people are seen as special people (the "troubled genius persona"), with creativity closely linked to the arts and not to business, science, or technology; further, the creative process is understood as essentially spontaneous, with the implicit assumption that creativity cannot be formally taught since it is a gift that some have and others do not.

Bilton (2007) observes that artists have become more circumspect about such understandings of creativity and increasingly interpret their activities through frameworks like performative research or practice-led research (Gray 2006; Haseman 2006) while the notion of creativity as the wild play of imagination has found new champions in the business community. This leads to assumptions that "creative people need to be protected from commercial realities, that budgets and deadlines might interfere with the eccentric, child-like world of pure inventiveness . . . [and] managers are warned from 'meddling' in the creative process because their rules and rationality have no validity in the world of art and innovation" (Bilton 2007: 8).

Such discourses in turn invoke skepticism about the value of the notion of creativity. In the context of debates about the creative industries, Donald (2004: 236) remains unconvinced that creativity is "anything other than a conceptual black hole" and that trying to teach creativity is "absurd and self-defeating" since demonstrated creativity is "invariably a by-product of learning to do other, more concrete . . . things." In a similar vein, Osborne (2003: 510) opposes the idea that creativity, as a feel-good concept, "as a combination of doctrine and morality . . . can be captured by business gurus and management writers, Californian lifestyle sects, new age groups, post-identitarian philosophers, literary critics turned cultural theorists, intellectuals, postmodern geographers, anti-globalization protestors, whoever."

Yet Clay Shirky, in *Cognitive Surplus: Creativity and Generosity in a Connected Age* (2010), describes how new digital technologies (especially social software and Web 2.0 technologies) are enabling forms of creativity that are not directly tied to making money but are in fact part of larger amateur contributions to the creative output of society. These amateur offerings are not just pale imitations of the professional side of creativity but something else entirely, created specifically to be shared (2010: 78).

Going even further, authors like Robinson (2001), Bilton and Leary (2002), Negus and Pickering (2004), and Bilton (2007) address some of the vagueness that has surrounded the concept of creativity and move the debate beyond the Platonic ideal of creativity as a unique individual gift. Robinson defines creativity as "imaginative processes with outcomes that are original and of value" and asserts that "creative ideas are more than novel; they are valuable" (2001: 116, 118). Bilton and Leary (2002) argue that the criterion of value is as central as newness or innovation, even if it is recognized that the value of a new idea, concept, or product may not be appreciated at the time and place in which it is presented to the world. Negus and Pickering (2004) draw attention to several aspects of creativity: (1) the need for creative activities to demonstrate extrinsic value and for creative acts to be not only expressed, but also effectively communicated; and (2) the need to draw upon symbolic and representational systems that can be understood and appreciated by a wider audience, whether a relatively discrete community of scholars or practitioners, or audiences in the wider sense of the general public.

One study that illustrates how conceptual understandings of creativity have been usefully extended into the policy realm is *Beyond Productivity: Information Technology, Innovation, and Creativity*, a report for the US National Research Council of the National Academies (Mitchell et al. 2003). *Beyond Productivity* makes much of the importance of domains of creativity, recognizing that "no intellectual domain or economic sector has a monopoly on creativity" (2003: 18). The report acknowledges that creativity manifests itself differently across the scientific, technological, economic, and cultural domains, in diverse forms such as patents and designs, entrepreneurship, and artistic product. Identifying information technologies as a unifying factor that can bring these domains of creative practice into a closer collaborative set of relationships, the report maps these interconnections in the manner set out in Figure 7.1.

The specific focus of *Beyond Productivity* is the extent to which developments in information technology and creative practice can be mutually reinforcing, generating dynamic forms of IT-related creative practice (ITCP) and new modes of research, collaboration, education, and wealth creation that bring together the fields of art, design, and information technology. Arguing that "to work within the realm of information technology and creative practice . . . individuals or groups need to be fluent in multiple disciplines" (Mitchell et al. 2003: 30), *Beyond Productivity* goes on to identify the main institutional and policy challenge for governments: how to better facilitate such cross-disciplinary interaction.

In the education context, Seltzer and Bentley (2000) seek to identify the implications of a growing stress on creativity in the knowledge economy for learning and for educational institutions. They reject claims that creativity is primarily associated with brilliance, a unique artistic sensibility, innate talents, or even acquired skills, arguing instead that

[creativity] requires the ability to solve problems progressively over time and apply previous knowledge to new situations. Creativity is also bound up with context—it can only be defined and assessed in relation to the context in which it is achieved. It must be developed through the interaction of the learner, her underlying goals and motivations, and the resources and context in which she operates. (2000: 19)

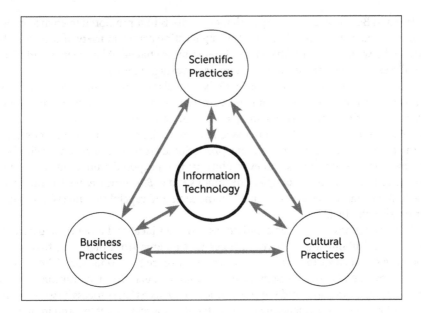

Figure 7.1 Domains of Creative Practice and the Role of
Information Technology
....
Source: Mitchell et al. (2003: 25).

Seltzer and Bentley identify four core characteristics of creativity, which they associate
with creative problem-solving:

1. the ability to formulate new problems, rather than depending on others to define
   them;
2. the ability to transfer what one learns across different contexts;
3. the ability to recognize that learning is incremental and involves making
   mistakes; and,
4. the capacity to focus one's attention in pursuit of a goal. (2000: 19)

For these writers, the educational paradox of the creative age is that the rapidly
changing socio-economic environment requires individuals to be increasingly adaptive; however, adding more and more content into course curricula so that people
can formally learn more and more skills (which is a model often used) does not
train people for a creative environment. Creativity, understood in this way, is not
seen as the unique property of an individual, but, rather, it is deeply shaped by the
domains in which it is applied (the arts, sciences, business, policy-making, community sector organizations, schools, etc.) and by those who are in a position to judge
creative output. The nature of creativity in a given field may vary, from the judgments
of teachers, professors, assessors, or peers, to the purchasing decisions made by
consumers. Given that the realization of creativity necessarily involves an interaction
between the person and the activity, the domains in which it is applied, and the fields
through which it is validated, creative outcomes can never be guaranteed by a school
curriculum, a government policy, or any single institutional instrument or form.

Seltzer and Bentley (2000: ix) argue that creativity is best promoted in environments characterized by trust, freedom of action, application across a variety of contexts, the balance between skills and challenges, interactive exchange of knowledge and ideas, and the experience of achieving concrete, real-world outcomes.

Burgess (2006) discusses the concept of vernacular creativity, linking it to a growing capacity for ordinary cultural participation—across the amateur/professional divide—with the democratizing and participatory potential of new media technologies. Game modding, which we discussed in Chapter 6, provides an excellent example of the potential of this type of amateur/professional creative endeavour. Machinima, the creation of short videos and even films using repurposed animations created by game engines, is another example. The famous *Red vs Blue* series, as well as the entire machinima.com website, was founded on the tools and capabilities unleashed by new forms of digital media.

Burgess defines vernacular creativity as "both an ideal and a heuristic device, to describe and illuminate creative practices that emerge from highly particular and non-elite social contexts and communicative conventions" (2006: 206). The concept of the vernacular is used "to distinguish 'everyday' language from institutional or official modes of expression" and Burgess defines creativity as "the process by which available cultural resources (including both 'material' resources—content, and immaterial resources—genre conventions, shared knowledges) are recombined in novel ways, so that they are both recognizable because of their familiar elements, and create affective impact through the innovative process of this recombination" (2006: 206). In developing a definition of vernacular creativity, it is described as "a productive articulation of consumer practices and knowledges . . . with older popular traditions and communicative practices" (2006: 207).

In his review of literature on management and creativity in the creative industries, Bilton (2007) draws attention to the phenomenon of "the genius and the water-carrier." Drawing on a comment by the former French soccer star Eric Cantona that his national-side teammate Didier Deschamps was "merely a water-carrier," Bilton argues that it is precisely the existence of workhorse players whose play is characterized by effort and unspectacular endeavour that allows the brilliant but sometimes undisciplined players such as Cantona to flourish. Even if, as is often the case, it is those who are perceived to be creative geniuses attract the most attention and, no less significantly, sponsorship. But flamboyant, creative individual talents such as Cantona, David Beckham, Lionel Messi, and others, are only as good as the teams around them. Bilton identifies in this a wider metaphor for the organization of creativity in the media entertainment industries, where creative teams and projects depend on uncreative people and activities:

> Creativity in the commercial creative industries is represented through the branding and packaging of individual talent and the personality cult fostered around stars and celebrities. Yet behind the scenes, a more realistic unit of analysis for creative processes and products is the team or partnership. At the core of this creative team is the double-act of the genius and the water-carrier. Creative thinking, like football, depends upon a union of contrasting abilities and styles of thinking or playing. (2007: 19)

The new media industry is rife with examples of the genius coupled with the more staid, diligent partner. Steve Jobs, the mercurial and creative side of Apple Computer, was famously paired with the quiet, reserved, and technically minded Steve Wozniak.

Whatever definition you choose, creativity is significant in considering larger social and economic practices and dynamics that are embedded in organizations, networks (as we saw in Chapter 5), and industries. In the next section of this chapter, we focus on the role that creative industries play in the economy and how digital new media are making it possible to turn creativity into commerce more quickly and across a wider geographic range than ever before.

Charles Davis

interview with a new media expert

Charles Davis is the Edward S. Rogers Research Chair in Media and Entrepreneurship at Ryerson University. He teaches and conducts research on innovation management and policy in industries that produce digital experience goods and has research projects on media product innovation, media audiences, and media labour.

What does the term *creative industries* mean to you?

There are several different definitions circulating, none of them completely satisfactory. The term does *not* refer to those industries that are "creative," as if other industries were not creative. It refers generally to industries that deliberately produce culture as a product or service, in which sustained introduction of novelty is critically important, and in which intellectual property is generally protected by copyright or trademark. Thus, exemplary creative industries are film and television, digital media, music, books, performing arts, advertising, architecture, art, design, crafts, video games, etc. A larger group of "cultural industries" is sometimes included: sports and recreation, hobbies, tourism, libraries, and so on.

What are the key policy questions relating to creative industries in Canada?

Should creative industries be promoted for purposes of *cultural sovereignty* (another problematic concept) or for purposes of economic growth, or both, or neither? If they are to be promoted, how should it be done?

How are the issues different at the level of the city, the region, and the nation?

Multiple overlapping jurisdictions make policy coordination difficult. Cities are generally where creative industries locate, so cities have a direct stake in the success or failure of creative industries, but cities have few policy instruments to use, and not much spending power for programs. Regions (let's say provinces) are often active in creative industry policy from the standpoint of economic development and workforce training. The national level has jurisdiction over key policy aspects of creative industries, notably broadcasting and telecommunications, IP legislation, and foreign trade.

What are some key emerging concepts or challenges or ideas?

A key challenge has to do with addressing labour issues in creative industries. Most workers are self-employed freelancers, not salaried workers, so employment legislation does not apply to them. Policies regarding employment equity and employment-related benefits such as insurance and pensions are difficult to apply.

A second challenge is to understand the role that creative industries play in larger economic development? Do they have wide spillovers by acting as a kind of R&D lab for the larger economy? Or are they more like specialized industrial sectors that can grow if properly managed, but which do not have important backward or forward linkages? And what characteristics make cultural products and services exportable?

A third challenge is to understand the critical success factors in various creative industries, notably with respect to critical acclaim and commercial success. Innovation, which is usually considered a key critical success factor in other industries, is pervasive in the creative industries. It is difficult to meaningfully measure innovation in creative industries and to tie the rate and direction of innovation with significant outcomes.

The Rise of Creative Industries

New media is a key part of the creative industries, both in terms of the size of the sector as well as its current and future growth. Games are big—$86 billion in 2013 when you include the fast-growing mobile and social gaming segments (Nayak 2013)—and employ large numbers of highly talented people, such as writers, artists/designers, and computer programmers. If you measure by employee numbers, Canada is the third largest game-producing country in the world (Rudden 2010). The rise of **creative industries** is related to several trends: the growth in cultural production and consumption; the increasing significance of knowledge and creativity to all aspects of economic production, distribution, and consumption; and the growing importance of the services sector. The expansion of creative industries is also linked to the dynamics of knowledge-based, global, and networked economies (Castells 2000a), as well as to the renewed attention given to the importance of location and place as drivers of creativity and innovation. This turn to the creative industries comes in part from the ability of ICTs to allow for greater flexibility in production—such as small-batch production rather than long production runs—as well as the increasingly common global separation of research and development activities from commodity production through global production networks (Ernst and Kim 2002). In industries such as film, television, and games, for example, this has been described as the Global Hollywood model, where concept development and content production are increasingly geographically separated (Miller et al. 2001). The rise of creative industries also reflects the growing significance of design and signification, to everything from urban spaces, offices, retail outlets, cars, mobile phones, and indeed, corporations and governments themselves in an era of "promotional culture" and electronic commerce (Graham 2006).

The rise of creative industries is commonly measured in economic terms. In 2005, Canada's Creative City Network published a series of reports called *Making the Case for Culture*. The first report, titled, *Culture as an Economic Engine*, makes many of these same arguments, highlighting culture's impact on economic growth and jobs, on building linkages between public sector and private foundations, in helping cities become tourism destinations, and noting the link to urban revitalization, attraction of skilled workers, and the creation of spinoff businesses (Dang et al. 2005). The latter point is reinforced in Richard Florida's argument on the importance of the **creative class** for innovation and economic development. In the earliest work that used the concept, the Department of Culture, Media, and Sport (DCMS) in the United Kingdom identified the creative-industries sectors as being worth £112 billion to the UK economy in 1997, accounting for 5 per cent of British GDP (DCMS 1998). Globally, John Howkins (2001) estimated the creative industries to be worth USD $2.2 trillion in 1999 and to account for 7.5 per cent of global GNP (Howkins 2001: 114), although it is important to note that this figure has been questioned on the basis of its inclusion of all research and development as well as the software industries into the creative industries (Cunningham 2002). An American study estimated that the copyright industries accounted for 7.75 per cent of US GDP and 5.9 per cent of national employment (Siwek 2002). In the European Union (EU), where there is certainly no shared definitional understanding among its members as to the nature of the sector, it has nonetheless been observed that employment growth rates in cultural occupations were four times the EU average (4.8 per cent growth between 1995 and 1999, compared to overall employment growth in the EU of 1.2 per cent) and that people working in cultural occupations were almost three times as likely to be self-employed as the EU average (40.4 per cent compared to 14.4 per cent for the EU as a whole), and twice as likely to have a tertiary educational qualification (MKW 2001: 84–6). In a recent international survey of the creative industries and their wider relevance to economic development, the United Nations Conference on Trade and Development (UNCTAD) proposed that this sector now accounts for 7 per cent of global GDP, with estimates of annual growth of 10 per cent or more per annum, with annual growth in some sectors of 20 per cent or more (UNCTAD 2004).

All these figures on the economic significance of the creative industries, however, draw attention to this question: What are the creative industries? The early approaches of DCMS had a dual focus. Creative industries were defined as "those activities which have their origin in individual creativity, skill and talent and which have the potential for wealth and job creation through the generation and exploitation of intellectual property" (DCMS 1998). More pragmatically, the Creative Industries Task Force identified 13 sectors as constituting the creative industries (see Table 7.1).

This list-based approach inherently carried a realistic element where, in the UK case, the inclusion of sectors such as architecture and antiques was based on the institutional alignment of culture with the heritage industry. Garnham (2005) has argued that the linking of arts, media, and IT sectors has involved an unduly optimistic take on more long-standing problems and issues in the arts and cultural sectors, in order to link arts and cultural policy to the more salient—government—domain of information policy. In a different but related vein, Healy (2002: 101) argues that the evidence for transition toward a new economy that has creativity as its "axial principle" is at best mixed, and cautions against "using new economy jargon to give a bullish defence of the arts in economic terms."

The model of creative cities championed by authors such as Landry and Florida has also been challenged. Peck (2005: 763) argues that Florida's creative cities solutions have the potential to destroy what they aim to celebrate, which is culture, uniqueness, and authenticity. He argues that "rather than 'civilizing' urban economic development by 'bringing in culture,' creativity strategies do the opposite: they commodify the arts and cultural resources, even social tolerance itself, suturing them as putative economic assets to evolving regimes of urban competition." Kotkin (2006) argues against urban development strategies aimed at attracting a mobile and footloose creative class, observing that cities where the creative economy is strongest—such

Table 7.1 Creative Industries in the United Kingdom (DCMS study)

Advertising	Interactive leisure software
Architecture	Music
Arts and antique markets	Performing arts
Crafts	Publishing
Design	Software
Designer fashion	Television and radio
Film	

Source: Based on DCMS (1998).

as Los Angeles, New York, and London—are also those where urban inequality is highest. Kotkin also questions the claims that the most creative US cities, such as San Francisco and Boston, are more economically vibrant than cities such as Phoenix and Denver, or that the case has been convincingly made that creativity needs cosmopolitan urban milieus and cannot happen in new suburban communities. In an astute insider's account, Oakley (2004: 72–3) identifies problems with such generic, cookie-cutter models of creative-industries strategies in the UK context: "Rather than trying to understand the difference between the creative economy of Glasgow and that of Cornwall, we currently seem hell bent on trying to replicate a single creative-industries model across the country. It appears that everywhere needs a university, some incubators and a 'creative hub,' with or without a café, galleries and fancy shops."

In *The Flight of the Creative Class: The New Global Competition for Talent* (2007), Florida concedes some of these points. He acknowledges that some of the most creative city-regions of the United States are also among the most unequal, with San Jose; Washington, DC; Raleigh-Durham; Austin; and San Francisco being in the top 10 in both the creativity and inequality rankings (2007: 190). He also addresses the criticism that the "Creativity Index," as developed in *The Rise of the Creative Class, and How It's Transforming Work, Leisure, Community and Everyday Life*, may have been overly focused on the gay population and bohemians and insufficiently focused on other indices of tolerance, such as tolerance of recent migrants, and that the question of openness relates more simply to "'low barriers to entry' for talent . . . from across the entire demographic spectrum" (Florida 2007: 53). In doing so, Florida proposes the need to move from thinking about a creative economy to that of building a creative society. He notes the need for reform of social institutions that harness and extend the benefits of the creative economy to those who may otherwise be excluded, in order to overcome the emergent class divide between those in creative sector and service industry jobs, in a manner parallel to the New Deal that Franklin Roosevelt proposed in the 1930s as a response to the Great Depression:

> The creative economy is the Schumpeterian growth engine of our age, and the socio-economic dynamic that it sets in motion is the modern-day equivalent of the divide Roosevelt faced—the growth of two divergent classes; the creative and service sectors. . . . We need a strategy that is the modern-day equivalent of the New Deal—one that stimulates the creative economic engine while at the same time extending its benefits to a broad base of people. . . . To be effective, a fuller, more creative society will require that a large number of individuals feel they have a real stake in its emergence and expansion. (Florida 2007: 243–4)

Is "Creative Industries" Still a Useful Organizing Concept?

In light of these various critiques of the creative-industries idea, associated policy developments, and related ideas, is it still a useful way to organize the concept of creativity? One influential line of thinking, coming primarily from UK writers such as Nicholas Garnham, questions this. Linking the shift from cultural industries to creative industries to the shift toward a "Third Way," made famous by the British Labour Party under Tony Blair's leadership in the 1990s and early 2000s, Garnham (2005: 20) argues that this discursive shift constituted "an attempt by the cultural sector and the cultural policy community to share in its relations with the government, and in policy presentation in the media, the unquestioned prestige that now attaches to the information society and to any policy that supposedly favours its development." In other words, the cultural sector hoped to gain the kind of unquestioning government support that the technology sector already seemed to have.

Hesmondhalgh and Pratt propose that creative-industries policy discourse constituted a pragmatic turn for cultural policy advocates:

> Cultural policy, previously on the margins in many areas of government, could be seen to be economically relevant in an era when policy was judged primarily in terms of its fiscal rewards. . . . The popularity of such policies was underpinned by an increasing acceptance amongst both neo-liberal conservatives and the postmodernist left that the commodification of culture was not something that could any longer be "resisted" through arts subsidies and other traditional forms of cultural policy. Moreover, creative industries policy could be portrayed as democratizing and anti-elitist, as opposed to the supposed elitism of arts policy aimed at subsidizing cultural production that could not meet its costs through the market. (2005:5)

Hesmondhalgh argues against the term *creative industries*, in favour of the concept of "cultural industries," on the grounds that the concept of creativity is vaguely defined, that creative-industries policy discourse is too imbued with hype about the creative or new economy, and that strategies to promote creative urban spaces may reproduce established inequalities of access and class-based social hierarchies (2007: 144–9).

Referring either to creative or cultural industries may only be a matter of preferred nomenclature. Within the United Nations, for instance, UNESCO (2003) refers to the cultural industries, while UNCTAD (2004) refers to the creative industries, yet both are referring to a broadly similar set of arts, media, and digital content industries. Definitional issues plague the creative-industries debate, in spite of the eminently pragmatic solution offered by the Singaporean Ministry of Trade and Industry, which proposed that cultural industries were engaged in the "upstream" activity of content creation, and the creative industries in the "downstream" activities of distribution and commercialization (MTI 2003). Both definitions and underlying assumptions about these terms exist within EU member states, ranging from the view in Germany that "culture" and "industry" remain antithetical since aesthetic excellence cannot be mass produced, to the more pragmatic Finnish position that mobile phones can be a part of the nation's cultural output. Long-standing differences can also be identified between the French perspective on the arts and culture as integral components of the state itself, as compared to the alleged British tendency to speak of culture only when it is associated with the media and sports (MKW 2001).

The definitional issues run deeper when they are connected to wider debates about the global cultural economy. Authors such as Hesmondhalgh (2007) broadly adhere to an understanding of the media-cultural system that is identified in the political economy of global media, whereby core–periphery relations continue to operate on a global scale. For example, Global Hollywood and its adjuncts in other related industries continue to dominate the flow of capital to creative projects through favourable intellectual property laws while they save money by outsourcing content production around the world (see Miller et al. 2005; Thussu 2006). By contrast, the creative-industries perspective tends to understand the global cultural economy as a positive-sum game in which new entrants create more value for everyone and the globalization of media and creative industries leads to a better and richer society. In this approach, new media and creative-industries production hubs emerge through processes of "creative destruction" in which some established production sites decline and others emerge, but where the geocultural space of media and cultural flows has nonetheless become far more complex than was the case in the second half of the twentieth century (see Curtin 2007; Scott 2004).

Flew argues that the latter tendency, to more complex and globalized cultural flows (Flew 2007), predominates in the twenty-first-century global cultural economy, as it is increasingly infused by the dynamics of the knowledge-based economy, multi-culturalism, diasporic media consumption patterns, and global production networks. Cunningham (2007) has undertaken an extensive documentary search of creative-industries policy statements outside the United Kingdom to defend the view (shared with Garnham) that there is much less of a top-down and more of a tentative and explorative trend to identifying both definitions and policy approaches in the creative-industries policy literature. The Asian case is instructive in terms of how such discourses do, or do not, travel. In their seven-country Asian study, King and colleagues (2006: 191) identify an "uneven geography of flows of creative economy dis-courses." They differentiate between nations where policy-makers drew upon estab-lished Western notions of the creative industries (Singapore, Hong Kong), to those where more localized understandings of the concept have gained prominence (South Korea, Taiwan), to those where the concept either translates into the preservation of existing cultural forms (Japan) or has no policy resonance at all (India). King and col-leagues note that China is a significantly ambiguous case, where the long-established interest in the cultural industries (*wenhua chanye*) on the part of the state sits along-side a demand for growth and international competitiveness in the cultural sectors, so that there is considerable experimentation at the level of city authorities in how to develop the creative industries (*chaungyi gongwe*).

Cunningham and Potts (2007) have proposed a new way of approaching the ques-tion of how to best understand the creative industries. They propose four models of the creative industries:

1. *the welfare model*, where the creative industries are a net drain on the economy (i.e., they consume more resources than they produce), but they receive public subsidy on the basis of their non-economic public good benefits;
2. *the competitive model*, where the creative industries are like other industries and have a neutral effect on the overall economy, albeit with different industry dynamics to other sectors;
3. *the growth model*, where the creative industries are experiencing above-average growth in the economy, and are growth drivers in the way that manufacturing was in the 1950s and '60s and ICTs were in the 1980s and '90s; and
4. *the creative economy model*, where complex new economy dynamics are evolving in the creative industries that have wider resonance throughout the

economy, so that they not only evidence above-average growth (as in point 3), but they also prefigure wider changes in national and international innovation systems.

Cunningham and Potts argue that while the evidence is not fully conclusive—due in part to the difficulties in agreeing on a single definition, as mentioned above—it tends to strongly support points 3 and 4 over points 1 and 2, as measured by indicators such as comparative growth rates, proportionate expansion of the number of firms involved in the creative-industries sectors, and average incomes of those working in the creative-industries sectors. If this is the case, Cunningham and Potts (2007:17) argue that "creative industries are a source of economic growth by their ability to generate and process change in the economic system. Irrespective of the social or cultural value of the creative industries, their economic value properly includes their role in the economic coordination in the face of uncertainty." An implication of this finding is that "cultural policy, traditionally based on model 1, may require some critical retooling to adapt to what appears to be a model 4 world [and] cultural and arts policy may work best as an adjunct to innovation policy." We are seeing some examples of this approach already in the ways that the Canadian government has begun to support new media forms. For example, the Canada Media Fund (CMF) has an "interactive" category and applicants are advised that for an application to be successful, it should include elements of social media and transmedia.

Underpinning these discussions are shifting understandings of culture and its nature, role, and significance. The historical tension between "culture as aesthetics" and "culture as everyday life" has been noted in the historical genealogy of the term (Bocock 1992; Williams 1976). What is now apparent is that there are three further overlays on the concept of culture that have significant implications for thinking about the creative industries:

1. culture as mediated symbolic communication, or the interaction between systems of mass-mediated representation of social reality and the everyday reality of lived experience, much of which occurs through mediated forms (TV and radio, computers, mobile phones, etc.);
2. culture as resource, or the tendency identified by Yúdice (2003: 9) for culture to be "increasingly wielded as a resource for both socio-political and economic amelioration" across a range of fields, and his associated concept of the expediency of culture, or the growing understanding of its role as being involved in the deployment of specific resources to identifiable ends; and
3. culture as policy discourse, or the role identified by Bennett (1998) for cultural policy as a mechanism for intersecting governmental priorities into everyday conduct, which have historically revolved around citizenship and the cultural sense of belonging to a nation, but are increasingly concerned with the management of culturally diverse populations.

The creative industries understood in this way become clearly significant and linked to economic and entrepreneurial issues. We look at these issues in the next section.

CASE STUDY

Toronto as a Creative City

If one were to imagine a case study of creativity, creative cities, and cultural industries in Canada it would be difficult not to look to Toronto. The largest city in the country and the home to some of Canada's most significant cultural enterprises— from professional sports to classical music and ballet to the Toronto International Film Festival— Toronto has fully embraced the notion of the city as an economic and social force. The city now boasts a *Creative City Planning Framework* (see www.creativecity.ca/database/files/library/ creative_city_planning_framework_feb08.pdf) and approved a cultural plan in 2011.[1]

Toronto's efforts to become a creative city predate the 2008 report and include a broad range of initiatives spanning most of the municipal planning, including the 2001 *Economic Development Strategy, The Toronto Culture Plan* (2003), and the 2006 *Imagine a Toronto: Strategies for a Creative City* (available at www.utoronto.ca/progris/imagineatoronto/ home.htm). The latter report, authored by Meric Gertler, Lori Tesolin, and Sarah Weinstock from the University of Toronto's Munk Centre for International Studies, provides an overview of the many faces of a creative city and creative economy policy. For example, the report lists the occupations and employment figures for the creative sector—68,000 by conservative estimate, swelling to almost a million if you use a broader definition, akin to Florida's creative class category; the firms in the creative industries— more than 8600 in 2005; and the creative spaces used by all these people and firms. While noting seven key strengths and lessons from their review of the Toronto situation, the authors conclude that there are serious challenges, including competition from other centres seeking to become creative capitals in their own right, the underutilization of much of the talented workforce, and the lack of a "strategic linked-up approach" to support and coordinate activity in the sector. One of the key players in conversations about creative cities in the context of economic growth, The Martin Prosperity Initiative, hosts a gathering of researchers each June in Toronto. The Experience the Creative Economy (ECE) conference brings together young researchers from around the world for presentations and discussions about the impact of creative industries on city life.

While Toronto boasts many advantages, not the least of which is a large population that provides the audiences for a diverse range of cultural

Economic Drivers of Creative Industries

A mix of economic and cultural factors, with a very significant public policy overlay, has sparked the rise of the creative industries. Factors driving the adoption of creative-industries policy discourse have included the rebranding of arts industries and arts policy to emphasize their significance as wealth-generating sectors (e.g., see Americans for the Arts 2007); the more general identification of creativity as a key driver of growth and innovation in a knowledge-based economy; the implications of digital convergence for bringing together the media and communications, cultural content, and information technology sectors; and the turn toward user-generated content in the context of Web 2.0. Hartley argues that "the idea of the creative industries seeks to describe the conceptual and practical convergence of the creative arts (individual talent) with cultural industries (mass scale), in the context of new media technologies . . . within a new knowledge economy, for the use of newly interactive consumer-citizens" (2005: 5).

A study by the US National Endowment for the Arts reports that "arts participation through media appears to encourage—rather than replace—live arts attendance.

productions, and a wealthy class of donors and foundations providing financial support where needed (opera, ballet, classical music), it would be unfair to suggest that the cultural industries have this prominence and success merely because of their history. It is clear, when you read the various reports and initiatives from this era, that culture is taken seriously in Toronto, at all levels of government, as well as by local firms and citizens. To have culture as a major platform in municipal elections may be a surprise to voters in other Canadian cities, but in Toronto, it is both expected and respected. The results are clear. To quote the 2008 *Creative City Planning Framework*,

> Toronto is riding an unprecedented wave of creative and cultural successes, at every scale. Major new and expanded facilities—ROM, AGO, Royal Conservatory of Music, National Ballet School, Gardiner Museum, Ontario College of Art and Design—designed by world renowned architects. The extraordinary success of Luminato—a major new festival created through private sector vision and leadership. The Toronto International Film Festival—the largest and many argue most influential [film] festival in the world. The Young Centre, the new home of Soulpepper

Theatre Company and a visionary new theatre school, a partnership with George Brown College District. The enormous success of Nuit Blanche Toronto. The groundbreaking adaptive reuse of the Don Valley Brick Works and the Wychwood Car Barns. (Toronto: 2008)

Culture is clearly big business in Toronto, but it is also a vital and fundamental part of life for residents and for the growing number of visitors who come purely to experience the magic of theatre, professional sports, ballet, music, festivals, and film.

Case Study Questions

1. See if you can find a "creative city" strategy for another Canadian (or international) city. Does it look similar to the Toronto one? Are the differences related to intrinsic characteristics of the city? What is the role of new media in the strategy?
2. How do you feel about culture being treated as an "industry" and having a strategy? Does this align with your thinking about culture? How would you enhance and protect culture in your community?

There is a strong relationship between media arts participation and live arts attendance, personal arts performance, and arts creation" (2010: 14). Similar studies have looked at the relationship between downloading of music, even illegal downloading, and attendance at live performances. The link is strong, with heavy downloads strongly correlated to live performance, which is not surprising when you think about it—people are more likely to wish to attend a performance that they have some familiarity with—but it goes against the notion that media are a replacement for live performance. The recent surge in touring by bands of all types reflects the growing awareness that the real money for musical acts is no longer in recordings but in touring and merchandising. Importantly, there is little opportunity to substitute a digital copy for a live show; people want the experience of being there and may even value it more highly in our extremely mediated lives.

The three key economic drivers of creative industries are (1) the rise of the service industry sectors, (2) the emergence of the knowledge-based economy, and (3) the culturalization of the economy as services become increasingly central. Arguably, the major trend in advanced capitalist economies since the 1970s has been the rise of the services industries (e.g., banking, insurance, telecommunications, retail) as the principal source of employment, wealth generation, and innovation. In terms of both employment and the share of total output, the services industries have grown in significance since the Second World War, and especially in the period after 1970. Castells and Aoyama note that, in 1990, services accounted for 75 per cent of employment in the United States and 70 per cent of employment in the United Kingdom, compared to 52 per cent in the United States and 47 per cent in the UK in 1920 (Castells and Aoyama 1994). Taking even more of a macro-historical perspective, Abramovitz and David (2001) observe that the growth in the share of intangible capital—devoted to knowledge production and dissemination on the one hand and education, health, and well-being, on the other—accelerated in the US economy for the whole of the twentieth century and its share of total wealth has exceeded that of tangible capital (e.g., physical infrastructure, equipment, inventories, natural resources) since the early 1970s. Such a trend can be partly explained by the movement of manufacturing to lower-wage economies in developing countries. This is increasingly true of many developing countries: India has established itself as a global leader in IT-based services, while revisions in 2003 to how GDP was calculated in China found that the services sector was twice the size (40 per cent of the Chinese economy) as was previously thought. Moreover, manufacturers are themselves increasingly engaged in the services industries. Giarini (2002) observes that the pure cost of production or manufacturing of goods rarely accounts for more than 20 per cent of the final price and that 70 to 80 per cent of the cost is attributable to service and delivery functions undertaken before manufacturing (R&D, financing), during manufacturing (quality control, safety), selling (logistics, distribution networks), during product and system utilization (maintenance, leasing), and after product and system utilization (waste management, recycling). New media, especially the Internet, is a key component in the creation and delivery of these services, many of which are aspects of the creative economy.

In *The Age of Access: How the Shift from Ownership to Access is Transforming Modern Life*, Jeremy Rifkin (2000) locates the rise of services industries in a wider pattern of transformation of the nature of property and markets that includes the following shifts:

- from markets and discrete exchanges between buyers and sellers, to networks based on continuing relationships between suppliers and users;
- from wealth based on the ownership of tangible assets (e.g., plant, equipment, inventory) to the outsourcing of production and wealth creation based on access to intangible assets, most notably goodwill, ideas, brand identities, copyrights, patents, talent, and expertise;
- from the ownership of goods to the accessing of services;
- from production and sales to customer relationship marketing; and,
- from production-line manufacturing and long product cycles to the Hollywood organizational model of project-based collaborative teams brought together for a limited time.

For Rifkin, these changes together mark the rise of cultural capitalism, developing out of new forms of linkage between digital communications technologies, culture, and commerce:

> More and more of our daily lives are already mediated by the new digital channels of human expression. And because communication is the means by which human beings

find common meaning and share the world they create, commodifying all forms of digital communications goes hand in hand with commodifying the many relationships that make up the lived experience—the cultural life—of the individual and the community. (2000: 138)

The nature of a knowledge-based economy, and the role played in it by networks and clusters, will be explored in more detail in the next chapter. It is nonetheless worth noting several key ways in which the development of a knowledge-based economy has contributed to the rise of the creative industries. The relationship between information, knowledge, and creativity, and the ways in which sustained technological and economic innovation are accompanied by social, cultural, and institutional innovation, is strongly connected to the rise of creative industries. According to Leadbeater, there is an increasingly significant role for knowledge in all sectors in the new economy of the twenty-first century:

In the new economy more of the value of manufactured products will come from the software and intelligence that they embody, and more of what we consume will be in the form of services. Across all sectors the knowledge content of products and processes is rising. . . . Knowledge push and market pull have made know-how the critical source of competitive advantage in the modern economy. (2000: 39)

We can see this phenomenon clearly in the way in which a smartphone, tablet, or computer is made much more valuable by the "ecosystem" of software (apps), content (music, movies, books), and services (texting, email, news, video streaming) that it enables. This doesn't mean that the hardware has no value, only that the value of the hardware is greatly enhanced by the knowledge and creative content that it brings to us.

The concept of knowledge push refers to the growth in outputs in education and scientific research arising from public and private investment, and the ways in which ICTs speed up the production, collection, and dissemination of such research outcomes, enabling more rapid transformation into new products, services, activities, and processes (David and Foray 2002). Market pull factors that promote the rise of a knowledge economy include economic globalization, increased competition, greater sophistication in consumer demand, and the growing importance of intangible assets, such as branding and know-how, to competitive advantage.

The fact that knowledge is not synonymous with information, as Brown and Duguid (2000) point out, also contributes to the rise of the creative industries. At an epistemological level, they distinguish knowledge from information on the basis of the personal dimensions of ownership of knowledge, the difficulties in disembedding knowledge as content from those who possess it, and that knowledge transfer requires a learning process, which takes time and effort. You cannot simply send knowledge to someone in the same way you might send that person information. Arguing that a knowledge economy is different not only from an industrial economy but also from an information economy, Brown and Duguid emphasize how "the importance of people as creators and carriers of knowledge is forcing organizations to realize that knowledge lies less in its databases than in its people" (2000: 121).

Brown and Duguid's observations about the embodiment of knowledge and learning in people and communities is supported by Andy Pratt's (1998) observation that knowledge in the new economy is characterized not only by its weightlessness but also by its embeddedness in people, locations, networks, and institutions, and the related point that cultural activity and employment is growing yet becoming more tied to places, especially cities. Justin O'Connor (1999) links this to new modes of cultural production and consumption among the young (18–35 years old) in urban centres where

- making money and making culture are one and the same activity;
- there is an antipathy to distinguishing between work time and leisure time;
- there is a heavy reliance on informal networks for information and ideas;
- there is an emphasis on intuition, emotional involvement, immersion in the field, and an enthusiast's knowledge of the market; and,
- cultural producers desire to work for themselves and outside the nine-to-five routine.

Finally, the culturalization of economic activity over the latter half of the twentieth century was an important factor in the rise of creative industries. Du Gay and Pryke (2002) and Amin and Thrift (2004) argue that there has been a growing "culturalization of economic life" and that evidence of this can be found in the increasing importance of organizational culture as a key to economic performance; the rise of the services sector, where there is a "more or less direct relationship . . . between one or more service provider and one or more service customer" (Du Gay and Pryke 2002: 3); and the growing role played by cultural intermediaries in sectors such as advertising, marketing communication, and public relations. Hauge and Hrac, in a 2010 paper on the link between indie music and local fashion designers in the Toronto area, provide an excellent example of this process at work. Indie music and indie fashion designers engage in a process of "synergistic collaboration" helping to reach their audiences with unique—and therefore distinctive and sellable—items that are nonetheless authentic by virtue of being anchored to each others' community and, importantly, the place in which they originate (Hauge and Hracs 2010). You want to buy a band T-shirt to support the band and show your support but it is much cooler to have a T-shirt (or shoes, or blue jeans) made by a local designer.

The creative industries also have their own distinctive dynamics, which authors such as Lash and Urry (1989), Rifkin (2000), Lash (2002), and McRobbie (2005) suggest are increasingly becoming the norm in many sectors in the twenty-first-century market economy. Harvard economist Richard Caves (2000) draws attention to core features of these sectors, whether publicly or privately supported:

1. considerable uncertainty about the likely demand for creative product, due to the fact that creative products are "experience goods," where buyers lack information prior to consumption, and where the satisfaction derived is largely subjective and intangible;
2. the ways in which creative producers derive non-economic forms of satisfaction from their work and creative activity, but rely on the performance of more humdrum activities (e.g., basic accounting and product marketing) in order for such activities to be economically viable;
3. the fact that creative production is frequently collective in its nature, which generates a need to develop and maintain creative teams with diverse skills, who often also possess diverse interests and expectations about the final product;

4. the almost infinite variety of creative products available, both within particular formats (e.g., videos at a rental store), and between formats;
5. vertically differentiated skills, or what Caves terms the "A list/B list" phenomenon, and the ways in which producers or other content aggregators rank and assess creative personnel;
6. the need to coordinate diverse creative activities within a relatively short and often finite time frame; and
7. the durability of many cultural products, and the capacity of their producers to continue to extract economic rents (e.g., copyright payments) long after the period of production.

Caves argues that these characteristics suggest major risk and uncertainty about the economic outcomes of creative activities. This insecurity and the need to spread risk and provide insurance to creative producers, is one reason for public funding for some creative activities. Society as a whole benefits from the presence of cultural actors—be they magicians or musicians—every time they perform. In the absence of government support, the risks of this lifestyle, the low pay and frequent unemployment, is born almost entirely by the individual, however. In earlier times, this sort of support might have been provided by a benefactor or patron, but these types of relationships are not nearly as common today.

In commercial terms, risk and uncertainty are also managed through contracts, whereby the various parties involved in the production and distribution of a creative product seek to manage risk and diversify rewards based on the skills and capacities they bring to the project and the need to ensure mutual obligation to meet commitments. The ongoing management of risks, contracts, and creative production processes is a factor that leads to industrial organization in the creative industries, in forms such as publishing, recording, broadcasting, and film companies commissioning production and managing distribution; guilds, unions, and legal arrangements protecting creative producers; and intermediaries such as agents managing the more commercial elements of a career in creative practice.

Policy Drivers of Creative Industries

Creative industries policy has been taken up enthusiastically in a variety of local, regional, national, and international contexts. While there is a long history of policy-making with cultural objectives—Canada advanced a number of initiatives in the 1920s and '30s, including the creation of the CBC (Dorland 1996: x)—the concept as a policy discourse has gained momentum since the early 1990s. For example, shortly after its election in 1997, Tony Blair's Labour government in the United Kingdom advanced policies that led to a variety of national and regional creative industries development strategies as well as some highly influential sectoral mapping documents. The British Council's economic unit, a non-profit advocacy and consulting organization that provides insight and education around cultural affairs even produced a "mapping toolkit" to help local groups better identify their priorities, manage the process, and ensure that the resulting documents were implemented (or at least implementable) in policy (British Council 2010). Since then, some of the policy initiatives that have been undertaken in different parts of the world include

- Canada: Creative-industries strategies have been adopted at both the national and regional level. Some of these date back several decades, including Canadian content (CanCon) incentives and regulations for film, television, and radio as well as subsidy programs for artists and new media productions. The Department of Canadian Heritage works closely with cultural industry actors, ranging from individual artists to major museums and symphonies, and coordinates its activities with Industry Canada. All of the provinces and many cities have their own culture strategies. A good example of this is Calgary, which has an organization called Calgary Arts Development working closely with the city's economic development office and explicitly linking a vibrant artistic sector with benefits in the broader community, claiming that "a strong Creative Industries sector leads to a vibrant culturally rich city that attracts and retains people" (see www.calgaryartsdevelopment.com);
- Sweden: The Knowledge Foundation was established by the Swedish government to examine the role and significance of what it terms "the experience industries," which it identified as constituting 6.5 per cent of the Swedish labour market (Nielsén 2004);
- Australia: A creative-industries strategy was adopted by the Queensland state government in 2001 and there is a proposed national strategy for developing the digital content industries, as well as a pioneering national mapping strategy that identified the sectors as being 50 per cent larger than was previously understood (Cunningham 2006);
- New Zealand: Creative industries are identified as one of the three pillars of the 2002 Growth and Innovation Framework (with biotechnology and information and communication technology);
- Singapore: The Remaking Singapore strategy has sought to redefine the economic base of the city-state around creativity and entrepreneurship (Leo and Lee 2004);
- South Korea: The Korean Wave (*Hallyu*)—or the growing international popularity of film, music, television, games, and entertainment software from South Korea—has been capitalized on by the Korean Ministry of Culture and Tourism, which is investing heavily in developing South Korea's digital content industries;
- Hong Kong: The *Baseline Study of Hong Kong Creative Industries*, undertaken by the Centre for Cultural Policy Research at the University of Hong Kong (CCPR 2003), identified the importance of creative industries to the image or branding of Hong Kong, as well as the opportunities to shift the local economy toward high-value-added services as labour-intensive manufacturing shifted to the Guangzhou (Pearl River Delta) regions of mainland China;
- China: The Eleventh Five-Year Plan, promulgated in 2005, drew attention to the need to develop the creative industries (*chaungyi gongye*) in order to take advantage of opportunities in the digital content sectors, which combine knowledge-economy priorities with the need for enhanced creativity. This is part of a wider set of debates about how China can move from being the

"world's factory" to a "created in China" agenda, which sees China as a leader in intellectual property development (Hartley and Keane 2006; Keane 2004).

Internationally, the United Nations Council on Trade and Development (UNCTAD) (2004) has estimated that the creative industries, which it identifies as lying at the crossroads between the arts, business, and technology, are growing at 10 to 20 per cent annually, or two to three times the growth rates of the global economy overall. UNCTAD has explicitly linked expansion of the creative industries to five trends of globalization:

1. deregulation of national cultural and media policy frameworks;
2. increasing average global incomes, which allow for more discretionary expenditure on arts, cultural, and entertainment products and services;
3. technological changes, particularly the role played by the Internet in the global distribution of digital media content;
4. the global rise of service industries, which place a higher premium on intangible forms of knowledge, and are demand sources for creative-industries outputs in areas such as design, advertising, and marketing; and,
5. the general expansion of international trade, and particularly trade in services.

Creative policy agendas have been even more marked at the municipal and regional levels. Stevenson describes this as the new civic gold rush in urban planning and cultural policy, where strategies are developed for "fostering strategically the cultures of cities and regions . . . [where] culture and creativity have become . . . forms of 'capital' that supposedly can be measured, developed, and then traded in an international marketplace comprised of cities eager to compete with each other on the basis of image, amenity, liveability and visitability" (2004:119–20). Examples of these strategies can be found throughout Europe, the United States, Canada, Australia, New Zealand, and increasingly throughout Asia. The role played by the European Capital (formerly City) of Culture initiative in developing such rebranding of cities has been noted, particularly with the redevelopment of cities such as Barcelona, Glasgow, and Dublin in the 1990s and 2000s (García 2004), and it can also be seen in the competition for cultural leadership between Beijing and Shanghai in China.

The public art boom in the United States has also been linked to the role of cultural infrastructure as a lever of new forms of "place competitiveness" (Weiss 2007). Most visible in this regard is New York City's Times Square. The growing role of public art saw a place that was in a serious downturn get revitalized and begin to flourish "during the '80s and '90s as redevelopment authorities and billboard companies sought to turn Times Square around, non-profits such as the Public Art Fund and Creative Time invigorated the space with Jumbotron videos and installations in empty storefronts. . . . Now the public arts have expanded to include dance, murals sculpture, music, participatory, videos and digital works in the new pedestrian spaces." (Weiss 2007).

In an evaluation of such public art initiatives in cities in the Netherlands such as Amsterdam, Rotterdam, Tilburg, and Utrecht, Mommaas (2004) observes that such creative city strategies have been driven by a heterogeneous—and sometimes contradictory—mix of policy priorities including

- attracting globally mobile capital and skilled labour to particular locations;
- stimulating a more entrepreneurial and demand-oriented approach to arts and cultural policy;
- promoting innovation and creativity more generally, through the perceived interaction between culturally vibrant locales and innovation in other economic sectors;
- finding new uses for derelict industrial-era sites in post-industrial economies; and,
- promoting cultural diversity and cultural democratization, and being more inclusive of the cultural practices of otherwise marginalized social groups.

Two key authors who have influenced these new urban cultural policy agendas are Charles Landry and Richard Florida. Landry (2000: 133) discusses the significance of a creative milieu to the development of creativity in modern cities and regions, which he defines as a combination of hard infrastructure (the network of building and institutions that constitute a city or a region) and soft infrastructure (defined as "the system of associative structures and social networks, connections and human interactions, that underpins and encourages the flow of ideas between individuals and institutions"). Making a case for considering London as a creative city, Landry (2005) proposes that culture constitutes a valuable resource for cities like London in the twenty-first-century global economy in six respects:

1. both the historical artifacts and the contemporary practices of a city's population generate a sense of local belonging and civic pride;
2. cultural activities are linked to innovation and creativity, and the capacity of cities to adapt and innovate is the key to their longevity;
3. the cultural sectors are linked to place image and place competitiveness in their ability to attract international capital investment and geographically mobile skilled workers;
4. culture and tourism are inextricably linked, as tourists seek both the high culture of a city (e.g., museums, galleries, historic buildings) and its popular culture (e.g., clubs, bars, restaurants, street festivals);
5. the growing economic significance of the creative industries in the global economy raises the importance of innovative forms of digital content and of networks that promote innovation and creativity; and
6. culture may be able to promote greater social inclusion and redress economic inequality and social disadvantage, through the ability to provide places where otherwise marginalized groups can engage in collective forms of cultural activity.

Landry provides a reasonable and well-argued rationale for creativity being part of a vibrant city, but who is going to do the hard work of building those shows, that public art, that music and architecture and dance? The people behind creative works—the "creative class", as Richard Florida terms them—are sometimes underappreciated. What will bring them to a city and ensure that they will stay?

Florida (2002) emphasizes the power of place in aiding the rise of the creative class, suggesting that creative people attach great importance to living in diverse, culturally vibrant cities with a distinctive identity and a variety of engaging experiences. He argues that urban centres with a strong wellspring of cultural creativity will thrive because their economic dynamism is driven, not by government incentives to attract new ICT-related industries, but by what he terms the "Three Ts": technology, talent, and tolerance. This is because "regional economic growth is powered by creative people who prefer places that are diverse, tolerant and open to new ideas. Diversity increases the odds that a place will attract different types of people with different skill sets and ideas" (Florida 2002: 249). While writers often focus on the "first tier" of creative cities—places like London, Paris, and New York—Florida uses American cities such as San Francisco, Boston, and Austin as examples of "second-tier" cities that can use their embedded reputations for diversity, tolerance, and openness to become dynamic new economic hubs.

Florida's work has come under increasing scrutiny of late, especially in the post-recession era in which restraint is limiting budgets and racial, ethnic, and class tolerance is seemingly in short supply. The advice to create, in some cases from scratch, a "creative city," is seen as misguided in some instances and far-fetched in others. Many city managers—attending seminars on how to make your locale a creative city—appeared to latch on to the idea as the latest panacea for their ills. Much as being "the next Silicon Valley" has preoccupied those who hope to build technology clusters in their city, being a creative city has inspired would-be creative-policy managers in cities from around the world. Their expectations were probably overambitious.

Another critique, that correlation does not amount to causation, can be found in a number of analyses. It is one thing to find diversity and a high level of cultural production in the same city, but it is another thing to say that the one brings about the other. Critics have argued that Florida's observations were lacking in this regard and questioned the theoretical underpinnings of his approach, wondering if it was just so much wishful thinking. It didn't help matters that a lively cottage industry of Florida "interpreters" sprang up, and media attention inevitably focused on the more celebrated and exceptional cases, downplaying the less interesting elements.

Recent work on **creative cities** has drawn upon some well-established historical lessons. Hall (2000) foregrounds the historic significance of creative cities, in which he includes Athens in the fifth century BCE, Florence in the fifteenth century, London in Shakespeare's time, Vienna in the nineteenth century, Paris between 1870 and 1910, and Berlin in the 1920s. He argues that what characterized these cities was not simply that they were sites of wealth creation and global trade, but that they were also centres of cultural achievement, large-scale migration, intellectual leadership, creativity, and public dissidence. In the same vein, Jacobs (1994 [1961]) argues for the centrality of diverse, mixed-use urban centres, and for the contribution and importance of urban villages not only to the residents' quality of life, but also to economic growth, since diverse and concentrated urban zones encouraged the productive cross-pollination of ideas. In the views of both Hall and Jacobs, cities play a key role in the evolution of ideas and the economy. It is not surprising, once you think about it, that cities—and especially cities with a high level of diversity—are hotbeds for new ideas and new economic growth, if one accepts Jacobs's argument that innovation arises when people encounter difference, whether it is different culture, different needs, or different abilities. Inevitably, this exposes the potent combination of an unfulfilled gap and an unrecognized solution, frequently brought together by people who see things just a little bit differently, perhaps because they are new in the area or because they have brought some new knowledge or object, device, or service with them from elsewhere.

Creative Industries and Evolving Arts and Cultural Policy

Public support for the arts, media, and culture has evolved in the past few decades and can be described as a three-stage process, culminating in something called the "creative industries approach". This is not to say that arts and culture were previously unsupported. Far from it. Instead, this policy evolution is one in which cultural policy and industrial policies—which had existed for a long time, but apart—were seen to be intertwined and even possibly as the same thing.

The first stage sees arts policy as a distinctive activity, associated with publicly subsidized excellence in the production and exhibition of art forms such as opera, orchestras, live theatre, the visual arts, dance, and literature. During this stage, areas that are primarily commercial in their operations, such as the media, are not considered relevant to arts policy, while government-supported activities in these areas—such as public broadcasting and national film production—are understood as being outside the domain of arts policy. Culture in this framework is associated with quality, excellence, national identity, and social improvement: it is by definition outside the economic domain. This approach underpinned the development of arts policy in many countries after the Second World War until the 1980s.

The second stage is cultural policy, which combines the media and other forms of popular cultural content production into an expanded policy domain. Cultural policy has been the dominant mode in many European countries, most notably France (since the 1960s) and UNESCO strongly promoted cultural policy development in newly decolonized developing nations (Flew 2005b, 2007: 174–8). In countries where more traditional forms of arts policy had prevailed, such as the United Kingdom, cultural policy was seen as a way of moving from an idealist conception of the arts that rejected the commercial market, to one that sought to intervene more actively in the cultural industries and markets (Garnham 1987; Lewis 1990; Mercer 1994). Traditional arts policies sought to focus the arts on the challenges presented by establishing greater commercial viability (marketing and audience development, value-chain analysis, and so on), new forms of advocacy such as "arts multiplier" studies,[2] and the opportunities presented by new digital media technologies. In the United Kingdom, cultural industries development strategies gained momentum from Labour Party–controlled local councils in cities like Sheffield and Glasgow that had faced the consequences of deindustrialization in the 1980s. Such approaches understood cultural industries as important in terms of their contribution to national economic development and drew attention to the value-adding possibilities arising from effective policy development, particularly in relation to developing the cultural industries value chain, or ensuring that the products and outputs of artistic creativity were better distributed and marketed to audiences and consumers.

While cultural policy is broader in its remit than traditional arts policy, and identifies the economic contribution of the arts and cultural industries, it nonetheless retains a certain "arts-centredness." To take one example, cultural economist David Throsby proposed a model of creativity that was "centred around the locus of origin of creative ideas, and radiating outwards as those ideas become combined with more and more inputs to produce a wider and wider range of products" (2001: 112). Arguing that "cultural goods and services involve creativity in their production, embody some degree of intellectual property and convey symbolic meaning" (2001: 112), Throsby proposed a "concentric-circles" model of the cultural and creative industries based on their level of cultural and non-cultural inputs and outputs "with the arts lying at the centre, and with other industries forming layers or circles located around the core, extending further outwards as the use of creative ideas is taken into a wider production context" (2001: 113; see Figure 7.2).

The third stage, a cultural industries approach, is distinct from both of the first two approaches. The differences between creative-industries policy and an arts policy or a cultural policy can be seen clearly in comparison (cf. Cunningham 2005). First, as we noted earlier in this chapter, it is difficult to sustain the argument that creativity is the exclusive provenance of the arts; in a knowledge-economy context, it is increasingly seen as integral to sustainability and competitive advantage across a range of sectors (a corollary is that entrepreneurship is no longer seen as the exclusive domain of business but also exists in the policy, social, arts, and cultural sectors [cf. Leadbeater 2000]). Second, drawing on Howkins's (2001) calculation of the value-adding sectors of the creative economy, it is apparent that the significance of the creative and performing arts is dwarfed by that of highly capitalized and globalized sectors such as publishing, software, design, and the audiovisual industries. Howkins argues that, in 1999, the creative and performing arts accounted for only 2 per cent of the market value of the creative industries overall (2001: 114). Third, creative-industries policies tend to work around the relationship between local initiatives and the global cultural economy, whereas the focus of cultural policy has tended to be resolutely national and relatively autonomous from wider economic policy concerns (cf. Flew 2005b). Finally, creative-industries policy draws on the impact of digitization and convergence to argue that such policies should enter into the mainstream of national innovation policies, linking the cultural sectors to the knowledge and service industries, presenting the promotion of creative innovation and the digital content industries as a central part of innovation strategies in the twenty-first-century knowledge-based economy (Cunningham et al. 2004; PMSEIC 2005).

There has been some disagreement with the tendency to simply fold arts policy and arts practice into a creative-industries policy template. McQuire (2001) expresses a concern that the creative-industries model runs the risk of blurring "the slender but significant difference between being market-savvy and being market driven," running the risk of losing sight of "the important role that art has assumed in generating a

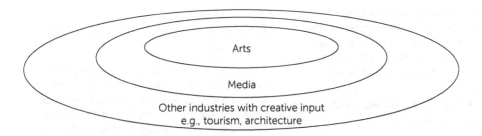

Figure 7.2 Throsby's Concentric Circles Model of Creative Industries

Source: Throsby (2001).

critical space within contemporary culture" (2001: 209, 210). McNamara (2002) notes that the creative-industries model may generate an unduly narrow definition of creativity as that which acquires commercial value, arguing instead for "an expansive rather than a narrowly functionalist approach" (2002: 73). In a more policy-related context, O'Regan wonders whether the rise of creative-industries policy models means that

> ... even in the domain of "creativity", which is a close attribute of "the arts", policy-making is no longer being carried out solely by the arts and cultural institutions who would normally be the main contributors of ideas and managing the process, but increasingly dominated by other actors and agents, such as economic councils, regional governments, and even trade associations and unions. It seemed that "creativity" was now too important to be left up to cultural policy institutions and frameworks. (2002: 23)

Finally, Rossiter questions the linkage of creative industries to intellectual property, arguing that it may too readily have attached these sectors to intellectual property regimes that are "reactionary" and can inhibit new forms of creativity (2006: 108–11). We will return to the issue of intellectual property laws in the digital environment in Chapter 9.

Useful Websites

Innovation Systems Research Network (ISRN) City–Region Initiative
www.utoronto.ca/isrn/city-region_initiative/index.html

This site is a network of scholars from across Canada, hosted at the University of Toronto. The research focus is on the role of cities in the social, cultural, and economic health of a region.

Canada's Creative City Network
http://creativecity.ca

This website is an outgrowth of a simple mailing list started by members of the Vancouver Office of Cultural Affairs and has emerged as a major initiative helping to coordinate activities and research by member cities across Canada.

Centre for Policy Studies on Culture and Creativity
http://cultureandcommunities.ca

The Centre for Policy Studies on Culture and Communities at Simon Fraser University promotes teaching, research, and public outreach on cultural politics, policy, and planning in communities from the local to the global.

Experience the Creative Economy
http://experience.martinprosperity.org

The annual Experience the Creative Economy conference is a forum for emerging scholars engaged in research related to the creative economy. The conference brings together researchers from around the world to share and discuss their research, present their work, receive feedback, refine and develop research methods, and join an ongoing network of collaboration and exchange.

Vancouver Digital Strategy
http://vancouver.ca/your-government/digital-strategy.aspx

Creative economy arguments have been distilled down into specific digital strategies, designed to ensure a city is well-positioned for the digital economy. Accordingly, "the City of Vancouver is developing a digital strategy that will outline both immediate and future areas of opportunity to enhance digital engagement and access, improve infrastructure and support the digital economy to the benefit of people who live, work and play in Vancouver."

Americans for the Arts Policy Research Center: Creative Industries
www.americansforthearts.org/information_
services/research/services/creative_industries/
default.asp

This website provides a national mapping of the creative industries in the United States with a strong focus on the creative and performing arts.

Creative Clusters
www.creativeclusters.com

This is a website for a UK-based, national, creative economy network.

Australia Policy Online: Creative and Digital
http://apo.org.au/creative-economy

This website provides online news and research on the creative industries, innovation and society. It is hosted by the ARC Centre of Excellence for Creative Industries and Innovation www.cci.edu
.au, which is a federally funded Australian university centre for research in the creative industries, with participants from six universities and extensive international collaborative networks.

UNESCO Culture Sector
http://en.unesco.org/themes/
protecting-our-heritage-and-fostering-creativity

This website contains a vast database on global resources on arts, culture, and creative industries developed by UNESCO.

Further Reading

Audience Labour: The Asymmetric Production of Culture, Geoff Glass (2006)
Creativity is not confined to the professionals. In this article, Glass shows some of the economic implications of audience creativity as he updates, expands, and extends Dallas Smythe's argument about audience labour (2001) for a twenty-first-century understanding of the work we engage in when we participate in Web communities such as YouTube or Facebook. The text is available online at www.geof.net/research/2006/
audience-labor.

Handbook of Creative Cities, David Andersson, Åke E. Andersson, and Charlotta Mellander (2011)
A collection of essays, articles, and short practical guides that pulls together key scholarship and policy recommendations, along with important implementation guidelines.

The Geography of Innovation: Twenty-first-Century Cities, David Wolfe (2009)
Wolfe summarizes the key insights and findings from a multi-year study of urban industrial clusters across Canada. Using the data from 15 Canadian cities, this book examines cities as key sites of economic activity—the places where leading-edge innovation generates new ideas, new products, and new industries. Canada, as a highly urbanized

nation (though we may not think of ourselves that way), has a particularly keen interest in policies and programs that can help cities enhance and continue their role as hubs for creativity and innovation.

Creative Cities, Cultural Clusters and Local Economic Development, Philip Cooke and Luciana Lazzeretti (2008)
In this volume, Cooke and Lazzeretti have collected essays from around the world that consider the role of culture in local economic development. For students interested in non–North American approaches to culture and economic development, including Asian and European examples, this collection is a useful starting place.

Under Construction: The State of Cultural Infrastructure in Canada, Nancy Duxbury (ed.), (2008)
The cultural industries are dependent on space, equipment, and most of all, people. This report brings together a national profile of those infrastructure resources and argues that merely updating our museums, galleries, and other cultural buildings is not sufficient, given the challenges ahead, particularly in the area of planning and policies for culture. The text argues that we need to invest in the intellectual as well as the physical capital of culture.

Discussion Questions

1. What are some examples of historic creative cities? In what ways were they (and are they still) significant?

2. What is meant by the concepts of "knowledge push" and "market pull"? What relevance do these have for cultural industries?

3. What new modes of cultural production and consumption in urban centres among young people (18–35 years old) are discussed in this chapter? Why is this shift significant?

4. In what ways are knowledge and information different from each other? Why is this relevant in understanding the knowledge economy and creative industries?

5. What is the significance of the rise of the service industry sectors in the knowledge-based economy and the "culturalization" of the economy?

6. What are the four models of the creative industries proposed by Cunningham and Potts?

7. In this chapter, we noted Healy's (2002: 101) caution against "using new economy jargon to give a bullish defence of the arts in economic terms." Why is this significant?

8. What is the "creative class", as discussed in this chapter? In what ways has the concept been challenged?

9. What are some of the creative-industries policy initiatives undertaken in Canada? How are these seen as affecting cultural industries?

Class Activities

1. Using the website for your city, locate and summarize the statement on cultural industries. Most large cities, and many smaller ones as well, have such a statement. If available, look for the local cultural industries website (e.g., Culture Montréal) or the ministry of culture for the province (e.g., Ministry of Culture, Saskatchewan). Divide into groups and identify the cultural policy in a selected city (see http://creativecity .ca for a number of useful resources, especially the Making the Case series at www.creativecity .ca/publications/making-the-case.php). Identify recent policy statements and consider them in light of the discussion of culture in this chapter. What bias or approach is being taken on the sites you visit?

2. In his March 2009 essay, "The Art of With" (available online at http://bit.ly/ArtofWith), Charles Leadbeater addresses the question of whether or not the Web is creating a more open, participative, and collaborative approach to culture. Read through the article and then engage with your classmates in a debate on the proposition that "the Web is creating a culture more inclined to thinking, working, acting with providing an alternative to the dominant principle of To and For. The principle of with can apply to art and culture as much as work,

politics, and learning. It would draw on a very different tradition of the avant-garde, one that has privileged participation and collaboration as the principles at the heart of modern art rather than shock and separation." Can you think of examples from your own lives? Can you imagine how a local cultural organization (e.g., gallery, museum, orchestra) might transform itself for the "art of with"?

3. Almost anything related to new media is subject to rapid change. Firms come and go, technologies change, and numbers of users, viewers, and creators for new media content and memes change every day. Look up a fact or figure in this chapter and verify whether it remains true today, using online sources. Identify corroborating or supporting sources for your findings. Not only will you have the new facts, but you'll also have an appreciation for how quickly things change and, most importantly, a visceral sense of the way in which the Internet and new media are self-revealing to the diligent and inquisitive scholar. If you discover a fact that needs updating, you can even submit your update (with page reference and new citation) in the form of a rewritten paragraph, to the author: Richard Smith (smith@ sfu.ca). He promises to reply.

1. A debate has arisen among scholars who question the existence of a "creative class." Split into two groups, one in defence of the concept, one critiquing it. Make references to recent commentary as well as examples from your own community.

2. If creative industries are to be treated like any other industry, as an engine of the economy, does this benefit artists and creators by putting them on more equal footing or does it deny their unique contributions to society?

3. Do you think education, and particularly post-secondary education in universities, colleges, and trade schools, should be seen as part of the creative economy?

8

The Global Knowledge Economy

Questions to Consider

- What is meant by the term *globalization*? Why is it significant for new media?

- What is the knowledge economy? In what ways is it important for new media?

- Why is it important to understand the differences between information and knowledge when thinking about investments in research and education in a global knowledge economy?

- How are creativity and culture relevant to understanding new media as fundamental to the knowledge economy?

Chapter Outline

In this chapter, we explore how new media are a powerful force for globalization. We saw in Chapter 2 how the telegraph provided an early version of global communication. Marshall McLuhan observed in the 1960s that television—and specifically television beaming live coverage via satellite—had made the world a global village. But this was a globalization driven by, and managed for, giant corporations and national governments. Most people didn't have their hands on a global mass medium until the rise of the Internet. Digital media and networks have taken that effect to a new level, by making globalization a "live" phenomenon. From Zapatistas to Occupy Wall Street to Idle No More, everyday citizens have been able to project power and influence at a scale that until recently was reserved for a privileged few. In this chapter, we explain the complexity of globalization and review some of the main criticisms of these developments as part of an overall knowledge economy. We examine both technological change and its role in the economy as well as more practical matters such as e-commerce strategies and the role that new media play in disintermediation in order to better understand the forces driving the global knowledge economy. We look at the nature of digital goods and how they have disrupted many industries that relied on the expense of reproducing and transporting ideas (e.g., news, music, movies) and now find themselves without that avenue for extracting value. In this context, we return to some of the themes on creativity from Chapter 7 and examine the creative economy more closely from a business perspective, focusing on topics such as technological innovation and the innovator's dilemma.

The Global Knowledge Economy

Economic activity—making things, providing services, and buying and selling—occurs at a global level these days. We experience this every time we purchase something manufactured in China, consume food grown in Mexico, or receive a service call from India. Canada is particularly active in the global economy, with over 45 per cent of our GDP accounted for by exports (Trading Economics 2012). As with many developed countries, knowledge—often embedded in services—is a key component of those export and import numbers. This buying and selling of knowledge is called the global **knowledge economy**. Importantly, a knowledge economy is different from an information economy because knowledge is learned over time and enables action. Knowledge cannot simply be purchased, so for a knowledge economy to succeed, it is important to invest in research and education.

The global knowledge economy arose from the convergence of three developments: the ubiquity of new media and globally networked ICTs, the ongoing and complex process of globalization, and the growing use of knowledge as a tool for wealth creation. We will look at each of these developments in some detail in the next few pages.

The first force behind the growth of the global knowledge economy, the increasingly ubiquitous nature of new media and globally networked ICTs, will be familiar to almost all citizens of the modern world. New media are central to globalization because they constitute the borderless technological and service-delivery platforms streaming the images, information, finance, and communication that make up a globalized world. New media industries are also leaders in the push for corporations to expand and integrate themselves globally. Moreover, the new media provide informational content and images of the world through which people make sense of events in distant places. The centrality of new media to globalization derives not only from their role as communications technologies that enable the international distribution of messages and meanings, but also from their perceived role in weakening the cultural bonds that tie people to nation-states and national communities (Flew 2007).

Earlier media forms such as radio and television, and even comic books, were similarly criticized for their roles in cultural assimilation and cultural imperialism (Dorfman and Mattelart 1984). It should be noted, however, that new media are not *necessarily* globalizing forces, or more precisely, they have local, regional, and national manifestations and implications as well. Some aspects of this have been discussed in our review of the creative industries, and Canadian support for new media in this context stems mainly from two impulses: to provide a place for local employment and capital accumulation within a larger global economy, and as a way of presenting Canadian perspectives and culture to that global knowledge economy. Government support for knowledge industries, and specifically that subset of the knowledge economy known as the new media industries, often has twin objectives: economic and cultural. So, while new media certainly are implicated in the weakening of cultural bonds, and have been criticized in this context, it is not necessary to see this as an essential aspect of them as media forms.

Globalization is the second development that has contributed to giving us a global knowledge economy—it is an *omnibus* term used to describe and make sense of a collection of interrelated processes, including the ever-increasing international flows of people, money, and information in support of trade, production, finance, and cultural industries. Think of the foreign workers, the presence of foreign goods, the importance of foreign investment in today's world. This isn't just a phenomenon in Canada but everywhere. Globalization can also be seen in the increasing reliance on international standards, rules, laws, and practices for everything from sizes of batteries to copyright laws to USB connectors to shipping containers. It has even given rise to global anti-globalization forces, and protest movements, such as Occupy Wall Street or Idle No More, that spill across national or regional borders. The United Nations and its many subsidiary and ancillary organizations, such as UNESCO or the World Health Organization (WHO), are also entities of globalization. Even the global war on terror—launched following the 9/11 attacks on the World Trade Center and the Pentagon—can be seen as part of globalization.

New media technologies, firms, and practices are very much a part of this process of globalization. A device such as a smartphone or a tablet is designed for a global consumer base. For example, smartphones and tablets have inputting methods that, directly out of the package, accommodate different writing methods and languages. They facilitate—by design—the creation, circulation, and consumption of images, sounds, and ideas from anywhere. International business people or backpackers are able to tweet their location, their lunch, and their love letters from any place at any time.

Extensive debates are ongoing about the degree to which globalization has become the central feature of our times, with positions ranging from those described as globalization enthusiasts (e.g., Friedman 2005) to others who are more skeptical of the significance of trends associated with globalization (e.g., Hirst and Thompson 1996). Overlaid on these analyses of the empirical evidence for and against globalization are debates between those who believe that globalization should be welcomed (Legrain 2002) and those who are concerned that it erodes local communities and identities (Barber 2000). Among critical theorists and activists, there are those who argue that the rise of global capitalism has reconfigured the entire terrain of political struggle (Hardt and Negri 2000, 2005), and those who argue that globalization is not something qualitatively new, but it is the latest stage in the development of capitalism as a world system (Callinicos 2001; Curran and Park 2000).

Economic globalization is arguably more established than political, legal, or cultural globalization. As Held and colleagues (1999) and Held and McGrew (2002, 2003) conclude, globalization is neither completely new nor has it eliminated the significance of nation-states and national sovereignty. Despite these caveats, there have been real and substantive changes in the relationship between political globalization and modern nation-states over the past three decades. This has meant that effective political power is increasingly shared and bartered across agencies at local, national, regional,

Michael Hardt and Antonio Negri

Michael Hardt and Antonio Negri's book *Empire* in 2000 would not have seemed like a likely bestseller, given that it was penned by a little-known American left-wing academic and a jailed Italian dissident. Their book looks at the way in which empires operate today, the role of the common person—Marx's proletariat—in society, and suggests that within the challenges of empire and the coordination and sense of common purpose among the masses—what they call the Multitude—there exists potential for a revolution with humanist and communist principles.

When interviewed by Ian Vulliamy for *The Observer* in July 2001, Hardt noted that global capitalism, like the Internet, has no centre: "The organising principle is similar to the principle of the Internet—it links the Internet age to the way power functions as a distribution network.

Even the North–South divide doesn't work—there is Third World in the First World and First World in the Third World—Brazil is the ideal example" (Vulliamy 2001).

Hardt and Negri's book took on considerable importance in part because it came out right at the time of some of the first global protests—in Seattle, Gothenberg (Sweden), and Prague (Czech Republic)—linked to the bilateral agreements and international treaties enforcing the rules that enabled global capital flows and trade.

Hardt and Negri's optimism about the decline of empire—they see the postmodernized global economy as containing the seeds of its own destruction—may have been premature, but their analysis has provided over a decade's worth of fodder for discussion among both left- and right-wing scholars and activists about the ways in which globalization is not simply a force of oppression but may also be a pathway to freedom.

and international levels, particularly with the emergence of supranational legal frameworks and authority structures. Many of these relate to new media, including copyright agreements that create or are creating global marketplaces for digital content and common legal frameworks for the protection from and prosecution of those who infringe on the intellectual property rights of creators. (We discuss this in more detail in Chapter 9.) As a result, citizens of all nation-states increasingly find themselves enmeshed within "overlapping communities of fate" (Held et al. 1999: 81). Examples of these communities go well beyond new media topics and include matters as diverse as the impact of environmental degradation on climates, drug trafficking, global terrorism, immigration controls, arms trading, and use of non-renewable resources.

In the cultural sphere, one of the complicating factors in these debates is the duality of culture as both a form of lived and shared experience and as mediated symbolic communication. Much of the discussion of cultural globalization relates to the latter, though Anthony Smith believes that the outcome of common access to global media systems will not be the emergence of a single world culture:

If by "culture" is meant a collective mode of life, or a repertoire of beliefs, styles, values and symbols, then we can only speak of cultures, never just culture; for a collective mode of life, or a repertoire of beliefs, etc., presupposes different modes and repertoires in a universe of modes and repertoires. Hence, the idea of a "global culture" is a practical impossibility . . . the differences between segments of humanity in terms of lifestyle and belief-repertoire are too great, and the common elements too generalized, to permit us to even conceive of a globalized culture. (1991: 171)

So far, we have seen how new media technologies and globalization have contributed to the growth of the global knowledge economy. In the next passages, we look at the third development, how ideas are turned into commodities, and how it contributes to a global knowledge economy.

In a knowledge economy, ideas and intangible assets are more valuable than tangible physical assets. In the present day, "the economy is more strongly and more directly rooted in the production, distribution, and use of knowledge than ever before" (Howells 2000: 51). This transition has not only occurred in the so-called post-industrial economies, as the "information society" theories of the 1960s and '70s believed (see Castells 1999 for a critique), but it has been a global phenomenon, particularly driven by the intersection of international economic competitiveness with direct foreign investment and the use of globally networked ICTs. The growth of call centres and software development houses in Bangalore, India, is a good example of this phenomenon. In Canada, New Brunswick leveraged its bilingual population and relatively low wages to become a major site for outsourced service work, often housed in call centres, for companies across North America. David and Foray argue that the global nature of the knowledge economy is indicated by the extent to which "disparities in the productivity and growth of different countries have far less to do with their abundance (or lack) of natural resources than with the capacity to improve the quality of human capital and factors of production: in other words, to create new knowledge and ideas and incorporate them into equipment and people" (2002: 9).

David and Foray observe that the rise of a knowledge economy is both a historical trend of the past hundred years and a process that has accelerated since the early 1990s. In an historical sense, the growth of intangible capital (encompassing both knowledge production and dissemination on the one hand, and education, health, and well-being on the other) has been accelerating in the economy for the whole of the twentieth century and into the twenty-first century, and its share has exceeded that of tangible capital (e.g., physical infrastructure, equipment, inventories, natural resources) since the early 1970s (cf. Abramovitz and David 2001). They attributed the more recent acceleration of knowledge production to

- the growing diversity of sources from which new knowledge is accessed (e.g., users as a source of innovation);
- the role played by networked ICTs in accelerating the diffusion of new knowledge and the possibilities for collaboration;
- the ways in which ICTs enable new forms of codification of once-tacit knowledge through knowledge-management systems; and,
- the importance of knowledge sharing through cross-institutional and cross-sectoral knowledge communities, of which the open-source software movement (discussed in Chapter 9) may be one of the most globally significant.

Batterham (2000) identifies the differences between the old paradigm of economic development, based on the more efficient use of existing physical resources, and the new paradigm, based on continuous innovation and the more effective deployment of intangible (weightless) capital in the new, knowledge-based economy in the terms set out in Table 8.1.

Table 8.1 The Old and New Paradigms of Economic Development

Old paradigm	New paradigm
1. Key factors: capital, resources, and labour	1. Rising importance of knowledge and creativity
2. More efficient application of existing resources	2. Addition of knowledge-based industry and knowledge-based parts of resource activity
3. Predominant focus on national markets	3. Firms going global and subject to global competition
4. Primary focus on cost competitiveness	4. The imperative to deliver superior value to customers through innovation
5. Relatively long product cycles	5. Trend to shorter product cycles
6. Getting more out of existing businesses	6. Creating new businesses and a new premium on risk-taking and entrepreneurship
7. Reliance on traditional capital sources, such as loans and stock market equity	7. Venture capital as central to new business development
8. Focus on individual achievement	8. Shift to strategic alliances and other forms of collaboration, such as networks and clusters

Source: Adapted from Batterham (2000: 10).

Hodgson (2000: 93) argues that the shift from a manufacturing economy to a knowledge economy, or one that is "relatively less 'machine-intensive,' and more and more 'knowledge-intensive'," has the following features: both production and consumption processes are becoming increasingly complex and sophisticated while at the same time increasingly advanced knowledge and skills are being required in many processes of production. Simultaneously, consumers also face increasingly complex decisions about evaluating the quality of goods and services on offer and there is an increasing reliance on specialist or idiosyncratic skills. Not only that, the use and transfer of information is becoming increasingly important in economic and social activities and uncertainty is increasingly central to all aspects of economic and social life.

Hodgson ultimately prefers the concept of a learning economy to that of a knowledge economy, since the latter implies a fixed stock of knowledge to be distributed throughout a society, whereas "in a complex and evolving, knowledge-intensive system, agents not only have to learn, they have to learn how to learn, and to adapt and create anew" (2000: 93).

Electronic Commerce

One important aspect of how new media have affected business has been through **electronic commerce (e-commerce).** While electronic transactions preceded the rise of the Internet, the latter dramatically broadened the scope for electronic transactions through features such as

- its open, non-proprietary access protocols based on TCP/IP;
- the development of the Web and its standard coding system based on HTML;

- ease of access to a diverse range of websites using web browsers and search engines;
- falling costs of personal computing and the growing ease of Internet access from the workplace or home; and
- the ways in which new media technologies based on the Internet allow for both one-to-many communication and direct one-to-one interaction (OECD 1999: 28–9).

Electronic commerce can take a variety of forms, depending on the degree of digitization of (1) the product or service sold; (2) the transaction process; and (3) the nature of the delivery agent or intermediary. There are varying degrees of physical or electronic commerce in transactions. For example, buying a book through a website (such as Amazon.ca or Abebooks.com) is not pure e-commerce unless one purchases an e-book, because although the agent and the process are both digital, the final product is delivered through physical transportation systems. By contrast, buying software online, acquiring a song from the Apple iTunes site, or purchasing an airline ticket online may constitute pure e-commerce, as the product, process, and agent all exist in digital form. It is also important to distinguish between business-to-business electronic commerce (B2B), which has been estimated to account for 80–90 per cent of all electronic commerce transactions (Lovelock and Ure 2002; OECD 1999) and business-to-consumer electronic commerce (B2C), to which the bulk of the discussion below is devoted, but which is not necessarily at the core of e-commerce transactions (see Figure 8.1).

It has become a commonly held view that businesses have no choice but to develop an e-commerce strategy. Andy Grove, the former chair of Intel, said that by the mid-2000s, all companies would become Internet companies, or they would not be companies at all (*The Economist* 1999). The implicit line of reasoning in Grove's remark suggests the competitive advantages that accrue to companies from harnessing the

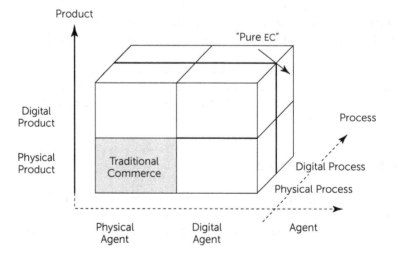

Figure 8.1 Dimensions of E-commerce

Source: Turban et al. (2000: 5).

Internet are of such significance that neglecting this aspect of operations would leave companies highly vulnerable to losing market share in an increasingly volatile economy. The benefits to business of developing an e-commerce strategy have been identified as being the following: the expansion of the available marketplace from geographically defined, local markets to national and international markets and the reduction of the costs of creating, processing, distributing, storing, and retrieving information, both within the organization and between the organization and its clients (both suppliers and consumers).

Companies can also benefit from the ability to develop highly specialized businesses, and they are able to target particular niche consumer groups while at the same time enjoy a reduction of inventory and overhead costs, through a move to toward "pull-type" supply-chain management, where processes begin with customer orders and enable just-in-time (JIT) production. Importantly, they are also better positioned to customize products and services to client and consumer needs, providing competitive advantages based on "first-mover" advantages and brand loyalty (Turban et al. 2000: 15).

For consumers, the advantages of e-commerce include the ability to undertake transactions 24 hours a day—all year round, from any networked location—for a vastly increased range of products and services. People can also compare prices online and find the lowest-cost provider with minimal search cost. Consumers also enjoy quick delivery of products and services, particularly if they are in digitized form and the ability to interact with other consumers in virtual communities, and exchange ideas and experiences. With the rise of sites such as eBay, consumers are also able to participate in virtual auctions (Turban et al. 2000: 15–6).

One of the most important implications of electronic commerce for distribution has been related to the processes of **disintermediation** and "reintermediation" (see Figure 8.2). In the manufacturing sector, the relationship between producers and consumers has traditionally been mediated through a supply chain that includes wholesalers, distributors, and retailers. Similarly, in the creative industries, the relationship between the creators and consumers of content has been mediated through those responsible for aggregating, promoting, marketing, and distributing content for final reception by consumers, giving these sectors their characteristic hourglass structure of many producers, many consumers, but a distributional filter that operates through a small and concentrated number of distributors (Hesmondhalgh 2007: 18–24). One consequence of the rise of both the Internet and new media has been disintermediation, where a more direct relationship emerges between the creators/producers of content, products, or services and their consumers. Another outcome has been reintermediation, where intermediary functions remain, but are conducted by organizations whose operations are driven by the new e-commerce marketing logics, such as a shift toward partnership with consumers, "permission" advertising, product and service customization, and multiple modes of communication with consumers (Shenton and McNeeley 1997; Turban et al. 2000).

The whole concept of e-commerce suffered a significant setback with the collapse of the NASDAQ share price index in 2001 (the US-based index for high-technology shares). The collapse brought with it the sense that e-commerce and dot-com enterprises had been seriously oversold and that most lacked a credible business plan to match their widely hyped ambitions. The rise and fall of the NASDAQ provides an illustration of the possibility of dramatic reversals of fortune for companies operating in this environment within a relatively short period of time (as shown in Figure 8.3).

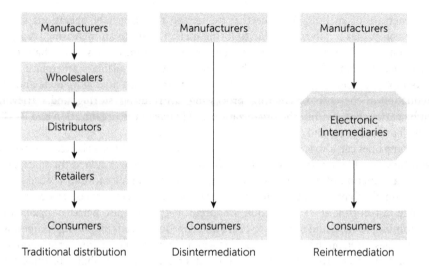

Figure 8.2 Disintermediation and Reintermediation
....

Source: Turban et al. (2000: 64).

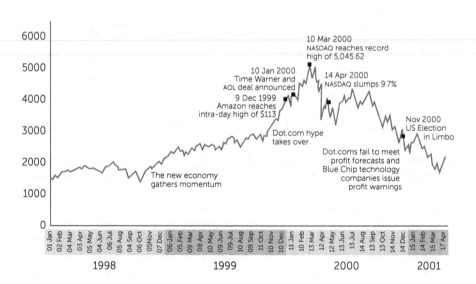

Figure 8.3 Rise and Fall of the NASDAQ, 1998–2001
....

Source: ABC Four Corners 2001, www.abc.net.au/4corners/dotcom/graphs/default.htm.

Volatility in the shares of new media and information and technology companies persisted throughout the decade, with many companies experiencing dramatic
price increases and then steep declines. Apple, for example, was at one time thought
to be almost worthless—prompting the claim by Michael Dell that if he owned the
company he would close it down—and then grew, by the summer of 2012, into the

most valuable company in the world before dropping almost 30 per cent from those highs by the end of the year. We will explore in more detail the forces at work in such volatility—including the perceived need to continuously update and innovate in order to remain valuable—later in this chapter.

Some of the companies that have been most successful in the 2000s—such as Amazon, eBay, and Google—have been able to leverage the advantages of what Anderson (2006) terms the **long tail**. Anderson argues that digitization of content has completely transformed the distributional models of the media and entertainment industries, as the availability of content is no longer constrained by distributional bottlenecks such as theatres, radio, television channels, and shelf space in bookstores and record outlets. This challenges the assumption that only media content with mass appeal is profitable, as it reveals that when a wider range of content is made more accessible through online distribution and retail, consumer tastes and preferences for books, movies, music, and so on are far more diverse and niche-oriented than the media and entertainment industries have traditionally assumed. With traditional constraints of geography and scale being eliminated, it is niche content that accounts for a rapidly growing proportion of total online sales, meaning that "popularity no longer has a monopoly on profitability" (Anderson 2006: 24). Digital production, distribution, and consumption enables an economic model that is not as dependent on blockbuster movies, bands, or books. We have recently seen the rise of a range of small creators—from indie game studios to self-published authors—who are able to connect with an audience and sell in sufficient numbers that ensures a living, if not wealth and fame.

Information and Knowledge

The nature and significance of information and knowledge has long been a problematic question in economics. Mainstream economic theories of perfect competition have assumed (to simplify) that both producers and consumers have perfect information and behave accordingly in economic markets. Since this is obviously not true, an extensive literature has emerged on the economics of imperfect information and related questions, such as information asymmetries (i.e., when sellers know more than buyers or when some agents have privileged access to information that gives participants market advantage [Akerlof 1970]). There is also a tradition of information economics, associated with writers such as economist Don Lamberton, which asks what it means when information is considered not simply as a component of how markets operate, but as a form of capital that "structures the knowledge base of the economic system" (Potts 2003: 477). As Lamberton noted in an early essay, "identifying information with the cost or time of transmission, and not with the value of a message, may be misleading" (1971: 10).

Lamberton's concerns about thinking of information as a form of capital that is central to the structure of all economic relations, rather than simply a factor in market exchange relations, have become more pressing for several reasons. Information as capital is important when considering how innovation has been a catalyst to economic growth and corporate competitive strategy, and it also figures into the way in which ICTs have become more central to the economy as a whole, and as knowledge flows proliferate with the emergence of the Internet (David and Foray 2002; Giddens 1998; Haltiwanger and Jarmin 2003; Lamberton 1999; OECD 2003). Two research questions have been central to these discussions. The first concerns the nature of **digital goods** in the new economy. Quah defines digital goods as "bitstrings, sequences of 0s and 1s, that have economic value," which includes "ideas and knowledge, computer software, digital images, music, databases, video games, blueprints, recipes, DNA sequences [and] codified messages" (2003: 289, 293). He argues that digital goods possess five characteristics that challenge conventional understandings of the economics of goods and services. They are

1. non-rivalrous: use by one agent does not degrade its usefulness to other agents;
2. infinitely expansible: every user can make and distribute as many copies of the digital good as they choose;
3. discrete: they show indivisibility, so that only the whole digital good contains all of its value (i.e., the whole of a film has value over and above that of its component parts);[1]
4. a-spatial: they exist in cyberspace, and are both everywhere and nowhere on the digital network simultaneously; and
5. recombinant: they arise in part from drawing together existing elements in new forms that have features that were absent from the original, parent digital goods.

These features have profound implications for those who founded their businesses on scarcity of information and the challenges of moving it around—i.e., the media industries in particular. As Clay Shirky (2010) points out, when anyone can press a button that says, "Publish!" there are considerable implications for publishers/producers, whether they are in the newspaper, book, music, or film business. Digital goods are infinitely and easily copyable—given this, it is not surprising that people are inclined to share them, as it would seem churlish to not share something if it costs almost nothing to do so.

Recombinant forms of new media are particularly popular, since they are so easy to create and engage an audience's desire to participate, but without the training required to make things from scratch. In this vein, you see the "mash-up" type of content that is so popular on video-sharing sites such as YouTube, or even the silly captions over pictures of cats (LOLCats) on http://icanhascheezburger.com (some recent examples include "Clark the talking dog," "Big Bird" and "McKayla is not impressed"). This return of the animated GIF—a digital form whose time seemed to be long in the past—has spawned sprawling and spiralling variations on a theme, with specialized sites and subsites making use of tools such as Tumblr to aggregate and curate collections.

While LOLCats might seem like a trivial and ridiculous example, as Shirky (2010) notes, this type of engagement with media is far different from the passive stance often taken with broadcast media. Importantly, these low-stakes sharing sites can become a gateway to fuller and richer creative activities. As a growing number of people are discovering, YouTube offers simple editing capabilities, annotations, and the ability to add a soundtrack (importantly, a legal, copyright-free, or licensed soundtrack), and they are also learning that if you can watch YouTube videos, you can *make* YouTube videos.

For the firms that host such DIY content sites, the rewards can be enormous. When the whole world can participate, then they benefit from the potential for selling advertising alongside that content. Importantly, the content is provided for free by the users. Some of that "free" content is so popular—for example "Charlie bit my finger" had more than 500 million views as of January 2013—that the (optional) revenue-sharing model provided by the hosting company has resulted in significant financial rewards for the creators (Sibary 2011).

A second key set of issues concerns the rise of **endogenous growth** theory or "new growth economics." Economists from Stanford University, Paul Romer (1994, 1995, 2007) and Paul David (1985, 1999), have argued that technological change and economic growth need to be seen as intrinsically connected, in contrast to the conventional approach that treats technology as an "exogenous variable" to growth models. An exogenous variable is something that has influence on a system—such as an economy—but originates from outside the system. Romer (2007) proposes that "economic growth springs from better recipes, not just from more cooking"; in other words, that it arises not from the discovery of new resources (e.g., labour, capital, physical resources) but, rather, from those occasions where "people take resources and rearrange them in ways that are more valuable." Growth, according to this way of thinking, is possible from internal (endogenous) activities. Romer argues that the central economic change of the past two decades has been the shift from people being primarily involved in the production of physical objects to the discovery and design of ideas and new ways of doing things, so that "the whole economy will start to look like Microsoft, with a very large fraction of people engaged in discovery as opposed to production" (1995: 70). David (1999) argues that it may take up to a generation for the longer-term economic impacts of new technologies to become apparent, not least because the nature of what needs to be measured changes as the structure of economic production and consumption changes, and as growth becomes increasingly driven by the hard-to-measure sectors of services and information.

The Internet makes many of these issues more pressing, as it is the largest repository of information gathered through a networked infrastructure in human history. It is estimated that there were about 45 billion web pages in existence on more than 108 million websites in February 2007 (Boutell.com 2007), all of which may lay claim to providing at least some information that is of interest to someone. Not long afterwards, in July 2008, Google engineers announced that their indices contained a trillion unique URLs (pages).[2] Even that is an underestimation by a significant degree since much of the Internet is behind authentication systems. So, for example, Facebook, which has a billion users, is partly "dark" to Google's searches because of privacy settings. More importantly, a growing part of "the Web" is not really represented in the form of pages but in the form of smaller chunks of information, known as "tweets" (Twitter), "status updates" (Facebook), and "pins" (Pinterest), not to mention photos on Flickr and Instagram, and items for sale on eBay and Craigslist. These little snippets of information are sometimes much more useful to people than a possibly outdated web page, because they are anchored to events, places, transactions, and news.

The Internet has also begun to bring forth more than just the professional knowledge embedded in the people who work in large organizations. Once it becomes

CASE STUDY

YouTube

Over the course of the 2000s, far more people acquired access to high-speed broadband Internet connectivity than in previous decades. In many cases, this was not due to their home service subscription decisions but rather to the availability of high-speed broadband access in workplaces, schools, universities, and other institutions. One consequence of the advent of high-speed broadband Internet was that access to audiovisual content became much more readily available, yet major film studios and television networks were reluctant to put much of their content online. The two main reasons for this were concerns about piracy and copyright infringement, and the potential for "channel conflict" with their traditional distribution sites, such as cinemas, video and DVD outlets, and television channels, from which the bulk of their advertising revenue was derived. Yet it has been increasingly apparent that users are keen to access their media content through personal computers, particularly when they are able to rate, reuse, and distribute this content among their peers. It was in this context that YouTube (www.youtube.com) was launched.

YouTube is a video-sharing site, where users can upload, share, rate, comment on, and distribute audiovisual material. Created in February 2005, it was ranked by *Time* magazine as the "Invention of the Year" for 2006, and

was subsequently acquired by Google for USD $1.65 billion. YouTube was a disruptive innovation in the sense discussed by Bower and Christensen (1999), because its developers determined that the Internet had made it far less costly to distribute audiovisual content, but this was not being exploited by established film and television industries because they had to recoup the high costs of production of their content through managed distribution via their existing channels. Drawing on the pro-am revolution identified by Leadbeater and Miller (2004), we can see that the production costs of making video had fallen, but that this was not recognized at the higher levels of the film and television industries, so YouTube encouraged the multitude of video producers to put their material up for distribution through the site.

The rise of user-generated content has sparked both criticism and praise. José van Dijck's 2009 article, "Users Like You: Theorizing Agency in User-Generated Content," suggests that we have insufficiently theorized the contributions that millions of amateurs and semi-professionals are making in the media landscape. As he points out, "agency" (the independence of action and reaction that individuals exhibit in their consumption of media) has until recently been tied to the medium being examined. So, for example, it is different to watch a film than it is to sit down in front of the television, and that in turn is different from listening to the radio. As the audience becomes users and even "prosumers"

possible for people to share the ambient or embedded knowledge that they have about the things for which they care, they are often willing or even excited to do so. In his examination of what happens when people have access to a **cognitive surplus** (spare time, used effectively) and a way to share their thoughts and ideas, Shirky (2010) reveals the power of Internet-connected hobbyists. A particularly telling example is his rough calculation of the number of person hours represented by Wikipedia (approximately 100 million, apparently) compared to the number of hours spent watching television (200 billion hours annually, in the United States alone). In fact, Americans watch 100 million hours of advertising on an average weekend (Shirky 2010). Even a small percentage of this, switched from watching television to participating on the Internet, can have profound implications. Not all this spare time is spent well, but some of it is dedicated to online discussions, updating web pages, or "produsers"—implying considerably more potential for action and independence—we need to reconsider many of our theoretical positions. Nevertheless, it is too simplistic to deem the television viewer as passive and the person with a YouTube account as active. A more nuanced perspective needs to be put forward, and, in particular, we need to take into account the fact that—for most participants, at least—this participation is wholly voluntary and unrewarded.

It was estimated that over 4 billion hours of video are watched each month on YouTube and its audience was about 800 million people worldwide each month in 2012 (YouTube 2013), with younger people (median age of 33) comprising a large majority of users.

YouTube also serves an increasingly important function as a feedback loop into the mainstream media. In January 2013, the most-viewed postings on the site were music videos: Psy's "Gangnam Style" had 1.2 billion views, followed by Justin Bieber's "Baby" (822 million views), and Jennifer Lopez and Pitbull's "On the Floor" (641 million views). Homemade video continues to have a place, however: as we noted, "Charlie bit my finger" garnered over 500 million views.

Copyright infringement remains an ongoing issue for YouTube. In January 2013, coincident with Internet Freedom Day, and just before Martin Luther King Day in the United States, King's famous "I have a dream" speech was repeatedly subject to "Take down" notices (issued as part of a claim under the Digital Millennium Copyright Act, or DMCA, part of the US legal structure for online copyright enforcement) because of legal action by King's descendants.

In the case of some of the most popular material uploaded to the site, such as excerpts from TV shows like *The Simpsons* and *South Park*, this proliferation is clearly more of an issue for the owners and distributors of the content—such as Viacom and News Corporation—than for its producers, who have long accepted that their material is accessed virally through the Internet community and forms part of an overall marketing and sales strategy.

Case Study Questions

1. Have you created a YouTube video with an eye to having it "go viral"? Were you motivated by the potential money to be made? Did you even select the box that allows your video to participate in YouTube's revenue-sharing program?
2. *The Innocence of Muslims*, a controversial movie made in the United States, caused YouTube to be blocked in several countries and is said to have sparked large, and sometimes violent, protests around the world. Does YouTube have a social responsibility to manage the content on its site? Does it do a good enough job, in your view?
3. Some schools block or filter access to YouTube as a way to "protect" their students. Should schools be held accountable for what students view on YouTube while they are on school grounds or using school networks?

doing research, and many other things that contribute to a substantial change in our information and knowledge environment.

Not every commentator is excited about the prospects of this mass participation or convinced of the quality of the results. Andrew Keen, in his 2007 book, *Cult of the Amateur: How Today's Internet Is Killing Our Culture*, takes aim at the demise of professionalism and the inevitable (in his view) dilution of quality journalism, music, and even movies in the face of a deluge of poorly conceived and executed amateur work. Nicholas Carr posed a provocative question in a 2008 essay when he asked, "Is the Internet making us stupid?" Carr followed up on that theme with a book, *The Shallows* (2011), in which he discusses the challenge presented by the prevalence of poor-quality online information combined with people's inability (or lack of time) to sort the wheat from the chaff.

Interestingly, William Leiss made this same argument over 20 years ago in his book *Under Technology's Thumb* (1990), which provided a wide-ranging examination of the role of technology in our society. In a chapter on the information economy and **information society**, Leiss—writing well before the Internet was widely known outside of research labs—made the point that we were not asking the most basic question of our information technologies: What did we *want* them to bring to our society? Should we not be expecting them to make us more knowledgeable (and not distracted)? And

Bill Leiss

William Leiss received his Ph.D. from University of California San Diego under the supervision of Herbert Marcuse and then moved to Canada in the 1970s. He has been a professor at the University of Regina, York University, Simon Fraser University, Queen's University, and the University of Ottawa. His work has spanned a broad range of topics including political theory and most recently social, environmental, and financial risk management. You can connect with him via his website, http://leiss.ca or his twitter account @ WilliamLeiss.

What has happened to the role of information in our economy in the twenty-first century?

Since the 1990s, the arrival and development of the Internet and high-speed data transmission has brought a sea-change in the use of "information" in both society at large and individuals within it. I place the key term in quotation marks because its meaning is increasingly problematic, in part precisely as a result of its abundance now. In earlier times, information was scarce and difficult to access for individuals, even if it was in the public domain; those who spent many fruitless days and weeks in library searches through random collections of print materials will remember this well. Then, once found, information was difficult to make use of, requiring first, laborious transcription in handwritten notes, then transfer to typewritten form using carbon copies, all of which was time-consuming and vulnerable to the accidental incorporation of errors. No one who hasn't had these experiences over long periods of time can possibly imagine how tedious and

onerous this process was! Thus, training in the techniques of information search (for example, in graduate education) was a high priority. This training required mental discipline of a very high order: for example, the ability to formulate precise research questions, to prioritize the sequence of searches in an ordered manner (so as to avoid doubling back), and, above all, to relate evidence to argument, using good judgment, in a well-structured and logical fashion. This type of training was essential if one was to develop even a modicum of efficiency in information search. In a sense, the sheer difficulty of this process, or, in other words, the high cost of relevant information, put a high premium on developing one's own methods for maximizing the value extracted from it in the service of advancing an argument.

Do we have too much information?

Now and henceforth, the situation is roughly reversed. Information is overabundant, ridiculously easy to access, and dirt cheap to appropriate in terms of personal time cost. Moreover, it is a trivial matter to copy it for personal use. Thus, information itself is cheap, and what becomes costly are the acts of "processing" and "packaging" (i.e., interpreting) it for purposes of argument and belief or credibility. The very cheapness and abundance of information, therefore, gives rise to an exponential increase in the social and institutional structures of "intermediation" through which information is filtered: professional commentators and "experts," social media discussions among friends, personal narratives in videos, use of visual should we not be better able to deploy this knowledge to address the serious issues of the day?

Leiss argued that when we try to extract value from these new sources of information, we are met with three considerable challenges: misinformation, disinformation, and excess information. Misinformation is the wrong information received by accident. Disinformation is purposefully misleading information. An example of excess information would be when your online search turns up 100,000 results and you are not

imagery to condense meaning, all ruthlessly shortened into sound bites and twitter feeds. The hard work has switched from information search to navigating the thickets of tendentious interpretive framing within which information now is presented to us. The United States appears to present this new reality to us in its most extreme forms: examples are the divisive discourse within never-ending political election cycles and contentious social issues such as abortion, environmental protection, and sexuality. Information, meant to be placed at the service of judgment (making good choices in personal and social affairs), is lost in the sheer amount of interpretive noise. Looking back from the present at earlier times, one sometimes thinks that the task of using information to support judgment was more efficient and effective when information was scarcer.

What about the role of health information?

One area very relevant to the lives of individuals is information about diseases and other health risks. Only two generations ago, this kind of information was very scarce; now it is hyper-abundant. Individuals are highly motivated to access it, in the belief that their own awareness of risks and remedies can be a factor in lifetime health outcomes. But in many cases, the Internet-based and social media resources people access for health information are a seething jungle of contending interpretations. For example, the relatively new vaccination designed to prevent infection by HPV (human papillomavirus) addresses a serious sexually transmitted disease,

especially for young people. Authoritative statements by qualified medical experts indicate a very large margin of health benefit as against side-effect risks from the vaccine itself. At the same time, Internet-based and social media sources are replete with anecdotal accounts of individuals who have allegedly suffered types of serious side-effect risks that are not even indicated in the medical literature. The information search in this area is trivially easy these days; the information value of the search results—in terms of using information as a support for well-considered judgment—is utterly problematic.

You have also written quite a bit lately on climate change. Is information helpful here?

A similar example, at the level of global societal risk, is given in the issue of climate change. There is a vast amount of scientific information available to the general public, drawn from technical literature in peer-reviewed publications. But navigating safely the interpretive jungle thrown up by Internet-based searches represents a huge challenge, and it is unsurprising that in the political discourse on this issue—which potentially threatens the future of industrial society itself—so little of the genuine information value derived from the scientific research record is ever referenced.

To sum up, the old need for training in efficient information search has been replaced by a very different need: for intensive training of individuals in practical techniques for extracting the latent value, buried within today's hyper-abundant information resources, that enables us to utilize evidence to make good choices.

sure where to start. The solution to these information challenges is better education, but Leiss was not optimistic that the population as a whole was up to the task. Both Keen and Carr have similarly dreary views of the potential of free information and widespread sharing: they see us drowning in a sea of our own mediocrity. Will the world blossom with a hundred Wikipedias as the population takes full advantage of their cognitive surplus, as Shirky imagines? Or will we soon dissolve into a group of imbeciles unable to tell fact from fiction because we will have been inundated with misinformation, disinformation, and excess information? Clearly, the stakes are high, and there is evidence on both sides. (Shirky, Carr, and Keen have their critics, and they have put forward strong criticism of each other.)

The embodiment of knowledge in people and practices as distinct from its capture and storage in databases becomes more significant when considering the distinction between explicit and tacit knowledge. **Explicit knowledge** is knowledge that is codified (i.e., written or recorded in some form as data), that can be formally taught and learned, and readily transferred from one context to another. The Internet is a remarkably cost-effective means of codifying, reproducing, and distributing explicit knowledge worldwide. As the Internet makes explicit knowledge more readily available, however, this has implications for tacit knowledge. **Tacit knowledge** is knowledge derived from direct experience and the processes through which it is acquired are often intuitive, habitual, and reflexive, best learned through practices of doing something and the trial-and-error processes associated with learning by doing. Both Leadbeater (2000) and Romer (2007) refer to the significance of cooking in this respect, as it is an activity that involves both the application of explicit knowledge (codified in the form of recipes) and forms of tacit knowledge, such as knowing when pasta is al dente or the quantity of a dab of butter or a pinch of salt. Leadbeater (2000: 28–30) sees celebrity chefs such as Jamie Oliver or Nigella Lawson as paradigmatic knowledge entrepreneurs in this sense, because they trade in both formal knowledge, which is acquired by purchasing their recipe books, and tacit knowledge, acquired by watching them cook these recipes on television. By contrast, the challenge for large organizations, in both the public and private sectors, is that their strength is also a weakness. They are powerhouses in the production, dissemination, and use of explicit knowledge. Organizations are able to manage large amounts of information—they can preserve information over time and distribute it across long distances (made easy now with the Internet)—but they are not well adapted to do those same things with informal and tacit knowledge. How can an organization that has invested heavily in storehouses for information, and rules around its distribution and protection, make the transition to working effectively with bits of information that are not anchored in documents or governed by rules?

A third important issue is found in the distinction between incremental knowledge creation and radical knowledge creation. Incremental knowledge creation is knowledge that is embodied in organizations. Those who become part of the organization are inducted into this embodied knowledge and gradually add to it. Within a company such as Disney, whose theme parks are the largest single-site employers of labour in the United States, there is a strong emphasis on the induction of new staff, who are not only trained in skills required to do their jobs but in understanding the "Disney way," which the company believes to be service that exceeds consumer expectations. Workers therefore bring both explicit and tacit knowledge to the performance of their roles in Disney, but the knowledge comes in forms that have been prepackaged by the Disney Corporation for mass distribution.

By contrast, radical knowledge creation is based on extensive experimentation and testing, and explicit recognition of the likelihood of ideas failing. Leadbeater argues that large companies will find it difficult to dominate sectors such as computer software, communications, and biotechnology, because the speed with which new ideas are being generated exceeds the capacity of such large companies to adopt new processes and unlearn previous practices.

In the twenty-first century, Facebook's rapid growth has been attributed in part to its embrace of "the hacker way," an approach to building and launching code that has put the site under constant change, and engineers have been encouraged to launch things quickly, even if they aren't perfect.

For Facebook, though, *hacker* means something different. It's an ideal that permeates the company's culture, involving a constant push to try new ideas (even if they fail), and to promote new products quickly (even if they're imperfect). The hacker approach has made Facebook one of the world's most valuable Internet companies (Ortutay 2012).

The relationship between the four forms of knowledge described by Leadbeater is outlined in Table 8.2. Although this is only one of many knowledge taxonomies, in considering Leadbeater's categories of knowledge, what becomes apparent is that, radical knowledge creation based on tacit knowledge and unproven assumptions is unlikely to thrive within large organizations, but it is increasingly important to competitive strategy in the new economy, particularly in knowledge-intensive industries. In Leadbeater's view, "big companies in knowledge-intensive fields will resemble a mother ship with a flotilla of smaller companies around it. To be creative a big company needs to be linked into a knowledge-creating network outside it, which gives it access to the places where counter-intuitive, unconventional ideas are being created" (2000: 105).

One way that large companies have been able to take advantage of this relationship is by making acquisitions. Large technology companies such as CISCO or Apple are not just innovation hubs, despite their large research-and-development budgets. They also buy small firms that complement their offerings or provide beachheads in new markets. The widely used and enormously important iTunes program, for example, was originally known as SoundJam and developed by a small software publisher called Casady & Greene.

Table 8.2 Forms of Knowledge and Organizational Strategy

	Formal knowledge	Tacit knowledge
Incremental knowledge creation	Organizational training	Induction into organizational culture
Radical knowledge creation	Promotion and distribution of "best practice" knowledge	Informal knowledge networks

Source: Leadbeater (2000: 111–12).

Innovation and the Innovator's Dilemma

The significance of both tacit knowledge and radical knowledge creation is drawn into even sharper focus when considering the changing nature of **innovation** or the application of new knowledge to new products, processes, and services. Dodgson and colleagues (2002) refer to a fifth-generation innovation process, linked to the rise of **disruptive technologies** that undercut established products, management practices, and industry players (Bower and Christensen 1999), and the greater role that is played by both global markets and end-users in the innovation process. In contrast to ideas-push or demand-pull models of innovation, or the recent focus on national innovation systems, fifth-generation innovation processes stress the links between suppliers and consumers, strategic integration through research and partnership networks, technological integration through both the fusion of different technologies (e.g., the linking of electrical and mechanical technologies to develop the hybrid car), and the development of new ICT-based tool kits that promote global collaborative knowledge networks (Dodgson et al. 2002: 54–7).

Indicators of the increasing importance of innovation can be seen in shortened product development cycles, reduced product life cycles, a greater range of products to cater to discrete market segments, and the high market-to-book ratios of many of the world's largest companies. Companies such as Microsoft and Apple possess few physical assets relative to their market valuation as measured in their share capital, when compared to established manufacturers (such as General Electric, General Motors, or Boeing), since much of their wealth creation arises from product innovation. The challenge of innovation, however, is not simply that it is both more complex and more vital to a firm or an organization's survival in increasingly competitive global markets. The challenge rests also in what Clayton Christensen (2003) famously referred to as the **innovator's dilemma** or the traps that exist in following two long-standing business orthodoxies: working to your established strengths and listening to your customers.

The innovator's dilemma is the outcome of two factors that are common to products and services based on new technologies. The first, which is derived from Everett Rogers's (2003) model of the **diffusion of innovation**, as well as from Donald Norman's (1998) work on technology users and their needs and expectations, leads to the model of the technology S-curve (see Figure 8.4).

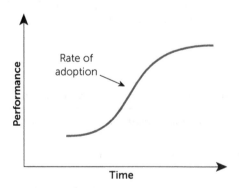

Figure 8.4 The Technology S-Curve

Source: Sood and Tellis (2005: 153).

The technology S-curve takes the shape that it does for two reasons. First, from the point of view of technological innovators, early applications of the technology may possess significant bugs or faults, or the relationship between the technology and its applications may remain unclear, but there is a threshold point where improvements are rapidly made to the technology as dominant standards emerge with the coalescence of product characteristics and consumer preferences, until the technology matures in a mass-market stage as most users find its performance to be good enough and the energies of researchers go to other, newer technologies. For example, the television would now be considered a mature technology, as most people now have one that is good enough for their purposes, but developing mobile and wireless devices from which you can access television content is at an early development stage. The second factor in the technology S-curve relates to users and the fivefold distinction between enthusiasts, early adopters, mainstream adopters, late adopters, and laggards, where, again, the bulk of the user population tends to sit in the middle rather than at either end of the spectrum, thus generating a bell-curve distribution.

The technology S-curve sits alongside the development of new technologies in terms of performance over time as identified by Bower and Christensen (see Figure 8.5).

If these two diagrams are mapped onto one another, they illustrate the innovator's dilemma, which is the risk on the one hand of providing a product or service that underperforms in terms of the expectations of early adopters in the early stage of the product life cycle, and the concern, on the other hand, of providing a product or

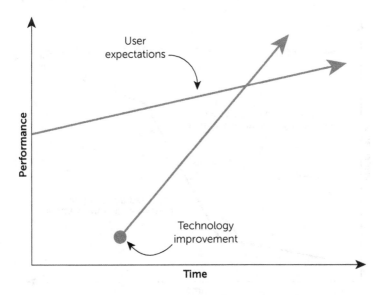

Figure 8.5 Assessing Disruptive Technologies

Source: Bower and Christensen (1999: 149).

service that exceeds the needs of most users in the later stages of a product life cycle (see Figure 8.6).

The innovator's dilemma can be the result of new products containing bugs or design flaws, to which early adopters are particularly likely to draw attention. What is known as "first-mover advantage" can become "first-mover disadvantage," or "second-mover advantage," as competitors who subsequently enter the market learn from the first mover's mistakes (Tellis and Golder 1996). For example, Apple's attempts to capture the PDA market with the release of the Newton in 1993 suffered from such problems, and more stable second-mover products such as the Palm Pilot and Pocket PC took advantage in the marketplace of Apple's popularization of the PDA concept.

The second case of innovator's dilemma is a more complex one and is linked to the growing disjuncture over time between the trajectory of performance improvement for technologies and the expectations of users over time as products and services become more mass-market commodities. It is quite clear, for example, that 95 per cent of the functionality of a software program such as Microsoft Excel is unlikely to be used by 95 per cent of its users, who are not specialists in statistics, finance, or such areas, and tend to use the program for a small number of basic tasks. The extent to which this matters depends in part on whether competitors can identify an opportunity for a product or service that is less sophisticated and less expensive than that of the established market leader, and on whether they can tap into this unmet demand for a pared-down product.

Christensen developed his theory with a detailed examination of one of the building blocks of the new media industry: the hard drive. Although we don't think of this very much today, hard drives were at one time very large, heavy, and expensive. They gradually became smaller, faster, and cheaper and are usually taken for granted these days. What Christensen noticed was that at several stages in the evolution of hard-drive technology, the leading manufacturer was displaced. It was not a story of the major player taking

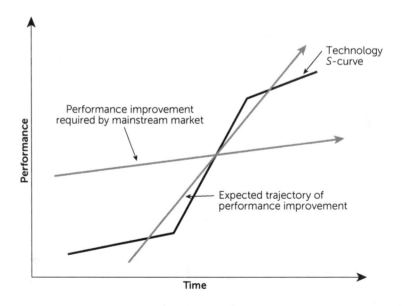

Figure 8.6 The Innovator's Dilemma

Source: Based on Christensen (1997).

the lead with subsequent breakthroughs, but instead he saw that successors repeatedly upset the incumbent and dominant player. Interestingly, they did so by introducing a product that, at first, seemed to be inferior. Looking more closely, Christensen noticed that the dominant player was often closely focused on the needs of existing customers while the new entrant was focused on emerging customers who had different needs. So, for example, the leading supplier of hard drives to minicomputers didn't pay much attention to the needs of microcomputer manufacturers and was unable to respond quickly enough when a new entrant emerged on the scene with smaller and cheaper hard drives. These drives wouldn't have been good enough for a minicomputer (a kind of business computer), but they were sufficient for the new desktop computers that people were buying for their homes. The existing firm had the dilemma: do we deliver what our existing customers want or do we shift gears and try to provide products for new customers? Time and again, across many industries but particularly in new media and information and communication technologies, this decision has proven difficult to make, in part because you have existing power structures within firms that are tied to existing lines of business. Who will give up their bonus today for potential business tomorrow?

There is a variant on these innovation theories, one that is finding a growing place in our wired world. This is called "lead-user innovation," named by Eric von Hippel of MIT. His book, *The Sources of Innovation* (1988), describes a world in which new generations of products seem to be emerging, not from the engineers and scientists who create them but from their most demanding customers. These customers modify the products, enhancing and extending their capabilities to solve specific problems or to go beyond their original specifications. Savvy businesses started to pay attention to this process and actively encouraged these people, helping them to form groups and working with them to design new versions of the product. Finding these people, helping them organize, and staying in touch with them was a herculean—and very expensive—task in the 1980s.

The Internet changed this situation dramatically. A more recent book, von Hippel's *Democratizing Innovation* (2005), describes how **lead-user innovation**, which involves manufacturers adopting and adapting ideas from their users by bringing the users back into the company, is being transformed into **user-centred innovation** processes. In this scenario, users are no longer simply a source of ideas but are actively engaged in designing and creating products that they want and need. Von Hippel offers a variety of examples, including windsurfing equipment, kites, and cars, but some of the most evocative come from Internet-based and new media industries such as open-source software, and most recently 3D printing communities. The people engaged in these activities are passionate and often—but not necessarily—have a high level of expertise and the ability to express themselves through tools such as 3D modelling software. The results of their imagination and dreams are posted to online forums and blogs, voted on by a community, and then produced for those who have placed orders.

A Creative Economy?

We noted in the previous chapter that the rise of the creative industries has drawn new attention to the relationship between creativity, innovation, and entrepreneurship in the new economy. While much policy attention in the 1990s was directed toward information policy, the need to develop skills and infrastructure for the ICT sector, and the promotion of electronic commerce, there is now a renewed focus on creativity and the unique skills and talents of individuals. The imperative to innovate is stronger every year, but some of the established models of research and development, based on incremental improvements and direct response to existing customers, are unable to cope swiftly enough. As we have seen, they are vulnerable to phenomena such as the innovator's dilemma. As a result, there is renewed interest in creativity and the creative process as a way of unlocking the potential for new knowledge to generate new and innovative products and services.

John Howkins, author of *The Creative Economy*, captured this shift in thinking from an information society to a creative economy and society in a 2002 presentation to the London Development Agency:

> The information society that we've been speaking about and living in for 30–40 years, and which is symbolized by the boom in information technology, telecoms, media and financial services, is losing its grip on our imaginations and may, indeed, be coming to an end. I define an IS as a society characterized by people spending most of their time and making most of their money by handling information, usually by means of technology. *If I was a bit of data I would be proud of living in an information society. But as a thinking, emotional, creative being—on a good day, anyway—I want something better* . . . I am talking about a change of perspective, a shift of emphasis. Ideas and information are symbiotically intertwined. But when I say I have an idea I am expressing a more personal view, and making a different claim, from when I say I have some information. . . . We need information. But we also need to be active, clever, and persistent in challenging this information. We need to be original, skeptical, argumentative, often bloody-minded and occasionally downright negative—in one word, creative. (Howkins 2005: 117–88; italics added for emphasis)

The new economy literature believes its dynamics are driven by creativity and culture. For "new growth" economists, creativity and economic dynamism are best promoted by institutional and policy frameworks that encourage a culture of innovation and entrepreneurship (PMSEIC 2005). Castells proposes that the dynamics of the new creative economy are cultural, not only in the sense that economic growth is associated with the development and diffusion of new ideas, but also in the more anthropological sense that the dynamics of ICT development will be dependent on "the culture of innovations, on the culture of risk, on the culture of expectations, and, ultimately, on the culture of hope in the future" (Castells 2001: 112). Mitchell and colleagues (2003) argue that supporting this new economy requires a shift toward promoting ICT development and measuring its influence, to move beyond productivity-based indicators, and to understand more fully the relationship between ICTs and new forms of creative practice. In particular, we need to better appreciate the extent to which a global information economy—built on digital devices and networks—is both enriching and complicating the information environment that we all live in. Out of this complexity, this soup of different ideas, arises the potential for new and useful ideas. Venturelli argues that culture and creativity are the gold that nations possess in the global information economy:

> Culture can be seen as the key to success in the Information Economy, because for the very first time in the modern age, the ability to create new ideas and new forms of expression forms a valuable resource base of a society. . . . Cultural wealth can no longer be regarded in the legacy and industrial terms of our common understanding, as something

fixed, inherited and mass-distributed, but as a measure of the vitality, knowledge, energy, and dynamism of the production of ideas that pervades a given community. (2005: 395–6)

In this vein, one can argue, as Richard Florida has, that if the nineteenth and early twentieth centuries were the heyday of industrial capitalism and the factory system, and the mid- to late twentieth century was dominated by organization and bureaucracy, the twenty-first century marks the rise of the creative class, whose core values are a commitment to individuality, meritocracy, mobility, diversity, openness, and the self-formation of identities (Florida 2002). The shift toward creativity becoming "the decisive source of competitive advantage" in the global economy has further implications since "creativity has come to be the most highly prized commodity in our economy—and yet it is not a 'commodity.' Creativity comes from people. And while people can be hired and fired, their creative capacity cannot be bought and sold, or turned on and off at will" (Florida 2002: 5).

Despite criticisms of Florida's analysis and the policy implications derived from it (e.g., Kotkin 2006; Peck 2005), one reason Florida's work has been so influential is that the notion of creative cities and regions can be linked to arguments about the embodied nature of knowledge that is valuable in particular people and their skills and talents, and the embeddedness of particular forms of knowledge in certain geographical places. Theories of dynamic economic clusters aim to capture the correlation between agglomerations of related firms, industries, or sectors and the economic success of particular cities and regions. Porter (1998) argues that successful geographical clusters generate sustained competitive advantage for the firms and institutions within them, by increasing productivity through access to specialist inputs, labour, knowledge, and technology, promoting innovation by making information about new opportunities more widely available, and promoting new business formation in related sectors through distinctive access to necessary labour, skills, knowledge, technology, and capital. Based on his study of different types of Quebec high-technology firms, Shearmur observes that "there is increasing evidence that innovation is also a spatial phenomenon: the propensity of establishments to innovate also varies with their location relative to major and minor metropolitan areas, independent of local context" (Shearmur 2010). Storper (1997) proposes that the interaction between new digital technologies, organizational changes such as networking, and competition among cities and regions to capture economic rents, means that sources of distinctiveness between cities and regions have become more, not less, relevant in the global economy. Scott (2004) argues that the creative industries (or what he terms the "cultural-products industries") demonstrate particularly strong tendencies toward location-based clustering due to

1. the importance of specific forms of labour input, and the quality of such specialized labour and associated forms of tacit knowledge;
2. the organization of production in dense networks of small- and medium-sized enterprises that are strongly dependent on each other for the provision of specialized inputs and services;
3. the employment relation in creative industries, which is frequently characterized by intermittent, project-based work, meaning that recurring job-search costs can be minimized through co-location in particular areas;

4. the indirect, synergistic benefits that result from the interaction of individual creativity with collective learning, tacit knowledge, and historical memory, through the coexistence of people and enterprises engaged in interrelated activities; and,

5. the development of associated services and institutional infrastructure, and the priority that the relevant industry sectors have in the thinking of local and regional governments.

Scott highlights the role of local, regional, and even national governments, often acting through regulatory mechanisms or other incentives, in fostering a creative economy. Creative industries were specifically exempted from many provisions of the Canada-US free trade agreement. As we will see in the next chapter, however, many legal mechanisms for both enhancing and constraining the creative and digital economies are at the same time often undermined by the technologies and business models that are enabled by new media.

Useful Websites

Annual Review of Sociology: The Knowledge Economy

www.stanford.edu/group/song/papers/powell_snellman.pdf

Powell and Snellman's contribution to the 2004 edition of the *Annual Review of Sociology* provides a foundational document for a student looking for basic information, definitions, and discussion. Although somewhat dated, the paper provides a useful baseline for further inquiry.

E-marketer.com

www.emarketer.com

This website aggregates international trends in e-business and online marketing trends, drawing from over 2800 worldwide sources.

The World Bank: Knowledge for Development (K4D)

www.worldbank.org/kam

This regularly updated website was developed by the World Bank as part of its Knowledge for Development program, which, using the Knowledge Assessment Methodology tool, aims to benchmark countries in terms of their preparedness to compete in a knowledge economy. In 2012, Canada sat seventh in their rankings. The top five countries (Sweden, Finland, Denmark, Netherlands, Norway) were all from Scandinavia, with New Zealand at number six. See also the Knowledge Economy Index at http://info.worldbank.org/etools/kam2/KAM_page5.asp

The Work Foundation—The Knowledge Economy

www.theworkfoundation.com

This website provides a major investigation into the nature of the global knowledge economy—with a particular focus on developments in Europe. Based at Lancaster University, The Work Foundation has, since 2006, conducted research and provided policy advice to UK and other European governments on the future of work.

Further Reading

Here Comes Everybody: The Power of Organizing without Organizations, Clay Shirky (2009)

In this book, Shirky explains how new technologies are making collective action online—through sites like Wikipedia—possible. Importantly, he begins with why the option of forming groups is (a) desirable and (b) significant. Humans are social animals, Shirky reminds us, and we form groups to get things done that we cannot do (easily) on our own. In the past, the creation of larger-sized groups has been hampered by logistics, and, as a result, we have long resorted to bureaucracies to get larger projects done. The promise of information and communication technologies is to have the advantages of large groups without the burden of bureaucracy. How this works, and how it is most successful, is explored with numerous examples and case studies, including one of the most famous Canadian contributions to social media: Flickr.

Cognitive Surplus: Creativity and Generosity in a Connected Age, Clay Shirky (2010)

In a follow-up to *Here Comes Everybody*, Shirky examines the impact of "free time" (time formerly spent watching television, mainly) that is deployed for collective action. While the first book examined how and why social action online was possible, this book suggests what the outcome(s) might be, given that we might actually find the time to contribute to our collective well-being. While this might sound hopelessly optimistic, it is important to remember that many of these collective acts are not something we have never done before but, in fact, are the retrieval of behaviours that humans commonly engaged in during a pre-industrial, pre-anonymized society.

Everything Is Miscellaneous: The Power of the New Digital Disorder, David Weinberger (2007)

Weinberger's book is a consolation for those of us who can never get our lives in order. Drowning in bits of paper, and the flotsam and jetsam of everyday life, we wonder how we can cope. The answer is to embrace the messiness of life and see it instead as an opportunity. Conceding that we can never get things into perfect order, but by applying the growing power of search engines, Weinberger argues that we can learn from the pioneers (digital music is one of his examples) and benefit from the shift to digital forms of knowledge and information. In simple terms, with computers, it is much faster and easier to leave things messy and search for them than putting them in (imperfect anyway) order in the first place. In particular, his prescription for greater use of search engines as a bridge between information and knowledge suggests there will be economic opportunities in the knowledge economy, despite the untidiness of information.

Discussion Questions

1. *Globalization* is defined in this chapter in terms of a series of interrelated processes. What are these processes and what evidence or examples of them can you identify in your own living, working, or educational spheres?
2. What is meant by the term *knowledge economy*? What are some of the features, processes, and dynamics involved?
3. What is an e-commerce strategy, what are some of its benefits, and why is it important for new media?
4. In this chapter, we describe the global knowledge economy as arising from the confluence of three developments. What are these and what are the dynamics that link them?
5. We present here both old and new paradigms of economic development. What are the characteristics of each of these paradigms? Why are they significant to new media studies?
6. What are the two examples of the innovator's dilemma given in this chapter? What are some real-world examples of this dilemma?
7. In this chapter, we take up discussion of the difference between information and knowledge. For example, the notion that knowledge is embodied in persons and practices, whereas information is captured and stored in databases and is readily accessible and increasingly reproducible through the Internet. What significance does this have for understanding the knowledge economy in terms of both creative and cultural aspects?

Class Activities

1. As a class, attempt to discover the country of origin for the collected electronic and fashion items present in the room. Try to account for raw materials and multiple points of origin for complex items with embedded components such as laptop computers. If you can, see how much—if anything—is "Made in Canada." What do your conclusions suggest to you about Canada's role in a knowledge economy?

2. Use the World Bank's Knowledge Assessment Methodology tool (see Useful Websites, on page 212) to compare Canada to another country. How do we compare? What are our strong points and what are our weak points?

3. In groups or individually, select a recent Internet meme or viral video and trace its history as well as spinoffs and variants of it. Identify, as best you can, the ways in which it is being monetized (e.g., pre-roll advertisements on YouTube videos) by the creators and by others.

4. Almost anything related to new media is subject to rapid change. Firms come and go, technologies change, and numbers of users, viewers, and creators for new media content and memes change every day. Look up a fact or figure in this chapter and verify whether it remains true today, using online sources. Identify corroborating or supporting sources for your findings. Not only will you have the new facts, but you'll also have an appreciation for how quickly things change and, most importantly, a visceral sense of the way in which the Internet and new media are self-revealing to the diligent and inquisitive scholar. If you discover a fact that needs updating, you can even submit your update (with page reference and new citation) in the form of a rewritten paragraph, to the author: Richard Smith (smith@sfu.ca). He promises to reply.

Debate Questions

1. Globalization has its proponents and its critics. Argue for or against a globalized knowledge economy, using examples from, and making reference to, new media content and Internet technologies.

2. Leiss points out that in a previous era, the challenges of acquiring information forced researchers to develop skills and techniques that have been lost or attenuated in our current age. Argue for or against the notion that mental discipline is lost in an era of easy access to information.

9

Internet Law, Policy, and Governance

Questions to Consider

- What are some examples of the domains covered by cyberspace law? What are the complications and issues specific to this type of law?

- How do policy initiatives or interventions taken by the Canadian government affect new media?

- Why is it important to consider the distinctions and balance between private ownership and public use of intellectual property when thinking about new media?

Chapter Outline

In this chapter, we examine the interesting and sometimes difficult issues that have appeared in a world in which two of the foundational principles of law—property and the state—have been significantly altered by digital and global information flows. We look at some of the major domains of law as they pertain to cyberspace and some of the legal implications that have arisen as that space has changed and expanded. That digital goods are ephemeral and easily cross borders is challenge enough, but a further pressure comes from the fact that there is currently little if any cyberspace law—the Internet is self-policing, but only in a loose sense and mainly at the level of technology standards. Beyond that, only national and local law can be applied, and that, as we will see, is often very difficult to do. Nations have attempted to establish priorities, programs, and policies designed to boost the power and role of their own citizens and corporations in information and communication technologies—first with computers and then networks. Given that the Internet originated in Western democracies, sometimes the laissez-faire attitude adopted online is incompatible with local standards in other countries, as we saw when the International Telecommunications

Union threatened to "regulate the Internet" in the fall of 2012 (Masnick 2012a). We examine these issues along with implications for copyright and property rights, and the open-source software movement.

Internet Law, Policy, and Governance

It takes little more than a cursory glance at the range of legal issues raised by the development of the Internet and networked ICTs to recognize that they are enormous in their scope, domain of application, and implications for different individuals and groups within societies. Examples of some of the domains covered by cyberspace law include

- cyberspace and business: e-commerce; online contract law, online financial law, online gambling, cyberfraud, Internet tax issues, especially relating to online retailers;
- cyberspace and medicine: telemedicine, online prescribing, online pharmacies;
- cyberspace and telecommunications fairness: broadband development, throttling and access, educational uses of the Internet, gender and race online, poverty and unequal access to the Internet (the digital divide);
- cyberspace and education: plagiarism, use of computers in schools, content filtering for minors, evolution of fair dealing and fair use in education;
- free speech issues: freedom of expression, obscenity, pornography and online indecency, protection of children, cultural rights, online defamation (libel and slander);
- intellectual property issues: copyright law, patent law, trademark law, gifts and online exchange;
- privacy issues: cryptography and privacy protection for online transactions, employment privacy, personal information privacy, data security;
- security issues: cybercrime, spamming, cyberstalking and online harassment, hacking, identity theft, the Internet and terrorism; and
- political rights: access rights, online democracy experiments, evolution of national firewalls.

This is a lengthy list and more could easily be added to it. The legal implications of the Internet's rapid development are further complicated by the way(s) in which it is situated in relation to existing laws, regulatory frameworks, and the ideas that underpin them. First, there are the unique characteristics of networked information: it is intangible, geographically distributed, recombinant, and continually changing in its form and character. These characteristics confront the legal tradition, where "existing legislation depends upon clearly demonstrable, localizable and liable legal persons and ownership titles. Information and evidence have to be, or must be able to be, set down on a data carrier that has still to be comparable to printed paper" (van Dijk 1999: 116). The contrast between the need for stability and tangible links to applicable subjects on which the legal system operates and the fluidity of the online environment is compounded by the difficulties that arise in implementing laws, since activities in networks are frequently non-transparent, communication can be anonymous or very hard to trace back to an original source, and evidence can be destroyed, hidden, erased, or altered by computer users and systems operators.

The second set of factors that greatly complicates Internet law arises from the global nature of the Internet and its network infrastructure, and the predominantly national basis of laws and legal systems. Froomkin observes that the transnational nature of the Internet as a communications medium promotes regulatory arbitrage, whereby people and corporations can, in certain circumstances, "arrange their affairs so that they evade domestic regulations by structuring their communications or transactions to take advantage of foreign regulatory regimes" (1997: 129). The problem of both Internet users and service providers being able to evade national laws by accessing content or undertaking transactions through other territorial domains—or, as others might see it, the enhanced freedom of Internet users to evade domestic laws that they may deem inappropriate—is magnified by the uncertainties related to legal and territorial jurisdiction in cyberspace. There have been many instances of jurisdictional conflict over content, ranging from attempts by the Chinese government to close down websites hosted in Taiwan and Hong Kong that promote the ideas of the Falun Gong movement (which is banned in China) (Kalathil and Boas 2003), to the French government's effort in 2000 to pressure the Yahoo! search engine into blocking French citizens' access to Nazi memorabilia on its English-language auction sites (Stein and Sinha 2002). These issues are ongoing and arise regularly. Twitter was required to reveal information relating to an Occupy Wall Street protester in the fall of 2012, and early in 2013, to respond to requests by the French government for information relating to anti-Semitic tweets, for example (Parnell 2013). While some Internet companies have been criticized for turning over this information too readily, a growing movement in the United States at least is for firms to request a warrant before releasing personal information.

This problem is also found in areas such as defamation and libel. Different jurisdictions have very different rules regarding what it is to defame someone else. In the era of print media, this was not so great a problem since it was usually straightforward to demonstrate that copies of a magazine or book had never been distributed—or intended to be distributed—in another country. That is much more difficult to prove in the Internet age, and this has given rise to the phenomenon of "libel tourism" (Stavely-O'Connell 2009). Canadians learned more about this phenomenon in 2010 and 2011 during Conrad Black's legal battle to have libel lawsuits heard in Ontario, but they were based on actions in the United States. The Supreme Court of Canada ruled in the spring of 2012 that the suit could proceed, on the basis that the material was available in Ontario and that Black's reputation was created, and, presumably, defamed, in that province (Schabas and Hoult 2012).

Libel and defamation have also been implicated in something called the "autocomplete feature" built into search engines such as Google's. In this case, typing a few letters of a person's name can result in "related" or "likely" search strategies being prepopulated in the search box. Mainly this is a convenience for users, who need only type "ju" into a Google.ca search in order for it to suggest that you might be interested in "Justin Bieber." This becomes problematic, however, when the autocomplete is—claimants feel—defamatory of them. Google has had to defend its autocomplete algorithms, which it claims are created by software, and result from real searches by real people, in a variety of jurisdictions (BBC 2012). One interesting aspect of these cases is that Google has tried to defend its actions by pointing to rights of free speech, but it has not been particularly successful—yet—in enshrining that right for a software program.

The third issue is that Internet law, in a sense, does not exist. Just as the Internet marks out a convergent space between computing, telecommunications, and media, what is termed "Internet law" is in truth rarely more than the application and extension of laws developed for other media and communications technologies, such as print, broadcasting, and telecommunications. The legal issues linked to the Internet have also extended, in a largely unplanned and incoherent manner, to areas of civil, criminal, and corporate law that were developed to address quite different issues from those presented by networked and convergent media. Similarly, what constitutes Internet policy in many countries is often an uncomfortable amalgam of policies developed for traditional media industries (most notably, broadcasting), telecommunications policies, and policies to promote production in media content sectors, with defence and national security making an occasional appearance in the mix. The problem is not simply one of law and policy lagging behind technological developments, since this, inevitably, will always be the case to some extent. Rather, as van Dijk observes, legal and policy responses to new media have largely been fragmentary and ad hoc adjustments that remain based on outdated assumptions: "There is no internal readjustment. Instead, detailed alterations are made to existing legislation including technical definitions that will soon be outdated. . . . Fragmentary adjustments to legislation are not suitable for the regulation of large-scale networks and their far-reaching consequences to individuals and society at large" (1999: 117).

In the plethora of national information policy statements that emerged in the 1990s, there was also often a curious dualism. On the one hand, there was confidence that the freely operating commercial market provided the best means of allocating resources and promoting technological development. The Global Information Infrastructure proposed in the 1990s by the Clinton–Gore administration in the States prioritized private investment, service development driven by free markets and competition, flexible regulatory systems, and the removal of barriers to foreign investment. In tandem with this, new international regulatory organizations such as the World Trade Organization (WTO, established in 1995) actively promoted the privatization of public telecommunications monopolies and fostered the promotion of competition policy and free trade, with an underlying view that communications companies were market-based service providers with sharply delimited universal service obligations (CRTC 1995; Flew and McElhinney 2005; Winseck 2002). The notion that telecommunications companies had public service obligations has been linked to the idea of Internet access as a human right (see below). At the same time, through national information policies, many governments heavily funded the ICT sectors in the hope of developing "national champions" in global markets and promoting a networked society and a Web-savvy population.[1] Melody (1996) observed at the time that in many of these programs, there was a misplaced priority given to development of information infrastructure as an end in itself, which was often accompanied by generous subsidies being given to multinational ICT corporations to produce locally, with insufficient attention being given to the relationship between content applications, user demand, and skills acquisition that would have provided a more sustainable, equitable, and democratic basis for Internet development policies (cf. Breen 2002).

Perspectives on Internet Governance

It has been proposed that, rather than understanding the various attempts at Internet regulation in terms of law (which raises the question of the origins of current laws) or policy (which presumes a national territorial jurisdiction, as well as government stewardship of a global, predominantly commercial medium), Internet regulation can be understood in terms of **governance**. The concept of governance recognizes links between the public and private sectors or between the market and the state: markets themselves can constitute powerful governance structures and governments act as often to promote markets and private sector interests as they do to regulate and constrain them (Jessop 1998, 2000). Moreover, from the perspective of governance, there is an understanding of the various roles played in Internet law and policy—by non-governmental and non-corporate institutions and by organizations of civil society and social movements, alongside state/public and corporate interests—as well as of the ways in which such processes increasingly cross territorial jurisdictions (Murphy 2002).

The concept of Internet governance is useful as an alternative to strong notions of **cyber-libertarianism**, commonly found among key user communities (particularly in the United States), which view the infrastructure of the Internet as essentially manageable through self-governance. Cyber-libertarianism was a key tenet of Internet pioneers like those associated with the Electronic Frontier Foundation (EFF), which saw in the Internet a "platform which will allow every person to speak their mind and query the world to create their own point of view" (Electronic Frontier Foundation n.d.). The non-hierarchical, decentralized, and networked nature of the Internet presented libertarian groups like the EFF with the opportunity to develop self-governing online communities which, being finally free of state interference and censorship, could truly realize the freedom of speech principles outlined in the First Amendment of the US Constitution. John Perry Barlow (1996a) stated in his "A Declaration of the Independence of Cyberspace," "We believe that from ethics, enlightened self-interest and the commonweal, our governance will emerge. . . . The only law that all of our constituent cultures would recognize is the Golden Rule." In one of the first high-level court decisions to rule on the distribution of materials via the Internet, the US Supreme Court cited the First Amendment in 1996 ("freedom of speech") when it struck down provisions of the US Communications Decency Act that it deemed went too far in restraining the communication rights of adults. The case helped establish the Internet as different from broadcast television and radio, for example, where stronger protection of the public was justified.

Mike Godwin, counsel for the EFF in the case, made the following argument:

> Give people a modem and a computer and access to the Net, and it's far more likely that they'll do good than otherwise. This is because freedom of speech is itself a good—the framers of the [US] Constitution were right to give it special protection, because societies in which people can speak freely are better off than societies in which they can't. (1998: 23)

The cyber-libertarian perspective is no longer articulated as strongly as a model for Internet governance as it was in the mid-1990s. One reason for this has been that as the Internet has grown exponentially and as the user base has become more diverse, the notion of a shared ethos that underpinned early forms of virtual communities is less applicable (Davies 2003). More significantly, the cyber-libertarian perspective was also deeply ambivalent about corporate power on the Internet. Authors and activists such as Lessig note the danger of the cyber-libertarian position and its failure to address questions of corporate power, observing that Internet activists operating from a cyber-libertarian position run the risk of "winning the political struggle against state control so as to entrench control in the name of the market" (Lessig 2001: 267). Early critics of cyber-libertarianism such as Barbrook and Cameron (1995) noted how an anti-statist vision of Internet self-governance (what they termed the "Californian Ideology") was likely to be conflicted about its relationship to the rise of corporate power on the Internet and associated neo-liberal ideologies that critique state power in the name of the commercial global market (e.g., Dyson et al. 1994).

A very different perspective on Internet governance emerged from critical political economy. For Mosco (1997), McChesney (1999), and Schiller (2000), the early promise of the Internet as a democratic and decentralized alternative to commercial mass media was quickly swept aside as governments around the world deregulated or eased their regulation of communications systems in the 1990s to give greater power to dominant commercial interests. These writers saw the emerging pattern of Internet governance closely mirroring that of the societies in which it operated, meaning that in corporate-dominated societies, it would be these powerful interests that most effectively shape government policy to suit their interests. McChesney argues that "if certain forces thoroughly dominate a society's political economy they will thoroughly dominate its communications system ... and so it is ... for the most part, with big business interests in the United States" (1999: 124–5). Schiller argues in *Digital Capitalism: Networking the Global Market System* (2000) that the development of the global Internet is best understood as being driven by the demands of transnational corporations and the US government for a globally integrated computing and communications network that could promote the expansion of operations and markets worldwide, minimizing the capacity of national governments to regulate such activities in the public interest.

As the Internet has developed as a global, decentralized network, it continues to challenge the two core tenets of nation-state sovereignty: sovereignty over territory and sovereignty over citizens. Not only will cyberspace always exist apart from national territories and borders (unlike air space, for example), but the Internet also enables, indeed actively promotes, communications activities and transactions that cross territorial boundaries (Kleinwächter 2002: 56–7). The Internet Corporation for Assigned Names and Numbers (ICANN) is one attempt to develop a framework for global Internet governance. ICANN was established in 1998 to address a very new problem: how to govern the allocation of Internet domain names, or the addresses that people, organizations, and governments adopt to direct people to their sites on the Web.

Before the mid-1990s, the allocation of Internet addresses had been a largely technical matter, undertaken by individuals or small groups with little discussion or controversy, and with little international consultation. As the Internet grew, however, this structure became inadequate. Commercial interests increasingly saw their domain name as a part of their branding and marketing strategies, and they sought to ensure that their brand, as embodied in their domain name, was protected in cyberspace. This was exacerbated by the phenomenon of "cybersquatting," where people buy up potentially popular domain names, sometimes in the hope of profit, sometimes to use them for "culture-jamming," in which critics of consumerism use mainstream media and advertising to critique popular culture (Lasn 2000). Kalle Lasn's Vancouver-based Adbusters Media Foundation, which produces a magazine and website that contain anti-consumer articles and advertising as well as the annual Buy Nothing Day event, is an example of culture-jamming. Others exploit domain names for less positive ends, directing unsuspecting users to pornography sites, or simply capturing an asset that they could then profitably sell. This was clearly problematic for commercial and other users, and a range of powerful interests collaborated to put in place a more cohesive structure for domain-name governance: the aforementioned ICANN.

ICANN is a private, not-for-profit agency representing both the global Internet community, business and otherwise, which includes both those involved in domain-name registration and those seeking to register online domain names in order to pursue electronic commerce. While governments clearly have an interest in the outcomes of ICANN decision-making, ICANN seeks to maintain an advisory, back-seat function for governments (Kleinwächter 2002: 66). It has also developed an approach to dispute resolution that is non-legalistic, based on a quick and low-cost resolution premised on whether a domain-name registrant could be considered to have acted in bad faith.

Paré (2003) and Froomkin (2003) find, however, that the US government (representing business interests in trademark and intellectual property protection) has heavily influenced both the structure and the conduct of ICANN. They question the claim that ICANN has developed a new form of decentralized global Internet governance that transcends national interests and appeals to the distinctive ethos of a global Internet community. Indeed, Paré argues that the consensus-oriented politics of ICANN have in fact generated a crisis of legitimacy for the organization, because it is seen as "a private organization which is exerting global public authority over a key information and communication resource in a manner that appears to be inconsistent with both the way in which decisions have traditionally been made in the public domain and the traditional norms and values associated with internet-working" (Paré 2003: 169). ICANN's legitimacy was addressed at the World Summit on the Information Society (WSIS) in Geneva (2003) and Tunis (2005), where developing countries and civil society organizations in particular argued for an alternative framework for Internet governance over issues such as domain names, one where the organizations of the United Nations would play a leading role (Froomkin 2003; Ó Siochrú 2004; Ó Siochrú et al. 2003).

This debate flared up again in the fall of 2012, at a related agency, the International Telecommunications Union, or ITU. The ITU dates from the era of the telegraph, and was originally set up to ensure standards compliance around the world—and mediate disputes—as the first electronic global networks were built. This type of standardization was not in place during the establishment of the railways, for example, and resulted in enormous logistical problems relating to the movement of trains across borders, when the width of the tracks (the gauge) varied. The ITU helped avoid that problem for telegraphs and ensured that a message sent from Montreal to Mumbai could get though. As telephone networks grew in the late nineteenth and early twentieth centuries, the ITU took over international regulation of these systems, too.

Importantly, the ITU governs the technical infrastructure, not the content of those systems. In other words, they have nothing to say about what you say during your phone call but everything to say about how interconnections between one system and another are managed. From time to time over the past 30 years, the ITU has made announcements about getting involved in the regulation of the Internet. Each time, these announcements went nowhere and did not result in any meaningful involvement by the ITU. But during meetings in the fall of 2012, the topic arose again. This time, it seemed to find traction among a group of member states, particularly around the issue of managing the flows of encrypted traffic that certain regimes regard as detrimental to their internal security. Various speakers, including the chair of the ITU, proposed a need for control of the use of the Internet in the name of state security (Masnick 2012a). As in the past, representatives from the United States, backed by the European Union and countries such as Canada and Australia, refused to sign the agreement (Masnick 2012b).

Canadian New Media Policy

Internet and new media policy in Canada has a long history. As we discussed in Chapter 2, the Internet and other present-day technologies did not emerge wholly formed but rather have evolved from, and in many cases are based on, antecedent technologies. To have an understanding of current new media policy in Canada, it is important to first examine some of the historical policy initiatives that the Canadian government has taken in these areas. Policy interventions can come in the form of laws and regulations but also in the form of public inquiries, investments, subsidies and tax benefits, and even decisions *not* to regulate at a particular time or in a particular area.

Philip Savage

Philip Savage is a professor of communication studies at McMaster University in Hamilton. With a long career in public broadcasting, Dr Savage received his Ph.D. from Toronto's York University, where he continued his interest in the evolutions of audiences and media in Canada. Co-director of the Communication Metrics Laboratory (COMMLab) at McMaster, Savage is active on twitter as @docsavagephd.

What does the term *policy* mean to you, in the context of new media?

First, policy is *not* just what governments do. It's a big mistake to think that in Canada, culture or telecom policy is just what the CRTC or minister of Canadian heritage does.

Policy is more broadly *decision-making* by any number of actors and the *environment* in which decisions are made. The policy process is dynamic, both very local and simultaneously worldwide. That doesn't mean governments are not involved in policy. Through laws and regulations (or decisions not to have laws), various levels of government can have a predominant impact on the policy environment. But for most policy decisions being made, there is increasingly little government involvement.

I like to use the example of movie rating systems. If a film is rated "G", "R" or "NC-17," a decision made in an LA suburb affects whether someone in Truro, Nova Scotia, can see a particular film. It also significantly changes the film's profits. The Canadian or Nova Scotia government doesn't decide that policy, nor does the US government; instead, a group of parents chosen by the MPAA (Motion Picture Association of America) makes the decision. In other words, a group comprised of the six major US film companies manages the whole decision-making process for that Truro teen and, indeed, countless viewers in Canada and around the world, both in theatres and on various digital platforms.

Public Inquiries

As with the establishment of the national radio broadcasting system, put in place as the result of a royal commission the Canadian government has often initiated public inquiries into issues of national concern. Just such an inquiry was established in the early 1990s, when the "information superhighway" (as it was then known) loomed on the horizon. In early 1994, Canada's Information Highway Advisory Council (IHAC) was formed to consider the implications and recommend actions for the government on concerns related to the arrival of digital information in Canadian homes and businesses.

IHAC provided advice to the federal minister of industry in a series of reports, which were condensed into an issues document published in April 1994 under the title, *The Canadian Information Highway—Building Canada's Information and Communications Infrastructure*. The issues document laid out the main concerns for the government in three broad areas: jobs, sovereignty, and access. The initial report set out four principles as important for a Canadian information highway: (1) interconnections and interoperability between networks; (2) mixed public and private sector investment in infrastructure; (3) competition in services, content, and equipment; and (4) adequate protection of privacy and network security. A series of public meetings and a wealth of commissioned research followed, with a series of reports published through 1995 and a final report at the end of that year. The following year (1996), the government issued an action strategy under the title, *Building the Information Society: Moving Canada into the 21st Century.*[2]

interview with a new media expert

What are the key policy questions relating to new media in Canada?

One of the broadest questions has to do with whether in fact as a community (or even subcommunities/regions within the country) Canadians have access to the forums by which they think, play, and exchange communication of various sorts. Traditionally in Canada, there has been a struggle to make sure we've had roads or radio networks that allowing Canadians to have some control over their own communication networks, the results being things like "CanCon" quotas or incentives to help Canadian-content producers compete against big Hollywood films or London publishers. Digital networks, including social media, often allow for new content providers to get their ideas/art to a broad Canadian or worldwide audience, but there still remains a need to develop well-financed, professional groups of content providers who are not at the very long end of the tail (i.e., lost very low in a typical Google search).

What are some key emerging concepts, challenges, or ideas?

One key idea emerging is the degree to which "ordinary" citizens are active in creating policy. For example, the over 500,000 Canadians who lobbied through openmedia.ca to stop telecommunications companies like Bell from developing types of "usage billing" (i.e., to preserve Net neutrality).

But on the other side off the coin, to digital activism it is becoming incredibly valuable to corporations and organizations to collect almost automatically huge amounts of fine-grained data about our use of media, especially online sites. A big issue for all of us will be the privacy laws to govern the use of such information, but also the degree to which the content—both editorial and advertising—is pre-selected for us and breaks down other types of large communities to which we belong.

Although the type of network that seemed imminent at the time of the IHAC report—a system more dominated by media giants than by the information and interaction-driven Internet that actually evolved—has not entirely come to pass, Canada's policy response to the Internet has been shaped and informed by IHAC. The Internet of today, as it is accessed from Canada and contributed to by Canadians, is largely interconnected and open, despite threats to that openness that occur from time to time. It is hard to say whether IHAC and the federal government or business interests (see Chapter 2 for a discussion of network economics) deserve the credit for this openness, but either way, Canadian citizens benefit when they are able to use one network connection to reach all of the potential sites in the world.

Although it is government policy to not restrict access to sites or based on provider or country of origin, commercial considerations and licensing terms continue to frustrate Internet users who come up against the dreaded "this video is not available in your territory." These licensing terms, which seemed sensible in the era of analog media and the need to have local distributors for content—and hence agreements to protect those local distributors' investment—seem archaic in the age of the Internet. And yet they

Archival Policy

Back in 1994, the information highway reports were released online—a novel and radical initiative at that time—but for a while, they were difficult to locate except in paper form. A thorough search of available websites in January 2010 failed to locate any current copies on federal government web servers. The "wayback" function provided by the Internet Archive Service can be used as an alternate route to locating documents, and the archived report can be found by going to http://web.archive.org and searching for the original URL for the report (which was http://strategis.ic.gc.ca/SSG/ih01650e .html)—the resulting complete URL is http://web .archive.org/web/19990117001335/strategis .ic.gc.ca/SSG/ih01650e.html. A more recent search (January 2013) revealed that the report was available again. This kind of "here now, gone tomorrow, (maybe) back again" phenomenon is a fact of life for digital documents.

While the Internet Archive Service makes the document available, it raises an interesting policy question: should government documents be allowed to go stale and disappear from public view? Was the decision to remove these documents made consciously or were they simply relegated to archive status when Industry Canada upgraded its website or server? Is

Canada relying on an Internet archive service to maintain access to its digital documents? Certainly, it is difficult to imagine a government directive that would remove a document like this from the many libraries around the world that maintain print copies. Yet a digital version can disappear completely. This case illustrates the complexity and subtlety of new media policies and in particular the challenges relating to aging digital documents.

Not only are there problems with deleted records, but also, the viability of various storage mechanisms is unknown. How long does a CD-ROM or DVD last? In 2050, will we be able to read a hard drive that was stored in 2010? What about file formats? Can we count on being able to read documents in Microsoft Word for 10 years? Twenty? Information on paper has the advantage of being immediately accessible in and of itself; digital files, on the other hand, will always be dependent on intermediary technology.

It is clear that questions relating to the archiving of digital documents extend far beyond the federal government, to other levels of government, universities, private industry, and even citizens. Every agency and institution is grappling with these issues in different ways.

persist for historical reasons, or because new agreements have not been worked out, or because content producers believe they can extract higher prices from one region of the globe than another. In this way the free and open Internet remains a patchwork with some content broadly and widely available and other content—usually of a commercial or politically sensitive nature—restricted by licensing terms or censorship.

Public Consultations

In recent years, the Canadian government has added a slightly different approach to their data collection, experimenting with wide-ranging public consultation initiatives. The hub for this, Consulting with Canadians, is housed at its own dedicated website (www.consultingcanadians.gc.ca) and links to initiatives in the various departments. Some of the experiments, such as the recent Digital Economy Consultation (May to July 2010) allow citizens who register on the site to submit an idea, and also to vote (up or down) the ideas of others, similar to sites such as Digg (http://digg.com) or Reddit (http://reddit.com). The site is not as well known or flamboyant as the equivalent US site, run by the Whitehouse, which in January 2013 featured a petition relating to the construction of a "Death Star," but instead seems to be focused on a blend of online and in-person consultations. Importantly, the site brings together all consultations run by government departments, regardless of where they are located, which agency initiated them, whether or not they involve an online component. This approach, often described as a "customer-focused" approach to government services, is one way in which corporate use of the Web has migrated over to governments. As organizations have tried to engage with their users, they have found that departmental structures or divisions are not meaningful or salient to customers or citizens. What people want is one point of contact. In a way, this is reflecting the transition that the Web underwent as we moved from a catalogue style of Web directory pioneered by Yahoo! to a single search-box approach, epitomized by the simple box that Google presents. Services such as Consulting Canadians, or the "3-1-1" telephone and websites that are springing up for cities around the world, are part of an overall trend to focus on a single point of contact and have the "back end" (often a search engine) figure out how to direct the inquiry or answer the question or provide the service.

While there have been controversies surrounding these initiatives, particularly on the question of whether the government will or will not follow the advice of Canadians who participate,[3] there is a strong sense that these new tools for public engagement with government, long championed by the proponents of Internet democracy, are finally being tested.

Public Investment and Regulation of Infrastructure

Internet infrastructure, while at times subsidized (especially at public institutions), remains a strong mix of private and public investment. On the public side, throughout the late 1990s and on through 2013, the federal government and several of the provinces have invested heavily in extending broadband networks to rural and remote communities as well as building a research network (Canarie) across Canada, linking universities and other research institutions. Often times these are not outright government-owned projects but rather subsidies to private operators or lease arrangements.

Despite continuing government involvement, there are concerns that the balance may have tipped too far to the side of private investment, leading to lawsuits and challenges relating to the shaping and filtering of the network by Internet service providers that may have a commercial interest in promoting one form of content over another. In most parts of Canada there is competition in the provision of Internet access, although this remains a challenge in rural areas and smaller cities and the prices remain uncomfortably high in rural and remote locations, relative to the speed of service and compared to offerings in other countries such as Korea and Japan.

Privacy and the Law

Law and regulation are continually engaged in the ongoing challenge of protecting privacy and safety in new media and particularly online (see Chapter 10 on surveillance and new media). Government agencies, including the Privacy Commissioner of Canada, have been able to require significant changes to how organizations handle personal and private information online. A celebrated case from 2009 saw Canada's Privacy Commissioner negotiate important changes to the privacy settings on Facebook, the giant social networking site used by many Canadians and hundreds of millions of people worldwide.

Privacy is also at risk when firms or agencies request information of Internet service providers, alleging crimes. Often the requests for information are related to alleged copyright infringement—typically downloading movies or music. Back in 2005, most of the large Canadian Internet service providers (Shaw, Telus, Bell, Rogers, Videotron) successfully resisted requests for the identity of their subscribers based on a list of Internet protocol (IP) addresses (Federal Court of Appeal 2005). Perhaps encouraged by new provisions in a new copyright law, a similar suit was launched in 2012 against a smaller Canadian Internet service provider, Tekksavvy (CBC 2012).

As more and more employers provide computers and network access as part of normal workplace equipment, we are seeing challenges to what has been understood as expectations of privacy in the workplace. In a remarkable case from October 2012, the Supreme Court of Canada ruled that an employee has a reasonable expectation of privacy with regard to their use of computer equipment and network access, if the employer condones or permits personal use of that equipment. So, for example, if your employer allows you to bring a workplace laptop home with you, they may be diminishing their ability to absolutely control what uses you make of that device. In the *R v. Cole* case, the Supreme Court ruled that "Canadians may reasonably expect privacy in information contained on workplace computers where personal use is permitted or reasonably expected" (Thiessen, York, and Friesen 2012). The specifics of the case were a teacher accused of possession of pornography and who objected to a warrantless search of his computer, initiated by a technician employed by the school board. His argument—supported by the court—was that in this case his right to be free from unreasonable search and seizure, under section 8 of the Charter of Rights and Freedoms, were violated by this search.

This is a particularly important ruling in light of a trend toward "bring your own device" (BYOD), wherein employees are permitted and even encouraged to select, purchase (perhaps with a subsidy), and maintain their own mobile phone and laptop for use at work. Companies are drifting toward these types of practices because employees enjoy the freedom of having their own computer or mobile device and may be resentful of the need to carry multiple devices, and are willing to bear the capital cost of purchasing as well as the overhead of maintaining and servicing the device. Depending on the type of business that you operate, this type of arrangement can seem compelling, but as *Cole* revealed, once a device has mixed use it also has mixed control from a legal point of view.

Public Investment in Underlying Technologies

Governments also influence new media policy through investments in underlying technologies such as computers and networking protocols and the Internet in Canada has benefited significantly in this regard. As early as the late 1940s and early 1950s, the Canadian government was an early customer, through the air force and the navy, of computers from Computing Devices Canada (Mussio 2001: 74). In the 1980s, the federal government, through the Communication Research Centre and the Department of Communication, helped pioneer a technology for the distribution of small text messages as part of a television signal. The technology, called Telidon, was a form of teletext and a pioneering service for the time.[4] It worked with televisions and cable television connections, somewhat like the crawl of information on a cable news channel, but with more interactivity because users could choose from streams of messages in a branching menu format.

The service was not a success in a commercial sense, but it did build capacity among content providers (firms were set up to create digital content) and manufacturers (that made the encoding and decoding devices), and perhaps most importantly, it increased awareness of the benefits of digital and interactive media among Canadians. As such, this serves as a good example of Canada's early investments in the development of digital broadcast satellites, of government investment in new media, and as direct intervention in a media form. This type of intervention in the economy is less popular today and governments by and large do not make direct investments in particular technologies, choosing instead to create the ideal conditions for business to flourish.

Subsidies and Tax Incentives

Subsidies and tax incentives are another way that governments can influence technology development and use. In the era of free trade, and particularly in the case of Canada in the North American Free Trade Agreement (NAFTA), it is sometimes difficult for governments to give local industries an advantage over companies in other countries. Quite often, this favouring of local firms is explicitly forbidden under the rules of such international agreements. Nevertheless, jurisdictions do what they can to attract business and encourage investment, especially in growing areas like new media.

Culture is often one of the exceptions in these agreements and national, regional, and local governments have taken advantage of the inherent cultural content in new media products to justify tax breaks for firms working in those fields. This has resulted in a wide array of tax incentives, subsidies, and rebates for the producers of animation, films, and even computer games. Recent examples include the Ontario Computer Animation and Special Effects Tax Credit[5] or the Canada New Media Fund (through Telefilm Canada). These types of incentives often provide exceptional tax breaks, subsidies on labour, or financial assistance for the distribution of products. New media industries are seen as environmentally friendly, future-oriented, and creative producers of indigenous content made from Canadian ingenuity, thereby contributing to job growth and economic growth for the country. In 2011–12, the Canada Media Fund provided $358 million in funding to digital media and television production.[6] Digital media creators are especially interested in the Experimental Stream division, which had $32.9 million in funding in 2011–12, as it "supports the creation of innovative Canadian interactive digital media content" (Canada Media Fund 2010).

The existence, continuation, and growth of tax incentives for specific industries remain a controversial topic around the world, and particularly in Canada. Local, regional, and national governments often create these tax incentives to attract and retain talent and then find that they are on the hook to maintain them in perpetuity and compete with other jurisdictions that offer even greater incentives. The video-game industry in Canada has been strongly affected by this phenomenon, with some studios moving from British Columbia to Ontario and Quebec specifically to take advantage of a more favourable tax-incentive structure in those provinces (Warnica 2012).

Declining to Regulate

It might at first seem to be an odd assertion, but declining to regulate (which is called **forbearance** in legal terminology) is also a policy option for governments. In Canada, this has had significant effects in two new media domains in particular: mobile phones and the Internet. When mobile phones were first developed, they were seen as an extension of the existing telephone system and, as such, logically subject to regulation by the CRTC. Mobile phones were also transmitting and receiving devices, which had implications for another regulatory body, the federal Department of Communication, now known as the Spectrum Management and Telecommunication division of Industry Canada. At first, mobile phones were considered a luxury item and were rarely seen except in the hands of the wealthy or people with exceptional—and perhaps tax-deductible—reasons to have one. As cell phones became a more common item, and particularly at the 2G or "personal communication system" stage (essentially, the small, digital cell phones we have now), the CRTC had to consider how they would regulate these devices.

Would cell phones be regulated as part of the telephone system and be subject to all of the requirements and obligations of justifying revenues, or would they be regulated as a separate, competitive business that would have modest oversight? The CRTC, following government policy as well as the economic thinking of the day, decided on the latter stance: they would forbear from making significant regulations and allow a more competitive open market, as with automobiles, home furniture, or computers.[7] There remain significant technical regulations, of course, especially because of the need for radio spectrum in order to operate, but on issues of how cell phones are priced, what services they provide beyond some basic needs like emergency access and so on, the regulator has decided to take a hands-off approach. This was a significant policy decision at the time, given that the government could have taken a similar approach to how they have regulated the wired telephone system.

A similar decision was reached in the case of regulating the Internet.[8] Although Internet access is typically provided through the infrastructure of existing regulated businesses (usually a cable or telephone provider), the CRTC decided to not regulate Internet services beyond a few basic aspects. Importantly, they decided not to get involved in Internet content. While content regulation was never a part of telecommunications regulation—the law is explicitly designed to ensure carriers are not liable for and need not monitor what people say on the telephone, apart from criminal prosecutions that are addressed in other parts of the law—content regulation is common in radio and television.[9] Both radio and television in Canada are required to have minimum amounts of Canadian content, they have obligations regarding hours of service and coverage areas, they have to abide by codes of conduct with regard to adult entertainment, and so on. The Internet being full of content (websites, video, music) could have been seen as an object for regulation (how that would be accomplished, of course, is another matter), but in the end the CRTC—which did hold hearings and has considered the matter seriously on at least two occasions—decided on a position of forbearance. They have persisted in this "hands-off" approach, most recently in consideration over whether Netflix should be considered a broadcaster as the cable and over-the-air television networks hoped (CBC 2011). The Internet— like mobile phones—has been allowed to evolve largely without regulatory oversight. This, too, is an important policy decision, which has significant implications for other domains. As a simple example, how people use the Internet to copy and share music or movies is considered a civil matter between individuals and not something in which the regulator is willing to get involved (or punish the Internet service provider for).

Next Generation New Media Policy

As Christopher Yoo (2008) has argued, the way in which broadcasting and telecommunications networks are becoming one and the same—with people making phone calls and watching video over the same Internet connection—has profound implications for countries such as Canada and the United States, which divide their new media regulation into content and carriage regulatory groups. In Canada, for example, there are the broadcasting division and the telecommunications divisions of the CRTC. The latter, based on regulation of telegraphs and telephones, and the former, based on regulation of radio and television, have struggled to come up with meaningful oversight of the Internet, as it seems to slip through their grasp at every opportunity.

Yoo's prediction, that content delivery networks, multicast protocols, and much more aggressive traffic management will affect network neutrality debates in the United States (2008), has already come true in Canada. In 2009, there was a request— ultimately unsuccessful—from small Internet service providers (ISPs) who argued that the CRTC should take action again against **traffic shaping** by Bell Canada.[10] Traffic shaping is a method of managing different protocols (the Web is a protocol, as is email, for example) on the Internet, differently. Bell, and other large ISPs, have reserved the right to restrict some protocols—mainly because of what they claim is exorbitant use of the network by users who are sharing media files using software such as BitTorrent. Smaller ISPs, who were selling unrestricted packages to these users, but who had to buy their Internet connections wholesale from Bell, were not able to deliver truly unrestricted service. They sought a ruling from the CRTC that would force Bell to offer unshaped Internet connections, under common carriage rules. The CRTC denied their request.[11]

Despite this setback, mass media content in the form of streaming video and audio continues to grow in importance on the Internet and the days of being able to govern the Internet purely as a telecommunication service, or ignore the content side of the Internet, are dwindling. How regulatory regimes will be restructured or recreated remains to be seen, however. The CRTC, particularly in its 2012 decision (CRTC 2012) to deny Bell and Astral Media's proposed merger, has shown a growing inclination to make decisions with a greater emphasis on "what is best for the consumer" rather than "what's best for the industry" (Ladurantaye 2012).

Copyright and Intellectual Property Law: An Overview

Copyright and intellectual property law has become, in many respects, the crucible for many of the issues and challenges that new media poses to law and policy. These legal and policy issues are being played out in a variety of national and international forums and are at the core of how the global knowledge economy or creative economy will develop. Among the issues raised are

1. the balance between public good and private benefit criteria for use of, and access to, information;
2. the balance between individual rights of ownership and social use for common benefit;
3. the nature of knowledge as both a commodity for commercial exploitation and as a public good for common use; and
4. the best ways in which to promote and equitably share the benefits of creativity in an age of digital networks for people, communities, nations, and global humanity.

Copyright law as it is understood today was first enacted in Britain in 1709 with the Statute of Anne, which established a term of protection (of 14 years) for the author of an original work as an incentive to produce new works, and set a limit (of 21 years) to the time before which control over the rights to previously published works was ceded from publishers to the public domain. The US Congress, in one of its first legislative acts after the Declaration of Independence, passed the Copyright Act of 1790, to "promote the Progress of Science and useful Arts, by securing for limited Times to Authors and Inventors the exclusive Right to their respective Writings and Discoveries" (Walterscheid 2005). This legislation both provided protection to the creators of original works ("Authors and Inventors") and set statutory limits to the time before such rights passed into the public domain. James Madison, one of the original authors drafting the US Constitution, saw in this an outcome where "the public good fully coincides . . . with the claims of individuals" (quoted in Vaidhyanathan 2001: 45).

Copyright presumes that original forms of creative expression can belong to individuals, who have both a moral right to ownership and a legitimate economic right to derive material benefit from the use of these ideas and works by others. It also presumes that the use of their original ideas and works should be subject to the laws of free and fair exchange, that there should be adequate compensation for use by others, and there should be safeguards against misuse. At the same time, copyright recognizes that original ideas and works are drawn from an existing pool of knowledge and creativity, and that there is, therefore, a need to guarantee that such ideas and works exist in the public domain for **fair use** (or **fair dealing** in Canada) by others. Moreover, since such information is the lifeblood of democracy, commerce, and the development of future knowledge, broad access by the community to the widest possible pool of information, knowledge, and forms of creative expression is a valuable end in itself, as a condition for participation in public life and the development of new knowledge. In order to balance these competing claims on knowledge, copyright law divides up the possible rights in and uses of a work, giving control over some of these rights to the creators and distributors and control over others to the general public (Litman 2001: 16).

The neat distinctions that copyright law seeks to make between private ownership and public use have often been difficult to sustain in practice. Three areas of distinction have been particularly contentious. First, facts, ideas, and concepts are not themselves copyrightable—they cannot be owned by individuals. What copyright protects is original forms of creative expression of such facts, ideas, concepts, and so on, or the ways in which they are expressed, selected, and arranged by individuals through physical works such as books, publications, artistic works, and so on. Second, what the author or creator has an exclusive right to is the creative expression contained in a work, not the physical form in which that work is produced and distributed. In the case of a book, for example, the original author retains exclusive ownership of the forms of creative expression that constituted that book, but is assumed to have contractually assigned the rights of reproduction of that book to a publisher, and in turn derives subsequent benefit from that publisher's activities in distributing the book, in the form of royalties or other forms of financial remuneration.

Finally, there has developed alongside copyright law a series of exceptions where it is deemed to be in the public interest to make material more widely available at no cost. These fair use or fair dealing provisions for private, non-commercial uses without authorization, have been typically applied to the photocopying of works in public libraries, but are now extensively applied in the copying of software applications, and the placing of materials on the Web (e.g., sections from books and academic journals used for teaching purposes). Embedded within copyright more generally are two competing visions of intellectual property: (1) as something that can be privately owned as property and (2) as something that is central to the principles of freedom of speech, equitable access to public information, and economic efficiency (see Table 9.1).

Table 9.1 Two Visions of Intellectual Property

	Information as public resource	Information as private property
Normative starting point	Free speech and free circulation of ideas and information in society	Individual property rights and rights of personal privacy
Vision of production of ideas	Primarily drawn from existing materials	Individual creativity and originality
Economic perspective	Information and efficiency	Innovation and incentives
Principal concern	Inequitable access to information in society	Denial of individual rights and creativity

Source: Adapted from Boyle (1997: 158).

It is notable that the US Copyright Act of 1790 constructed issues relating to copyright upon what can be described as a horizontal axis of content creators, distributors, and users, where each was a broadly equal player in terms of power resources. Subsequently, in a process tracked by authors such as Bettig (1996), Vaidhyanathan (2001), and Perelman (2002), this horizontal axis has been overlaid by a vertical axis, whereby those who have established ownership of copyrighted works—who are, by the nature of contracts in the creative industries, typically the distributors of creative content rather than its originators—have constituted themselves as a powerful group whose interests sit over and above, and frequently in opposition to, the much larger, but far more dispersed, group of end-users of copyrighted or copyrightable material (see Figure 9.1).

Copyright law is derived from the principle that neither the creator of a new work nor the general public should be able to appropriate all of the benefits that flow from the creation of a new, original work of authorship. In Canada, this has taken the form of a balance: "between promoting the public interest in the encouragement and dissemination of works of the arts and intellect and obtaining a just reward for the creator" (Supreme Court of Canada 2002).

Canadian copyright law is similar to US and UK copyright law and contains many of the same provisions and characteristics. In some areas, the law is stricter; in others, it is more relaxed. As with US and UK law, Canadian law preserves a right of fair dealing, which has been interpreted broadly in recent court decisions.[12] However, as

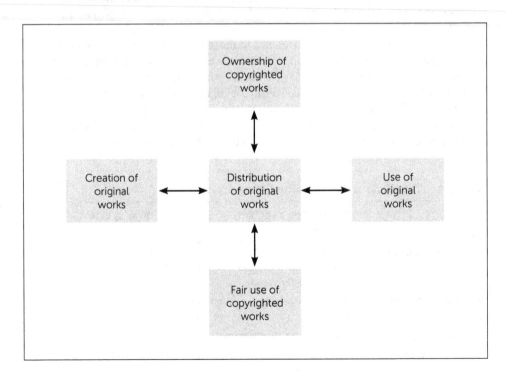

Figure 9.1 Relations within Copyright and Intellectual Property Regimes

copyright law is an area of considerable importance in an information and knowledge economy, there has been a fair bit of pressure from creator groups—many of which are based in the United States—that would like to see Canadian laws more restrictive. Changes to the Canadian Copyright Act were proposed in 2009 and 2010 and finally passed into law in 2012, with many of the new provisions seemingly inspired by US law. One of the most controversial aspects of the new law is the provision to legally protect **digital locks**, even when a fair dealing/fair use right may exist. Digital locks—also known as copy protection—are technical ways of preventing people from copying material or otherwise infringing on the rights of copyright holders. The controversy over protection of digital locks arises when users have rights—to back up a DVD, for example—but cannot exercise those rights because in order to do so, they would have to break the digital lock and the lock itself is protected by law.

The new copyright law in Canada, and especially as it is interpreted in light of important Supreme Court of Canada decisions in 2012, can also be seen as more supportive of user rights with regard to copyright. Legal scholars speak of copyright not as a fundamental right but rather a policy "bargain" made by governments to encourage creators and benefit users, often with an explicit reference to science and education. These user rights are enshrined in the law, and have been reinforced by recent court decisions. The result has been a move back toward a balance of rights between creators and consumers of content.

Importance of the Public Domain

Another way of looking at copyright has been suggested by a group of European academics working on topics related to the digital public domain. Known as COMMUNIA, this group has created a statement focused on those things that are *not* covered by copyright, encouraging people to ensure that as much material as possible goes into and stays in the **public domain**. They lay out a number of principles that help clarify why the public domain is so important and how it can be protected.

- The Public Domain is the rule, copyright protection is the exception.
- Copyright protection should last only as long as necessary to achieve a reasonable compromise between protecting and rewarding the author for his or her intellectual labour and safeguarding the public interest in the dissemination of culture and knowledge.
- What is in the Public Domain must remain in the Public Domain.
- The lawful user of a digital copy of a Public Domain work should be free to (re) use, copy, and modify such work.
- Contracts or technical protection measures that restrict access to and reuse of Public Domain works must not be enforced. (COMMUNIA 2009)

It is unclear whether this initiative will gain the recognition necessary to shift people's thinking about copyright, but it provides an important alternative perspective, given that the language is quite often heavily weighted by the groups and organizations with the most to gain from an expansive interpretation of copyright: the owners and distributors of copyrighted movies, music, and books.

Copyright and New Media

Of the many issues that render copyright law ever more complex and significant in an age of new media and the Internet, there are four particularly worthy of attention. First, the rapid development and mass dissemination of technologies that enable low-cost reproduction of data and information have dramatically changed the issues associated with copyright law. Whereas copyright law developed at a time when the reproduction of a work bore significant costs (e.g., the costs of reprinting a book), the development of low-cost duplication technologies, readily available at home, work, or school, has meant that more and more people have the ability to copy materials at near-zero cost. With the development of the Internet, email, and file-sharing technologies, these copies can be distributed to any number of people across electronic networks.

Second, the rise of a knowledge-based or creative economy has seen intellectual property rights become a key source of new corporate wealth. The commercial creative industries are characterized by a high initial cost to produce original material, a high failure rate for new commercial products, and near-zero costs of content reproduction (Caves 2000; Hesmondhalgh 2007). As a result, a very high premium is attached to successful creative product that is likely to accrue economic worth over time. The value of Mickey Mouse to the Disney Corporation, or the value of the Beatles' back catalogue of songs, remains high decades after the content was originally produced. Associated with the enhanced economic value of intellectual property rights has been the rise of the copyright industries, which are defined as those industries "engaged primarily in the generation, production, and dissemination of new copyrighted material" (Siwek 2002: 9).

Third, copyrighted products are now a part of global popular culture to a historically unprecedented degree. Corporate trademarks are reproduced and often parodied, musical fragments are sampled, references to other pop-culture forms are frequently made in television programs such as *The Simpsons* and *South Park*, films and television programs increasingly draw on generic conventions established in other films and television programs, and advertising undertakes a relentless co-optation of cultural referents derived from other media. Coombe observes that the growth and extension of legal protections to intellectual property has occurred at a time when "the texts protected by intellectual property laws signify: they are cultural forms that assume local meaning in the life worlds of those who incorporate them into their daily lives" (1998: 7).

Fourth, copyright and intellectual property law has been progressively globalized over time. The European states agreed on a common framework for copyright law through the Berne Convention for the Protection of Literary and Artistic Works (1886), although the United States was a conspicuous non-signatory to this convention (Drahos and Braithwaite 2002: 34–5). In more recent times, the United States has been a leader in promoting international intellectual property regimes, not least because its copyright industries are seen as most at risk from product piracy. The US-based Software Protection Agency estimated in 1994 that as much as 98 per cent of software used on computers in China was pirated, as was 95 per cent of computer software used in Russia and 92 per cent of that used in Thailand (Baase 1997: 174–5), and the International Intellectual Property Alliance estimated that the cost to the US economy of intellectual property piracy has been about USD $40 billion annually (Boyle 1997: 121). As the world's leading net exporter of intellectual property rights, the United States has been the principal driver of the Trade-Related Aspects of Intellectual Property Rights (TRIPS) Agreement, signed by more than a hundred nations in 1994 after agreement by the signatories to the General Agreement on Trade in Services (GATS). The entry of China into the WTO is perhaps particularly significant in this regard, as China has been seen, particularly by US interests, as the nation that is most frequently in breach of copyright and intellectual property law (Montgomery and Keane 2006; Y. Zhang 2006).

Cyber-libertarians such as John Perry Barlow predicted the collapse of copyright law under the weight of new media, arguing that "intellectual property law cannot be patched, retro-fitted or expanded to contain the gasses of digitized expression. . . . We will need to develop an entirely new set of methods as befits this entirely new set of circumstances" (Barlow 1996b: 10). However, copyright and intellectual property law have not only proved more resilient, they have been strengthened since the rise of the Internet, raising the question of how best to manage the balance of interests (identified in Figure 9.1 on page 232). Litman (2001) observes that the problem with applying old rules to new media is that they are likely to inhibit the development of new technologies in the short term and to fail completely in the medium term.

At the same time, the call for a generalized copyright exemption for new media developments, which follows from the cyber-libertarian position, is unlikely to satisfy the creators of copyrightable content, who are concerned about who would pay for their work and their ability to continue in creative or intellectual pursuits, if content were made more freely available to users. Litman instead proposes that there is a need for more direct dialogue between the creators and users of copyrightable content, or between creative people and the wider public, because their interests are less clearly opposed than is presented to be the case by content distributors. Initiatives such as the Creative Commons digital content licensing scheme (see the accompanying case study) have sought to address such concerns, in ways that are legally robust, readily understood, and applicable to producers of original content in the creative industries and related sectors.

Others have drawn attention to the position of institutions such as public libraries, accepted and honoured for the role they play in education and the furtherance of the objectives of a democratic society. In a satirical blog posting about the "cost" of libraries in the United States, Eric Hellman writes,

> As soon as I got off the train, I was surrounded by even more of this crowd. Calling themselves "Librarians," they talk about promoting literacy, education, culture and economic development, which are, of course, code words for the use and dispersal of intellectual property. They readily admit to their activities, and rationalize them because they're perfectly legal in the US, at least for now.[13]

The "at least for now" closing line is a not-so-subtle reference to the ever widening scope of copyright extension and inclusion.

CASE STUDY

Creative Commons

Creative Commons (CC) is a worldwide project that aims to make copyright material more accessible and its terms of access more negotiable in the digital environment (Creative Commons 2007). In order to do this, Creative Commons asks content owners who wish to contribute to the commons to generically give permission in advance to certain types of use of their content, through the labelling of their content with a CC badge and an agreement in advance to the terms and conditions attached to this use through a legally binding CC licence. It aims to overcome three bottlenecks that current copyright and intellectual property laws present in the digital environment: (1) the difficulties faced by users of already existing content in locating and negotiating with the initial content creators; (2) the question of rights and conditions attached to use of existing digital content in other domains, for commercial or non-commercial purposes; and (3) the extent to which existing copyright and intellectual property laws circumvent direct negotiation between content creators and prospective users of copyrighted material through the assignation of rights to content distributors, who then manage all legal aspects of content use and repurposing rather than the direct producers of the original content. Creative Commons was founded in 2001 by a series of high-profile intellectual property experts and creative practitioners, including Lawrence Lessig, James Boyle, Hal Abelson, Eric Saltzman, Joi Ito, and Eric Aldred, with financial support from the Center

for the Public Domain and other organizations. It is currently supported in the United States by the Berkman Center for Internet and Society at Harvard Law School and the Stanford Law School Center for Internet and Society. By 2007, Creative Commons licences had been developed in 35 countries outside the United States, including Argentina, Australia, Austria, Slovenia, South Africa, South Korea, Spain, Sweden, and Switzerland, with a further 14 countries being in discussion (Creative Commons 2007). Central to this international expansion of Creative Commons have been initiatives to ensure legally effective harmonization of the Creative Commons licence to the specific national legislation that governs copyright and intellectual property law within different countries. Creative Commons Canada (http://creativecommons.ca) was set up in 2003 and provides English and French versions of the Creative Commons licences, adapted to Canadian law. It is housed at the University of Ottawa and supported by the Canadian Internet Policy and Public Interest Clinic (CIPPIC).

A key aim of Creative Commons has been to simplify the range of choices available to creative people across the artistic, educational, scientific, and digital production domains about how they can, in advance and independently of those who distribute their content as commercial product, designate rights to use and repurpose their work. There are four categories of Creative Commons licence that are available to those who choose to place their content under a CC licence:

1. Attribution: Content developers allow others to copy, distribute, display, and perform the copyrighted work—and derivative works based

Recent Developments in International Copyright and Intellectual Property Law

The 1990s saw two very significant extensions in both the scope and the domain of copyright law. In the United States, the Digital Millennium Copyright Act was passed by Congress in 1998, along with the Sonny Bono Copyright Term Extension Act, 1998, which extends the term of copyright protection for copyright works from the life of the author plus 50 years to the life of the author plus 70 years. Despite widespread upon it—but only if they give credit to the original work in the way it was requested.

2. Non-commercial: Others are permitted to copy, distribute, display, and perform a copyrighted work—and derivative works based upon it—but only if it is for non-commercial purposes. If there is an intention to use the work for commercial purposes, then there needs to be a different legal basis for discussion. An example of this would be Alberto Korda's famous photograph of Che Guevara in 1960, which has been made freely available to radical organizations and groups that broadly share Che's ideals. Korda successfully defended the right for this image not to be used by Smirnoff to promote its vodka products in 2000, as he argued that this was clearly at odds with Che's own socialist ideals and Korda's moral rights as the photographer.

3. No derivative works: Others are permitted to copy, distribute, display, and perform only verbatim copies of the copyrighted work, but not derivative works based upon it. In this way, the integrity of the original work can be preserved, as well as the moral rights of the creator.

4. Share alike: Original content creators allow others to distribute derivative works only under a licence identical to the licence that governs their own work. It should be noted that a licence cannot feature both the "share alike" and "no derivative works" options, since the "share alike" requirement applies only to derivative works.

Creative Commons describes its purpose as providing "free tools that let authors, scientists, artists, and educators easily mark their creative work with the freedoms they want it to carry" so that creative producers can change "copyright terms from 'All Rights Reserved' to 'Some Rights Reserved'" (Creative Commons 2007). In doing so, the aim has also been to avoid complex and costly legal disputes by dramatically simplifying the plethora of legal questions that face providers of original creative content about how to deal with others who draw upon their creative work. As Fitzgerald puts it, "Models such as Creative Commons rely on the power of copyright ownership and law to structure access downstream. In this sense CC is not anti-copyright. Rather, it uses copyright as the basis for structuring open access. However, CC is designed to provide an alternative for managing copyright in digital content" (2006: 222).

Case Study Questions

1. When you are uploading pictures to a service, such as Flickr, that provides the option of selecting a Creative Commons licence, do you choose that option? Why or why not?

2. If you were participating in a site, such as Wikipedia, that declares all of its material to be covered by a Creative Commons licence, does that encourage you to participate or discourage you from participating?

3. Many people argue that academic journals, where the writing is the result of salaries and research grants that come from the public, should be uniformly available under a Creative Commons or other "free" licence. Do you agree? What would be the impact of such a policy on traditional, for-profit, publishers?

criticism of these legislative initiatives from both a legal and policy perspective (e.g., Litman 2001; Perelman 2002; Rimmer 2003b; Vaidhyanathan 2001), their impact has been significant within and outside the United States. Cases such as *Eldred v. Ashcroft* were unsuccessful in challenging the extension of copyright, despite 17 leading US economists, including five Nobel laureates, arguing that such copyright extension was not in the nation's economic interest (Moore 2005). Rimmer (2003b) terms the Sonny Bono Copyright Extension Act the "Mickey Mouse Bill" because it arose at a time when Disney's copyright on Mickey Mouse and its other famous cartoon characters was about to expire, but the resultant legislative changes have guaranteed that Mickey Mouse will not pass into the public domain until 2023.

The second major development was the passing of the Trade-Related Aspects of Intellectual Property Rights (TRIPS) Agreement in 1995, at the conclusion of the Uruguay Round of trade negotiations that led to the formation of the WTO. The TRIPS Agreement was signed by more than a hundred countries in April 1994, with all members of the WTO bound by the conditions of the agreement, including recent members such as China (Braithwaite and Drahos 2000: 57). Unlike previous multilateral conventions governing intellectual property, such as the Paris and Berne Conventions struck by the European powers in the late nineteenth century, TRIPS is not based on the setting of minimum standards and mutual adjustment of national laws over time. Rather, it establishes a global framework for the protection of intellectual property to which significant legal and economic sanctions can be applied to nations that fail to comply with its highly prescriptive standards to protect the rights of those holding patents, copyright, trademarks, and trade secrets. Sell describes TRIPS as

> A stunning triumph for commercial interests and industry lobbyists who had worked so tirelessly to achieve the global agreement. TRIPS institutionalized a conception of intellectual property based on protection and exclusion rather than competition and diffusion. By extending property rights and requiring high substantive levels of protection, TRIPS represented a significant victory for US private sector activists from knowledge-based industries. (2002: 172)

One of the factors that links US legislation and developments through TRIPS and the World Intellectual Property Organization (WIPO) is the impact of bilateral free-trade agreements. TRIPS established an important beachhead for uniformity in international patent legislation through the Patent Cooperation Treaty, which enables developers of patentable products to file an international patent application through the WIPO. This has force for 136 member nations, which agreed in 2007 that, if the application is accepted, the patent is binding in all of those nations. Bilateral free-trade agreements between the United States and other nations have typically involved the extension of US-based forms of copyright protection to the signatory nations. Canada has so far not completed a rationalization of its copyright laws to coincide with US law, much to the concern of the United States, as signalled by Canada's placement on a piracy blacklist in April 2009 (Koring 2009). The pressure for Canada to amend its law has been considerable, but progress has been slow and there have been significant countervailing pressures, both from activists and scholars, such as Michael Geist as well as representatives from Internet industry groups concerned about the costs of implementing some of the measures.

Two critical questions arise from these measures to extend copyright protection into the indefinite future and to establish a legally binding global intellectual property regime. The first is whether or not it is beneficial to society as a whole. The economic argument for copyright protection has revolved around the rights of content creators to receive remuneration for the expression of their ideas and concepts, and the idea that such returns provide incentives for future development of new ideas. Critics have argued that while these are valid arguments in principle, the extension of copyright protection through recent legislation not only shifts the balance too far away from other users and, therefore, heightens the possibility of inadvertent copyright infringement, but it also is a hindrance to economic and social innovation. Given the capacity of the digital media environment to promote collaboration, content sharing, content reuse and repurposing, and P2P file-sharing, which is arguably "both the origin and the future of the Internet" (Haussmann 2002), the case can be made that the media and entertainment industries would be better served by fostering such networks, rather than seeking to restrict or criminalize such activities (Benkler 2006; Lessig 2004; Perelman 2002; Vaidhyanathan 2001, 2004).

Moreover, the economic case for extending copyright protection is considered weak: the extension of copyright protection to 70 years under the Sonny Bono Copyright Extension Act only provides an increase in compensation to creators of less than 1 per cent (cited in Moore 2005: 74). This needs to be balanced against the economic costs of extending copyright protection and extending the capacity to extract monopoly rents for existing copyright holders over time, in ways that would likely be detrimental to the creation of new works. In its criticism of these changes, the US Committee for Economic Development emphasized how copyright law can inhibit the capacity of "follow-on" and "second" innovators to build upon copyrighted innovations, thereby dampening the overall scope for innovation by artificially restricting the public domain (CED 2004). Perelman argues that information is not only a public good and, hence, deserves government oversight of how it is produced and distributed, but it also is, in fact, a "metapublic" good, which generates positive benefits to a community when it is freely available in ways that cannot be calculated, since "information is not scarce, except to the degree that society allows agents to create artificial scarcity through secrecy and property rights . . . as the economy becomes increasingly dependent on information, the traditional system of property rights applied to information becomes a costly fetter on our development" (2002: 178).

The issues that arise from the global application of US-derived copyright and intellectual property laws, as pursued through agreements such as TRIPS, are considerable (e.g., see Bannermann 2006; Shanker 2006). These tend to involve debates about the equity of such arrangements between economically developed and developing countries, for two reasons. First, the vast bulk of intellectual property rights are held in a small number of countries: in 2004, five patent offices (Japan, United States, South Korea, China, and Europe) accounted for 75 per cent of patent applications and 74 per cent of patents granted worldwide (WIPO 2006). Second, the near-zero costs of reproduction of digital goods enabled by new media technologies create strong incentives in lower-wage countries to make illegal copies of such materials (DVDs, computer software programs, etc.) and resell them at substantially lower prices than those offered to consumers in higher-wage nations.

Drahos and Braithwaite (2002: 188–9) draw attention to this paradox, which is that strong protection of intellectual property rights may lead to monopolies, while weak protection may lead to "free-riding" on the innovations of others, and underinvestment in innovation. Drahos and Braithwaite also identify a positive correlation between democratic societies and efficient intellectual property rights, but note that this is in turn dependent on (1) an inclusive policy culture, where all relevant interests participate in negotiation of the final outcomes; (2) full provision of information to all relevant parties; and (3) the absence of coercive power by one party over others.

Significantly, they find all of these to be absent from international negotiations about the TRIPS Agreement: developing countries were largely excluded from the forums in which TRIPS was debated, awareness of possible adverse consequences of TRIPS (e.g., on the availability of low-cost generic drugs to address the AIDS crisis in Africa) was low, and the United States, in its view, threatened trade sanctions and foreign-aid withdrawals for nations that did not share its views on the merits of a uniform multilateral agreement on intellectual property rights (Drahos and Braithwaite 2002: 189–92).

Using the public goods framework derived from economic theory, Drahos and Braithwaite conclude that current tendencies on copyright and intellectual property law have the potential to lead to information feudalism on a global scale. They characterize information feudalism as involving the use of intellectual property rights to inhibit competition (e.g., through the patenting of basic business processes); the withholding of valuable information about diseases and suitable treatments from poorer developing nations; and the locking up of basic research outcomes from institutions that once treated knowledge as a pure public good for social use, such as universities and colleges.

Some countries, most notably Brazil, have made strong statements that attempt to balance the rights of consumers with the rights of authors in copyright statements. In a recent proposal from that country, initiatives such as digital locks are permitted as long as they do not hinder fair use/fair dealing rights (e.g., using a work for education, research, or criticism). Canada has similar fair-dealing rights (as do most countries), recently reaffirmed in the CCH case by the Supreme Court of Canada. In that case, the Law Society of Upper Canada was accused of copyright infringement for allowing students and members of the Law Society to make copies of decisions that were held in the library. Three large publishers of legal materials, led by CCH Canadian Limited, sued for copyright infringement. In a unanimous decision, the court ruled that this form of copying was fair dealing in that it constituted research or private study and as such was protected under Canadian law.

There have also been concerns that proposals in Canada relating to digital locks would trump users' rights. In other words, you might have a right to use something but not the right to remove the lock that would let you have access, effectively negating your right of access. Passed in 2012, Canada's new Copyright Act (Bill C-11) retained these protections of digital locks, despite widespread criticism of the provision.[14]

On the other hand, the new act contained important provisions that enhanced fair dealing, format shifting, backup copies, and user-generated content, among others (Geist 2012). This, coupled with an important decision by the Canadian Supreme Court later in the summer of 2012, created a new climate for the use of copyrighted works in Canada.

The more recent Anti-Counterfeiting Trade Agreement (ACTA) can be expected to have significant consequences for new media law and policy. Even before being finalized, the negotiations for the trade agreement, conducted mainly behind closed doors in countries around the world, stirred up considerable debate in 2009 and 2010. In a sense, the way in which ACTA has been negotiated in secret is itself a challenge to many of the principles of open source and the free exchange of information. The agreement, which covers a broad range of topics, including the way in which countries are expected to control the production, sale, and export of counterfeit goods (e.g., fake

Rolexes or knock-off Gucci handbags), also covers "piracy over the Internet."[15] *Piracy* is a term that is widely (mis)used to refer to copyright **infringement**, however, and its use there is inappropriate: no ships have been commandeered, no goods are missing, no one has been deprived of the use of their movies, music, or books.

There is a law against piracy in Canada (R.S., c. C-34, s. 75; 1974-75-76, c. 105, s. 3.), but it is entirely related to ships and their cargo. The lobby groups for those who make their money distributing copyrighted material (mainly movies, music, and books) use the term *piracy* in order to equate copyright infringement with the more rhetorically loaded concept of piracy, with its long history and considerable cultural reference points. Using such language also serves as a tactic to conjure images of swashbuckling ruffians on the bounding main or present-day pirates off the coast of Somalia in order to garner support for a cause. Effective as it may be, it should be understood as a tactic of persuasion by lobbyists and not a legal term when speaking of copyright.

ACTA began as an initiative between the United States and Japan, in 2006. It has since been expanded to a growing number of countries, in part because the United States has begun to encourage countries that it trades with to sign the agreement as a way of harmonizing regulation over copyright and intellectual property around the world. The proposed trade agreement has not yet been ratified and the terms of the agreement were unknown for many years. The objectives of the agreement, however, have been broadly referenced in a document released by the US Trade Representative and includes the following opening statement:

> The ACTA initiative aims to establish international standards for enforcing intellectual property rights in order to fight more efficiently the growing problem of counterfeiting and piracy. In particular, the ACTA is intended to establish, among the signatories, agreed standards for the enforcement of intellectual property rights that address today's challenges by increasing international cooperation, strengthening the framework of practices that contribute to effective enforcement of intellectual property rights, and strengthening relevant enforcement measures. The intended focus is on counterfeiting and piracy activities that significantly affect commercial interests, rather than on the activities of ordinary citizens. ACTA is not intended to interfere with a signatory's ability to respect its citizens' fundamental rights and civil liberties, and will be consistent with the WTO Agreement on Trade-Related Aspects of Intellectual Property Rights (TRIPS Agreement) and will respect the Declaration on TRIPS and Public Health (US Trade Representative 2010).

Section 4 of the proposed agreement covers "intellectual property rights enforcement in the digital environment" and, presumably, will have the most impact on new media productions. The final version of the treaty was published in the spring of 2011 and is available on a Canadian government website (http://www.international.gc.ca/trade-agreements-accords-commerciaux/topics-domaines/ip-pi/acta-text-acrc.aspx). While Canada and many other countries have signed the agreement, ratification is proceeding slowly with only Japan formally ratifying as October 2013.

One of the most controversial elements of the treaty may very well be the "graduated response" system for people accused of copyright infringement. Graduated response is a type of copyright-infringement punishment regime, commonly known as a **three- strikes** law, in which people who have three accusations of copyright infringement (e.g., downloading movies or music illegally) would no longer be permitted to have Internet access. There is some ambiguity about whether all members of a household would lose their access to the Internet in the case of infringement by one individual in the family or home (e.g., a child accused of file sharing).

These types of laws are in place in a few countries (France, for example), however, there is little experience with them to date. The most controversial aspect of this type of law is that the punishment is meted out not for a conviction but for an accusation, which opens the law to possible abuse by malicious or mistaken claims of infringement. In July 2009, a French court struck down this key component of that country's three-strikes law when the justices ruled that "under the Declaration of 1789, every man is presumed innocent until proven guilty." The ruling further stated that "the Internet is a fundamental human right that cannot be taken away by anything other than a court of law, only when guilt has been established there."[16] The law has also been criticized as excessive in its levels of punishment, since banning someone from the Internet could be a serious impairment in his or her life, especially if the allegation is unproven. Again, there are few accounts of how these laws have been applied. New Zealand, for example, had a three-strikes law before Parliament in 2009, but it was withdrawn after widespread public protests. A revised law is now in place, but as of this writing, there have been no reported convictions.

The Internet as a Human Right or Universal Service Obligation

Several countries have begun to treat Internet use as a fundamental human right. One of the first to do so was Estonia, which made Internet access a fundamental human right in that country in 2000.[17] Greece has also taken this approach, with Finland[18] and Spain[19] adding service-level obligations for the telecommunication carriers to provide broadband access. The Conservative Party in the United Kingdom made broadband access for the majority of homes part of their election platform in early 2010.[20] And in Germany, courts held that Internet access was fundamental to modern life, and having access withdrawn or denied—in this case by a service error—was something worthy of compensation (*The Local* 2013).

Canada has long had **universal service** objectives for both telephone and broadcasting services. In urban areas, these are non-problematic, as the market is prepared and welcomes the opportunity to serve large populations gathered closely together. Canada, with a high percentage of its population in urban centres in close proximity to the United States, and its massive Internet industry, generally has excellent Internet service for its urban citizens. Rural Canadians, however, are not so well served and remote and northern residents have either slow service or no service. Satellite services are available in most of the country, but they are private, commercial services, which are either slow or expensive or both. For residents of narrow mountain valleys where satellite coverage does not reach, prospects for getting high-speed Internet service are even more limited.

Universal access to the Internet was discussed as early as 1995 in the CRTC report, *Competition and Culture on Canada's Information Highway: Managing the Realities of Transition*.[21] Chapter 4 of that report dealt explicitly with "public spaces in a digital world" and considered universality as a key element. While the commission supported the idea of public access as being important, it declined to impose a cross-subsidization scheme on telecommunication providers:

> While basic telephone services can continue to be supported in part by subsidized rates, the Commission considers that decisions on funding and priorities for infrastructure development on the information highway in high-cost areas should be made by governments (CRTC 1995).

Since the time the report was released, the federal government has, at various times, initiated a number of programs that provide funding; subsidized access; and provided access for community drop-in centres, training groups, schools, health services, and a number of other programs. Some of these have persisted for many years, such as the Community Access Program, which provides computers, training, software, and Internet access for community centres, libraries, and other places where the public can have access to, and learn to use, the Internet.

Although universal service is a policy objective for telephone service in Canada, as we noted earlier, there is not yet an equivalent obligation on the part of telecommunications providers to deliver subsidized or universal Internet service, and, in particular, there is no obligation to deliver broadband speeds. The question of if and when a neighbourhood is served with high-speed Internet is a business decision being made by telephone companies or cable providers. It should be noted that this business decision became easier for a while, as the federal government and the governments of several provinces stepped in with subsidy programs for rural and remote Internet initiatives (Smith and Godfrey 2009). Regardless of the degrees of success of these programs, the question of how to continue to support and extend the reach of high-speed Internet connectivity outside of urban areas remains a policy debate in Canada and elsewhere.

Digital Gatekeepers and the Open-Source Movement

While the challenges of copyright in a digital age have generated different responses both within and across the creative industries, responses in the media and entertainment sectors have often been reactive and defensive. These responses have frequently involved legal action against those perceived to be transgressors of copyrighted material, as seen in the 2007 USD $1 billion lawsuit lodged by Viacom against YouTube (cf. Butt and Bruns 2005; O'Brien 2007), as well as in heavy lobbying efforts. In the lawsuit, Viacom sued YouTube (and its corporate parent, Google) for allowing users to upload material—largely clips from television programs—that were owned by Viacom. Lobbying for increased terms of copyright by copyright owners associations—typically, the recording, television, and movie industries—is both ongoing and effective, as in the case of the Sonny Bono Copyright Term Extension Act that we discussed.

At the technological level, there has also been a focus on the development of technological protection measures (TPMs), generally, and digital rights management (DRM), in particular (Flew 2005b; Flew et al. 2006). DRM can be defined as the set of technical and legal mechanisms applied to help control access to, and distribution of, copyrighted and other protected material in the digital environment. Development of DRM systems are technically complex, requiring client rendering devices with trusted processing, input, and output paths, as well as modifications to current personal computing architecture. A key question arising from DRM strategies as a means to regulate access to digital content is whether or not the costs of DRM, and the more general strategy of defence-in-depth of the current copyright regime, justifies its status as the primary solution to the current dilemma. The DRM-driven approach is criticized as an insufficient solution, as it has at least three adverse consequences:

- diminished consumer privacy, as DRMs generate significantly increased functional capability to monitor online user behaviour;
- reduced innovation potential, as the development of new methods to attack peer-to-peer file-sharing networks and applications can inhibit the capacity for "follow-on" or "second" innovators to build on copyrighted innovations (as we noted above); and
- greater imbalances in the relationship between copyright holders and users of copyrighted materials; it is impossible to program fair use exceptions into DRM systems, since fair use is a complex legal mechanism, with outcomes dependent on individual aspects of each case.

An important alternative paradigm, and one that is very much grounded in the collaborative, DIY ethos that has underpinned the Internet from its inception (Castells 2001; Flichy 2007), is the paradigm arising from the **open-source** movement. The open-software and free-software movements[22] have pioneered decentralized, networked, and collaborative initiatives to develop new forms of software, licensed through non-proprietorial general public licences (GPLs). This means not only that users can acquire the software without cost, but they also can acquire access to the source code, which they can in turn apply, modify, or reconfigure. The influence of open-source thinking can be seen throughout the Web 2.0 environment, with the idea that "back-end" systems should be relatively open and flexible.

Underpinning the emergence of this large community of software developers, from which software such as the Linux operating system has emerged as a major alternative to proprietary systems such as those developed by Microsoft, are a series of broad principles whose domain of application moves well beyond the realm of software. The first is a general belief in freely available content. This is not, as Lessig notes in *Free Culture: How Big Media Uses Technology and the Law to Lock Down Culture and Control Creativity* (2004), "free" as in "free beer" (no one having to pay for anything), but, rather, free in the sense that creativity and innovation are best served by information and culture that is as widely available as possible. In this respect, belief in the intrinsic value of an "information commons" or a "creative commons" is threatened by recent initiatives to strengthen the intellectual-property rights regime, which is seen as presenting the danger of creating "a 'permission culture'—a culture in which creators get to create only with the permission of the powerful, or of the creators of the past" (2004: xiv).

Second, there is a belief that collaborative, non-proprietorial initiatives ultimately generate better product, and that open source has a compelling commercial as well as a moral logic. Eric Raymond contrasts the "cathedral" model of corporate- or government-controlled initiatives to that of the "bazaar" model, or initiatives generated by cooperating autonomous communities such as software developers. Raymond (1998) argues that "perhaps in the end the open source culture will triumph not because cooperation is morally right or software 'hoarding' is morally wrong ... but simply because the commercial world cannot win an evolutionary arms race with open source communities that can put orders of magnitude more skilled time into a problem." Third, there is an implicit belief in the value of a gift economy, whereby people will freely choose to participate in a collaborative initiative on the basis that sharing and collaboration are good things to do, and that the benefits they derive from such participation can be principally non-material in form (Best 2003).

The rise of the open-source movement has focused attention on different possible Internet futures and on the varying layers of control—over physical infrastructure and code as well as over content—in digital communications networks. This attention has sharpened the distinction between a policy environment that reproduces the old ways of broadcast media with its high barriers to entry for new competitors and its sharp demarcation between content producers and consumers, and an uncertain but potentially more open and democratic future based on the collective empowerment of users of digital media backed by an open and robust public information domain. Yochai Benkler identifies the new public interest in policies to develop open source and an information commons in these terms:

> We are in the midst of a pitched battle over the spoils of the transformation to a digitally networked environment and the information economy. Stakeholders from the older economy are using legislation, judicial opinions and international treaties to retain the old structure. . . . As economic policy, letting yesterday's winners dictate the terms of tomorrow's economic competition is disastrous. As social policy, missing an opportunity to enrich our freedom and enhance our justice while maintaining or even enhancing our productivity is unforgivable. (2001: 90)

Rennie also terms this a "new public interest" model that "involves embracing a range of possible publics that may conflict with or contradict each other. There is no claim to what the 'good' is, only a striving for it: more players and more ideas means a greater chance that some kind of progress will emerge, either in the form of economic advancement or the advancement of democracy" (2003: 56).

More generally, the open-source movement is characterized by its tendency toward the new and innovative. As Lawrence Lessig articulates, "We as a society should favour the disrupters. They will produce movement toward a more efficient, prosperous economy" (2001: 92). What this debate produces is not left–right politics as it has been traditionally defined—the state versus the market, the public sphere versus commercialization, socialism versus capitalism—but, rather, a shifting field of more contingent alliances, which recognizes the capacity of incumbent interests, both public and private, to effectively block innovation in order to protect existing monopoly privileges, and the difficulties in forming constituencies for change where the outcomes are uncertain. Arguably, creativity and innovation are best served by information and culture that is as widely available as possible, "to guarantee that follow-on creators and innovators remain as free as possible from the control of the past" (Lessig 2004: xiv).

Useful Websites

OpenNet Initiative and the Citizen Lab
https://citizenlab.org/tag/opennet-initiative

The OpenNet Initiative is a collaborative undertaking that involves four major partners, one of which is the Citizen Lab (http://citizenlab.org), based at the University of Toronto and led by scholar Ron Deibert. The partners also include Harvard's Berkman Center and the Oxford Internet Institute (see those two entries in this section), as well as Cambridge University. Together, they are pioneering research and interventions in the realm of open and free Internet connections. The partners study how censorship is being conducted on the Internet and how activists are working to get around it; they also develop tools to better assist in anonymous and secure use of the Internet.

Berkman Center for Internet Law & Society
http://cyber.law.harvard.edu

This is a resource site developed at Harvard Law School that is a leader in addressing intellectual property issues, as well as a range of areas of Internet law and policy. It is the host site for a series of major international research initiatives, including the Center for Citizen Media, FreeCulture, and the OpenNet Initiative.

Oxford Internet Institute
www.oii.ox.ac.uk

This is a major site for international and interdisciplinary Internet research, working out of the University of Oxford. Key research strands include Internet governance and democracy, the Internet and everyday life, and the wider implications of the open source software movement.

World Intellectual Property Organization
www.wipo.int/portal/index.html.en

The World Intellectual Property Organization is a specialist agency of the United Nations responsible for information gathering and promotion of shared international intellectual property standards. The site is a key source of information on what copyright, patents, and trademarks are, how they are distributed worldwide, and how policy and regulation is developing on an international scale.

Further Reading

From "Radical Extremism" to "Balanced Copyright": Canadian Copyright and the Digital Agenda, **Michael Geist (ed.), (2010)**
Canada Research Chair in Law, Technology and Society Michael Geist, based at the University of Ottawa, will be familiar to many Canadians from his high-profile campaign on Facebook relating to the copyright law. He also pens regular columns for the *Globe and Mail* and maintains a blog on various topics relating to technology law. This book brings together a wide range of authors writing about copyright for a Canadian audience and speaking directly to some of the changes happening currently. See also Geist's ongoing coverage of Canadian copyright issues at his Speak Out on Copyright site: http://copyright.michaelgeist.ca.

Free Culture: How Big Media Uses Technology and the Law to Lock Down Culture and Control Creativity, **Lawrence Lessig (2004)**
Lessig is a popular and dynamic public speaker (make sure to search for his name on Ted.com) who famously popularized thinking about the role of free culture and then shifted his work to devote his time to combating corruption and influence in government. His 2004 book lays the foundation for much of what we know and think about the value and importance of free materials in our culture.

Free: The Future of a Radical Price, **Chris Anderson (2009)**
Anderson, editor of *Wired* magazine, delivered this follow-up to *The Long-Tail* on the concept

of free material, though this book is more oriented to the business aspects and the prospects and opportunities for companies that want to take advantage of the potential for delivering goods and services for free. All of this sounds too good to be true, but behind the packaging is often another

source of revenue, such as the freemium approach that Flickr uses: give away a basic version in the hope that enough people will upgrade to the pro (premium) account, which is not free. Anderson discusses this and many other models for making money from things priced as free.

Discussion Questions

1. What are some of the domains covered by cyberspace law?
2. What are some of the policy initiatives or interventions that the Canadian government has taken in regard to new media? How are these important to understanding current new media policy in Canada?
3. What are some of the recent developments in international copyright and intellectual property law? What critical questions arise from measures to extend copyright protection and to establish a legally binding global intellectual property regime?
4. In what ways does the Internet, as it is situated in relation to existing laws and regulatory frameworks, complicate efforts to establish binding legal guidelines?
5. Copyright law seeks to make distinctions between private ownership and public use,

though these have often been difficult to sustain in practice. What three areas of distinction have been particularly contentious?
6. In the case involving the US Communications Decency Act (1996), Mike Godwin, counsel for the Electronic Frontier Foundation (EFF), argued (1998: 23), "Give people a modem and a computer and access to the Net, and it's far more likely that they'll do good than otherwise." How is this view characteristic of cyber-libertarian perspectives and why do you think such views are not now articulated as strongly as they once were?
7. Copyright law is derived from the principle of balanced interests. What are these interests and in what ways have new media and the Internet brought challenges to maintaining such balance?

Class Activities

1. Take a look at the CRTC website (www.crtc .gc.ca), noting the recent decisions relating to new media. Pick a recent decision that has general applicability (e.g., Net neutrality, or ISPs as carriers versus broadcasters) and consider how it fits with the concepts and analyses in this chapter. Does the approach of the commission or the tone of the decisions match with the views of this text? Does it match your own views?
2. Consider the implications of making Internet access either a human right or a fundamental right of Canadians. Are these similar to the universal service provisions adopted in Canada (and elsewhere) to ensure telephone service was made widely available outside of urban

areas? If you or any of your fellow students are from rural or remote areas in your class, speak about the challenges of getting Internet access at home.
3. Almost anything related to new media is subject to rapid change. Firms come and go, technologies change, and numbers of users, viewers, and creators for new media content and memes change every day. Look up a fact or figure in this chapter and verify whether it remains true today, using online sources. Identify corroborating or supporting sources for your findings. Not only will you have the new facts, but you'll also have an appreciation for how quickly things change and, most

importantly, a visceral sense of the way in which the Internet and new media are self-revealing to the diligent and inquisitive scholar. If you discover a fact that needs updating, you can even submit your update (with page reference and new citation) in the form of a rewritten paragraph, to the author: Richard Smith (smith@sfu.ca). He promises to reply.

Debate Questions

1. Some people would regard new media and the Internet as best served by a "hands-off" approach, leaving operations of businesses and technologies to market forces. Others note the considerable harm that can be done, or opportunity lost, when governments don't intervene. Select a type of new media technology or category and present the arguments for and against regulatory oversight or government involvement.
2. Imagine someone who has been cut off from the Internet for a whole day, because of a billing error or other fault of their Internet provider. Using a courtroom-style presentation, make the case for and against compensation—and the proposed amount of compensation—for that person.
3. The federal government has recently been winding down or eliminating government subsidies relating to the provision of Internet service in Canada. Is it the case that such financial support is no longer needed? Argue against the elimination of subsidies, taking the position of someone living in a rural and remote part of Canada. What is the argument for dropping this support system?

10

Conclusion

Questions to Consider

- What are some of the negative aspects of new media? What aspects of human relations does it disrupt that we would not necessarily wish to have disrupted?

- How can new media be used to go beyond mere entertainment to affecting real change? How can new media—and social software in particular—be used professionally and responsibly, rather than frivolously and hurtfully?

- New media have been "screen-oriented" until recently, but there is nothing to say that we can't have new media in the form of robots or digital media–enabled objects through 3D printing, or even projected onto our eyes, as Google Glass proposes. What are the implications for new media as it moves beyond screens?

Chapter Outline

As new media are currently evolving at the start of the second decade of the twenty-first century, there are several additional topics that are particularly relevant, whether in terms of personal and professional use of new media, the new media industry, or new media policy. The first of these is mobility, which has a number of implications, both for users and providers. The second is the notion of the Internet of things rather than an earlier concept of the Internet as being made up of hosts and people. A third significant consideration involves an understanding of a network as something that is always on and always there. The fourth area worth attention is social media and its implications for social interaction, whether for personal, business, political, or other purposes. Finally, we will look in some detail at the surveillance implications of our networked, digital new media. In concluding the discussion of this text, each of these merits attention, once more, in terms of identifying further considerations.

Key Concerns and Future Considerations

As we have discussed in previous chapters, new media is a technical and social achievement with a remarkable history, and yet enormous challenges lie ahead. If new media as a resource is to be made even more broadly available—as recent moves to include access to the Internet as a human right would suggest—how can new media be extended without negating social and cultural boundaries? There are also concerns related to the environment: Will the development, use, and waste from the expansion of information technology continue to weigh more and more heavily on the planet?

Much of the evolution of new media has brought with it an almost gleeful acceptance and adoption of whatever developments come from the minds of software and hardware engineers working in universities and start-up companies around the world. Regulation has been light or non-existent and no one has (yet) proposed anything as radical as an "Internet driver's licence," except as a joke. Yet as new media matures, it may be necessary to consider how more established industries such as automobiles or home construction approach development: as important to the economy, but also with certain risks, inputs and by-products to be minimized or curtailed. In other words, it may be necessary to be more critically aware of and engaged with the changes and consequences of the continued evolution of new media.

As an example, it is estimated that most of the spam in the world is not sent directly from spammers, but instead, travels through "botnets," or personal computers that have been hijacked and used by others for nefarious purposes. This may at first glance seem to be insignificant, however, spam represents more than 80 per cent of the email traffic in the world[1] and computers operating as part of a botnet can be harnessed for tasks even more malicious and dangerous than spam; for example, distributed denial-of-service (DDOS) attacks that periodically rise up to disable even the most well-protected Internet hosts.

This example raises a number of questions. Is this botnet activity something we will allow to continue? Should governments require virus checkers on computers? Should we insist that people properly maintain their network-connected device, just as we require periodic safety inspections of cars and trucks? What about an operator's permit, which cannot be obtained without demonstrating a certain level of training and competence? Initiatives such as these would fly in the face of some interpretations of freedom of speech and yet we insist on them for drivers of automobiles, for example, even though there is an equivalent "freedom of movement" in bills of rights and freedoms.

Similarly, the environmental cost of new media is certain to be an important personal, policy, and corporate issue in the years to come. Just as society began to realize in the 1960s that the unconstrained growth of automobile use—and automobile culture—was having deleterious effects on cities (Jacobs 1994 [1961]), some of the costs of new media may draw attention. Indeed, there have already been concerns raised about new media, but these have not often taken the form of serious, critical inquiry—rather, new media are more likely to be blamed for some societal malady (game addiction or violence caused by computer games are perfect examples), for which there is very little credible evidence. Alternatively, the mainstream media also tend to run new media stories in which attention is given to little more than how new media is a novelty and the supposed quirky nature of things online. These kinds of stories are often about typical human foibles played out—for example, on Facebook or in text messages. This may garner some attention, but, ultimately, the focus on new media as novelty diverts attention from larger, underlying questions or problems.

This edition of *New Media: An Introduction* highlights the extent to which, in the two decades that the Internet and digital media technologies have established themselves as the dominant media and communication forms, there have been major changes to those technologies and how they are used. Canadians recently passed a significant milestone in this regard: in 2010, a prominent research firm reported that, for the first time, Canadians spent more time on the Internet, on average, than watching television (Ipsos Reid 2010). As Canadians, we are not just *watching* the Internet, however. The rise of social media and Web 2.0 technologies have accelerated the trend of making the users of digital media into new media's primary content producers as well. While the 1990s saw concepts such as convergence, interactivity, and the virtual world dominating both popular and academic discourse, in the 2000s, there has been an increasing focus on participation, collaboration, collective intelligence, and user-led innovation. This emphasis on participation may partially explain another phenomenon: the co-consumption of media. A recent Neilson study reports that Americans use the Internet, television, and their cell phone, all at once, for three and a half hours per week, an increase of 35 per cent over the previous year (Neilson 2010). This "three-screen" activity suggests that there is a modification underway, at least in part, not just in the amount of television being consumed but also in the way it is being consumed. It would appear that Canadians, too, are participating in the "cognitive surplus" generated by declining television viewing and outlined by Shirky (2010).

At the heart of such changes, the Internet continues to evolve as a dense, ubiquitous, global, socio-technical network. While early Internet studies posed questions about the relationship of this technology to the culture surrounding it, new media is now clearly embedded in global media culture to the extent that people now live in a network society. This has a range of economic, cultural, political, legal, and other implications. In the economic sphere, new media is linked to the shift toward a global knowledge economy, or an economy increasingly driven by knowledge-based and creative industries, and by user-led innovation, rather than industrial production, science-based research and development, and mass consumption. Culturally, new media have allowed participatory culture to flourish through blogs, social media sites, and DIY media production and distribution outlets such as YouTube. Politically, new media presents a challenge to established sites of institutional authority—be they governments, political parties, and indeed the traditional news media—as looser, more fluid and collaborative networks constitute increasingly dynamic sites of innovation and new ideas, information, as well as forms of power, resistance, and activism (Milberry 2009).[2] In the legal domain, remix culture and the almost limitless scope for repurposing and remediating of digital content confront traditional copyright and intellectual property laws. Indeed, even issues of personal and professional identities are increasingly located within global networks of information and communication, whether through online affiliations that people have or from the information stored on various databases as a result of their electronic transactions.

The rise of social media, blogs, and social software is linked, as Benkler (2006) describes, to the rise in types of social production that are collaborative in form, strongly motivated by non-market behavioural factors, and over which it is difficult to directly claim ownership or control. Benkler argues that social production models find their most favourable ecologies in industries involved in information, communications, culture, and creativity, meaning that social production models are having their most significant impact in knowledge-based media and creative industries, but that the ruptures they promote in these industries resonate throughout the economic system. This is particularly evident in how information and creativity have become, as authors such as Howkins (2001) and Florida (2002, 2007) argue, the core productive forces of the twenty-first century global economy. Benkler observes that the more important non-contractual factors, such as gift relations, reciprocity, and trust, are to an economic relationship, the more social production will flourish, and the more of a challenge these new models will present to incumbent producers: the rise of Wikipedia and YouTube are perhaps the most illustrative examples of this. The core challenge, not surprisingly, concerns the status and application of copyright and intellectual property laws in this environment, and it is notable that both the laws themselves have been strengthened over the past decade and the propensity among incumbent media and information companies to seek their enforcement has increased, even as alternative socio-legal models such as Creative Commons have been evolving.

The copyright wars, or the tensions involving information and creative content as both public resources and private property, are salutary reminders to avoid being overly drawn into new media hype, and that critical analysis and empirically sound investigations of trends in new media are required. This becomes particularly apparent when considering two boom areas in the new media environment: multiplayer online games and new forms of news production such as citizen journalism. In the case of online games, the dynamism of the sector and the pleasurable experiences of gaming need to be considered alongside issues such as exploitative working conditions in the industry and the ongoing debates about ownership of user-generated content in the online games themselves, as well as issues such as identity, pedagogy, and other complex social phenomena linked to gaming.

The online environment has also spawned new forms of journalism and news production, with the shifts in production infrastructures associated with Web 2.0, as well as new patterns of distribution and use, leading to the rise of what has been termed "citizen journalism." While citizen journalism emerges in a context where there are growing questions about the professionalism of journalists and their tendency to be subject or beholden to powerful individuals and organizations—which can ruin a journalist by excluding him or her from access to official news or information (Levine and Forrence 1990)—there is also the concern that eroding traditional revenue bases for news organizations may see an undermining of news values in the online space, as lower-cost alternatives such as celebrity blogging seem to cater more effectively to the target demographics of marketing divisions. Both instances offer reminders that an understanding of the political economy of new media remains vitally important, even as new opportunities for participatory media culture and the expression of what Leadbeater (2007) refers to as "mass creativity" are emerging and multiplying.

Mobility

After some false starts, it is clear that one of the accelerating trends in new media is for data and digital content to be accessed from mobile devices. As we make clear in Chapter 4, the rise in mobile phone ownership and use has been astounding since the early 1990s, when phones for the most part functioned as devices for voice communication and simple text messaging, while more complex data, such as Web content, continued to be accessed almost exclusively from personal computers. That has all changed in the 2000s. The development of third generation (3G) wireless networking and the wiring up of spaces (particularly cities) has been accompanied by the development of devices that fully integrate phone, computing, and PDA functions, such as RIM's BlackBerry, the Android series of phones developed by Google, and the Apple iPhone. At the same time, smaller and smaller laptop computers (netbooks) and the emerging tablet format suggest that there is a transition away from the desktop to Internet in your hand.

The implications of mobile computing becoming a user expectation are only now being considered. One fallout may be that wireless networking access will inform locational decisions made by people and organizations, as part of the global competition for talent (Florida 2007). As we noted in Chapter 4, studies have shown that employers are starting to expect that employees will be available outside of work hours or when on the road, even if their job is white collar or not associated with traditional "on call" professions (Ladner 2008). Another implication of growing mobile access to the Internet may be further nomadism in terms of when and where people undertake work-related activities. This, too, can be something that employees take up initially as a source of freedom only to discover the negative aspects of being at work when at home (Ladner 2008). Mobility will also have an impact on how people consume leisure and entertainment products, with access to information about major sporting events (cricket scores in India, soccer scores in Europe, baseball and hockey information in North America) already proving to be a major driver of demand for wireless hand-held devices. It is also important to consider how relentless access to networked information affects its users: the BlackBerry has already been referred to as the "crackberry" because it facilitates a kind of dependence on email and other forms of text messaging.

Much of the 1990s and early 2000s involved adoption of and adaptation to the ability to have access to people at any time. The mobile phone has transformed everything from movie plots to business meetings with its potential to reach someone at any time, anywhere. In the coming decades, further transformation can be expected, as people reach out at any minute to the global knowledge storehouse that is at their fingertips. This raises different kinds of questions. For example, what are the effects of having constant access to Wikipedia, when everything from settling bar bets to establishing the location of one's next meeting is in the palm of one's hand? In one sense, this capacity can offer promising possibilities in terms of communication, knowledge exchange, informing opinions, and decision-making. But at the same time, with such changes, life experiences become increasingly mediated by technology, which suggests hints of the hive mind predicted in science fiction stories, or it at least raises the question of what is also lost with such advances.

The Internet of Things

Up until recently, the Internet was understood as comprising computers used by people. The unit of analysis was the Internet host computer and the web pages it contained. It was reasonable, in the earlier days of the Internet, to use measures such as counting the number of computers and the websites visited, for example, then extrapolate to the people using them. Gradually, it has become evident that the people—and the relationships among them—have greater significance than can be measured by counting information housed on host computers. Now, for example, it is more meaningful to know about the users of Facebook (and their use of Facebook) than how many computers Facebook uses to manage its site. The next frontier involves not only better understanding the complexity of how these technologies are used among people (and to what effects), but also to go beyond people and apply an Internet address to every object that they create using these technologies.

The phrase, *Internet of things*, was coined in the late 1990s by a group based at MIT known as Auto-ID (Dodgson 2003). In the Internet of things, rather than hosts or even people, what are followed are objects. In this emerging world every—or nearly every—object with any significant value is given an Internet address that is used to locate it, communicate with it, and determine certain pertinent facts about its state. A typical example is in the tracking of shipping containers or pallets in trucks. Instead of the former waybill (or, more recently, the barcode), these objects have computer chips with memory and a low-power radio frequency identification device (RFID) that allows (typically nearby) receivers to query the object and determine its status. The chip may be connected to sensors that indicate the temperature inside the container or perhaps track memory to indicate past encounters (shocks from being dropped or transit points completed, for example).

At first glance, perhaps assigning an address to an online object or querying the status of the content of shipping containers may not appear to fall under the rubric of new media. Artifacts and their relationship to humans, however, have been central to understanding new media in every era and in fact, form the foundation of archaeology. An enormous amount can be learned about a civilization—long lost or otherwise—by looking at their things, how those things were arranged, and how they were used. In addition, people attribute and derive enormous power from their possessions. Knowing where these possessions are and their status can be very useful: in commerce (stocking shelves, pricing goods, doing inventory, shipping and delivering supplies are all necessary); in war (issues of logistics are one of the most important elements in warfare); in family life (whether there is milk in the fridge and if it is expired); and so on. Objects have information linked to them, which, if communicated via networks and computers, endow them with greater value.

Networks: Always on and Always There

The rise of mobile computing intersects with another major trend in new media, which is increasing access to high-speed broadband services and, at the same time, rapidly diminishing costs associated with Internet access (e.g., usage time, network infrastructure constraints, download times, storage device capacity). As a result, it is becoming the norm for more and more people to leave their computers on at all times, and to consume a growing amount of material—increasingly audiovisual—via their computers.

While this consumption, for now, often consists of downloading (movies or music) and tends to be through software, like BitTorrent, which does not always adhere to or enforce copyright regulations or collect appropriate copyright fees, a growing amount of use does not involve creating a copy but instead is more transient and involves streaming Internet content, as has been popularized by YouTube and Internet music services such as Pandora. Many of the world's broadcasters—for example Canada's national public broadcaster, the CBC—have adopted this mode as a way of reaching people who might otherwise not bother to turn on a television or radio but still enjoy music and video entertainment.

Even for items of a personal and private nature, some Internet users have given up or greatly reduced their use of local storage. The notion of downloading and uploading content is fading away as the material is no longer anywhere in particular and instead is everywhere by virtue of its presence in the so-called cloud of data in online servers and services. This is most vividly experienced through the collection of software, services, and storage known as Google apps. Here, email does not permanently reside on a computer that the user owns, but rather, is accessed from a variety of terminals or devices, including mobile devices. Photographs, documents, music, and even spreadsheets and computer programs exist either exclusively or largely in the online world. Such a computing and network experience is free from the perils of lost files (backups are part of the service and no longer the user's responsibility), misplaced files (users search for rather than file things), or viruses (virus-checking is done by the service provider).

This vision of the network computer was one of the signature claims of computer and Internet pioneer, Bill Joy, whose company, SUN, had the motto, "the network is the computer," back in 1980s. In many ways, Joy's vision was almost 20 years ahead of its time: home computers and networks of that era were not up to the task that he saw for them, and the sort of network attached terminals without any local storage that he envisaged are even less likely to be adopted now. Nevertheless, the notion that most of the value of using a computer comes from its network connection is certainly true for many people and is sure to become increasingly true for most people. Even the idea of having more storage off your computer than on it is now a possibility with cloud storage. More recently, Joy was quoted in *The Register*, an online magazine, as saying, "The answering machine put voicemail by the desk, and then it went back into the network. . . . Your iPod is like your home answering machine. I guarantee you it will be hard to sell an iPod five or seven years from now when every cell phone can access your entire music library wherever you are" (Ashlee 2006). In this case, Joy might have underestimated how quickly things would evolve, since iPhones became able to access an almost limitless variety of streaming music and video less than five years later. Although the cost of this level of access has not dropped far enough that people have stopped buying iPods, such affordable access is ever closer on the horizon.

The broader socio-cultural implications of increasing speed and volume of communications or what can be termed "always on" culture, both for users and for the wider communications ecology, is an increasingly significant research question. For example, as we discussed in an earlier chapter, to be denied access to a network as a result of a court sentence is regarded as draconian and an unfair limiting of freedom of speech and association (Kravets 2010), if access to the Internet is understood as a human right.[3] The cost is economic as well: a US District Court ruling turned at least in part on the fact that it was almost impossible for the appellant to obtain or retain even blue-collar work without some access to computers. There are also concerns about far-reaching and profound environmental impacts related to new media, from the building of new media devices, to their use, and how they are discarded. Governments have started to wrestle with some of the challenges relating to electronic waste and overburdened landfills. Many Canadian provinces have e-waste recycling programs as well as special fees on new electronic devices, similar to what are imposed on new tires and car batteries.

Energy use for new media is one aspect of always-on that is becoming increasingly salient as climate change concerns mount. The power consumption of networks and network devices is non-trivial, estimated by some to be equivalent to the global air travel industry. Yet, new media can also bring net environmental benefits: the use of networks can make the movement of goods more efficient and using new media for video-conferencing can take the place of flying to a meeting, for example. Information technology systems themselves can also be made far more environmentally friendly, as is evident in emerging efforts for green data centres. Leading consumers of computing power are looking at creative ways to reduce their burden on the system by shifting computational demands to locations where power is greener or less contested.[4] In fact, there have been efforts to move data centres closer to sources of renewable energy (e.g., hydroelectric, solar, geothermal), where power is plentiful and green, rather than pulling the electricity across the country to where the computers are, wasting power as it travels across long distances.[5]

Ubiquitous always-on networks can transform existing businesses and create new ones (and destroy others). One example can be found in the long-tail phenomenon identified by Chris Anderson (2006), where businesses can increasingly profit from low-volume sales to niche consumers based on a wider inventory of virtual products (as seen with Amazon and eBay). In this scenario, while it is not profitable or even possible for a bricks-and-mortar bookstore to stock vast inventories of obscure books, centralized inventory coupled with powerful search engines and social features such as commentary and recommendations makes it possible for Amazon to profitably sell books that have very low sales volume. Traditional bookstores have difficulty competing against a network-enabled competitor and have been closing all over the world. Another example of these business transformations can be found in the area of news production, where a 24/7 news cycle is now the norm, rather than the traditional cycles of print or broadcast news production. There are also questions about the quality of communication: if people are receiving more than 100 emails per day and there is an expectation from senders that these will be read and responded to quickly, will the quality of responses deteriorate? How will communication be affected in a society where people lack the time away from work that was previously the basis for leisure and well-being? Will such changed expectations result in more people choosing to downsize by accepting a lower income for reduced workload as a necessary condition for an enhanced quality of life?

Meeting People Made Easy: Social Media

With estimates that there are about 100 million bloggers worldwide and social media sites such as Facebook claiming to have more than one billion accounts, the critical mass of people involved in online social activities has clearly reached a substantial level. Such trends are consistent with meta-theories such as those of the network society, participatory culture, and social production. There remains a need, however, to continue research on the implications of such a volume of online networkers using social media.

Researchers in the social sciences and humanities are confronted with the challenge of establishing empirical measures for identifying the significance of these trends and developing sound theoretical and analytical frameworks to better understand the implications of these phenomena. Research has shown, for instance, that open-source software development is effective because it can produce a powerful operating system such as Linux. What are equivalents for social media? Do bands and musicians that have Twitter feeds achieve more sales and downloads of their music than those who do not? Do people with a personal social networking site do better in the employment market? Research in the digital humanities has also opened up discussion about changing forms of texts, discourse, and, by extension, knowledge itself. What are the reasons that people have for going into these online spaces and what are the effects of doing so, whether personal, professional, political, or otherwise?

As another example, Facebook has become a force to be reckoned with in political circles. Politicians no longer dismiss user groups and fan groups on Facebook, as they now know that these online manifestations of popular sentiment are not simply virtual. This much was clarified in the winter of 2009-10 when the Canadian Parliament was briefly suspended (or prorogued) for procedural reasons and more than 200,000 people joined a Facebook group in protest. The group became the hub for on-the-street protests in cities across Canada, with some marches and rallies attracting more than 20,000 people.

Online services are not just for protest and reaction, however: the spring of 2010 saw Canada's prime minister interviewed on YouTube, with the questions coming from an online polling system.[6] In the United Kingdom, millions of Britons participated in online polls and other events during the 2010 election, leading politicians in that country to turn to Facebook in their quest for deficit-reduction ideas. The initiative, dubbed "the largest public engagement project" ever launched by the UK government, was hosted on the Democracy UK Facebook page, and it linked citizens—there are roughly 26 million Britons on Facebook—to information sources, places to voice their opinions on initiatives, and places to post ideas (Warren 2010).

It is no longer sufficient to see online activities as peripheral or unimportant when the online connections that people have are regarded as an aspect of their full, real, lives. A Facebook friend might be different from a face-to-face friend, but many of them are one and the same and, more importantly, the real world is being organized to a growing degree by those online tools and connections. Online contacts matter locally but also internationally, as was evident in the summer of 2009, when protests over election results in Iran spilled out onto the Internet through text messages posted on Twitter. It is by no means clear that these text messages had any impact in terms of changing the outcome of the elections and many would argue that the texting resulted only in people being identified and targeted for reprisals. Nevertheless these types of services were seen as a legitimate and important outlet for concerns and a way for people involved in the protests to stay in touch with each other.

Surveillance and New Media

New media enables many things for our society, our communities, and for us as individuals. We can coordinate our actions, locate new information, and share aspects of our lives with friends. These capabilities arise in many ways because new media are based on digital electronic technologies and are arranged into systems that facilitate easy exchange and sharing of bits. Mostly, these are beneficial and positive outcomes of the use of digital shared media. Unfortunately, new media also enable an unprecedented—and dangerously unremarked—level of **surveillance**. Some of this surveillance is purposeful and targeted and some of it is incidental and a side effect of other features. But all of it results in lives lived under an increasingly sharp lens and an increasingly long memory. In this section, we will discuss how this has come about, what it might mean, and how we can cope with this phenomenon.

Watching each other is something that humans are used to and participate in from birth. It is how parents know when their babies need something, how babies learn, and how we know when our clothes are out of style; we habitually watch each other and learn from what we see. Surveillance includes watching, but we nowadays regard surveillance as something a bit more sinister and organized. David Lyon defines surveillance as "focused, systematic and routine attention to personal details for purposes of influence, management, protection, or direction" (Lyon 2002:14). This definition includes the more benign aspects, and directs our attention beyond merely the gaze of the watcher but further into the many other ways in which "attention to personal details" might occur.

As various commentators have noted, surveillance is deeply connected to the existence and viability of the modern state, and modernity itself (Giddens 1990). We simply could not exist in the modern world (or postmodern world, for that matter) without surveillance. We need surveillance for industrial production and distribution of goods, for example. How else to determine that the work is getting done, that the products are being made to specifications, that they are delivered on time to the people who want them, and that the payments are made and distributed to those who participated in the process? All aspects of an automated industrial society are closely monitored for efficiency and effectiveness and all of this is a kind of surveillance.

New media are heavily implicated in that sort of systemic surveillance. We no longer, or rarely, require a boss to be watching the workers or a clerk to be counting inventory. Those tasks are relegated to machines, and in almost all cases to digital computers and networks. In consumption, as well, the watching that ensures that our favourite TV show gets the ratings that bring in the advertising that pays for the actors and the producers is almost all automatic, digital, and networked. Using surveillance to ensure the smooth operation of a modern economy seems like a good thing, and often it is. But surveillance is not always benign or confined to accepted industry uses. It is used to enforce the rules, punish the guilty, identify the perpetrators, and ensure compliance. New media participates in those aspects as well.

What do we think about surveillance? In the aftermath of the Second World War, with the horrors of technology-driven killing machines and the terrible force of totalitarian regimes still felt, George Orwell wrote the chilling novel *1984*, about a total surveillance state in which Big Brother was always watching (Orwell 1949). This vision came to dominate mid-century thinking about surveillance as a force of government. Later, philosopher and sociologist Michel Foucault theorized the impact that being watched has on society as a whole, applying the concept of a "panopticon"—a prison design based on the premise that, as all inmates are within view of an unseen guard, they would police themselves because they would never know when they were being watched (Foucault 1975). As it turned out, surveillance by the state and large bureaucratic institutions such as prisons and hospitals has been far eclipsed by the watching being done in the name of consumer capitalism. Throughout the latter years of the twentieth century, elaborate and interconnected systems were developed to optimize both the buying experience and the knowledge that advertisers and marketers were able to deploy to fine-tune their pitches to specific audiences. The fields of demographics (who we are), geo-demographics (where we are), and psychographics (how we think and what we think about) became the powerful tools they are in large part because of the enormous amounts of data and processing power in computers. We played along, using loyalty cards and seeing barcodes on everything we buy, in a kind of passive acquiescence to a system that delivered the goods.

This has changed dramatically in the twenty-first century. We can see the results in two very different places. First, the events of 11 September 2001 (9/11) crystallized a phenomenon that had been taking place for some time, namely the growing desire to remove risk from our lives and the willingness to give up freedoms in the name of safety (Ericson and Haggerty 1997). A surveillance state, imagined and anticipated by Orwell in 1948–49, grew up in the early 2000s. Much of US society, because of the actions of the federal government, was driven by fear after 9/11, and Homeland Security often heightened this fear by issuing orange and yellow alerts supposedly as a warning of potential terrorist attacks. Since then, this policing has taken on a profoundly technological aspect, with a vast array of scanners, cameras, databases, and sensors deployed at borders, airports, and around cities. And many of these tools have their basis in the computers and networks that we see as foundational to new media. For the most part, we accept this imposition in the name of safety and security.

The second way in which surveillance has come into our lives through new media is not imposed at all, but rather embraced and even advanced by our own actions. This is the growing use of new media for social purposes. In almost every case, these tools have an explicit or implicit surveillance aspect to them. Take, for example, the photo-sharing site Flickr. Here, people upload photos from their daily lives. The act of everyday people capturing the events of their life, and sharing them with others, is not new. Amateur painters and photographers have existed for a long time. New media, however, has profoundly changed the depth, extent, quality, and quantity of the capturing since, as we noted in the chapter on mobile technologies, almost half of the planet is carrying a phone and almost all of those have a camera. More importantly, these images are shared to a degree, scale, and scope that are unprecedented. From a surveillance perspective, the photos are not just available but tagged with a rich array of information including where, when, and how they were taken (even the model of camera and its settings are shared). People are often unaware of how widely the photos they add to Facebook or send via phone messages are shared by their friends and then friends of friends. Children typically do not have the same sensibilities around privacy that their parents do, with at times dire consequences.

The ability to embed information in databases and expose them to search engines, even more than the existence of the information, is what makes this type of casual and friendly undertaking reusable for surveillance. The surveillance can be mundane ("How many pictures are being taken with the new iPhone4?")[7] or potentially suspect ("Who is that person?" "Who is beside them?"), but the fact that we take pictures, upload them, and then tag them, makes it possible to use computers, databases, and networks to use those photos in a focused, systematic, and routine way—in other words, for surveillance purposes.

Many other new media technologies and services discussed in this book have similar or even more significant surveillance aspects. The popular social software site Facebook, for example, has even more users than Flickr, more pictures, and even greater ability to tag people in photos. It isn't just photos, of course. To give some idea on the volume of material going into Facebook, consider these facts from 2010:

- Users spent more than 16 billion minutes on Facebook each day.
- Every week users shared more than 6 billion pieces of content, including status updates, photos, and notes.
- Each month, more than 3 billion photos were uploaded to Facebook.
- Users viewed more than 1 million photos every second.
- Facebook's servers performed more than 50 million operations per second, primarily between the caching tier and web servers.
- More than 1 million websites implemented features of Facebook Connect.[8]

Some services (e.g., Picasa) are experimenting with automated tagging—giving names to the faces in your pictures by recognizing those faces using a computing algorithm. In almost all cases, these services have privacy settings that potentially limit the ability of these images and tags to be shared, but, in practice, a great deal of information is placed online because people want to share it. And much of the surveillance that is done is not malicious but merely commercial (for example a camera manufacturer might wish to see how popular their cameras are among photo sharers on Flickr, or look for trends in the ways photos are taken in order to develop new features to enhance their latest model).

Another important example can be found in the transition to digital cable. Previously, networks had no way of knowing—unless you were a participant in a monitoring project, like the Neilsen Ratings System—whether or not you were watching TV at all, let alone what you were watching. The new cable boxes, however, do not simply provide a dumb pipeline to an always-on stream of content. Instead, they are like little computers that have to be activated on the network, that are addressable by the system operator (thereby enabling pay-per-view features), and request a single channel at a time from the "head end." This means that your local cable provider knows when your cable box is on, and what channel is selected. Moreover, the cable company can tell when the channels are being changed and—if it bothers to couple this with an analysis of the programs—this could be turned into an incredibly rich data set about what attracts, retains, and repels audiences. This is a fountain of information that cable television companies are only just beginning to exploit.

Whether they are related to commercial interests, security, or just curiosity, these surveillance capabilities are both powerful and often misunderstood and it is for this reason that new media developments, especially those that allow or encourage sharing as a default setting, deserve our attention from a policy and regulatory point of view.

Regulating new media is a controversial topic in some ways, since the freedom to innovate and create new media forms without having to seek prior approval is considered one of the hallmarks of the Internet and online media forms in general. Even if we did hope to impose a regulatory framework on new media, the mechanisms for doing that are imperfect and in their infancy, as we discovered in Chapter 9. Nevertheless, there are good reasons to question the automatic approval of new media and a growing trend to question both institutional and personal sharing of information as wholly beneficial. A recent example was the request—ultimately successful—by Canada's privacy commissioner that Facebook revise its default privacy settings, the language used in the instructions, and, most importantly, the ability of third parties to access information of the site's members through the use of apps. A growing number of people are, on their own, taking advantage of more restrictive privacy settings in services such as Facebook or Flickr and not unthinkingly sharing information about themselves. This is a good first step and through dialogue, consumer demand, and occasional regulator intervention we should see better protection of consumer rights to privacy from potential breaches via social software manipulators.

The rapidly changing power of new media, driven forward by the investments in computers and networks being made by manufacturers, systems operators, as well as consumers, is part of the challenge for regulators. Many of our surveillance laws are decades old, having been introduced in an era of film photography and analogue telephones. When microscopic mobile cameras can record digitally, on infrared in the dark, in high definition and with excellent sound, and when the results can be linked to databases and analyzed automatically and in real time, you have a technological capability that has far outstripped both our casual understanding and our legal framework.

These capabilities confound both the police and security establishment—who are vexed by the built-in encryption that is available on Skype and in BlackBerrys—and consumers, who don't realize what they are sharing or how much information is really being gathered when they walk down a street covered by cameras with face-detecting software. At present, the pressure has been on commercial enterprises to greatly improve their protection of personal privacy, but in the coming years we may very well see pressure on states to limit their monitoring so that basic democratic freedoms, such as freedom of speech, freedom of movement, and freedom of association are not compromised. In a simple example, if you worry about who you are speaking to on the street—a person with a pamphlet, for example— because you wonder if you will be tied to them in a surveillance database, then our democracy has suffered a (tiny, perhaps) blow. Agencies around the world, including Canada's privacy commissioner, are working hard to ensure that civil rights are respected and to educate citizens on how to live responsibly in these news times. The recent digital comic, *Under Surveillance*, from European Digital Rights, is a great example of both building awareness and pushing for stronger protection.[9] Ultimately, it is the responsibility of

CASE STUDY

Citizen Lab (http://citizenlab.org)

Political activism is increasingly found not just on the streets but on the online networks of the world. The information-sharing and organizing capabilities of computers and networks is unprecedented, but using these tools is dangerous in some countries. A growing number of technologically inclined and politically aware people are engaging in something called "hacktivism"—the use of computers and networks for an activist agenda (Milberry 2009). One of the most well known of these is the Citizen Lab.

The Citizen Lab is based at the Munk Centre for International Studies at the University of Toronto. The lab focuses on advanced research and development "at the intersection of digital media, global security, and human rights." Their activities have brought international recognition in the form of funding support from large foundations as well as notoriety for their unflinching criticism of the use of information technology to impinge on freedom and undermine liberty. Their research has led to the publication of numerous reports and articles which have documented the ways in which regimes use the Internet to track down

dissidents or infiltrate activist computer networks to disrupt and deter them. The Citizen Lab is directed by Professor Ron Deibert of the University of Toronto's Department of Political Science (Mitrovica 2009).

In April 2010, the group published a report, titled *Shadows in the Cloud*, which shows how hackers based in Chengdu, China, were able to use a network of malware,[10] botnets, web-hosting services, and online social networks to infiltrate computers belonging to the Indian government as well as the Dalai Lama and steal classified and sensitive documents. All of this was released in the form of a lengthy report (Citizen Lab 2010); a press release; and coverage in the media, including the *New York Times*. As Ron Deibert and Rahel Rohozinski point out in an op-ed piece in the *Globe and Mail* released the day the report was published,

> Today, no country is secure in the global sea of information. Preserving cyberspace requires a strategy to address the dark side of the Internet. This requires urgent international co-operation, level-headed judgment and a commitment to preserve our values of freedom of speech and access to information, so as to ensure that in

citizens and governments to ensure that these tiny cuts to civil rights do not devolve into a killing blow for a free and democratic society.

Augmented Reality, 3D Printing, and Robots

Earlier in the book, we mentioned Paul Levinson's distinction between "new media" and "new new media" (Levinson 2012). He makes the case for social media as "new new media" in order to draw a distinction between that which is merely digital and that which goes beyond the technical underpinnings and into the relationships we have with the content and each other. For Levinson, "new new media," such as Facebook, Twitter, YouTube, and Wikipedia, are defined by their social nature and the extent to which they are largely comprised of user-generated content. But what comes next?

In this section, we discuss a type of media that goes even further, and along a new dimension: the physical world. Digital media used to be epitomized by terms such as *cyberspace* and *virtual reality*, as if it was not part of the real world. People often spoke of real life and online life, for example, as if they were wholly separate. Recently, this our quest for online security we do not secure ourselves into a new dark age (2010).

The report was completed in collaboration with a private security company in Ottawa (SecDev Group) and a volunteer organization of security professionals known as the Shadowserver Foundation.

This collaboration is typical of Citizen Lab, which has ongoing collaborations with Internet research groups at Oxford, Cambridge, and Harvard (through the OpenNet Initiative, http://opennet.net), and has formed a spinoff company, called Psiphon, to market censorship circumvention and managed content delivery systems.

As the exercise of democratic rights, and particularly the organization of protests and civic action, has moved online to computers, governments have responded against such activities. On a positive note, support by organizations such as Citizen Lab has gone beyond pure research and moved into software development. Citizen Lab has helped to develop—and package—software that can help hide or secure the work of activists (e.g., Occupy Wall Street, Arab Spring) by encrypting communications and files, and by getting around the growing number of firewalls and filters that

are in place around the world. These tools are made available for free download to help those who wish to protect their communications and to access websites or content previously unavailable to them. Some of the tools are being commercialized by Citizen Lab's spinoff company, Psiphon.

The lab has also produced a guide to avoiding censorship, titled *Everyone's Guide to Bypassing Internet Censorship*, downloadable from their website: http://citizenlab.org.

Case Study Questions

1. What issues arise in a democratic society from the use and proliferation of privacy enhancing and online activism tools such as those advocated by Citizen Lab?
2. When does Internet activism go too far and stray into irresponsible behaviour or even terrorism?
3. What if these privacy enhancing and online activism tools described in the case study get into the wrong hands? Search online for discussions relating to the use and abuse of LOIC (low orbit ion cannon) software for some background on this kind of development.

distinction has started to erode, and some scholars have actively rejected the premise entirely while poking fun at what they call "digital dualism" (Jurgensen 2013). More importantly, the distinction may soon be irrelevant because of the growing place of digital media as an enabler and integral part of the everyday, material life of human beings. The three examples we will explore here are augmented reality, 3D printing, and robots/cyborgs.

Augmented Reality

As in our earlier discussions, it is sometimes very difficult to draw a hard line that delineates the start of a new media form. Drawing such a line can often blur our understanding of how humans might make use of a media form or obscure the extent to which it is anchored in the past, at least at first. This is the case for augmented reality.

Simply stated, augmented reality is a blend of digital media (images, text, sound) with the world around us. Sometimes, these things are projected onto a surface; other times, they are presented as a "layer" on a view through a mobile phone or other device; still other times, they exist as an additional or replacement soundscape, via headphones. Augmented reality is distinct from virtual reality (in which participants wear goggles), in that the objective is not to displace the material world but rather to add to it. It can serve educational, informational, and entertainment purposes.

Augmented reality sounds new and exciting, but in its most elemental forms it is both commonplace and has a long history. Anything that uses the world around us as a setting or backdrop for additional information could be considered a form of augmented reality, but these days the tool of choice is a network-connected mobile computer with a sensor array—in other words, a smartphone or tablet. These devices provide a display, location (via GPS and other positioning technology), orientation (which way is it pointing), and a camera, all connected to a powerful computing and graphics engine and a high-speed network connection. Using these capabilities, service providers and software developers can add layers of information based on where you are, what you are looking at, and even the kind of person you are, based on past searches and profile information.

A great example of this sort of capability in action is Yelp (www.yelp.ca). It is a web service that provides ratings and information about restaurants and other services. If you have Yelp's mobile app, and a smartphone, you can choose an option called "Monocle" that activates the camera—what you see on the screen is not just your surroundings, but also restaurant names and reviews. The items that float into view are based on your location and the direction you are pointing. The type of food and your distance from the restaurant are indicated. An augmented layer—showing pertinent restaurant details—has been placed on top of your view.

It might seem a bit silly to be standing on the street waving a cell phone around looking for restaurants, but in many ways this is no more improbable than the increasingly common practice of snapping pictures with a phone. New technology—for example, glasses that project images onto your eyes, and voice recognition for making choices and activating features—may soon make the necessity of taking your phone out of your pocket a thing of the past.

The uses of augmented reality go well beyond restaurant reviews. Google has been experimenting with an augmented reality game, called *Ingress*. To play, you need an Android phone or a tablet with a data network connection. In many ways, it is a conventional "capture the flag" style of game, with teams who hack, claim, and defend portals. But the distinction is that this game is played on a mobile device, out on the streets. In fact, it is impossible to play indoors, on your couch, because portals are visible only when you are standing next to them. And the portals are objects (mainly public art and iconic buildings) that exist in the city. The game world is actually just a (darker, less-detailed) map view of your city, extracted from Google Maps. Even the "energy" (akin to the "gold" that has to be mined in an MMO) is not randomly placed there by the game engine but, in fact, is simply a representation of people using Google's services in the real world. As such, it clusters in places where people gather and search for things, such as downtown streets, tourist locations, transit hubs, libraries, and university buildings.

Museums have also explored the use of augmented reality as a way to break free from the limitations of traditional audio tours and signage. With a suitably equipped mobile device, visitors can point at something in a museum and learn as much (or as little) additional information as they wish. People in organizations coping with high degrees of visual complexity—for example, employees who assemble the wiring systems inside jet airplanes see augmented reality as a way to break free from the burden of assembly manuals, blueprints, and parts lists. Technical challenges abound—particularly pinpointing the location of people inside a building—but the advantages are manifold. Importantly, it seems entirely probable that this kind of layering is something that people will come to expect (Schell 2010).

3D Printing

New media is augmenting our daily lives in another way, by helping us create in three dimensions what we imagine in our heads and then design on our screens. Back in the early days of graphical user interfaces and "what you see is what you get" (WYSIWYG) breakthroughs in printing, graphic designers were astonished at the ability of new laser printers that could produce, seemingly as if by magic, typography and graphic design on paper that rivalled the printing press. Later advances provided home printers that recreated photographs, even colour ones, with resolution and colour balance to rival a professional service.

But all that was in two dimensions: taking the things you see on a flat screen and recreating them on a flat piece of paper. A new type of printing is emerging, enabling creators to print in three dimensions. These printers are, in many ways, an evolutionary step up (literally) from the original ink-jet printers that work a print head back and forth across a moving piece of paper spraying ink as they go. In the new 3D printers, the print head moves back and forth and up, spraying a type of plastic that hardens into the shape sent from the computer. For the early adopters of these technologies, it is exciting to watch the design that you have sketched on a screen take shape—slowly—in front of your eyes.

Many still question the quality of 3D objects produced in this way. The printers tend—like early dot-matrix and ink-jet printers—to produce objects with visible "graininess" or layers. The materials and colours, and the sizes of objects you can print, so far, are limited. And, not surprisingly, it still takes quite some time (sometimes hours) to print something. Materials, and the printers themselves, are expensive and finicky. But the prices are falling, quality is increasing, and anyone who lived through the early days of home printers can clearly see where things are headed. A generation of people who watched Jean-Luc Picard say, "Tea. Earl Grey. Hot."—and then receive a steaming beverage in an instant—may think that this sort of thing is only natural. Three-dimensional printing, however, has a long way to go before it has that kind of impact on our lives.

The fact that 3D printing is still rudimentary, expensive, and slow does not necessarily lessen its impact. For the student of new media, 3D printing provides an excellent example of the impact of digital media in the world. More importantly, it is a very interesting and current case study that provides insight into the way in which new media technologies emerge today. If you start to look into the world of 3D printing, you will find that—like the computer and the Internet—it started life as a large, industrial-strength technology. Students, who had been exposed to the possibilities of 3D printing in a lab, set out to recreate those capabilities in something that was cheaper to operate. These project ideas were shared online, and a community arose.

One of the defining features—and great enablers—of the computer era was the extent to which it was a technology that revealed itself to people. You could use a computer to learn about computers. And you could enhance your computer through use. Similarly, early network and then Web technologies were shared, extended, and enhanced by the people who were using them. The 3D printing era is enjoying a similar boom, with people sharing plans, suppliers, and designs online. As with software and websites, you can use a 3D printer to make (many of) the parts for a 3D printer. In fact, some community groups have the notion of a "replicator"—a device that can recreate itself—as their objective.

As with previous eras, the time of the hard-core hacker is giving way to the hobbyist and amateur. It is not longer necessary to build your 3D printer from a kit, or even assemble modules. If you like, you can buy the whole thing, pre-assembled. Nor is it necessary to know all about physics and material science in order to turn a 3D design into something that won't cave in or break. New types of software automatically adds reinforcement, thickens walls, and identifies design flaws that would create "impossible-to-print" ideas. Even the designs themselves are being shared online, so it is not necessary to be an artist or an artisan to have something to print. And, as we did in the early days of the Web, many people get started by taking an existing design (a figurine, or a teapot) and modifying it.

Although there is still a long way to go before every home has a 3D printer, these devices are taking their place in design and production processes that are changing the way that people approach the idea of making things. Whereas in a pre-industrial world, people often made (or knew the person who made) almost all of their things—clothing, shoes, tools, shelter—we have gradually turned the responsibility for the creation of those things over to an often-mysterious and usually distant industrial process. Three-dimensional printing returns the possibility of design—if not for the final product, then at least for the prototype—to the user. And in this way, it is adding another dimension to user-generated content, as YouTube did for video and Blogger did for words.

Robots

Although it might seem a bit of a stretch to call a robot a form of new media, we will argue here that—at least in some respects—robots deserve that designation and the attention of new media scholars. In Chapter 4, we made reference to the importance of cybernetics and cybernetic systems in the history of computers and networks. A cybernetic system is one that has a feedback and control loop. In a simple form, it is merely adjusting a machine based on environmental conditions. In the present day, we have robots that do everything from cleaning floors to building automobiles. But in the new media world, robots are also hard at work, maintaining and enhancing our user-generated content.

YouTube famously receives dozens of hours of video content from its users every minute. The figure is hard to pin down, as it is always growing, but you can find the latest information on this by searching for "YouTube statistics"—as of January 2013, it was 72 hours uploaded per minute (YouTube 2013). Behind the scenes, a robot (in this case, a software robot) called Content ID is scanning the video to ensure that it isn't pornography, that it doesn't infringe others' copyright, that it isn't a hate message, and so on. Although the Content ID system is augmented with human operators, there is no way that the 100 years of video it scans each day (again, as of January 2013) could be handled solely by any reasonable team of people.

Software robots (bots) also play a major role in maintaining Wikipedia, and, as of February 2013, more than 1600 automated tasks played an important role in helping people maintain, improve, and fend off malicious entries and edits, of the world's largest encyclopedia. In both the YouTube and Wikipedia cases, it is fair to say that the content is generated not just by users but actually by users and bots.

Automation is not solely the domain of large corporations and enormous community projects run by nerds. We are all, to varying degrees, making use of these software robots on an everyday basis. Spam filters, anti-virus software, automated vacation messages—these and many other software tools are part of the regular life of most computer users. And, like augmented reality, these tools have found their place in our lives off screen. Automobiles are full of automation these days, ranging from anti-lock brakes (fairly common) to self-parking features to lane-drift avoidance reminders, and even—in field testing—self-driving cars.

A robot that cleans your living room, made by iRobot, is still somewhat of a novelty, but this sort of robot companion is a growing part of everyday life for people. There are robot toys for children and robot caregivers for seniors. Each one brings new media further into the material world and expands our definition of what new media are and opens up new avenues for scholarship and inquiry.

New Media Scholarship: The Next Frontiers

To conclude this second Canadian edition of *New Media: An Introduction*, it is worth noting two areas of research whose significance and implications warrant further consideration by scholars as new media technologies evolve. The first, a proposal for critical information studies, is something that students in communication and information science programs may be familiar with, although the emphasis here is on new media and a specific proposal by Vaidhyanathan (2006). The second, a call for the de-westernization of new media scholarship, is something that is being taken up to varying degrees by researchers around the world. Issues related to the limitations of the dominant, Western perspective in numerous fields of inquiry are part of a growing discourse to which Canadian scholars are well positioned to contribute (and have been active in), given the diversity of the Canadian population and the strong historical and cultural connections that Canada has to other countries.

Critical Information Studies

Vaidhyanathan (2006) proposes that the complex set of legal, social, political, economic, and cultural issues arising from new media should be approached from a multidisciplinary perspective that he terms "critical information studies" (CIS). He proposes that CIS would consider "the ways in which culture and information are regulated, and thus the relationships among regulation and commerce, creativity, science, technology, politics, and other human affairs" (Vaidhyanathan 2006: 293). Identifying how this would translate more specifically into research agendas, Vaidhyanathan proposes examining the following:

- the abilities and liberties to use, revise, criticize, and manipulate cultural texts, images, ideas, and information;
- the rights and abilities of users (or consumers or citizens) to alter the means and techniques through which cultural texts and information are rendered, displayed, and distributed;
- the relationship between information control, property rights, technologies, and social norms; and
- the cultural, political, social, and economic ramifications of global flows of culture and information (2006: 293).

Vaidhyanathan observes that an interdisciplinary framework such as CIS makes it more exciting to do research in a field such as digital copyright law, as it brings together researchers in debates across cultural studies and political economy as well as law and information studies. Critical information studies also present the possibility that such scholarly research will engage quite directly with issues that are in the public domain:

> As the sets of cultural producers and consumers intersect, the marginal price of distribution of information and cultural products drops to zero, and global communication networks link disparate bodies of work and people who engage with that work. More people take an interest in the policies that govern how information and information technology get distributed and used. (Vaidhyanathan 2006: 303)

Considerations such as these also link research to the activities of various public interest organizations, legal groups, and policy-makers, as well as providing academic researchers with direct questions about how they wish their own work to circulate in the public domain. (For example, should it have a Creative Commons licence? Should it be published in open-access journals?)

The possibilities of CIS as an emergent field of critical and interdisciplinary sociolegal research are considerable, both drawing from and contributing to a rich range of "knowledges" from across a variety of other academic disciplines. At the same time, Vaidhyanathan identifies three key challenges for those working within this emergent field. The first is that it is dominated by research from the English-speaking world, in particular from the United States. As the Internet has increasingly become a genuinely global domain, he notes that some of the underlying assumptions in the existing research may "ring flat in parts of the world where liberalism is not taken for granted," pointing to a need for "CIS [to] get beyond its American roots and consider how every change in the information ecosystem is global" (Vaidhyanathan 2006: 306). A second challenge relates to the institutional location of many researchers within universities that increasingly see themselves not simply as the users and providers of information in the public domain, but also as significant *holders* of copyright materials, from which they extract revenues and develop research commercialization strategies. Finally, there is the question of whether scholars committed to a CIS agenda would practise what they preach by dealing only with publishers and journals that enable more open access to scholarly materials through legal mechanisms such as Creative Commons licences.

De-westernizing the Internet (and Internet Studies)

Following Curran and Park's (2000) proposal that there is a need to de-westernize media studies, the data we looked at in Chapter 1 on trends in global Internet use suggest a similar need in relation to understanding new media and the Internet. The fastest growth in global Internet use is happening in Asia, Africa, Latin America, the Caribbean, and the Middle East; with North America, Europe, and Australia/New Zealand moving from a position of dominance in the 1990s to one where they are becoming, or may indeed have already become, a minority of the global Internet community. In fact, as of March 2010, there are more users of the *mobile* Internet in China than there are people in the United States.[11] The role of mobile Internet—an emerging phenomenon—is what is largely driving the rapid growth of the Internet outside of its traditional home countries. Mobile access is growing quickly in North America, Europe, and the developed parts of Asia. Communities in the rest of the world that have not previously had any access to the Internet now see this access arriving through a phone (or another mobile device). As long as it is useful and afford-able, people will make use of it, and the Internet is proving to be both of those things around the world.

Canada has benefited through the early years of the Internet by its close proxim-ity to the United States—we share a common language and have compatible legal and social systems. Being close to both the large consumer base and the major US fibre-optic networks has meant that Internet start-ups in Canada have had relatively low barriers to entry and great opportunities. Sites such as HootSuite, Flickr, and Club Penguin[12] are premised on very significant bandwidth as well as cultural aware-ness, such as knowing what would attract people to use a website and how to make it useful and friendly. These offer illustrative examples of how Canada has been able to leverage compatibility with the first major Internet market. Although we have not yet leveraged to any notable degree the multicultural and multilingual aspects of this country's social fabric, it is not unreasonable to expect some of the country's future Internet success stories to involve a being savvy to a Chinese or Indian market (as opposed to the US market). The majority of the world's Internet users do not com-municate primarily through the English language, yet how this is changing the nature of the global new media ecology is little understood.

Just as Curran and Park note that early paradigms in global media and communi-cations tended to understand much of the world's media as an underdeveloped or state-controlled "other" to a Western (typically North American) norm, Internet stud-ies as a field of inquiry is still strongly influenced by its emergence in the United States during the freewheeling 1990s. One example of this is the degree of focus on Internet censorship in a number of countries, with China being the largest and perhaps most significant. It is certainly the case that there are varying degrees of censorship, state control, and surveillance of online communication in many parts of the world, and that this may well run at odds with the democratizing potential of new media. Yet this is not the whole picture, and it addresses only some aspects of new media use in some parts of the world. Establishing the significance of state control over the Internet in China, for instance, tells little about how the Internet is developing as a new media form in countries such as India, Korea, Brazil, and Russia, to take some examples. It also acts as a filter to more grounded case studies of comparative new media use in different socio-cultural and political-economic environments.

The problems here are twofold. The first arises from the strong historical association of the Internet with libertarian discourses (Flichy 2007). As the Internet was first popularized in the United States and the first major political campaigns around new media tended to focus on questions of free speech, there has been a tendency in Internet studies to focus on the more heroic, political, or resistant aspects of use of new media, as opposed to more mundane, everyday, convivial, or conversational uses (Burgess 2006).

This is not to say that attention should not be drawn to Internet censorship in different parts of the world, or that support should not be given to those who seek to use new media to achieve a legitimate right to free expression of opinion and ideas. But focusing only on these aspects may lead to some significant omissions in understandings of new media use in cross-cultural perspectives. The enthusiasm of Chinese Internet users to vote in televised talent programs, to take one example, may have much to tell about how a popular demand for the right to vote may be expressing itself in that country, if it is given significance as an aspect of new media use.

A second gap is clearly that of language, interspersed with isolation between different research communities, and an associated reluctance on the part of Western new media researchers to learn from developments in other parts of the world. South Korea provides a fascinating case study of how digital media content may evolve where there is near-universal access to high-speed broadband networks, yet published research in English-language new media journals on developments in Korea is patchy and sporadic. To make these points is not to discount what is most valuable in the Western intellectual and political traditions, such as the right to free speech and free expression of ideas and opinions. It is to say that more needs to be done to foster international and intercultural research and collaboration in the new media field (indeed, as in other fields), so that patterns of mutual learning and dialogue can emerge that are more reflective of the dynamics of global new media production, distribution, and use.

Final Words

New media are always changing. They are, by their very nature, fluid in ways that traditional media—tied to a technological form—are not. As such, new media are difficult to define if we confine our view to the physical tools that produce them. Instead, it is more useful to see new media in terms of the outcomes of the exploitation of certain fundamental characteristics (which we laid out in Chapter 1), namely that new media are manipulable, networkable, dense, compressible, and impartial. These characteristics are then expressed in a variety of artifacts, activities, and arrangements in such a way as to create an interactive experience (Lievrouw and Livingstone 2005).

The nature of those interactive experiences, however, is forever changing—and new and different forms emerge frequently. A student of new media, therefore, is well advised to be on the lookout for new forms and new experiences and to consider, as we have done in this book, the underlying characteristics that not only make the existence of new media possible but also what links them to the past. New media forms are quite often echoes or recreations of previous media forms, but with an interactive element. In trying to understand a new form, it can be very helpful to see if there are recognizable aspects or elements, something that may reflect a common human communication pattern or practice, something that recreates a business model or value proposition in a new and interesting way. Although it may be easy to be distracted by the claims of "new" and "different," existing knowledge is often a good guide to how these media can be used and how they affect our society, our culture, our economy, and our government.

Glossary

Actor network theory An approach to the study of networks and society that pays attention to both human and non-human (such as technology or organizations) actors.

App An abbreviation for *application*, commonly referring to computer applications, especially on mobile devices.

Augmented reality The use of networks, databases, computers, and sensors (camera, GPS) to overlay location- or time-specific information on top of a "live" display of the scene in front of the device. A typical consumer application is the provision of restaurant information over top of a view of a restaurant when a customer holds a camera phone up in front of it and selects the Yelp application.

Blogging (blog, blogger, blogosphere) The weblog was initially a simple reverse chronological listing of (typically) web pages encountered in one's daily surfing habits. Elaborated, refined, and expanded with dedicated software that made it easier to start, add multimedia content to, and maintain, blogging became a widespread amateur and commercial activity and a way to not just share links but commentary, photos, and videos.

Broadcasting The practice of sending a signal from one transmitter to many receivers; first done with radio, and later television. On the Internet, there are some equivalents, such as multicasting, that simulate a broadcast model.

Cellular (phone, radio, system) A method of mobile radio communication that distributes the transmitting/receiving responsibilities into small hexagonal cells that are responsible for a small area—a few blocks in highly populated areas—with participating devices engaging with many different antennae/towers as you move around. When the device moves from one cell to another there is a seamless handoff, without interruption in the call, even when you are travelling at highway (or high-speed train) speeds. The small cells require less power on the part of radios,

enabling smaller phones, and the reuse of radio spectrum.

Cognitive surplus A term coined by Clay Shirky to describe the human mind-power that is liberated when we stop doing something that has been taking up lot of time (in Shirky's example, it is watching television) and turn our attention to something else.

Computer-mediated communication (CMC) The use of computers to exchange messages, as with email, forums, blogs, wikis, and instant messaging.

Convergence Media forms and media businesses coming together, as when America Online (AOL Internet services) bought Time Warner (publishing and cable television); the term is sometimes used to describe technical convergence, as when various modes of entertainment, such as music, movies, and magazines, are all available on one Internet-connected device.

Convergence culture A term popularized by Henry Jenkins to describe media forms and consumption that cross many different sites and formats and incorporate both professional and amateur aspects.

Creative cities (creative class) A term coined by Richard Florida to describe cities that attract and retain a specific kind of creative people (the creative class), and as a consequence prosper in a world where intellectual property is highly valued.

Creative industries Those industries with a heavy emphasis on creativity, including architecture, filmmaking, fashion, music, and theatre. There is a growing recognition of the role of these industries both for their direct and indirect economic impact.

Critical theory of technology An approach to the study of technology that emphasizes the importance of understanding how power (especially economic power) has and continues to influence the operation and evolution of technology in society.

Cyber-libertarianism See **libertarianism**.

Cyberspace A metaphor for online networks and virtual worlds popularized in the early 1990s, first in fiction and then in the mass media. The term is in declining use at present as the online and offline worlds merge.

Diffusion of innovations model The spread of innovations within a society or market.

Digital Made of discrete (usually binary, 1 and 0, on and off) units.

Digital divide The gap between those who have access to the Internet and those who do not; the term is sometimes expanded to include gaps related to speed of access as well as capabilities to use the services (as for example when it is not in your native language).

Digital goods Items that can be digitized and sold (or given away) through electronic networks, these include music, movies, books, house plans, images, even dress patterns. Importantly, these goods are non-rivalrous, infinitely and perfectly copyable, can exist in many places at once, and can be easily recombined to form new digital goods.

Digital locks An encryption or other scheme to prevent copying of digital goods. DVDs are often protected by anti-copying codes (widely broken by software available on personal computers), for example.

Disintermediation The ability of buyers to directly connect with suppliers (and vice versa), eliminating the need for wholesalers or other brokers. A simple example is the musician who sells songs and albums directly to fans via her website.

Disruptive technologies Technologies or services that undermine or overwhelm the value proposition of an existing product or service thereby hastening its demise in the market. They are often unappreciated by suppliers of existing solutions, since they (at first) seem unrefined or unsuited to the task that their customers demand.

Dot-com crash A rapid devaluation of the stock prices in technology companies in late 2000 and 2001, especially those that were based on the Internet. Many people attributed this decline to a rationalization in a market that had become inflated by outlandish expectations and hyperbole.

Electromagnetic spectrum The full range of radiant energy, in the form of electromagnetic radiation, typically arranged from the highest to the lowest frequencies for reference—the higher the frequency, the shorter the wavelength and the more energy that is contained. The spectrum includes everything from gamma rays and X-rays at the high end, ultraviolet, visible and infrared light in the middle, and radio waves at the low end. Radio waves range from longer frequencies, used in AM radio, to very high frequencies, used in cell phones, WI-FI routers, and microwave transmission systems. This part of the electromagnetic spectrum is very important for communication, and is called the **radio spectrum**.

Electronic commerce (e-commerce) Online transactions including consumer (buying via the Web) and business to business (B2B; ordering new stock from a supplier); the term applies to both physical and virtual goods. For a growing number of industries, a fully electronic model is becoming the norm, even for the goods that are consumed (e.g., Apple's iTunes Store).

Endogenous growth A theory from economics that recognizes the importance of innovation in the growth of an economy and, importantly, that it is not outside of the economy (exogenous) but a part of it.

Explicit knowledge Knowledge that is or can be written down, shared, and sold; it is usually taught in a formal way.

Fair use (US) / Fair dealing (Canada) The principle of copyright law that some users, some times, have the right to use copyrighted material without paying a fee or obtaining a licence. Examples of fair dealing include research and criticism.

Folksonomy A definition or description (tag) for an object (photo, webpage) that is generated by users of a Web service such as Delicious or Flickr. It contrasts with "taxonomy" or the official naming of things. See **tag** and **hashtag**.

Forbearance (forbear) The decision not to fully regulate in an area where a regulatory commission has jurisdiction. The decision by the CRTC not to regulate mobile phones or the Internet has been a significant aspect of new media governance in this country.

Globalization The process by which markets, technologies, cultures, and businesses are homogenizing and becoming accessible everywhere on the planet. The term also refers to the process of moving jobs and capital to the place where they will reap the largest return (as when jobs move to low-wage countries).

Governance An amalgam of policy, regulation, law, commercial and consumer practices, and organizational behaviour. In the face of considerable uncertainty as to who has control of the Internet, there is much concern over "Internet governance," especially as a partial antidote to the free rein of "cyber-libertarian" notions.

Granularity According to Benkler, "the smallest possible individual investment necessary to participate in a project."

Hashtag A tag prefaced by the "hash" or pound character (#) to demarcate it as a tag and thereby render it more visible for searches, this usage has been popularized on Twitter.

Hypertext Now associated almost exclusively with the blue underlined words that provide links on web pages, the term was coined by Ted Nelson in 1963 for his Project Xanadu.

Information society A society dominated by the movement and use of information, as well as information and communication technology.

Infringement The act of misusing copyrighted material (often mislabelled as "piracy" or "stealing") by failing to obtain a licence where necessary. See also **fair use**.

Innovation The process by which people or organizations turn ideas into new products and services that are brought to the market.

Innovator's dilemma A choice that confronts those who develop new technologies, of whether or not to work on new (replacement) technologies, even while the existing ones are doing well in the marketplace. The term was coined by Clayton Christensen to describe a trap that many companies fall into, failing to notice the next big thing.

Interactive The ability to contribute to as well as consume media; it is generally reserved for activities that extend beyond merely changing channels. Internet services are almost all interactive.

Interface The way users experience software or hardware, epitomized by the WIMP (windows,

icons, menu, pointer) desktop that has become the standard for computer operating systems.

Knowledge economy An economy characterized by a high level of dependence, internally and in the form of trade, on knowledge creation, distribution, and exports.

Lead-user innovation Attending to, and adopting if possible, the changes made by your leading customers when they adapt or extend your product.

Libertarianism A political and economic theory that posits the primacy of freedom and especially economic freedom to allow markets to regulate human affairs. Often associated with Russian-American author Ayn Rand (1905–1982) and also linked to some early Internet activists.

Long tail The large number of items which make up a small sales volume individually but together may account for a non-trivial opportunity for retailers—such as Amazon.com—who can deliver these goods to people who want them. The term was coined by Chris Anderson of *Wired* magazine to illustrate the power of online access to the enormous number of books (and other items) that wouldn't merit stocking in a bricks-and-mortar store.

Luddite A follower of nineteenth-century labour activist Ned Ludd, who advocated smashing what was then the new weaving machine. Now often used as a blanket term for someone who opposes all things new, it has been revived as "neo-Luddism" by critics of new technologies in the late twentieth and early twenty-first centuries who have pointed out the rationality in Ludd's resistance to forces that were destroying families and communities.

Metcalfe's Law More of an observation than an actual law of nature, Robert Metcalfe predicted that the value of a network lay in the number of possible connections between the members—or nodes—in the network.

Microblogging Posting short messages (typically the length of a mobile phone text message, on which the business was premised, at first) to a website for sharing with others. Twitter is the best known of these, but this would also include the posting of short status updates to your Facebook wall.

Modding The modification, typically by end-users or groups of end-users, of the content or user interface of a game, usually with the tacit approval of the game designers, who make it possible by exposing their game engine to alternative content.

Modularity According to Benkler, the properties of a project that determine "the extent to which it can be broken down into smaller components, or modules, that can be independently produced before they are assembled into a whole."

Multiplayer games Games that are connected, via computer network, to servers enabling many people to play together at the same time. These are also known as massively multiplayer online games (MMOG), or massively multiplayer online role-playing games (MMORPG; e.g., *World of Warcraft*). These terms had their origins in earlier multi-user dungeons (MUDs) and MUDs object-oriented (MOOs).

Multiplexing The process of encoding multiple streams of information into a single stream to make maximum use of a scarce resource such as a telegraph or telephone line, and, more recently, mobile phone radio channels and fibre optics.

Network neutrality A principle, borrowed from transportation regulation, whereby the company agreeing to carry goods cannot discriminate between customers who wish to transport similar goods. This is sometimes referred to as the separation of carriage and content. It is widely applied in telecommunications pricing and regulation and most recently in the management of the Internet.

Network operator The provider of service to mobile telephones. The provider arranges for the radio spectrum licences, creates the billing and customer-service functions, installs the infrastructure for transmitting and receiving calls and—if necessary—transferring them to other networks (wireless or land line). Network operators also provide additional features, such as text messaging, caller identification, voice mail, and Internet service.

Network society A society in which individuals and groups are organized as a type of richly interconnected network rather than a hierarchy, with a resulting emphasis on trust and reciprocity rather than power. Information, and information and communication technology, occupy a special place in such societies.

Open source Computer software that is offered with full access to the underlying coding, enabling users to change and adapt the software. It is also known as free software. A variety of licences have evolved for this type of software, covering a range of applications and "freeness." In some cases, you are required to keep any derivative works similarly free; in other cases, you are free to create a proprietary commercial product.

Packet switching The process by which messages are converted into small bundles (packets), each with its own address information, to permit message passing by simple computers.

Paper tape Developed during the days of the telegraph, this was a method of storing messages to be transmitted later, or recording incoming messages for later decoding. Recording was done by punching holes in a paper tape and reading was accomplished by sensing those holes with a light or metal rods. This technique was adapted for use in early computers.

Participatory culture A culture in which citizens are not just media consumers but also media producers, usually through social media such as Flickr, Facebook, Twitter, and YouTube. Such users of media are sometimes referred to as "prosumers."

Political economy approach An examination of society that regards law, economy, and the political environment being interrelated and help to establish and sustain the social order. In new media studies this typically focuses on an examination of the regulation and ownership of media.

Post-Fordist A production logic that differs from the classic assembly-line factory pioneered by Henry Ford. Post-Fordist production is characterized by multiple small players and independent ownership of the various components and suppliers. The ability to economically manage the complicated relationships in a post-Fordist production chain is dependent on information and communications technology.

Predictive text (autocomplete) A software service embedded in many mobile phones to allow for faster and more accurate entry of words in text messages from a simple numeric or alphanumeric keyboard. It works by predicting, based on a statistical analysis of the entry language, the most likely next character or characters.

Pro-am revolution The emergence of "professional amateurs," people who are producing media content that rivals professional media in terms of quality. This process is often enabled by new technologies such as digital recording and editing that are cheaper, smaller, and nearly as capable as their professional equivalents. It is controversial to the extent that pro-ams begin to siphon funding away from professionals, or lower the prices paid for media (e.g., stock photography).

Public domain Works of art (including software, movies, music) that are no longer or have been explicitly removed from copyright protection. Works can be placed into the public domain or they can move into the public domain after a period of time has elapsed.

Radio spectrum See **electromagnetic spectrum**.

Recombinant The characteristic of digital goods that allows them to be repurposed and reused relatively easily by users with simple tools found on a computer, also known as the "mash-up."

Remediate In the Bolter and Grusin sense, this describes how new media adopt and extend old media.

Scanning A method of breaking a picture (or later, a series of pictures) into discrete elements for encoding and transmission to a remote location. This process was pioneered with the telegraph (wire photos) and was repurposed for fax machines, television (as a series of pictures), and again for computers.

Smartphone A mobile phone that has the ability to surf the Internet and download and install third-party applications. Examples include the BlackBerry, iPhone, and various Android phones.

Social capital An attempt to describe in economic terms the assets one possesses in the form of relationships with others. This takes the form of bonding (strong ties between closely connected individuals, as in a family), bridging (weaker ties, as within a community or group), and linking (connections between different groups or levels).

Social network The face-to-face or electronic relations between people for formal and informal purposes. In the context of this book, the social network especially includes those aspects enabled or harmed by new media.

Social network analysis (network analysis) A method for the academic study of social networks, with special attention to actors, ties between actors, network structure (patterns of ties), and major influences (such as culture) on the formation and durability of networks.

Social networking (social software, social networking software) Websites that are designed around connections between users.

A key feature of these sites is the ability to identify friends or followers and to keep up to date with their activities online.

Social production The creation of goods and services, including "informational goods," in a social or collaborative fashion. Many aspects of user-generated content can be included here, but social production is not necessarily outside the market economy. Wikipedia is an excellent example of social production.

Social shaping of technology An alternative approach to **technological determinism** that seeks to explain technological change in terms of the influence of key social groups.

Spime A neologism invented by science fiction writer Bruce Sterling to describe an object that can be tracked through space and time. The typical application would be inventory control, but this is being expanded in all directions as low-cost sensors and memory chips (and especially radio-frequency identification chips, or RFID) combined with ubiquitous wireless networks make it feasible to embed these capabilities in more and more objects.

Surveillance The coordinated and organized observation of someone in order to control or affect his or her behaviour. Surveillance has commercial, state, personal, and criminal aspects and all of these are greatly influenced by new media. A simple example would be analyzing purchasing trends according to status updates on Twitter.

Tacit knowledge Knowledge that is not written down, not codified, and thereby more difficult (than **explicit knowledge**—see above) to share. It is often acquired via a learning-by-doing process, rather than in a classroom.

Tag (tagging) A descriptive term for a piece of content or a key word, also the act of applying these tags. See also **folksonomy**.

Technological determinism An approach to technology that posits unmediated outcomes from the use of technology, and in its extreme form, a kind of self-determination and internal logic to the evolution of technology (often the result of short-hand thinking: e.g., "Computers are getting faster all the time."). The writer, if pressed, probably does not believe that, somehow, computers are getting faster on their own, but it is easy to say things like this, given the regular and predictable progress in many technological forms.

Technology S-curve A description of the diffusion of innovations over time, with a few people adopting at first (the bottom of the *S*), a great number once it is well known (the middle of the *S*) and then gradually tapering off as fewer and fewer new users are found (the top of the *S*).

Telegraph A device developed in the early nineteenth century for sending coded messages long distances over wires (and later via radio waves). This technology formed the first global network, prompting one writer to call it "the Victorian Internet."

Tetrad A mode of inquiry into new media, proposed by Canadian media theorist Marshall McLuhan. He suggested that when one is considering the impact of a new media form, we should ask four questions: *What does it enhance? What does it retrieve from the past? What does it change into when pushed to the extreme? What does it erode or obsolesce?*

Text messaging (texting, SMS) The process of using mobile telephones to send short messages (140 characters or fewer, typically) using a signalling channel built into the phone system. Messages can come from the system operator, or, more commonly, from other mobile phone users.

Three strikes A provision in the copyright-enforcement provisions in some countries whereby there is a graduated response to infringing acts (typically, file sharing on the Internet). The third accusation results in an automatic punishment of some type, usually being cut off from the Internet. Modelled on three-strikes laws in the United States that result in mandatory incarceration for some crimes, the provision has been deemed unconstitutional in some countries in part because of the accusation aspect—no conviction is required—and in part because access to the Internet is increasingly seen as a basic human right. The impact on families—where a child may have done the infringing—is also a concern.

Traffic shaping The application of rules to restrict the bandwidth allocated to some protocols on the Internet in order to provide more bandwidth to others. This technique is commonly used to restrict the speed of file sharing and ensure swift Web surfing. It is considered by some to be a violation of **network neutrality** rules.

Universal service A policy objective common in Canada during the early days of telephone service and rural electrification that sought to extend these services beyond their urban origins to rural areas. There has been pressure in Canada and elsewhere to apply the same principles to Internet access and even broadband Internet access.

User-centred innovation Innovation led by the users, who may create amateur or home-built versions of what they hope to use, but which is then adopted, refined, and manufactured by companies.

User-generated content The unpaid contributions of the users of a service, which often times constitutes the bulk of the content (over 90 per cent in the case of YouTube). This is also known as peer production.

Web 2.0 Sometimes called the "read–write Web," Web 2.0 refers to any website in which the contributions to and evolution of the site happens through the Web, via the users of the website.

Notes

....

Chapter 1

1. See www.techvibes.com/blog/as-crtc-hearing-nears-canadians-rally-against-monopolistic-media-merger-2012-09-08.

2. The term *information* is being defined broadly as all forms of message and symbol that are communicated to others, which include those forms that can be considered original knowledge, but also a vast range of other forms that are communicated. One of the difficulties in using the term in relation to new media, such as theories of the "information society," is that it implies a second, narrower definition, where information is associated with forms of knowledge that advance the understanding of the receiver about their social and physical environment. Any cursory glance at the Web, or any other digital media platform, will find an abundance of content that would constitute information in the former sense, but not the latter. The common tendency to conflate access to more information with greater personal and social knowledge has been widely critiqued (e.g., Castells 1999; Graham 1999).

3. The best histories of the Internet have been written by those directly involved in its development, such as Leiner et al. (2003), Berners-Lee (2000), and Gillies and Cailliau (2000), who provide important insiders' accounts of the development of the Web. A useful chronology of the development of computers that is very much informed by the development of the Internet can be found in Hirst and Harrison (2006: 207–12).

4. This question is discussed in Rheingold (1994), Hafner and Lyon (1996), Castells (1996a: 41–6; 2001: 39–46), Leiner et al. (2003), and Hassan (2004). Castells (2001) argues that it is more useful to see the culture of early Internet developers as being a techno-meritocratic one, strongly grounded in academic protocols of the common pursuit of science, peer review, and shared research findings rather than a culture grounded in military service. The research centres of universities such as MIT, Harvard, and Stanford were focal points for the Internet's development.

5. The Internet was already changing with the arrival of "gopher," but that is a prehistory of the Web that is beyond the scope of the present discussion. Those with an interest can do a search and read up on gopher.

6. See the original press release on the Flickr blog: http://blog.flickr.net/en/2005/03/20/yahoo-actually-does-acquire-flickr.

7. See http://dealbook.nytimes.com/2012/04/09/facebook-buys-instagram-for-1-billion.

8. You can still watch the video of the trip to the zoo: www.youtube.com/watch?v=jNQXAC9IVRw.

9. You can check the latest numbers yourself (and add to them, if you watch to the end) here: www.youtube.com/watch?v=kffacxfA7G4&feature=plcp.

10. Statistics on YouTube are notoriously unreliable, as a "view" is counted only when the video is watched to the end. Also, a video may appear many times on the site and can easily be referenced in hundreds or even thousands (as the Bieber video is) "response" videos. If you haven't seen "The Evolution of Dance," here it is: www.youtube.com/watch?v=dMH0bHeiRNg.

11. It wasn't just the news media that solicited and used amateur video. The UK police actively encouraged people with cell phone footage to come forward and contribute anything that might help solve the crime. See this story from the BBC, "Police appeal for bombing footage," available at http://news.bbc.co.uk/2/hi/uk_news/4668675.stm.

12. See http://newsroom.fb.com/content/default.aspx?NewsAreaId=22.

13. The description of the Internet as a place to help people "understand the world around them" came in an interview with CNN, in the fall of 2006, when Zuckerberg was just 22 years old and starting to open the Facebook site up to people outside of its initial target, university and college students. At that point, the site already had 10 million members. See http://money .cnn.com/2006/10/06/magazines/fortune/ fastforward_facebook.fortune.index.htm.

14. See this article in *Fortune* magazine: "'FarmVille' Gamemaker Zynga Sees Dollar Signs," Jessica Shambora, 26 October 2009, http://brainstormtech.blogs. fortune.cnn.com/2009/10/26/ farmville-gamemaker-zynga-sees-dollar-signs.

15. The number of Internet hosts is inevitably lower than the number of users, since multiple users will connect from a single host, as seen in the worldwide proliferation of Internet cafés for travellers. The number of Internet hosts, or sites from which connection to a server is made, is easier to measure than the number of people who access the Internet.

16. See Kate Milberry, "Geeks and Global Justice: Another (Cyber) World is Possible," doctoral thesis, Simon Fraser University: *Geeks and Global*.

17. See www.foreignaffairs.com/articles/67325/ malcolm-gladwell-and-clay-shirky/ from-innovation-to-revolution#.

18. Based on an interview with Robert Ouimet, executive producer of three websites (120seconds.com, newmusiccanada.com, and justconcerts.com) that made up the component parts Radio 3, a pioneering online initiative created by the Canadian Broadcasting Corporation between 2000 and 2005. The site has evolved, and the three parts have been merged in to one main site (music.cbc. ca/#/radio3), but the history of Radio 3 is an important milestone in Canadian new media.

Chapter 2

1. This historical approach to new media is presented in much greater detail, and with a warm and eminently readable style, by Canadian scholar Wade Rowland in his excellent book, *Spirit of the Web: The Age of Information from Telegraph to Internet* (Toronto:

Thomas Allen Publishers, 2006). Now in its third edition, Rowland's book is an excellent resource in the field of new media and media studies generally.

2. Morse code was created in the 1840s for Samuel Morse's first telegraph. Although based on dots and dashes, there were also different pauses between these elements (which were transmitted as a buzz or click on early systems), resulting in six different discrete elements. An even earlier system for binary encoding of messages, the Braille system for creating letters with raised dots on paper, was invented in 1821 and is still in widespread use today to enable the blind to read by touch. See http://en.wikipedia. org/wiki/Braille for details.

3. Some of these models for revenue sharing and technical standards had already been worked out for the international postal network that existed prior to the telegraph, and in many countries the telegraph was set up as an extension of the post (PTT, or "post, telegraph, and telephone," is an acronym that you still see in Europe).

4. See also James Carey for his important chapter on the telegraph and its role in breaking the link between transportation and communication in *Communication as Culture: Essays on Media and Society*, (New York and London: Routledge, 1992), Chapter 8.

5. As Briscoe, Odlyzko, and Tilly point out in their 2006 *IEEE Spectrum* article, this "law" is "a rough empirical description, not an immutable physical law." See http:// spectrum.ieee.org/computing/networks/ metcalfes-law-is-wrong/0.

6. The story of the origins of telegraph regulation is told masterfully by Matthew Lasar in an *ars technica* post called, "How Robber Barons Hijacked the 'Victorian Internet'," http:// arstechnica.com/tech-policy/2011/05/how-the-robber-barons-hijacked-the-victorian-internet. Accessed 30 December 2009.

7. Walter P. Phillips, *The Phillips Code, Telephone and Telegraph Age* (New York, 1879 [1975]). Available at www.radions.net/philcode.htm. Accessed 29 December 2009.

8. Phillips, *The Phillips Code* p. 2.

9. This is chronicled in a fascinating article published in the 17 December 2009 issue of *The Economist*. The article, entitled "Network

Effects," appeared as part of a series on newspapers and technology. It is available here: www.economist.com/node/15108618?story_id=15108618. Accessed 11 November 2010.

10. Stillman, "Journalism and Literature," p. 689.

11. Thoreau, *Walden* vol. 1, p. 84.

12. *The Economist*, "Network Effects."

13. According to the Wikipedia page on "The Victorian Internet" (a euphemism for the telegraph), "Besides news reporting, telegraphy, as the first true global network, permitted applications such as message routing, social networks (between Morse operators—with gossip and even marriages among operators via telegraph being observed), instant messaging, cryptography and text coding, abbreviated language slang, network security experts, hackers, wire fraud, mailing lists, spamming, e-commerce, stock exchange minute-by-minute reports via ticker tape machines, and many others." See http://en.wikipedia.org/wiki/Victorian_Internet. If you're inspired to find out more, see also Thomas Standage's excellent book, *The Victorian Internet: The Remarkable Story of the Telegraph and the Nineteenth Century's On-line Pioneers* (New York: Walker & Company).

14. Although it would seem clear enough that taking the coding out of the telegraph process would make the ability to transmit messages useful for most people, as it happens, the largest operator of telegraph networks at the time—Western Union—turned down a chance to buy Bell's emergent telephone company when given the chance. Western Union did not see the innovation as a viable business and declined to purchase the company.

15. A rival telephone inventor arrived moments after Bell. Eventually, his technology was incorporated into the Bell telephone design via a licence. As we continue to see, new media technologies are often tangled up in patent disputes—the patent war between Apple and Microsoft a few years ago about the "Windows" interface is an example—and these sometimes delay or distract the inventors in their early days.

16. Ralph de la Vega, head of AT&T's wireless unit, said that "AT&T is considering incentives to keep [iPhone] subscribers from hampering the experience for everyone else" (9 December 2009). See http://blogs.wsj.com/digits/2009/12/09/att-to-new-york-and-san-francisco-were-working-on-it.

17. There are some wonderful old instructional films available on YouTube, showing people how to dial a telephone. See, for example, www.youtube.com/watch?v=ClDw75mUl6c, complete with an example of what "dial tone," "ringing," and "busy" sound like, along with a call using the then-usual "5-digit" dialling. These instructional films would have been played at the beginning and end of feature films in theatres, as a way of informing the public of important issues, just as we now have advertisements and movie trailers. Many cell phone users are unfamiliar with dial tone, of course, and quite often never hear a busy signal either, as the cell service provider merely pops up an offer to redial.

18. Early telephones, which relied on a hand crank or buzzer to "ring Central" (get the operator's attention), did offer users a crude form of direct dialling, which they could use to contact their immediate neighbours—people could buzz or crank a special code to get their neighbours on the line without bothering the operator. This worked for the small number of people who shared that wire, called a "party line". Other niceties were practised, such as making a small ring when you were done a call, so others knew the line was available, and doing a special ring for emergencies. In a way, these practices foretold later uses such as chat rooms and chat lines (commonly used for phone sex these days) that have been recreated using modern technologies. Recreating existing practices is a common occurrence in new media.

19. See Daniel G. Dorner, "The Essential Services Policy Network: Organizational Influence in Canada's Information Highway Policy Development Process," *The Library Quarterly*, vol. 72, no. 1 (Chicago: University of Chicago Press, January 2002), pp. 27–84, www.jstor.org/stable/4309581. See also Glenn Fleishman, "The Killer App of 1900," *Publicola*, 11 December 2009 (retrieved 15 December 2009 from http://publicola.net/?p=20687). The telephone regulator in Canada, the Canadian Radio-television and Telecommunications Commission (CRTC), issued a call for a review of the definition of essential service in 2006 (see www.crtc.gc.ca/eng/archive/2006/pt2006-14.htm)

and issued a decision in 2008 (www.crtc.gc.ca/ eng/archive/2008/dt2008-17.htm). In the main, however, these regulations are applicable to telephone companies regarding their wholesale operations and how they are required to share infrastructure (essential services) to ensure effective competition.

20. Manovich, *The Language of New Media*, p. 50.

21. See this interview from the CBC archives with the tale of Fessenden's invention of radio: http://archives.cbc.ca/science_technology/ technology/clips/10258. Read more about Fessenden at this page honouring the centenary of his achievement (the first broadcast was Christmas Day 1906): http://blogs.voices.com/ voxdaily/2007/01/radio.html.

22. The early history of radio is quite detailed, but you can get a nice sense of it from the wonderful chronology, presented in a series of overlapping "eras," at http://earlyradiohistory. us. The story of Frank Conrad's early radio broadcasts is told there and in a number of books and articles. A useful starting point can be found here: http://en.wikipedia.org/wiki/ Frank_Conrad.

23. Godfrey (1982) points out that radio regulation in Canada was "tentative" and left to a civil servant, variously in the office of public works, fisheries, or the navy. A royal commission on broadcasting did not take place until 1928, and the first piece of legislation wasn't enacted until 1934 (1982: 60).

24. In Britain, with a single government-run broadcaster for many years, there was a form of subscription broadcasting through radio licenses that everyone who owned a radio (and later a television) had to pay. This money subsidized the creation of programs and meant that radio programs were mostly free of advertising. In Canada, the government "sponsored" the CBC but allowed it to also run advertising. When television came along, the decision was made to remove all advertising from CBC radio.

25. A detailed timeline, not only of television but also of radio, can be found here: www. hammondmuseumofradio.org/dates.html.

26. Details of the coronation, including a copy of the video, can be found in the CBC archives: Coronation of Queen Elizabeth II, http:// archives.cbc.ca/on_this_day/06/02.

27. For more information on the "media ecology" literature, a good source is the Media Ecology Association (MEA), "a not-for-profit organization dedicated to promoting the study, research, criticism, and application of media ecology in educational, industry, political, civic, social, cultural, and artistic contexts, and the open exchange of ideas, information, and research" (MEA 2010). The MEA website (www. media-ecology.org) highlights the work of prominent scholars in the field, such as Walter Ong, Elizabeth Eisenstein, Eric Havelock, Jacques Ellul, Harold Innis, Marshall McLuhan, and others.

Chapter 3

1. A marvellous and easy-to-follow explanation of tetrads can be found on Anthony Hempell's website, www.anthonyhempell.com/papers/ tetrad/concept.html. See also the Wikipedia page for the concept: http://en.wikipedia. org/wiki/Tetrad_of_media_effects. Libraries and Archives Canada maintains an Innis and McLuhan page that includes a section on the tetrad as well (www.collectionscanada.gc.ca/ innis-mcluhan/030003-2030-e.html), including a variety of multimedia elements and recordings of McLuhan using his tetrad analysis.

Chapter 4

1. This process of licences for wireless devices continues, but the design of the cellular system makes so many available that the government issues spectrum in aggregate to the cellular operator (e.g., Bell Mobility) and they manage the process—by having you subscribe to their service—for you. It is completely transparent— and requires no training—to the end-user.

2. ". . . [T]he best general arrangement of frequency assignments for the minimum interference and the minimum number of frequencies is a hexagonal layout in which each station is surrounded by six equidistant adjacent stations." From page 3 of the original 1947 memo, titled "Mobile Telephony—Wide Area Coverage," by D.H. Ring of Bell Telephone.

3. This switching from tower to tower is called "hand off" and it is a very tricky business. Thankfully, the whole process is invisible

to users of mobile phones and we can quite happily make a call while zooming along at highway speeds.

4. The price per megabyte is not what people are thinking about when they send text messages, of course. Nevertheless, at 15 cents per 140 characters—current cost for a single message in Canada—that is over $100 per megabyte. By comparison, data on a mobile phone is available for under $10 per megabyte ($100 per gigabyte) and under $2 per megabyte ($20 per gigabyte) on a home connection.

5. There is even HSDPA and HSUPA (the d and u being "down" and "up," respectively) and sometimes a + sign is added to indicate that it is even better for data services. In reality, a lot of this is like the specifications for automobiles, great on paper but "your mileage may vary."

6. Much of the nomenclature relating to mobile networks is an endlessly confusing array of acronyms and code words. These are made even more confusing because the most widely used terms—like 3G—are little more than marketing terminology or shorthand for engineers. Sometimes there are efforts to more rigidly define the terms, but these inevitably fall victim to "fast and loose" application of the terminology by vendors keen to sell their technology as the solution to a particular problem. LTE is already being marketed as 4G, for example, although it is not entirely clear that this is justified or that the delivered products fully support the specified capabilities. This is a replay of the situation with 3G, which was delivered by various vendors through various telecommunications service providers at various speeds and prices and continues to be remarkably variable.

7. Current numbers are available at http://148apps.biz/app-store-metrics.

8. Similar alarms have been raised about so-called L33T-speak as used in instant messaging programs like MSM and in the chat rooms of games.

9. BBC, "Over 5 Billion Mobile Phone Connections Worldwide," 9 July 2010, http://news.bbc.co.uk/2/hi/technology/10569081.stm. Accessed 11 July 2010. See also this analysis of the implications of 5 billion subscribers (and the estimate of 7 billion by 2015): Sam Churchill, "5 Billion Mobile Subscribers," dailywireless.org,

11 July 2010, www.dailywireless.org/2010/07/11/5-billion-mobile-subscribers. Accessed 11 July 2010.

10. Incorporated in 1984, Research In Motion won both an Emmy Award and an Academy Award for Technical Achievement for the DigiSync Film KeyKode Reader. See http://www.berryreview.com/2009/02/12/the-history-of-rim-the-blackberry-smartphone-part-1-the-origins.

11. See the RIM web page on super apps here: http://uk.blackberry.com/apps/super-apps.html.

12. The founders of RIM have donated generously to the Perimeter Institute among other things at the University of Waterloo. Jim Balsillie, alone, donated $170 million to the institute.

13. Details of the 2008 request can be found in a PC World article by John Ribeiro, "RIM Says It Can't Provide E-mail Interception in India," 26 May 2008, www.pcworld.com/businesscenter/article/146306/rim_says_it_cant_provide_email_interception_in_india.html. The 2010 dispute is covered by Mike Masnick of Techdirt, in "Indian Government Demands Right to Spy on Skype, Gmail, BlackBerry Messages," 7 July 2010, http://techdirt.com/articles/20100702/17551510065.shtml.

14. See the story here: "100 Fastest Growing Companies, 2009," Fortune, http://money.cnn.com/magazines/fortune/fortunefastestgrowing/2009/index.html. Accessed 7 July 2010.

15. The CBC has a timeline with many milestones in the life of Research In Motion. It is available here: http://www.cbc.ca/news2/interactives/timeline-rim/.

16. The "war" is ongoing, of course, and things are never as they seem. Early in 2010, the Amazon Kindle suddenly acquired a "developer's kit" and news emerged about its App Store, making it much more of a general-purpose device, albeit one focused on reading, than it was the week before. Amazon has continued to evolve its mobile platform, focusing on consumption of books, music, and movies. The Kindle Fire, Amazon's media-focused device, is based on the Android operating system, so it is not impossible that they might offer smartphone capabilities as well.

17. "A Review of the Potential Health Risks of Radiofrequency Fields from Wireless Telecommunications Devices," expert panel report prepared by the Royal Society of Canada

for Health Canada (Ottawa: Royal Society of Canada, RSC.EPR 99-1, 1999).

18. Modern mobile phone and data services typically use very high frequencies but low power settings. The combination means that the signal is effectively limited to a "line of sight" and cannot easily penetrate obstructions. This, along with the cell approach to creating capacity, means lots and lots of antennae (unlike the old days of radio and television where one large tower could suffice for a major city).

Chapter 5

1. For example, more than 100 *hours* of video are uploaded every minute to YouTube. See this posting from the YouTube blog: www.youtube.com/yt/press/statistics.html.

2. See www.govexec.com/magazine/2002/04/hierarchies-and-networks/11261.

3. For a useful primer on the social graph, see Alex Iskold's 12 September 2007 article, "Social Graph: Concepts and Issues," in *The Read Write Web*, available at www.readwriteweb.com/archives/social_graph_concepts_and_issues.php.

4. Quoted from CBS News, "Facebook: One Graph to Rule them All?" 21 April 2010, www.cbsnews.com/stories/2010/04/21/tech/main6418458.shtml. Accessed 12 November 2010.

5. Steve Whittaker, Loren Terveen, Will Hill, and Lynn Cherny, "The dynamics of mass interaction," Proceedings of CSCW 98, the ACM Conference on Computer-Supported Cooperative Work (Seattle, WA, 14–18November 1998), pp. 257–64. See also Nielsen's summary of the research at www.useit.com/alertbox/participation_inequality.html.

Chapter 6

1. Nicholas Carr, "The Economics of Digital Sharecropping," *Rough Type*, May 2012. Available online at www.roughtype.com/?p=1600.

2. This historical foundation in research is being rearticulated in the twenty-first century as more and more games, game mechanics, and game design philosophy draw upon sophisticated research and apply data to social challenges. Many firms, for example, build in detailed "analytics" in their game software, resulting in large data sets that can reveal how people play. This information can then be applied to real challenges in health, security, education, and fitness.

3. Hollywood and the games world have, of course, had more successful subsequent liaisons, most notably with the *Lara Croft: Tomb Raider* films, starring Angelina Jolie as the versatile action heroine.

4. It is estimated, for instance, that Microsoft lost USD $1.5 billion in the first 18 months of launching its Xbox, but saw this as a necessary condition for its being able to capture market share from more established players like Sony and Nintendo, as well as establishing its credibility in the games-development community as an industry player in for the long haul.

5. Cleverly, the makers of Lego have recognized the connection and made available *Minecraft* kits made up of blocks that are created to mimic the game.

6. Industry insight on this and almost any other aspect of the games industry can be found on the MobyGames website. You can get more details on Mattrick and the company he co-founded, Distinctive Software, here www.mobygames.com/company/distinctive-software-inc.

7. Full details on the Ontario program are available at the Ontario Media Development Corporation (OMDC) website: www.omdc.on.ca.

8. Florence Chee and Richard Smith, "Online Gamers and the Ambiguity of Community: Korean Definitions of Togetherness for a New Generation," in M. Consalvo and C. Haythornthwaite (eds.), *aoir Internet Annual*, vol. 4 (New York: Peter Lang Publishers, 2007), pp. 165–84.

9. For a fascinating account of the difficulties in presenting academic research on games to politicians and in the media that does not draw on the "moral panic" cause-and-effect model, see Henry Jenkins's description of his appearance before the US Congress shortly after the Littleton shootings: Henry Jenkins, (2006). "Congressional Testimony on Media Violence," MIT Communications Forum. Available at http://web.mit.edu/comm-forum/papers/jenkins_ct.html. Accessed 13 November 2010.

10. Florence Chee and Richard Smith, "Is Electronic Community an Addictive Substance? An Ethnographic Offering from the Everquest Community," in S. Schaffer and M. Price (eds.) *Interactive Convergence in Multimedia—Probing the Boundaries*, vol. 10 (Freeland, UK: The Interdisciplinary Press, 2005), pp. 137–56.

11. The "pink software movement" was a focus of this particular debate. In the 1990s, a number of companies were formed to make "pink" software—games that were designed to appeal to girls and women. The most notable of these was *Purple Moon*. However, there was much disagreement about whether creating "special" games for girls had the effect of marginalizing them, and whether a better tactic would be to integrate different styles into more mainstream games. It was also disputed that current games were not appealing to girls (de Castell and Bryson 1998) and that the nature of play was in fact gendered at all. See also Sara M. Grimes, "Deconstructing the Girl Gamer: From the Girls' Games Movement to Rule of Rose," paper presented at the Canadian Communication Association (CCA) Annual Conference, University of British Columbia, 4–6 June 2008, Vancouver.

12. For more on this topic, see J. Kucklich, "Precarious Playbour: Modders and the Digital Games Industry," *Fibreculture* 5 (2005).

Chapter 7

1. The term *arts multiplier* refers to those studies that seek to demonstrate that investment of public funds in arts activities generates economic and non-economic benefits greater than the cost of the original investment (e.g., a tourism industry that benefits from a town that hosts a major festival). Seaman (2000) has argued that such studies are plagued by the problem of double-counting, and the tendency to ignore what economists call "opportunity cost," or the question of whether the same investment of funds on another activity may have generated greater benefits. The fact that such studies are usually linked to advocacy on the part of a particular arts organization or arts funding agency has not helped to diminish their reputation among economists for being a form of industry-specific special pleading (or lobbying) that lacks methodological rigour (cf. Madden 2001).

2. The notion that culture is an important part of municipal politics resurfaced in the 2010 campaign as well. See, for example, this review of some of the position statements released in the middle of 2010 by mayoral candidates in Toronto: Shannon Litzenberger, "Will Toronto's Next Mayor Champion the Arts?" *The Mark News*, 9 July 2010, http://pioneers.themarknews.com/articles/1837-will-torontos-next-mayor-champion-the-arts/#.UozJTSembyA. Accessed 9 July 2010.

Chapter 8

1. This "discreteness" claim is debatable, since in some cases, a small piece is more valuable than the totality. A good example is a six-second drum sequence (the "Amen Break") that was included in a forgettable and long-forgotten B-side from a 1969 hit pop single but has since been "sampled" and included in dozens of other songs, making it much more valuable. See the fascinating story of this process explained in Nate Harrison's 2004 YouTube video: http://youtu.be/5SaFTm2bcac. Accessed 15 July 2010.

2. Google Blog, "We Knew the Web Was Big . . .," 2008, http://googleblog.blogspot.ca/2008/07/we-knew-web-was-big.html. Accessed 2 July 2010.

Chapter 9

1. Among the key national information policy statements of the 1990s were the US government's *National Information Infrastructure Task Force* (1993); the European Union's *Europe and the Information Superhighway* (Bangemann Report) (1994); Singapore's *IT2000-Vision of an Intelligent Island* (1992); the Canadian government's *The Canadian Information Highway: Building Canada's Information Infrastructure* (1994); Japan's *Program for Advanced Information Infrastructure* (1994); the Australian government's *Creative Nation* (1994) and *Networking Australia's Future* (1995); the Malaysian government's *Multimedia Super Corridor* (1995); Korea's *Information Strategies for Promoting National Competitiveness* (1996); and the OECD's *Global Information Infrastructure–Global Information Society* (1997). See Northfield (1999) for an extended commentary on these; cf. Barr (2000), pp. 169–74.

2. This report was published in *Canada, Industry Canada, Connection, Community, Content: The*

Challenge of the Information Highway, Final Report (Phase 1) of the Information Highway Advisory Council, Ottawa, September 1995.

3. In June 2010, the heritage minister (James Moore) famously claimed that opponents to a bill he was proposing in Parliament (C-32, relating to new copyright provisions) were "radical extremists," seemingly including the 8000 Canadians who had participated in the government's own consultation process. See commentary and analysis here: Michael Geist, "Who are James Moore's 'Radical Extremists'?" *Michael Geist Blog*, 22 June 2010, www .michaelgeist.ca/content/view/5137/125. Accessed 15 July 2010.

4. See H.G. Bown, *Telidon*, CRC Technical report; no. 697-E. (Ottawa: Communications Research Centre, 1978).

5. See Government of Ontario, "Ontario Computer Animation and Special Effects Tax Credit," 2009, www.omdc.on.ca/film_and_tv/tax_credits/ OCASE.htm. Accessed 29 January 2010.

6. See Telefilm Canada, "Canada New Media Fund—Product Assistance," 2009, www .telefilm.gc.ca/03/311.asp?lang=en&fond_id=3. Accessed 28 January 2010.

7. Forbearance was specifically inserted into the Telecommunications Act of 1993, as the government sought to increase market competition in telecommunication services. The first decision that took advantage of the new "power to forbear" (i.e., to opt not to regulate in an area in which the regulator had a legal jurisdiction), was in 1994 in relation to "non-dominant" (small, or new) cellular phone providers. Full text of the decision can be found on the CRTC website: www.crtc.gc.ca/eng/ archive/1994/PT94-44.htm.

8. Internet forbearance came in July 1998 in Telecom Public Notice CRTC 98-17, "Internet Forbearance." The full text of the decision can be found on the CRTC website: www.crtc .gc.ca/eng/archive/1998/PT98-17.htm.

9. The principle was confirmed in a July 2010 ruling from the Federal Court of Canada. Details are available at *Michael Geist*, "Federal Court of Appeal Rules ISPs Not Broadcasters," 7 July 2010, www.michaelgeist.ca/content/ view/5176/125. Accessed 8 July 2010.

10. CRTC decisions are available from your library or at the CRTC website. Here is the link to decision 2009–677, "Canadian Association of Internet Providers et al. and Vaxination Informatique–Application to Review and Vary Certain Determinations in Telecom Decision 2008-108 Related to Bell Canada's Internet Traffic Management Practices," Ottawa, 29 October 2009: www.crtc.gc.ca/eng/ archive/2009/2009-677.htm.

11. See Telecom Decision 2008-108 (in which the case against Bell is considered, and dismissed) and Telecom Decision 2009–677 (in which the appeal is dismissed). Both decisions are available at the CRTC website: www.crtc.gc.ca.

12. Importantly for scholars, these fair dealing rights have been preserved in recent court cases such as CCH, in which a legal publisher sued a law library for sending copies of articles printed in its journals to researchers. The law library was deemed to be exercising a fair dealing right for the purposes of research. See CCH Canadian Ltd. v. Law Society of Upper Canada, 2004 SCC 13, [2004] 1 S.C.R. 339, available at http://csc.lexum.umontreal.ca/ en/2004/2004scc13/2004scc13.html. Accessed 15 July 2010.

13. Read the full posting here: Eric Hellman, "Offline Book 'Lending' Costs U.S. Publishers Nearly $1 Trillion," 15 January 2010, http:// go-to-hellman.blogspot.ca/2010/01/offline- book-lending-costs-us.html. Accessed 28 January 2010.

14. Michael Geist outlines the concerns, and provides a link to the Brazilian proposal, in this blog post: www.michaelgeist.ca/content/ view/5180/125.

15. The term *piracy* is used six times in a briefing document created by the US Trade Representative, titled, "The Anti-Counterfeiting Trade Agreement—Summary of Key Elements Under Discussion." It can be downloaded from the Web, here: www.ustr.gov/sites/default/ files/uploads/factsheets/2009/asset_upload_ file917_15546.pdf.

16. See Ian Sparks, "Internet Access Is a Fundamental Human Right, Rules French Court," *Daily Mail*, 12 June 2009, www.dailymail. co.uk/news/worldnews/article-1192359/ Internet-access-fundamental-human-right- rules-French-court.html#ixzz153SwOtiH. Accessed 12 November 2010.

17. See www.csmonitor.com/2003/0701/p07s01-woeu.html.
18. The Finnish law came into effect 1 July 2010. Press release from the Finnish Ministry of Transport and Telecommunications, "1 Mbit Internet Access a Universal Service in Finland from Beginning of July." Available at www.lvm.fi/web/en/pressreleases/view/1169259.
19. See www.cebit.com.au/news/technology/spain-decrees-broadband-access-rights.
20. See http://news.bbc.co.uk/2/hi/uk_news/politics/8489870.stm.
21. See CRTC 1995, www.crtc.gc.ca/eng/HIGHWAY/HWY9505.htm.
22. The underlying principle of open software is not simply that it is freely available but that the source code is made available to all users, who can modify it accordingly. The concept of *free software* has been associated with Richard Stallman, who founded the Free Software Foundation.

Chapter 10

1. The actual percentage of spam arriving in your email box or in your company's or university's main email service varies day to day, month to month, and year to year according to the activities of the organization's members—have their email addresses been "harvested" and sold to spammers, for example? Current data is maintained by a variety of agencies, including WebSense, a spam and virus-prevention company, based in the United States. Their "Spam Percentage" page is here: http://securitylabs.websense.com/content/spamPercentage.aspx.
2. There is an emerging body of work that is remarking on the importance of mobile social media in protests and resistance. Recent examples include the use of YouTube in the aftermath of the Iran election in 2009 or the use of Twitter during the 2010 G20 protests in Toronto. See, for example, Antonia Zerbisias, "Coverage of the G20 Proved Twitter's News Edge," *Toronto Star*, 11 July 2010, www.thestar.com/news/insight/article/834367. Accessed 11 July 2010. See also the case study on the Citizen Lab in this chapter.

3. See also United States Court of Appeals, District of Columbia Circuit, USA v. Mark Wayne Russell, No. 08-3120, 2 April 2010. Available at http://www.wired.com/images_blogs/threatlevel/2010/04/mark_wayne_russell.pdf.
4. The world of "green broadband" is chronicled in detail by Canadian researcher—and former head of the CANARIE research network—Bill St Arnaud. His blog, http://green-broadband.blogspot.com, is a gold mine of information on the topic and provides links to research papers, conference proceedings, and recent tests and trials.
5. See Richard Smith, "University Data Centres and Climate Change," International Association for Management of Technology, Orlando, Florida, March 2009.
6. David Eaves, a political commentator and blogger from Vancouver, provided an after-the-fact evaluation of the outcome of the interviews on his blog: http://eaves.ca/2010/03/17/youtube-interviews-strengths-and-weaknesses.
7. Check the answer for yourself, by visiting this page: www.flickr.com/cameras/apple/iphone_4.
8. These numbers were given by Jonathan Heiliger at a conference (Structure 2010) in June 2010. The remarks were quoted in an article by Alex Williams, "Twitter: Comparing its Velocity, not Downtime," *Readwrite Cloud*, 10 July 2010, www.readwriteweb.com/cloud/2010/07/twitter-how-its-down-time-comp.php. Accessed 10 July 2010.
9. See European Digital Rights, *Under Surveillance*, 2010, www.edri.org/campaigns/comic-book-under-surveillance. The site has this overview: "The comic book *Under Surveillance* is an information and awareness tool for young adults created in the European project 'sensitization and information of young European citizens on the protection of their personal data,' where EDRi was one of the partners. The project is coordinated by the French League of Human Rights (LDH), in partnership with the European Association for the Defense of Human Rights (AEDH), European Digital Rights (EDRi), the Czech Association Iuridicum Remedium (IuRe) and the Spanish Association Comunicació per a la Cooperació (Pangea)." Accessed 15 July 2010.

10. Malware is an abbreviation of "malicious software." Malware is an omnibus term that includes many different types of software designed to harass, annoy, or steal. It is generally introduced without the owner's knowledge or consent, often through downloaded programs, images, or web pages.

11. See Noah Elkin, "Looking Beyond the Staggering Mobile Stats in the BRIC Countries," *eMarketer Daily*, 17 March 2010, www.emarketer.com/blog/index.php/staggering-mobile-stats-bric-countries. Accessed 20 March 2010.

12. That these online services were later sold to large US companies is both testimony to their success as business initiatives and an unfortunate commentary on this country's ability to sustain homegrown firms to the highest level of global competition.

Bibliography

Aarseth, Espen. 2001. "Computer Game Studies: Year One," *Game Studies: The International Journal of Computer Game Research* 1(1), www.gamestudies.org/0101. Accessed 25 April 2007.

Abramovitz, Moses, and Paul David. 2001. "Two Centuries of American Macroeconomic Growth: From Exploitation of Resource Abundance to Knowledge-Driven Development," SIEPR Discussion Paper No. 01–05, Stanford Institute for Economic Policy Research, Stanford, CA: Stanford University.

Agar, Jon. 2004. *Constant Touch: A Global History of the Mobile Phone*. London: Totem.

Ahonen, Tomi. 2010. *Tomi Ahonen Almanac 2010: Mobile Telecoms Industry Review*. Hong Kong: Tomiahonene Consulting.

Akerlof, George. 1970. "The Market for 'Lemons': Quality Uncertainty and the Market Mechanism," *Quarterly Journal of Economics* 84(3): 488–500.

Aksoy, Asu, and Kevin Robins. 1992. "Hollywood for the 21st Century: Global Competition for Critical Mass in Image Markets," *Cambridge Journal of Economics* 16(1): 1–22.

Aldridge, Stephen, David Halpern, and Sarah Fitzpatrick. 2002. "Social Capital: A Discussion Paper," Performance and Innovation Unit, London, April.

Amabile, Teresa. 1996. *Creativity in Context*. Boulder, CO: Westview Press.

———. 2004. "The Six Myths of Creativity," *Fast Company* 89, December. Accessed from www.fastcompany.com/magazine/89/creativity.html 22 April 2007.

Americans for the Arts. 2007. "Research Services: Creative Industries," www.artsusa.org/information_resources/research_information/services/creative_industries/default.asp, updated 12 March. Accessed 3 May 2007.

Amin, Ash, and Nigel Thrift, (eds.). 2004. *The Cultural Economy Reader*. Oxford: Blackwell.

Anderson, Chris. 2006. *The Long Tail: Why the Future of Business Is Selling Less of More*. New York: Random House.

———. 2009. *Free: The Future of a Radical Price*. New York: Hyperion.

Andersson, David Emanuel, Åke E. Andersson, and Charlotta Mellander (eds.). 2011. *Handbook of Creative Cities*. Cheltenham, UK: Edward Elgar Publishing.

Anthony, Ian. 2000. Radio Wizard: Edward Samuel Rogers and the Revolution of Communication. Toronto: Gage Publishing Company.

Arnison, Matthew. 2003. "Open Publishing Is the Same as Free Software," first published March 2001. Accessed from www.purplebark.net/maffew/cat/openpub.html 28 April 2007.

Arthur, W. Brian. 1999. "Competing Technologies and Economic Prediction," in D. MacKenzie and J. Wacjman (eds.), *The Social Shaping of Technology*, 2nd ed. Buckingham, UK: Open University Press.

Ashlee, Vance. 2006. "Sun and Apple Almost Merged Three Times—Bill Joy," *The Register*, 12 January 2001. Accessed from www.theregister.co.uk/2006/01/12/sun_apple_snapple 11 November 2010.

Atton, Chris. 2001. "Approaching Alternative Media: Theory and Methodology." Paper presented to Our Media, Not Theirs, International Communications Association pre-conference, Washington, DC, 24 May. Accessed from www.ourmedianet.org/papers/om2001/Atton.om2001.pdf 1 May 2007.

———. 2002. *Alternative Media*. London: Sage.

———. 2004. *An Alternative Internet*. Edinburgh: Edinburgh University Press.

Australian, The. 2007. "Ghosts of Blogging Haunt Net Celebrity," www.theaustralian.news.com.au/story/0,20867,21445581-2703,00.html, posted 26 March 2007. Accessed 26 March 2007.

Australian Broadcasting Corporation. 2001. "This Time It's Different," broadcast on *Four Corners*, 30 April, www.abc.net.au/4corners/dotcom.

Australian Research Council Centre of Excellence for Creative Industries and Innovation 2005, CCI National Mapping Project: Conceptual Background https://wiki.cci.edu.au/display/NMP/Conceptual+Background, created 11 November. Accessed 12 December 2006.

Baase, Sara. 1997. *A Gift of Fire: Social, Legal, and Ethical Issues in Computing.* Upper Saddle River, NJ: Prentice Hall.

Bannermann, Sara. 2006. "Copyright and the Common Good: An Examination of 'the Public Interest' in International Copyright Regimes," in P.N. Thomas and J. Servaes (eds.), *Intellectual Property Rights and Communications in Asia: Conflicting Traditions.* New Delhi: Sage, pp. 58–78.

Bakardjieva, Maria. 2005. *Internet Society: The Internet in Everyday Life.* London: Sage.

Barabási, Albert-László. 2003. *Linked: How Everything Is Connected to Everything Else and What It Means.* London: Penguin.

Barber, Benjamin. 2000. "Jihad versus McWorld," in F. Lechner and J. Boli (eds.), *The Globalization Reader.* Oxford: Blackwell, pp. 21–6.

Barbrook, Richard, and Andy Cameron. 1995. "The Californian Ideology," *Muse* 3: 3–17.

Barlow, John Perry. 1995. "Is There a There in Cyberspace?" *UTNE Reader*, March–April, pp. 31–6.

———. 1996a. "A Declaration of the Independence of Cyberspace," www.eff.org/pub/Publications/John_Perry_Barlow. Accessed 22 January 2001.

———.1996b. "Selling Wine without Bottles: The Economy of Mind on the Global Net," in P. Ludlow (ed.), *High Noon on the Electronic Frontier.* Cambridge, MA: MIT Press, pp. 9–34.

Barnes, Brooks. 2007. "Disney Acquires Web Site for Children," *New York Times*, 2 August. Accessed 30 June 2010 at www.nytimes.com/2007/08/02/business/02disney.html.

———. 2010. "Club Penguin Misses Goals, Giving Disney a Half-Price Deal," *New York Times*, 12 May. Accessed 30 June 2010 at www.nytimes.com/2010/05/13/business/media/13penguin.html.

Barney, Darin. 2004. *The Network Society.* Cambridge, UK: Polity Press.

Barr, Trevor. 2000. *newmedia.com.au: The Changing Face of Australia's Media and Communications.* Sydney, AU: Allen & Unwin.

Bassett, Caroline. 2007. "Cultural Studies and New Media," in G. Hall and C. Burchall (eds.), *New Cultural Studies: Adventures in Theory.* Edinburgh: Edinburgh University Press, pp. 220–37.

Batterham, Robin. 2000. "The Chance to Change: Discussion Paper by the Chief Scientist," August, www.isr.gov.au/science/review/ChanceToChange_17aug.pdf. Accessed 1 June 2002.

Baudrillard, Jean. 1988a. "For a Critique of the Political Economy of the Sign," in M. Poster (ed.), *Jean Baudrillard: Selected Writings.* Cambridge, UK: Polity Press, pp. 57–97.

———. 1988b. "Simulacra and Simulations," in M. Poster (ed.), *Jean Baudrillard: Selected Writings.* Cambridge, UK: Polity Press, pp. 166–84.

Baym, Nancy. 2005. "Interpersonal Life Online," in L. Lievrouw and S. Livingstone (eds.), *The Handbook of New Media: Social Shaping and Consequences of ICTs*, 2nd ed. London: Sage, pp. 35–54.

BBC (British Broadcasting Corporation). 2005. "Building Public Value: Review of the BBC's Royal Charter," May. Accessed from www.bbc.co.uk/info/policies/bpv.shtml 22 April 2007.

———. 2006. "Blogosphere Sees Healthy Growth," http://news.bbc.co.uk/2/hi/technology/6129496.stm. Accessed 17 March 2007.

———. 2007. "What Is Digital Storytelling?," www.bbc.co.uk/wales/digitalstorytelling/about.shtml. Accessed 22 April 2007.

———. 2012. "Google Loses Australia 'Gangland' Defamation Lawsuit," www.bbc.co.uk/news/technology-20153309. Accessed 26 January 2013.

Bell, Daniel. 1974. *The Coming of Post-Industrial Society.* Harmondsworth, UK: Penguin.

Bell, Steven, and Douglas Kellner. 1991. *Postmodern Theory: Critical Interrogations.* London: Macmillan.

Beniger, James. 1986. *The Control Revolution: Technological and Economic Origins of the Information Society.* Cambridge, MA: Harvard University Press.

Benkler, Yochai. 2001. "The Battle for the Institutional Ecosystem in the Digital Environment," *Communications of the ACM* 44(2): 84–90.

———. 2006. *The Wealth of Networks: How Social Production Transforms Markets and Freedom.* New Haven, CT: Yale University Press.

Bennett, Tony. 1994. "Research and Cultural Development," in M. Breen (ed.), *Enhancing Cultural Value: Narrowcasting, Community Media and Cultural Development.* Melbourne, AU: Centre for International Research on Communications and Information Technologies, pp. 17–23.

———. 1998. *Culture: A Reformer's Science*. Sydney, AU: Allen & Unwin.

Berland, Jody. 1992. "Angels Dancing: Cultural Technologies and the Production of Space," in L. Grossberg, C. Nelson, and P. Treichler (eds.), *Cultural Studies*. New York: Routledge, pp. 38–55.

Berners-Lee, Tim. 2000. *Weaving the Web: The Past, Present and Future of the World Wide Web by Its Inventor*. London: Texere.

Best, Kirsty. 2003. "Beating Them at Their Own Game: The Cultural Politics of the Open Source Movement and the Gift Economy," *International Journal of Cultural Studies* 6(4): 449–70.

Bettig, Ronald. 1996. *Copyrighting Culture: The Political Economy of Intellectual Property*. Boulder, CO: Westview Press.

Bilton, Chris. 2007. *Management and Creativity: From Creative Industries to Creative Management*. Oxford, UK: Blackwell.

———, and Ruth Leary. 2002. "What Managers Can Do for Creativity: Brokering Creativity in the Creative Industries," *International Journal of Cultural Policy* 8(2): 49–64.

Blizzard. 2012. "October Press Release." *Activision*, http://investor.activision.com/releasedetail.cfm?ReleaseID=711219. Accessed 15 December 2012.

Blumler, Jay, and Stephen Coleman. 2001. *Realising Democracy Online: A Civic Commons in Cyberspace*. London: Institute for Public Policy Research.

Bocock, Robert. 1992. "Consumption and Lifestyles," in R. Bocock and K. Thompson (eds.), *Social and Cultural Forms of Modernity*. Cambridge, UK: Open University Press, pp. 119–67.

Boden, Margaret. 1990. *The Creative Mind: Myths and Mechanisms*. London: Cardinal.

———. 1995. "Creativity and Unpredictability," *Stanford Humanities Review* 4(2), www.stanford.edu/group/SHR/4-2/text/boden.html. Accessed 22 April 2007.

Bogost, Ian. 2011. *How to Do Things with Video Games*, vol. 38. Minneapolis, MN: University of Minnesota Press.

Bolter, Jay David, and Richard Grusin. 2000. *Remediation: Understanding New Media*. Cambridge, MA: MIT Press.

Bosman, Julie. 2006. "Chevy Tries a Write Your Own Ad Approach, and the Potshots Fly," *New York Times*, 4 April, www.nytimes.com/2006/04/04/business/media/04adco.html. Accessed 2 November 2012.

Boutell.com. 2004. "WWW FAQs: How Many Web Sites Are There?," www.boutell.com/newfaq/misc/sizeofweb.html. Accessed 19 December 2006.

———. 2007. "WWW FAQs: How Many Web Sites Are There?," www.boutell.com/newfaq/misc/sizeofweb.html. Accessed 19 May 2007.

Bower, Joseph, and Clayton Christensen. 1999. "Disruptive Technologies: Catching the Wave," in *Harvard Business Review on Managing Uncertainty*. Cambridge, MA: Harvard Business School Press, pp. 147–73.

Bowman, Shayne, and Chris Willis. 2003. *We Media: How Audiences Are Shaping the Future of News and Information*, www.hypergene.net/wemedia/weblog.php.

boyd, danah. 2008. *Taken Out of Context: American Teen Sociality in Networked Publics*, Ph.D. dissertation, Berkeley, CA: University of California–Berkeley, School of Information.

Boyle, James. 1997. *Shamans, Software, and Spleens: Law and the Construction of the Information Society*. Cambridge, MA: Harvard University Press.

Braithwaite, John, and Peter Drahos. 2000. *Global Business Regulation*. Melbourne, AU: Cambridge University Press.

Brand, Jeffrey. 2007. *Interactive Australia 2007: Facts About the Australian Computer and Video Game Industry*. Sydney, AU: Interactive Entertainment Association of Australia.

Breen, Marcus. 2002. "Convergence Policy: It's Not What You Dance, It's the Way You Dance It," in G. Elmer (ed.), *Critical Perspectives on the Internet*. Lanham, MD: Rowman & Littlefield, pp. 165–82.

Briscoe, Bob, Andrew Odlyzko, and Benjamin Tilly. 2006. "Metcalfe's Law Is Wrong—IEEE Spectrum," *IEEE Spectrum* online: Technology, Engineering, and Science News, http://spectrum.ieee.org/computing/networks/metcalfes-law-is-wrong.

British Council. 2010. *Mapping the Creative Industries: A Toolkit*. London: British Council. Available online at www.britishcouncil.org/mapping_the_creative_industries_a_toolkit_2-2.pdf. Accessed 1 December 2012.

Brockman, John. 1996. *Digerati: Encounters with the Cyber Elite*. London: Orion Business Books.

Brook, James, and Iian Boal (eds.). 1995. *Resisting the Virtual Life: The Culture and Politics of Information*. San Francisco: City Lights.

Brown, Jesse. 2008. "The Face of Anonymous," *Search Engine*, CBC, 7 February. Archived version available at http://web.archive.org/web/20080211091428/http://www.cbc.ca/searchengine/blog/2008/02/this_weeks_show_feb708_1.html. Retrieved 23 September 2013.

Brown, John Sealy, and Paul Duguid. 2000. *The Social Life of Information*. Boston: Harvard Business School Press.

Bruns, Axel. 2005. *Gatewatching: Collaborative Online News Production*. New York: Peter Lang.

——. 2006. "Wikinews: The Next Generation of Alternative Online News?," *SCAN: Journal of Media Arts Culture* 3(1), http://scan.net.au/scan/journal/display.php?journal_id=69. Accessed 28 April 2007.

——, and Joanne Jacobs. 2006. "Introduction," in A. Bruns and J. Jacobs (eds.), *Uses of Blogs*. New York: Peter Lang, pp. 1–7.

Bryce, Jo, and Jason Rutter. 2002. "Killing Like a Girl: Gendered Gaming and Girl Gamers' Visibility," in F. Mayra (ed.), *Computer Games and Digital Cultures Conference Proceedings*. Tampere, Fl: Tampere University Press.

Buckingham, David. 2000. *After the Death of Childhood: Growing Up in the Age of Electronic Media*. Cambridge, UK: Polity Press.

——. 2005. "Children and New Media," in L. Lievrouw and S. Livingstone (eds.), *Handbook of New Media*, 2nd ed. London: Sage, pp. 75–91.

Burgess, Jean. 2006. "Hearing Ordinary Voices: Cultural Studies, Vernacular Creativity and Digital Storytelling," *Continuum: Journal of Media and Cultural Studies* 20(2): 201–14.

——, Marcus Foth, and Helen Klaebe. 2006. "Everyday Creativity as Civic Engagement: A Cultural Citizenship View of New Media." Paper presented to Communications Policy and Research Forum 2006, Sydney, AU, 25–26 September. Accessed from http://eprints.qut.edu.au/archive/00005056 22 April 2007.

Burnet, Robert. 1996. *Canadian Railway and Telegraph History*. Etobicoke, ON: Telegraph Key & Sounder.

Burnett, Ron, and P. David Marshall. 2003. *Web Theory: An Introduction*. London: Routledge.

Bush, Vannevar. 1996. "Excerpt from 'As we may think'," in M. Stefik (ed.), *Internet Dreams: Archetypes, Myths, and Metaphors*. Cambridge, MA: MIT Press, pp. 15–22.

BusinessWire. 2010. "Club Penguin Waddles onto Wii," *New York Times*, 10 June. Accessed 30 June 2010 at http://markets.on.nytimes.com/research/stocks/news/press_release.asp?docTag=20100610080181ZWIRE_USPRX____BW5430&feedID=600&press_symbol=89999.

Butt, Danny, and Axel Bruns. 2005. "Digital Rights Management and Music in Australia," *Media and Arts Law Review* 10(4): 265–78.

Cahoone, Lawrence. 2003. *From Modernism to Postmodernism: An Anthology*. Malden, MA: Blackwell.

Cairncross, Frances. 1998. *The Death of Distance: How the Communications Revolution Will Change Our Lives*. London: Orion Business Books.

Calabrese, Andrew. 1999. "The Information Age According to Manuel Castells," *Journal of Communication* 49(3): 172–86.

Callinicos, Alex. 2001. *Against the Third Way: An Anti-capitalist Critique*. Cambridge, UK: Polity Press.

Campbell, Cole. 2000. "Citizens Matter—And This Is Why Public Journalism Matters," *Journalism Studies* 1(4): 689–94.

Canada Media Fund (CMF). 2010. "Recoupment Policy: Experimental Stream," www.cmf-fmc.ca/downloads/create/Recoupment_exp_en.pdf. Accessed 10 September 2010.

Carey, James. 1992. *Communication as Culture: Essays on Media and Society*. New York and London: Routledge.

——. 1995. "The Press, Public Opinion, and Public Discourse," in T.L. Glasser and C.T. Salmon (eds.), *Public Opinion and the Communication of Consent*. New York: Guilford Press.

——, and John J. Quirk. 1992. "The History of the Future," in J. Carey, *Communication as Culture*. New York: Routledge, pp. 173–200.

Carr, Diane, Andrew Burn, David Buckingham, Gareth Schott, and John Thompson, (eds.). 2006. *Computer Games: Text, Narrative and Play*. Cambridge, UK: Polity Press.

Carr, Nicholas. 2005. "The Amorality of Web 2.0," www.roughtype.com/?p=110. Accessed 17 March 2007.

——. 2008. "Is Google Making Us Stupid?," *Yearbook of the National Society for the Study of Education* 107(2): 89–94.

——. 2009. *The Big Switch: Rewiring the World, from Edison to Google*. New York: W.W. Norton & Company.

———. 2010. *The Shallows: How the Internet Is Changing the Way We Think, Read and Remember*. London: Atlantic Books.

———. 2011. *The Shallows: What the Internet Is Doing to Our Brains*. New York: W.W. Norton & Company.

———. 2012. "The Economics of Digital Sharecropping," available online at www.roughtype.com/?p=1600. Accessed 7 January 2013.

Cassell, Justine, and Henry Jenkins (eds.). 1998. *From Barbie to Mortal Kombat: Gender and Computer Games*. Cambridge, MA: MIT Press.

Castells, Manuel. 1977. *The Urban Question: A Marxist Approach*, trans. A. Sheridan. London: Edward Arnold.

———. 1978. *City, Class, and Power*. London: Macmillan.

———. 1983. *The City and the Grassroots: A Cross-Cultural Theory of Urban Social Movements*. London: Edward Arnold.

———. 1989. *The Informational City: Information Technology, Economic Restructuring, and the Urban-Regional Process*. Oxford, UK: Blackwell.

———. 1996. *The Rise of the Network Society*, vol. 1 of *The Information Age: Economy, Society and Culture*. Malden, MA: Blackwell.

———. 1998. *The Power of Identity*, vol. 2 of *The Information Age: Economy, Society and Culture*. Malden, MA: Blackwell.

———. 1999. "Flows, Networks, and Identities: A Critical Theory of the Informational Society," in M. Castells, R. Flecha, P. Freire, H.A. Giroux, D. Macedo, and P. Willis, *Critical Education in the New Information Age*. Lanham, MD: Rowman & Littlefield.

———. 2000a. *End of Millennium*, vol. 3 of *The Information Age: Economy, Society and Culture*. Malden, MA: Blackwell.

———. 2000b. "Materials for an Exploratory Theory of the Network Society," *British Journal of Sociology* 51(1): 5–24.

———. 2001. *The Internet Galaxy: Reflections on Economy, Society and Culture*. Oxford: Oxford University Press.

———. 2004. "Afterword: Why Networks Matter," in H. McCarthy, P. Miller, and P. Skidmore (eds.), *Network Logic: Who Governs in an Interconnected World?* London: DEMOS, pp. 221–24.

———, and Yuku Aoyama. 1994. "Paths towards the Informational Society: Employment Structure in G-7 Countries, 1920–90," *International Labour Review* 133(1): 5–33.

Castronova, Edward. 2005. *Synthetic Worlds: The Business and Culture of Online Games*. Chicago: University of Chicago Press.

Caves, Richard. 2000. *Creative Industries: Contracts Between Art and Commerce*. Cambridge, MA: Harvard University Press.

CBC. 2010. "*World of Warcraft* Gamers Can Stay Anonymous," www.cbc.ca/technology/story/2010/07/12/blizzard-world-of-warcraft-forums.html. Accessed 15 July 2010.

CBC. 2011. "CRTC Opts Not to Regulate Netflix," www.cbc.ca/news/technology/story/2011/10/05/technology-crtc-netflix-online-video.html. Accessed 26 January 2013.

CBC. 2012. "TekSavvy Asked to Reveal Customer Info by Film Studio," www.cbc.ca/news/technology/story/2012/12/11/business-teksavvy-customer-info.html. Accessed 26 January 2013.

CCH Canadian Ltd. v. Law Society of Upper Canada, 2004 SCC 13, [2004] 1 S.C.R. 339

CCPR (Centre for Cultural Policy Research). 2003. *Baseline Study of Hong Kong's Creative Industries*, University of Hong Kong, September.

CDS (Centre for Digital Storytelling). 2007. "What Is Digital Storytelling?," www.storycenter.org/whatis.html. Accessed 22 April 2007.

CED (Committee for Economic Development). 2004. *Promoting Innovation and Economic Growth: The Special Problem of Digital Intellectual Property*, Report by the Digital Connections Council for the Committee for Economic Development, CED, Washington, DC.

Centre for Citizen Media. 2007. "About the Centre," www.citmedia.org/about. Accessed 28 April 2007.

Chakravartty, Paula, and Katharine Sarikakis. 2006. *Media Policy and Globalization*. Edinburgh: Edinburgh University Press.

Chandler, Alfred. 1977. *The Visible Hand: The Managerial Revolution in American Business*. Cambridge, MA: Harvard University Press.

Chee, Florence, Marcelo Vieta, and Richard Smith. 2006. "Online Gaming and the Interactional Self: Identify Interplay in Situated Practice," in J.P. Williams, S.Q. Hendriks, and W.K. Winkler (eds.), *Gaming as Culture: Essays on Reality, Identity and Experience in Fantasy Games*. Jefferson, NC: McFarland Publishing, pp. 154–74.

Cho, Kevin. 2006. "Samsung, SK Telecom, Shinhan Sponsor South Korean Alien Killers," *Bloomberg News*, www.bloomberg.com/apps/

news?pid=email_us&refer=asia&sid=a2JvzciDnpB4, 15 January. Accessed 15 July 2007.

Christakis, Nicholas A., and James H. Fowler. 2009. *Connected: The Surprising Power of Our Social Networks and How They Shape Our Lives*. New York: Little, Brown.

Christensen, Clayton. 1997. The Innovator's Dilemma: When New Technologies Cause Great Firms to Fail. Boston: Harvard Business Press.

Christensen, Clayton. 2003. *The Innovator's Dilemma: The Revolutionary Book That Will Change the Way You Do Business*. New York: HarperCollins.

Christopherson, Susan, and Michael Storper. 1986. "The City as Studio, the World as Back Lot: The Impact of Vertical Disintegration on the Location of the Motion Picture Industry," *Environment and Planning D: Society and Space* 4: 305–20.

Citizen Lab (University of Toronto). 2007. *Everyone's Guide to Bypassing Internet Censorship*. Available at www.nartv.org/mirror/circ_guide.pdf.

———. 2010. *Shadows in the Cloud*. Toronto: Munk Centre for International Studies, University of Toronto. Available at https://citizenlab.org/2010/04/new-iwm-report-shadows-in-the-cloud.

Clift, Stephen. 2000. "The E-Democracy E-Book: Democracy Is Online 2.0," www.publicus.net/ebook/edemebook.html. Accessed 7 April 2002.

Club Penguin website, *Coins for Change 2009*. Accessed 30 June 2010 at www.clubpenguin.com/parents/coins-for-change-2009.htm.

Coase, Ronald H. 1937. "The Nature of the Firm," *Economica* 4(16): 386–405.

Coleman, Stephen. 2006. "New Mediation and Direct Representation: Reconceptualising Representation in the Digital Age," *New Media and Society* 7(2): 177–98.

———, and John Gøtze. 2001. *Bowling Together: Online Public Engagement in Policy Deliberation*. London: Hansard Society.

Collins, Jim. 1992. "Postmodernism and Television," in R.C. Allen (ed.), *Channels of Discourse, Reassembled*. London: Routledge, pp. 327–53.

COMMUNIA. 2009. "The Public Domain Manifesto." Accessed from www.publicdomainmanifesto.org/node/ 8 September 2013.

Community Broadcasting Foundation. 2007. "What is Community Broadcasting?" Accessed from www.cbf.com.au/Content/templates/sector.asp?articleid=30&zoneid=13 1 May 2007.

Cooke, Philip N., and Luciana Lazzeretti (eds.). 2008. *Creative Cities, Cultural Clusters and Local Economic Development*. Cheltenham, UK: Edward Elgar Publishing.

Coombe, Rosemary. 1998. *The Cultural Life of Intellectual Properties: Authorship, Appropriation, and the Law*. Durham, NC: Duke University Press.

Cortada, James. 2006. *How Computers Changed the Work of American Financial, Telecommunications, Media, and Entertainment Industries*, vol. 2 of *The Digital Hand*. Oxford: Oxford University Press.

Couldry, Nick. 2002. "The Digital Divide," in D. Gauntlett and R. Horsley (eds.), *Web Studies*. London: Arnold, pp. 185–94.

———. 2003. "Beyond the Hall of Mirrors? Some Theoretical Reflections on the Global Contestation of Media Power," in N. Couldry and J. Curran (eds.), *Contesting Media Power: Alternative Media in a Networked World*. Lanham, MD: Rowman & Littlefield, pp. 39–54.

Coupland, Douglas. 2009. *Extraordinary Canadians: Marshall McLuhan*. Toronto: Penguin.

Cowan, Ruth Schwartz. 1997. *A Social History of American Technology*. New York: Oxford University Press.

Cox, Melissa. 2000. "The Development of Computer-Assisted Reporting." Paper presented to the Association for Education in Journalism and Mass Communication, University of North Carolina, Chapel Hill, NC.

Crandall, Robert, and J. Gregory Sidak. 2006. "Video Games: Serious Business for the US Economy," Entertainment Software Alliance, www.theesa.com/archives/files/2006%20WHITE%20PAPER%20FINAL.pdf. Accessed 30 April 2007.

Cranny-Francis, Anne. 2005. *Multimedia: Texts and Contexts*. London: Sage.

Crawford, Kate. 2003. "Control-SHIFT: Censorship and the Internet," in C. Lumby and E. Probyn (eds.), *Remote Control: New Media, New Ethics*. Cambridge, UK: Cambridge University Press, pp. 173–88.

Creative Commons. 2007. "Creative Commons," Creative Commons, http://creativecommons.org. Accessed 24 April 2007.

Creeber, Glen, and Ben Hills. 2007. "Editorial—TV III," *New Review of Film and Television Studies* 5(1): 1–4.

Critcher, Chas (ed.). 2006. *Critical Readings: Moral Panics and the Media*. Maidenhead, UK: Open University Press.

Cross, Robert. 2004. *The Hidden Power of Social Networks: Understanding How Work Really Gets Done in Organizations*. Boston: Harvard Business School Press.

CRTC. 1995. Competition and Culture on Canada's Information Highway: Managing the Realities of Transition. Available at www.crtc.gc.ca/eng/HIGHWAY/HWY9505.htm.

——. 2012. Broadcasting Decision CRTC 2012–574, "Bell Astral Media Merger." Accessed from www.crtc.gc.ca/eng/archive/2012/2012-574.htm 26 January 2013.

Csikszentmihalyi, Mihaly. 1996. *Creativity: Flow and the Psychology of Discovery and Invention*. New York: HarperCollins.

Cubitt, Sean. 2006. "Tactical Media," in K. Sarikakis and D. Thussu (eds.), *Ideologies of the Internet*. Cresskil, NJ: Hampton Press, pp. 35–46.

Cunningham, Stuart. 2002. "From Cultural to Creative Industries: Theory, Industry and Policy Implications," *Media International Australia* 102, February: 54–65.

——. 2005. "Creative Enterprises," in J. Hartley (ed.), *Creative Industries*. Oxford: Blackwell, pp. 282–98.

——. 2006. "What Price a Creative Economy?" Platform Paper No. 9. Sydney, AU: Currency Press.

——. 2007. "Creative Industries Policy Discourse outside of the United Kingdom," *Global Media and Communication* 3(3), 347–52.

——, and Jason Potts. 2007. *Four Models of the Creative Industries*. Unpublished paper.

——, Terry Cutler, Greg Hearn, Mark Ryan, and Michael Keane. 2004. "An Innovation Agenda for the Creative Industries: Where Is the R&D?" *Media International Australia* 112: 174–85.

Curran, James, and Myung-Jin Park (eds.). 2000. *Dewesternizing Media Studies*. London: Routledge.

Curtin, Michael. 2007. *Media Capitals: The Cultural Geography of Globalization*. Oxford: Blackwell.

Cutler & Company. 2002. *Producing Digital Content: A Report for the Department of Communications, Information Technology, and the Arts*, Melbourne, August.

Dang, Steven, Elise Finnigan, and Katie Warfield. 2005. *Making the Case for Culture*, a series of six papers. Vancouver: Creative City Network of Canada (www.creativecity.ca).

David, Paul. 1985. "Clio and the Economics of QWERTY," *American Economic Review* 75(2): 332–7.

——. 1999. "Digital Technology and the Productivity Paradox: After Ten Years, What Has Been Learned?" Paper prepared for Understanding the Digital Economy: Data, Tools and Research, held at US Department of Commerce, Washington, DC, 25–26 May.

——, and Dominique Foray. 2002. "An Introduction to the Economy of the Knowledge Society," *International Social Science Journal* 171: 9–23.

Davies, William. 2003. You Don't Know Me But . . . Social Capital and Social Software. London: iSociety.

DCMS (Department of Culture, Media, and Sport, United Kingdom). 1998. *Mapping the Creative Industries*, www.culture.gov.uk/creative/creative_industries.html. Accessed 5 May 2001.

de Bono, Edward. 1995. *Serious Creativity*. London: HarperCollins.

de Castell, Suzanne, and Mary Bryson. 1998. "Retooling Play: Dystopia, Dysphoria, and Difference," in J. Cassell and H. Jenkins (eds.), *From Barbie to Mortal Kombat: Gender and Computer Games*. Cambridge, MA: MIT Press, pp. 232–61.

——, and Jennifer Jenson (eds.). 2007. *Worlds in Play: International Perspectives on Digital Games Research*. New York: Peter Lang.

de Certeau, Michel. 1984. *The Practice of Everyday Life*. Berkeley: University of California Press.

Deibert, Ronald, and Rafal Rohozinski. 2010. "Breaking up Dark Clouds in Cyberspace," *Globe and Mail*, 5 April, www.theglobeandmail.com/news/opinions/breaking-up-dark-clouds-in-cyberspace/article1524064.

de Kerckhove, Derrick. 1998. *Connected Intelligence: The Arrival of the Web Society*. London: Kogan Page.

Department of Communications and the Arts. 1994. *Creative Nation: Commonwealth Cultural Policy*. Canberra: AGPS.

Deuze, Mark. 2003. "The Web and Its Journalisms: Considering the Consequences of Different Types of News Media Online," *New Media and Society* 5(2): 203–30.

——. 2005. "What Is Journalism? Professional Identity and Ideology of Journalists Reconsidered," *Journalism* 6(4): 442–64.

———. 2006. "Participation, Remediation, Bricolage: Considering Principal Components of a Digital Culture," *The Information Society* 22: 63–75.

Dewar, Kenneth C. 1982. "The Origins of Public Broadcasting in Canada in Comparative Perspectives," *Canadian Journal of Communication*, 8(2).

Dietz, Jason. 2012. "Metacritic's 2nd annual game publisher rankings." *Metacritic*, www.metacritic.com/feature/game-publisher-rankings-for-2011-releases. Accessed 13 November 2012.

DiMaggio, Paul, Eszter Hargittai, W. Russell Neuman, and John P. Robinson. 2001. "Social Implications of the Internet," *Annual Review of Sociology* 27: 307–36.

Disappearing Computer. 2004. "The Disappearing Computer Initiative," www.disappearing-computer.net/artefacts.html. Accessed 20December 2006.

Dobb, Maurice. 1973. *Theories of Value and Distribution since Adam Smith: Ideology and Economic Theory*. Cambridge, UK: Cambridge University Press.

Doctorow, Cory. 2006. "Technorati State of the Blogosphere, Q3 2006." Accessed from BoingBoing: A Directory of Wonderful Things, www.boingboing.net/2006/11/07/technorati_state_of_html, 26 March 2007.

———. 2010. *For the Win*. New York: Tor Teen.

Dodgson, Mark, David Gann, and Ammon Salter. 2002. "The Intensification of Innovation," *International Journal of Innovation Management* 6(1): 53–83.

Dodgson, Sean. 2003. "The Internet of Things," *The Guardian*, 9 October, www.guardian.co.uk/technology/2003/oct/09/shopping.newmedia. Accessed 11 November 2010.

Donald, James. 2004. "What's New: A Letter to Terry Flew," *Continuum: Journal of Media and Cultural Studies* 18(2): 235–46.

Doremus, Paul, William Keller, Lewis Pauly, and Simon Reich. 1998. *The Myth of the Global Corporation*. Princeton, NJ: Princeton University Press.

Dorfman, Ariel, and Armand Mattelart. 1984. *How to Read Donald Duck: Imperialist Ideology in the Disney Comic*. New York: International General.

Dorland, Michael. 1996. *Cultural Industries in Canada*. Toronto: James Lorimer & Company.

Dovey, Jon, and Helen Kennedy. 2006. *Game Cultures: Computer Games as New Media*. Maidenhead, UK: Open University Press.

Drahos, Peter, and John Braithwaite. 2002. *Information Feudalism: Who Owns the Knowledge Economy?* London: Earthscan.

Du Gay, Paul, and Michael Pryke. 2002. "Cultural Economy: An Introduction," in P. du Gay and M. Pryke (eds.), *Cultural Economy: Cultural Analysis and Commercial Life*. London: Sage, pp. 1–19.

Duxbury, Nancy (ed.). 2008. *Under Construction: The State of Cultural Infrastructure in Canada*. Vancouver: Centre of Expertise on Culture and Communities.

Dyer-Witheford, Nick. 2002. "E-Capital and the Many-Headed Hydra," in G. Elmer (ed.), *Critical Perspectives on the Internet*. Lanham, MD: Rowman & Littlefield, pp. 129–63.

———, and Greg de Peuter. 2006. "'EA Spouse' and the Crisis of Video Game Labour: Enjoyment, Exclusion, Exploitation, and Exodus," *Canadian Journal of Communication*, 31(3).

———, and Zena Sharman. 2005. "The Political Economy of Canada's Video and Computer Game Industry," *Canadian Journal of Communication* 30(2).

Dyson, Esther. 1999. *Release 2.0: A Design for Living in the Digital Age*. New York: Broadway Books.

———, George Gilder, George Keyworth, and Alvin Toffler. 1994. "Cyberspace and the American Dream: A Magna Carta for the Knowledge Age," www.pff.org/issues-pubs/futureinsights/fi1.2magnacarta.html. Accessed 3 February 2000.

Eco, Umberto. 1976. *A Theory of Semiotics*. Bloomington, IN: Indiana University Press.

Economist, The. 1999. "The Net Imperative, Economist Survey: Business and the Internet," 26 June, pp. 3–5.

———. 2009. "Network Effects," 17 December. Retrieved from www.economist.com/displayStory.cfm?STORY_ID=15108618 30 December 2009.

Electronic Frontier Foundation. (n.d.). "Preserving Free Expression: Our Fundamental Rights of Freedom of Speech and Press," www.eff.org/freespeech.html. Accessed 20 July 2001.

Elmer, Greg (ed.). 2002. *Critical Perspectives on the Internet*. Lanham, MD: Rowman & Littlefield.

El-Nawawy, Mohammed, and Adel Iskandar. 2002. *Al Jazeera: How the Free Arab News Network*

Scooped the World and Changed the Middle East. Cambridge, MA: Westview Press.

El Oifi, Mohammed. 2005. "Influence without Power: Al Jazeera and the Arab Public Sphere," in M. Zayani (ed.), *The Al Jazeera Phenomenon: Critical Perspectives on New Arab Media.* London: Pluto Press, pp. 66–79.

Engelbart, Douglas. 1962. "Augmenting Human Intellect: A Conceptual Framework," October, www.bootstrap.org/augdocs/friedewald030402/augmentinghumanintellect/ahi62index.html, posted September 1997. Accessed 23 April 2007.

Ericson, Richard, and Kevin Haggerty. 1997. *Policing the Risk Society.* Toronto: University of Toronto Press.

Ericsson (multinational company). 2010. "Mobile subscriptions hit 5 billion mark," Ericsson press release, 9 July. Accessed from www.ericsson.com/thecompany/press/releases/2010/07/1430616 11 July 2010.

Ernst, Dieter, and Lin Su Kim. 2002. "Global Production Networks, Knowledge Diffusion, and Local Capacity Formation," *Research Policy* 31: 1417–29.

ESA (Entertainment Software Alliance). 2006. "Essential Facts about the Computer and Video Games Industry," www.theesa.com/archives/files/Essential%20Facts%202006.pdf. Accessed 6 April 2007.

———. 2011. "Industry Facts," www.theesa.com/facts. Accessed 1 December 2012.

Farmer, James. 2006. "Citizen Journalism Sucks," *The Age,* http://blogs.theage.com.au/media/archives/2006/10/citizen_journal.html, 5 October. Accessed 27 April 2007.

Federal Court of Appeal. 2005. BMG et. al. v. Shaw et. al., 19 May. http://decisions.fca-caf.gc.ca/en/2005/2005fca193/2005fca193.html. Accessed 26 January 2013.

Feenberg, Andrew. 2003. "Democratic Rationalization: Technology, Power, and Freedom," in R.C. Scharff and V. Dusek (eds.), *Philosophy of Technology: The Technological Condition.* Malden, MA: Blackwell, pp. 652–65.

Feldman, Curt, and Tor Thorsen. 2004. "Employees Readying Class-Action Lawsuit against EA," Gamespot, 11 November, http://au.gamespot.com/news/2004/11/11/news_6112998.html. Accessed 7 April 2007.

Fiske, John. 1987. *Television Culture.* London: Routledge.

———. 1992. "The Cultural Economy of Fandom," in L.A. Lewis (ed.), *The Adoring Audience: Fan Culture and Popular Media.* London: Routledge, pp. 30–54.

Fitzgerald, Brian. 2006. "Creative Commons: Accessing, Negotiating and Remixing Online Content," in P. Thomas and J. Servaes (eds.), *Intellectual Property Rights and Communications in Asia.* New Delhi: Sage, pp. 219–25.

Flanagan, Mary. 2009. *Critical Play: Radical Game Design.* Cambridge, MA: MIT Press.

Flanagin, Andrew J., Craig Flanagin, and Jon Flanagin. 2010. "Technical Code and the Social Construction of the Internet," *New Media & Society,* 12(2): 179–96.

Flew, Terry. 2001. "The 'New Empirics' in Internet Studies and Comparative Internet Policy," in H. Brown, G. Lovink, H. Merrick, N. Rossiter, D. Teh, and M. Willson (eds.), *Fibreculture Reader: Politics of a Digital Present.* Melbourne: Fibreculture Publications, pp. 105–13.

———. 2002. *New Media: An Introduction,* 1st ed. Melbourne: Oxford University Press.

———. 2004a. "Creativity, the 'New Humanism' and Cultural Studies," *Continuum: Journal of Media and Cultural Studies* 18(2): 161–78.

———. 2004b. "Creativity, Cultural Studies and Services Industries," *Communication and Critical/Cultural Studies* 1(2): 176–93.

———. 2005a. *New Media: An Introduction,* 2nd ed. Melbourne: Oxford University Press.

———. 2005b. "Creative Commons and the Creative Industries," *Media and Arts Law Review* 10(4): 257–64.

———. 2005c. "Creative Economy," in J. Hartley (ed.), *The Creative Industries Reader.* London: Blackwell, pp. 344–60.

———. 2007. *Understanding Global Media.* Basingstoke, UK: Palgrave Macmillan.

———, and Stephen McElhinney. 2005. "Globalisation and the Structure of New Media Industries," in L.A. Lievrouw and S.M. Livingstone (eds.), *The Handbook of New Media: Social Shaping and Consequences of ICTs,* 2nd ed. London: Sage, pp. 287–96.

———, and Jason Sternberg. 1999. "Media Wars: Media Studies and Journalism Education," *Media International Australia* 90, February: 9–14.

———, Greg Hearn, and Susanna Leisten. 2006. "Alternative Intellectual Property Regimes in the Global Creative Economy," in P.N. Thomas and J. Servaes (eds.), *Intellectual Property Rights and*

Communications in Asia: Conflicting Traditions. New Delhi: Sage, pp. 226–40.

———, Jason Sternberg, and Debra Adams. 2007. "Revisiting the 'Media Wars' Debate," *Australian Journal of Communication* 34(1).

———, and Richard Smith. 2011. *New Media: An Introduction*, Canadian ed. Don Mills, ON: Oxford University Press Canada.

Flichy, Patrice. 2005a. "New Media History," in L.A. Lievrouw and S.M. Livingstone (eds.), *The Handbook of New Media: Social Shaping and Consequences of ICTs*, 2nd ed. London: Sage, pp. 185–204.

———. 2005b. "Internet: The Social Construction of a 'Network Ideology,'" in O. Couthard, R. Hanley, and R. Zimmerman (eds.), *Sustaining Urban Networks: The Social Diffusion of Large Technical Systems*. London: Routledge, pp. 103–16.

———. 2007. *The Internet Imaginaire*. Cambridge, MA: MIT Press.

Florida, Richard. 2002. *The Rise of the Creative Class, and How It's Transforming Work, Leisure, Community and Everyday Life*. New York: Basic Books.

———. 2007. *The Flight of the Creative Class: The New Global Competition for Talent*. New York: HarperCollins.

Forte, Andrea, Vanessa Larco, and Amy Bruckman. 2009. "Decentralization in Wikipedia Governance." *Journal of Management Information Systems* 26(1), pp. 49–72.

Foucault, Michel. 1975. *Discipline and Punish: The Birth of the Prison*, trans. A. Sheridan. New York: Random House.

Foundation Radiomuseum Luzern. n.d. History of the Radio Manufacturer Rogers-Majestic; Canada. Online resource. www.radiomuseum.org/dsp_hersteller_detail.cfm?company_id=8085. Accessed 31 March 2010.

Friedman, Thomas. 2005. *The World Is Flat: A Brief History of the twenty-first Century*. New York: Farrar, Straus & Giroux.

Friel, Brian. 2002. "Hierarchies and Networks," Openflows, www.openflows.org/article.pl?sid=02/08/02/2118227&mode=nocomment&tid=12, 2 August. Accessed 21 January 2007.

Froomkin, Michael. 1997. "The Internet as a Source of Regulatory Arbitrage," in B. Kahin and C. Neeson (eds.), *Borders in Cyberspace*. Cambridge, MA: MIT Press, pp. 129–64.

———. 2003. "International and National Regulation of the Internet," http://law.tm/docs/International-regulation.pdf, 8 December. Accessed 21 May 2007.

Frow, John. 1994. *When Was Postmodernism?* Sydney: Local Consumption Publications.

———. 1995. *Cultural Studies and Cultural Value*. Oxford: Clarendon Press.

Galperin, Hernan. 2004. *New Television, Old Politics: The Transition to Digital TV in the United States and Britain*. Cambridge, UK: Cambridge University Press.

Gandy, Oscar. 2002. "The Real Digital Divide: Citizens versus Consumers," in L. Lievrouw and S. Livingstone (eds.), *Handbook of New Media*. London: Sage, pp. 448–60.

García, Beatriz. 2004. "Urban Regeneration, Arts Programming and Major Events: Glasgow, 1990, Sydney, 2000, Barcelona, 2004," *International Journal of Cultural Policy* 10(1): 103–18.

Garnham, Nicholas. 1987. "Concepts of Culture: Public Policy and the Cultural Industries," *Cultural Studies* 1(1): 23–37.

———. 2004. "Information Society Theory as Ideology," in F. Webster (ed.), *The Information Society Reader*. London: Routledge, pp. 166–83.

———. 2005. "From Cultural to Creative Industries: An Analysis of the Implications of the 'Creative Industries' Approach to Arts and Media Policy Making in the United Kingdom," *International Journal of Cultural Policy* 11(1): 15–29.

Gartner [press release]. 2013. "Gartner Says Smartphone Sales Grew 46.5 Percent in Second Quarter of 2013 and Exceeded Feature Phone Sales for First Time," Gartner website, August. Accessed from www.gartner.com/newsroom/id/2573415 7 September 2013.

Gary, Loren. 1999. "Beyond the Chicken Cheer: How to Improve Your Creativity," *Harvard Management Update*, July.

Gates, Bill. 1999. *Business @ the Speed of Thought: Succeeding in the Digital Economy*. London: Penguin.

Gauntlett, David. 2000. *Web.Studies: Rewiring Media Studies for the Digital Age*. London: Arnold.

———. 2004. "Web Studies: What's New," in D. Gauntlett and R. Horsley (ed.), *Web Studies*, 2nd ed. London: Arnold, pp. 2–18.

———, and Ross Horsley (eds.). 2002. *Web Studies*, 2nd ed. London: Arnold.

GBN (Global Business Network). 2002. "Social Software and the Next Big Phase of the Internet," interview of Clay Shirky by Peter Leyden, www .gbn.com, December. Accessed 8 November 2005.

Geist, Michael (ed.). 2010. *From "Radical Extremism" to "Balanced Copyright": Canadian Copyright and the Digital Agenda.* Toronto: Irwin Law.

———. 2010. "Who Are James Moore's 'Radical Extremists'?" *Michael Geist blog,* 22 June. Accessed from www.michaelgeist.ca/content/view/5137/125 15 July 2010.

———. 2012. "The Battle over C-11 Concludes: How Thousands of Canadians Changed the Copyright Debate," June 18. Available online at http://www .michaelgeist.ca/content/view/6544/125.

George, Cherian. 2006. *Contentious Journalism and the Internet: Towards Democratic Discourse in Malaysia and Singapore.* Singapore: Singapore University Press.

Giarini, Orio. 2002. "The Globalisation of Services in Economic Theory and Economic Practice: Some Conceptual Issues," in J.R. Cuadrado-Roura, L. Rubalcaba-Bermejo, and J.R. Bryson (eds.), *Trading Services in the Global Economy.* Cheltenham: Edward Elgar, pp. 58–77.

Gibson, William. 1984. *Neuromancer.* London: Gollancz.

Giddens, Anthony. 1990. *The Consequences of Modernity.* Cambridge, UK: Polity Press.

———. 1998. *The Third Way.* Cambridge, UK: Polity Press.

Gilder, George. 1994. *Life After Television.* New York: W.W. Norton & Co.

Gill, Rosalind. 2002. "Cool, Creative and Egalitarian? Exploring Gender in Project-Based New Media Work in Europe," *Information, Communication, and Society* 5(1): 70–89.

———. 2006. "Technobohemians or the New Cybertariat? New Media Work in Amsterdam a Decade after the Web." Report prepared for the Institute of Network Cultures, Amsterdam.

Gillies, James, and Robert Cailliau. 2000. *How the Web Was Born: The Story of the World Wide Web.* Oxford,: Oxford University Press.

Gillmor, Dan. 2006. *We the Media: Grassroots Journalism by the People, for the People.* Sebastopol, CA: O'Reilly.

Gitelman, Lisa, and Geoffrey Pingree. 2003. *New Media 1740–1915.* Cambridge, MA: MIT Press.

Glass, Geoff. 2006. *Audience Labor: The Asymmetric Production of Culture,* A Whole Minute, 22 January, www.geof.net/research/2006/audience-labor. Accessed 11 November 2010.

Glasser, Theodore. 2000. "The Politics of Public Journalism," *Journalism Studies* 1(4): 683–96.

Gleick, James. 2000. *Faster: The Acceleration of Just about Everything.* New York: Vintage.

Godfrey, Donald G. 1982. "Canadian Marconi: CFCF: The Forgotten Case," *Canadian Journal of Communication,* vol. 8, no. 4.

Godwin, Mike. 1998. *Cyber Rights: Defending Free Speech in the Digital Age.* New York: Times Books.

Golding, Peter, and Graham Murdock. 2000. "Culture, Communications, and Political Economy," in J. Curran and M. Gurevitch (eds.), *Mass Media and Society,* 3rd ed. London: Arnold, pp. 60–83.

Google Research. 2012. "The New Multiscreen World," August 2012. Available at www .thinkwithgoogle.com/insights/library/studies/the-new-multi-screen-world-study.

Gore, Al. 1994. "Remarks Prepared for Delivery by Vice-President Al Gore to the International Telecommunications Union," 21 March. Accessed from www.goelzer.net/telecom/al-gore.html 26 December 2006.

Gow, Gordon, and Richard Smith. 2006. *Mobile and Wireless Communications: An Introduction.* London: Open University Press.

Graham, Gordon. 1999. *The Internet: A Philosophical Inquiry.* London: Routledge.

Graham, Philip. 2000. "Hypercapitalism: A Political Economy of Informational Idealism," *New Media and Society* 2(2): 131–56.

———. 2006. *Hypercapitalism: Language, New Media, and Social Perceptions of Value.* New York: Peter Lang.

Gramsci, Antonio. 1971. *Selections from the Prison Notebooks of Antonio Gramsci,* Q. Hoare and G. Nowell-Smith (eds.). New York: International Publishers.

Granovetter, Mark. 1985. "Economic Action and Social Structure," *American Journal of Sociology* 91: 481–510.

Gray, Carole. 2006. "A Different Way of Knowing: Inquiry through the Creative Arts," Proceedings of 1st International Symposium of Visual Studies, Production as Research, Centro de las Artes, Monterrey, April, http://publicoutputs.rgu.ac.uk/CREDO/open/additionalpublication.php?id=3661. Accessed 22 April 2007.

Green, Lelia. 2002. *Technoculture*. Sydney: Allen & Unwin.

Grey, Michael. 2008. "World of Warcraft hits 11 million subscribers," WoW.com, www.wow.com/2008/10/28/world-of-warcraft-hits-11-million-subscribers-worldwide. Accessed 15 July 2010.

Grimes, Sara M. 2008a. "Deconstructing the Girl Gamer: From the Girls' Games Movement to Rule of Rose." Paper presented at the Canadian Communication Association (CCA) Annual Conference, University of British Columbia, 4–6 June 2008, Vancouver.

———. 2008b. "The Exploitation of Children's Affective Labour in Corporately Owned Virtual Worlds." Paper presented at the Joint Annual Meetings of Law and Society Association and Canadian Law and Society Association, Montreal.

———. 2008c. "Saturday Morning Cartoons Go MMOG," *Media International Australia* (126), Special Issue: *Beyond Broadcasting: TV for the Twenty-First Century*, pp. 120–31.

Grossman, Lev. 2006. " You—Yes, You—Are *Time's* Person of the Year," *Time*, www.time.com/time/magazine/article/0,9171,1569514,00.html, 25 December. Accessed 17 March 2007.

Habermas, Jürgen. 1995. "Institutions of the Public Sphere," in O. Boyd-Barrett and C. Newbold (eds.), *Approaches to Media: A Reader*. London: Hodder, pp. 235–44.

Haddon, Leslie, and Nicola Green. 2010. *Mobile Communications: An Introduction to New Media*. New York: Berg Publishers.

Hafner, Katie, and Matthew Lyon. 1996. *When Wizards Stay Up Late: The Origins of the Internet*. New York: Simon & Schuster.

Hague, Barry, and Brian Loader (eds.). 1999. *Digital Democracy: Discourse and Decision Making in the Information Age*. London: Routledge.

———. 1999. "Digital Democracy: An Introduction," in B.N. Hague and B.D. Loader (eds.), *Digital Democracy: Discourse and Decision Making in the Information Age*. London: Routledge, pp. 3–22.

Halavais, Alex. 2008. *Search Engine Society*. Cambridge, UK: Polity Press.

Hall, Peter. 2000. "Creative Cities and Economic Development," *Urban Studies* 37(4): 639–49.

Hall, Stuart. 1982. "The Rediscovery of 'Ideology': Return of the Repressed in Media Studies," in M. Gurevitch, T. Bennett, J. Curran, and J. Woollacott (eds.), *Culture, Society and the Media*. London: Methuen, pp. 56–90.

———. 1986. "Cultural Studies: Two Paradigms," in R. Collins, J. Curran, N. Garnham, P. Scannell, P. Schlesinger, and C. Sparks (eds.), *Media, Culture and Society: A Critical Reader*. London: Sage, pp. 33–48.

Hallin, Daniel. 1994. *We Keep America on Top of the World: Television Journalism and the Public Sphere*. London: Routledge.

Haltiwanger, John, and Ron Jarmin. 2003, "A Statistical Portrait of the New Economy," in D.C. Jones (ed.), *New Economy Handbook*. Amsterdam: Elsevier, pp. 3–24.

Hamilton, Ian. 2012. "Game Developer Sets Kickstarter Record," *Orange County Register*, www.ocregister.com/articles/game-374766-games-obsidian.html. Accessed 13 November 2012.

Hammond Museum of Radio. n.d., The Rogers Collection. Online resource: www.hammondmuseumofradio.org/rogers.html. Accessed 31 March 2010.

Hardt, Michael, and Antonio Negri. 2000. *Empire*. Cambridge, MA: Harvard University Press.

———. 2005. *Multitude*. London: Penguin.

Hargreaves, Ian. 1999. "The Ethical Boundaries of Reporting," in M. Ungersma (ed.), *Reporters and the Reported*. Cardiff: Centre for Journalism Studies, pp. 1–15.

Hartley, John. 1999a. *Uses of Television*. London: Routledge.

———. 1999b. "The Frequency of Public Writing: Time, Tomb and Tome as Technologies of the Public," presented to MIT Media-in-Transition Conference, 8 October, http://web.mit.edu/comm-forum/papers/hartley.html. Accessed 17 August 2001.

———. 2003. *A Short History of Cultural Studies*. London: Sage.

———. 2005. "Creative Industries," in J. Hartley (ed.), *Creative Industries*. Oxford: Blackwell, pp. 1–39.

———. 2008. "Journalism as a Human Right: The Cultural Approach to Journalism," in M. Löffelholz and D. Weaver (eds.), *Global Journalism Research*. Oxford: Blackwell, pp. 39–51.

———, and Michael Keane. 2006. "Creative Industries and Innovation in China," *International Journal of Cultural Studies* 9(3): 259–62.

Harvey, David. 1990. *The Condition of Postmodernity*. Oxford: Blackwell.

Haseman, Brad. 2006. "A Manifesto for Performative Research," *Media International Australia* 118, February: 98–106.

Hassan, Robert. 2004. *Media, Politics and the Network Society*. Maidenhead, UK: Open University Press.

Hauge, Atle, and Brian J. Hracs. 2010. "See the Sound, Hear the Style: Collaborative Linkages between Indie Musicians and Fashion Designers in Local Scenes," *Industry and Innovation*, 17: 1, pp. 113–29.

Haussmann, Frank. 2002. "Protecting Intellectual Property in the Digital Age," in A. Thierer and C.W. Crews (eds.), *Copy Fights: The Future of Intellectual Property in the Information Age*. Washington, DC: Cato Institute, pp. 205–20.

Hawn, Carleen. 2004. "If He's So Smart . . . Steve Jobs, Apple, and the Limits of Innovation," *Fast Company* 78, January, www.fastcompany.com/magazine/78/jobs.html. Accessed 22 April 2007.

Healy, Kieran. 2002. "What's New for Culture in the New Economy?," *Journal of Arts Management, Law, and Society* 32(2): 86–103.

Hearn, Greg, Abraham Ninan, Ian Rogers, Stuart Cunningham, and Susan Luckman. 2004. "From the Margins to the Mainstream: Creating Value in Queensland's Music Industry," *Media International Australia* 112: 101–14.

Heilbroner, Robert. 2003 [1967]. "Do Machines Make History?," in R.C. Scharff and V. Dusek (eds.), *Philosophy of Technology: The Technological Condition*. Malden, MA: Blackwell, pp. 398–404.

Held, David, and Anthony McGrew (eds.). 2002. *Governing Globalization: Power, Authority and Global Governance*. Cambridge, UK: Polity Press.

——— (eds.). 2003. *The Global Transformations Reader: An Introduction to the Globalization Debate*. Cambridge, UK: Polity Press.

———, David Goldblatt, and Jonathon Perraton. 1999. *Global Transformations: Politics, Economics, and Culture*. Cambridge, UK: Polity Press.

Hermes, Joke. 2005. *Re-Reading Popular Culture*. Oxford: Blackwell.

Herring, Susan. 2004. "Slouching towards the Ordinary: Current Trends in Computer-Mediated Communication," *New Media and Society* 6(1): 26–36.

Herz, J.C. 2002. "The Bandwidth Capital of the World," *Wired*, no. 10.08, August, www.wired.com/wired/archive/10.08/korea.html. Accessed 30 April 2007.

———. 2005. "Harnessing the Hive," in J. Hartley (ed.), *Creative Industries*. Oxford: Blackwell, pp. 327–41.

Hesmondhalgh, David. 2007. *The Cultural Industries*, 2nd ed. London: Sage.

———, and Andy Pratt. 2005. "Cultural Industries and Cultural Policy," *International Journal of Cultural Policy* 11(1): 1–13.

Heyer, Paul. 2003. *Harold Innis*. Lanham, MD: Rowman & Littlefield.

Hill, David, and Krishna Sen. 2005. *The Internet in Indonesia's New Democracy*. London: Routledge.

Hirst, Martin, and John Harrison. 2006. *Communication and New Media: From Broadcast to Narrowcast*. Melbourne: Oxford University Press.

Hirst, Paul, and Grahame Thompson. 1996. *Globalization in Question*. Cambridge, UK: Polity Press.

Hodgson, Geoffrey. 2000. "Socio-Economic Consequences of the Advance of Complexity and Knowledge," in *Organization for Economic Co-operation and Development: The Creative Society of the 21st Century*. Paris: OECD, pp. 89–112.

Hofstede, Geert. 1980. *Culture's Consequences: International Differences in Work-Related Values*. London: Sage.

Horst, Heather, and Daniel Miller. 2006. *The Cell Phone: An Anthropology of Communication*. Oxford: Berg.

Howells, Jeremy. 2000. "Knowledge, Innovation, and Location," in J.R. Bryson, P. Daniels, N. Hentry, and J. Pollard (eds.), *Knowledge, Space, Economy*. London: Routledge, pp. 50–62.

Howkins, John. 2001. *The Creative Economy: How People Make Money From Ideas*. London: Allen Lane.

———. 2005. "The Mayor's Commission on the Creative Industries," in J. Hartley (ed.), *Creative Industries*. Oxford: Blackwell, pp. 117–23.

Hudson, Heather. 2002. "Universal Access to the New Information Infrastructure," in L. Lievrouw and S. Livingstone (eds.), *Handbook of New Media*. London: Sage, pp. 369–83.

Human Rights Watch. 2006. "How Censorship Works in China: A Brief Overview," www.hrw.org/reports/2006/china0806/3.htm, August. Accessed 5 May 2007.

Humphreys, Sal. 2004. "Productive Players: Online Computer Games' Challenge to Conventional

Media Forms," *Communication and Critical/ Cultural Studies* 2(1): 37–51.

IEEE (Institute of Electrical and Electronics Engineers). n.d. "The Alternating Current Tube," online resource, www.ieee.ca/millennium/ alternating_current/ac_about.html. Accessed 31 March 2010.

IGDA (International Game Developers Association). 2004. *Quality of Life in the Game Industry: Challenges and Best Practices*, www.igda.org/qol/ whitepaper.php. Accessed 26 April 2007.

Innis, Harold. 1972 [1950]. *Empire and Communications*. Toronto: University of Toronto Press.

———. 1951. *The Bias of Communication*. Toronto: University of Toronto Press.

Internet Software Consortium (ISC). 2006. *Internet Domain Name Survey* www.isc.org/index.pl?/ops/ ds. Accessed 3 December 2006.

Internet World Stats. 2012. "Internet Usage Statistics—The Big Picture, World Internet Users and Population Stats," www.internetworldstats .com/stats.htm.

Intven, Hank (ed.). 2000. *Telecommunications Regulation Handbook*, prepared for the World Bank, Washington, DC.

Ipsos Reid. 2010. "Weekly Internet Usage Overtakes Television Watching," *Ipsos News & Polls*, 22 March 2010, www.ipsos-na.com/news- polls/pressrelease.aspx?id=4720. Accessed 11 November 2010.

Ito, Mizuko, Misa Matsuda, and Daisuke Okabe (eds.). 2005. *Personal, Portable, Pedestrian: Mobile Phones in Japanese Life Hardcover*. Cambridge MA: MIT Press.

ITU (International Telecommunications Union). "Global ICT Developments," www.itu.int/ ITU-D/ict/statistics/ict/index.html. Accessed 17 March 2010.

———. 2004. "The Evolution to 3G Mobile-Status Report," www.itu.int/itunews/issue/2003/06/ thirdgeneration.html. Accessed 9 April 2004.

Jacobs, Jane. 1994 [1961]. *The Death and Life of American Cities*. Harmondsworth: Penguin.

Jameson, Fredric. 1992. *Postmodernism, or, the Cultural Logic of Late Capitalism*. London: Verso.

Jenkins, Henry. 1992. *Textual Poachers: Television Fans and Participatory Culture*. New York: Routledge.

———. 2006a. *Convergence Culture: When Old and New Media Collide*. New York: New York University Press.

———. 2006b. *Fans, Bloggers and Gamers: Exploring Participatory Culture*. New York: New York University Press.

Jessop, Bob. 1998. "The Rise of Governance and the Risks of Failure: The Case of Economic Development," *International Social Science Journal* 50(1): 29–45.

———. 2000. "The State and the Contradictions of the Knowledge-Driven Economy," in J.R. Bryson, P.W. Daniels, N. Henry, and J. Pollard (eds.), *Knowledge, Space, Economy*. London: Routledge, pp. 63–78.

Johnson, Steven. 2005. *Everything Bad Is Good for You: How Today's Popular Culture Is Actually Making Us Smarter*. New York: Riverhead Books.

Jones, Steven G. (ed.). 2003. *Encyclopedia of New Media*. Thousand Oaks, CA: Sage.

Jurgensen, Nathan. 2013. "Digital Life Is a Hoax . . . Because There's No Such Thing," *The Society Pages*. Available at http://thesocietypages. org/cyborgology/2013/01/18/digital-life-is-a- hoaxbecause-theres-no-such-thing. Retrieved 2 February 2013.

Juul, Jesper. 2003. "The Game, the Player, the World: Looking for a Heart of Gameness," in M. Copier and J. Raessens (eds.), *Level Up: Digital Games Research Conference Proceedings*. Utrecht: University of Utrecht, pp. 30–47.

Kahn, Robert, and Vinton Cerf. 1996. "Excerpt from 'The Digital Library Project, vol. 1: The World of Knowbots,'" in M. Stefik (ed.), *Internet Dreams: Archetypes, Myths, and Metaphors*. Cambridge, MA: MIT Press.

Kalathil, Shanthi, and Taylor Boas. 2003. *Open Networks, Closed Regimes: The Impact of the Internet on Authoritarian Rule*. Washington, DC: Carnegie Endowment for International Peace.

Katz, James E. 2008. *Handbook of Mobile Communication Studies*. Cambridge, MA: MIT Press.

Keane, Michael. 2004. "Brave New World: China's Creative Vision," *International Journal of Cultural Policy* 10(3): 265–79.

———. 2007. *Created in China: The New Great Leap Forward*. London: RoutledgeCurzon.

Kedrosky, Paul. 2007. "Viacom v. YouTube: The Real Issue Is a Consumer Rebellion, Not Intellectual Property," *OpinionJournal* (in *The Wall Street Journal*), www.opinionjournal.com/editorial/ feature.html?id=110009788, published 15 February. Accessed 14 October 2010.

Keen, Andrew. 2007. *The Cult of the Amateur: How Today's Internet Is Killing Our Culture*. New York: Doubleday.

Keene, Jamie. 2012. "Unity Users," *Polygon*, www.polygon.com/2012/4/10/2938040/unity-game-tools-one-million-registered-developers. Accessed 20 November 2012.

Kelly, Kevin. 1997. "New Rules for the New Economy," *Wired*, no. 5.09, September, www.wired.com/wired/archive/5.09/newrules.html. Accessed 9 January 2001.

Kenney, Keith, Alexander Gorelik, and Sam Mwangi. 2000. "Interactive Features of Online Newspapers," *First Monday* 5(1), http://firstmonday.org/issues/issue5_1/kenney/index.html. Accessed 27 December 2006.

Kerr, Aphra. 2006. *The Business and Culture of Digital Games: Gamework and Gameplay*. London: Sage.

Kingston, Margo. 2003. "Diary of a Webdiarist: Ethics Goes Online," in C. Lumby and E. Probyn (eds.), *Remote Control: New Media, New Ethics*. Cambridge, UK: Cambridge University Press, pp. 159–72.

Kitchin, Rob. 1998. *Cyberspace: The World in the Wires*. Chichester, UK: John Wiley & Sons.

Klein, Naomi. 2000. *No Logo*. London: Flamingo.

Kleinwächter, Wolfgang. 2002. "Trilateralism, Co-regulation and Governance in the Global Information Society," in M. Raboy (ed.), *Global Media Policy in the New Millennium*. Luton, UK: University of Luton Press, pp. 55–76.

Kline, Stephen, Nick Dyer-Witheford, and Greg de Peuter. 2003. *Digital Play: The Interaction of Technology, Culture and Marketing*. Montreal and Kingston: McGill-Queen's University Press.

Knights, David, Faith Noble, Theo Vurdubakis, and Hugh Willmott. 2002. "Allegories of Creative Destruction: Technology and Organisation in Narratives of the e-Economy," in S. Woolgar (ed.). *Virtual Society? Technology, Cyberbole, Reality*. Oxford: Oxford University Press, pp. 99–114.

Kong, Lily, Chris Gibson, Louisa-May Khoo, and Anna-Marie Semple. 2006. "Knowledges of the Creative Economy: Towards a Relational Geography of Diffusion and Adaptation in Asia," *Asia Pacific Viewpoints* 47(2): 173–94.

Koring, Paul. 2009. "Canada Placed on Copyright Blacklist," *Globe and Mail*, 10 April. Retrieved from www.theglobeandmail.com/news/technology/download-decade/article1127052.ece 28 January 2010.

Kotkin, Joel. 2006. *The City: A Global History*. New York: Modern Library.

Kravets, David. 2010. "US Courts Split on Internet Ban," *Wired*, 12 January, www.wired.com/threatlevel/2010/01/courts-split-on-internet-bans.

Kress, Gunther. 1997. "Visual and Verbal Modes of Representation in Electronically Mediated Communication: The Potentials of New Forms of Text," in I. Snyder (ed.), *From Page to Screen: Taking Literacy into the Electronic Era*. Sydney: Allen & Unwin, pp. 53–79.

Kumar, Krishan. 1995. *From Post-Industrial to Post-Modern Society: New Theories of the Contemporary World*. Oxford: Blackwell.

———. 2005. *From Post-Industrial to Post-Modern Society: New Theories of the Contemporary World*, 2nd ed. Oxford: Blackwell.

Kuo, David. 2001. *Dot.Bomb: My Days and Nights as an Internet Goliath*. New York: Brown & Co.

Ladly, Martha, and Philip Beesley (eds.). 2008. *Mobile Nation: Creating Methodologies for Mobile Platforms*. Toronto: Riverside Architectural Books.

Ladner, Sam. 2008. "Laptops in the Living Room: Mobile Technologies and the Divide between Work and Private Time among Interactive Agency Workers," *Canadian Journal of Communication*, 33 (3), pp. 465–98.

Ladurantaye, Steve. 2012. "CRTC Head Blais Lays down Law at Bell–Astral Hearing," *Globe and Mail*, 12 September 2012. Accessed from www.theglobeandmail.com/globe-investor/crtc-head-blais-lays-down-law-at-bell-astral-hearing/article4532188 26 January 2013.

Lambert, Joe. 2002. *Digital Storytelling: Capturing Lives, Creating Community*. Berkeley, CA: Digital Diner Press.

Lamberton, Don. 1971. "Introduction," in D. Lamberton (ed.), *Economics of Information and Knowledge*. London: Penguin, pp. 5–17.

———. 1999. "Information: Pieces, Batches, or Flows?" in S.C. Dow and P.E. Earl (eds.), *Economic Organization and Economic Knowledge: Essays in Honour of Brian J. Loasby*, vol. 1. Cheltenham UK: Edward Elgar, pp. 209–24.

Landry, Charles. 2000. *The Creative City*. London: Earthscan.

———. 2005. "London as a Creative City," in J. Hartley (ed.), *Creative Industries*. Oxford: Blackwell, pp. 233–43.

Lapsley, Robert, and Michael Westlake. 2006. *Film Theory: An Introduction*, 2nd ed. Manchester: Manchester University Press.

Lash, Scott. 1994. *Economies of Signs and Space*. London: Sage.

——. 2002. *Critique of Information*. London: Sage.

——, and John Urry. 1989. *The End of Organized Capitalism*. Cambridge, UK: Polity Press.

Lasn, Kalle. 2000. *Culture Jam*. New York: Quill.

Latour, Bruno. 2005. *Reassembling the Social: An Introduction to Actor–Network Theory*. Oxford: Oxford University Press.

Lavery, David (ed.). 2002. *This Thing of Ours: Investigating the Sopranos*. New York: Columbia University Press.

Leadbeater, Charles. 2000. *Living on Thin Air: The New Economy*. London: Penguin.

——. 2007. *We-Think: The Power of Mass Creativity*, www.wethinkthebook.net/home.aspx. Accessed 18 April 2007.

——, and Paul Miller. 2004. *The Pro-Am Revolution: How Enthusiasts are Changing Our Economy and Society*. London: DEMOS, p. 23.

Lee, Terence. 2006. "Going Online: Journalism and Civil Society in Singapore," in A. Romano and M. Bromley (eds.), *Journalism and Democracy in Asia*. London: Routledge, pp. 15–27.

Legrain, Philippe. 2002. *Open World: The Truth About Globalisation*. London: Abacus.

Leiner, Barry, Vinton Cerf, David Clark, Robert Kahn, Leonard Kleinrock, Daniel Lynch, Jon Postel, Larry Roberts, and Stephen Wolff. 2003. "A Brief History of the Internet," www.isoc .org/internet/history/brief.shtml, Version 3.32, last revised 10 October 2003. Accessed 3 December 2006.

Leiss, William. 1990. *Under Technology's Thumb*. Montreal: McGill-Queen's University Press.

Lenhart, Amanda, and Susannah Fox. 2006. *Bloggers: A Portrait of the Internet's New Story Tellers*. Washington, DC: Pew Internet and American Life Project, www.pewinternet.org/PPF/r/186/ report_display.asp, published 19 July. Accessed 13 January 2014.

——, Kristen Purcell, Aaron Smith, and Kathryn Zikuhr. 2010. *Social Media and Young Adults*. Washington, DC: Pew Internet and American Life Project, http://pewinternet .org/Reports/2010/Social-Media-and-Young-Adults.aspx, published 3 February. Accessed 2 February 2013.

Leo, Patrice, and Terence Lee. 2004. "The 'New' Singapore: Mediating Culture and Creativity," *Continuum: Journal of Media and Cultural Studies* 18(2): 205–18.

Lessig, Lawrence. 2000. *Code and Other Laws of Cyberspace*. New York: Basic Books.

——. 2001. *The Future of Ideas: The Fate of the Commons in a Connected World*. New York: Vintage Books.

——. 2004. *Free Culture: How Big Media Uses Technology and the Law to Lock Down Culture and Control Creativity*. New York: Penguin.

Levine, M.E., and J.L. Forrence. 1990. "Regulatory Capture, Public Interest, and the Public Agenda: Toward a Synthesis," *Journal of Law Economics & Organization* 6, pp. 167–98.

Levinson, Paul. 1997. *The Soft Edge: A Natural History and Future of the Information Revolution*. New York: Routledge.

——. 2012. *New New Media*, 2nd edition. New York: Pearson/Penguin Academics.

Levitt, Steven. 2008. "Club Penguin Anonymous," *New York Times*, 15 September 2008. Accessed from http://freakonomics.blogs.nytimes.com/2008/ 09/15/club-penguin-anonymous 30 June 2010.

Lévy, Pierre. 1997. *Collective Intelligence: Mankind's Emerging World in Cyberspace*. New York: Plenum Trade.

——. 1998. *Becoming Virtual: Reality in the Digital Age*. New York: Plenum Trade.

Lewis, Justin. 1990. *Art, Culture and Enterprise: The Politics of Art and the Cultural Industries*. London: Routledge.

Lewis, Michael. 2001. *The Future Just Happened*. London: Coronet Books.

Liestøl, Eve. 2003. "Computer Games and the Ludic Structure of Interpretation," in G. Liestøl, A. Morrison, and T. Rasmussen (eds.), *Digital Media Revisited*. Cambridge, MA: MIT Press, pp. 327–57.

Lievrouw, Leah, and Sonia Livingstone. 2005. "Introduction to the Updated Student Edition," in L. Lievrouw and S. Livingstone (eds.), *The Handbook of New Media: Social Shaping and Consequences of ICTs*, 2nd ed. London: Sage, pp. 1–14.

Ling, Rich. 2004. *The Mobile Connection: The Cell Phone's Impact on Society*. Amsterdam: Morgan Kaufman/Elsevier.

Lipsey, Richard, Kenneth Carlaw, and Clifford Bekar. 2006. *Economic Transformations: General Purpose Technologies and Long-Term*

EconomicGrowth. New York: Oxford University Press.

Lister, Martin, Jon Dovey, Seth Giddings, Iain Grant, and Kieran Kelly. 2003. *New Media: A Critical Introduction*. London: Routledge.

Litman, Jessica. 2001. *Digital Copyright*. Amherst, NY: Prometheus Books.

Litzenberger, Shannon. 2010. "Will Toronto's Next Mayor Champion the Arts?" *The Mark News*, 9 July. Accessed 9 July 2010 from www .themarknews.com/articles/1837.

Livingstone, Sonia. 1998. *Making Sense of Television*, 2nd ed. London: Routledge.

———. 1999. "New Media, New Audiences," *New Media and Society* 1(1): 59–68.

———. 2002. *Young People and New Media*. London: Sage.

———. 2005. "Critical Debates in Internet Studies: Reflections on an Emergent Field," in J. Curran and M. Gurevitch (eds.), *Mass Media and Society*, 4th ed. London: Hodder Arnold, pp. 9–28.

Local, The. 2013. "Court Rules Internet Access a Basic Right," 25 January. Accessed from www.thelocal .de/sci-tech/20130125-47553.html#.UQRos-gRFo4 26 January 2013.

Lockard, Joseph. 1997. "Progressive Politics, Electronic Individualism and the Myth of Virtual Community," in D. Porter (ed.), *Internet Culture*. New York: Routledge, pp. 219–32.

Lovelock, Peter, and John Ure. 2002. "The New Economy: Internet, Telecommunications and Electronic Commerce?," in L. Lievrouw and S. Livingstone (eds.), *Handbook of New Media*. London: Sage, pp. 350–68.

Lovink, Geert. 2002. *Dark Fiber: Tracking Critical Internet Culture*. Cambridge, MA: MIT Press.

Lyon, David. 1988. *The Information Society: Issues and Illusions*. Cambridge, UK: Polity Press.

———. 2002. *Surveillance Society: Monitoring Everyday Life*. Buckingham, UK: Open University Press.

McChesney, Robert W. 1999. *Rich Media, Poor Democracy: Communication Politics in Dubious Times*. New York: New Press.

———. 2000. "So Much for the Magic of Technology and the Free Market: The World Wide Web and the Corporate Media System," in A. Herman and T. Swiss (eds.), *The World Wide Web and Contemporary Cultural Theory*. New York: Routledge, pp. 5–35.

———. 2003. "Corporate Media, Global Capitalism," in S. Cottle (ed.), *Media Organization and Production*. London: Sage, pp. 27–40.

———, and Dan Schiller. 2003. *The Political Economy of International Communication: Foundations for the Emerging Global Debate about Media Ownership and Regulation*, United Nations Research Institute for Social Development, Technology, Business and Society Programme Paper No. 11, October.

McKay, George. 1998. "DIY Culture: Notes towards an Intro," in G. McKay (ed.), *DIY Culture: Party and Protest in Nineties Britain*. London: Verso.

MacKenzie, Donald, and Judy Wacjman. 1999. "Introductory Essay: The Social Shaping of Technology," in D. MacKenzie and J. Wacjman (eds.), *The Social Shaping of Technology*, 2nd ed. Milton Keynes, UK: Open University Press, pp. 3–27.

McLuhan, Eric, and Frank Zingrone (eds.). 1997. *Essential McLuhan*. London: Routledge.

McLuhan, Marshall. 1962. *The Gutenberg Galaxy: The Making of Typographic Man*. Toronto: University of Toronto Press.

———. 1964. *Understanding Media: The Extensions of Man*. New York: Mentor Books.

———, and Quentin Fiore. 1967. *The Medium is the Massage*. New York: Bantam.

———, and Eric McLuhan. 1988. *Laws of Media: The New Science*. Toronto: University of Toronto Press.

———, and Bruce R. Powers. 1989. *The Global Village: Transformations in World Life and Media in the 21st Century*. Toronto: University of Toronto Press.

McMillan, Sally. 2005. "Exploring Models of Interactivity from Multiple Research Traditions; Users, Documents and Systems," in L. Lievrouw and S. Livingstone (eds.), *Handbook of New Media*, 2nd ed. London: Sage, pp. 205–29.

McNair, Brian. 2003. "From Control to Chaos: Toward a New Sociology of Journalism," *Media, Culture and Society* 25(6): 547–55.

———. 2006. *Cultural Chaos: Journalism, News and Power in a Globalized World*. New York: Routledge.

McNamara, Andrew. 2002. "How 'Creative Industries' Evokes the Legacy of Modernist Visual Art," *Media International Australia* 102, February: 66–76.

McNamee, S. 1998. "Youth, Gender and Video Games: Power and Control in the Home," in T. Skelton and G. Valentine (eds.), *Cool Places: Geographies of Youth Cultures*. New York: Routledge.

McPhail, Thomas, and Brenda McPhail. 1990. *Communication: The Canadian Experience*. Toronto: Copp Clark Pitman.

McQuail, Dennis. 2002. *Mass Communication Theory*, 3rd ed. London: Routledge.

——. 2005. *McQuail's Mass Communication Theory*, 5th ed. London: Sage.

McQuire, Scott. 2001. "When is Art IT?," in H. Brown, G. Lovink, H. Merrick, N. Rossiter, D. Teh, and M. Willson (eds.), *Fibreculture Reader: Politics of a Digital Present*. Melbourne: Fibreculture Publications, pp. 205–13.

McRobbie, Angela. 2005. "Clubs to Companies," in J. Hartley (ed.), *Creative Industries*. Oxford: Blackwell, pp. 375–93.

McWilliams, I. 2013. "Saskatchewan Audio Drama," *Canadian Theatre Review* 154, 50–54. Retrieved 14 August 2013 from the Project MUSE database.

Madden, Christopher. 2001. "Using 'Economic' Impact Studies in Arts and Cultural Advocacy: A Cautionary Note," *Media International Australia* 98, February: 161–78.

Malaysiakini. 2007. "About Malaysiakini.com," www.malaysiakini.com/pages/general. Accessed 27 April 2007.

Malmstein, Ernst. 2001. *Boo Hoo: A Dotcom Story from Concept to Catastrophe*. New York: Random House.

Mander, Jerry, and Edward Goldsmith. 1996. *The Case Against the Global Economy: And for a Turn Toward the Local*. San Francisco: Sierra Club Books.

Manovich, Lev. 2001. *The Language of New Media*. Cambridge: MIT Press.

Marshall, David (ed.). 2006. *The Celebrity Culture Reader*. London: Routledge.

Marvin, Carolyn. 1988. *When Old Technologies Were New: Thinking about Electric Communication in the 19th Century*. New York: Oxford University Press.

Masnick, Mike. 2012a. "ITU Boss Explains Why He Wants the UN to Start Regulating the Internet," *Techdirt*. 7 November 2012. Retrieved from www.techdirt.com/articles/20121107/21233320970/itu-boss-explains-why-he-wants-un-to-start-regulating-internet.shtml 19 January 2013.

Masnick, Mike. 2012b. "ITU Boss in Denial: Claims Success, Misrepresents Final Treaty, as US, UK, Canada and Many More Refuse to Sign," *Techdirt*. 14 December 2012. Retrieved from www.techdirt.com/articles/20121214/05385721386/itu-boss-denial-claims-success-misrepresents-final-treaty-as-us-uk-canada-many-more-refuse-to-sign.shtml 26 January 2013.

Matlin, Julie. 2009. "Digital Storytelling Workshops," NFB.ca blog, http://blog.nfb.ca/2009/08/24/digital-storytelling-workshops, 24 August. Accessed 5 September 2010.

Mattelart, Armand. 2003. *The Information Society: An Introduction*, trans. S.G. Taponier and J.A. Cohen. London: Sage.

Mayfield, Antony. 2007. "What is Social Media?" Spannerworks e-Books, www.spannerworks.com/ebooks. Accessed 28 April 2007.

Mayfield, Ross. 2006. "Power Law of Participation," Ross Mayfield's Weblog: Markets, Technology and Musings, http://ross.typepad.com/blog/2006/04/power_law_of_pa.html, 27 April. Accessed 27 December 2006.

Meadows, Daniel. 2003. "Digital Storytelling: Research-Based Practice in New Media," *Visual Communication* 2(2): 189–93.

Melody, William. 1996. "Towards a Framework for Designing Information Society Policies," *Telecommunications Policy* 20(4): 243–59.

Menser, Michael, and Stanley Aronowitz. 1996. "On Cultural Studies, Science, and Technology," in S. Aronowitz, B. Martinsons, and M. Menser (eds.), *Technoscience and Cyberculture*. New York: Routledge, pp. 7–36.

Mercer, Colin. 1994. "Cultural Policy: Research and the Governmental Imperative," *Media Information Australia* 73, August, pp. 16–22.

Merrin, Chris. 2005. *Baudrillard and the Media: A Critical Introduction*. Cambridge: Polity.

Miège, Bernard. 2004. "Capitalism and Communication: A New Era of Society or the Accentuation of Long-Term Tendencies?," in A. Calabrese and C. Sparks (eds.), *Toward a Political Economy of Culture: Capitalism and Communication in the Twenty-First Century*. Lanham, MD: Rowman & Littlefield, pp. 83–94.

Milberry, Kate. 2009. *Geeks and Global Justice: Another (Cyber) World is Possible*. Ph.D. dissertation, Simon Fraser University, Burnaby, BC. Available online: http://geeksandglobaljustice.com/wp-content/Milberry-Dissertation-for-Library.pdf.

Miles, Ian. 1997. "Cyberspace as Product Space: Interactive Learning about Interactive Media," *Futures* 29(9): 769–89.

Miller, Daniel. 1998. "Conclusion: A Theory of Virtualism," in J. Carrier and D. Miller (eds.), *Virtualism: A New Political Economy*. Oxford: Berg, pp. 187–216.

———, and Don Slater. 2000. *The Internet: An Ethnographic Approach*. London: Routledge.

Miller, Paul. 2004. "The Rise of Network Campaigning," in H. McCarthy, P. Miller, and P. Skidmore (eds.), *Network Logic: Who Governs in an Interconnected World?* London: DEMOS, pp. 207–17.

Miller, Toby. 2007. *Cultural Citizenship: Cosmopolitanism, Consumerism and Television in a Neoliberal Age*. Philadelphia: Temple University Press.

———, Nitin Govil, John McMurria, and Richard Maxwell. 2001. *Global Hollywood*. London: British Film Institute.

———, ———, ———, and ———. 2005. *Global Hollywood 2*. London: British Film Institute.

Mills, C. Wright. 1956. *The Power Elite*. New York: Oxford University Press.

Milner, Andrew. 2006. "Theorize This! Cultural Studies versus Utilitarianism," *Continuum: Journal of Media and Cultural Studies* 20(1): 111–25.

Milstein, Sarah. 2009. "What Would Jane Austen Have Twittered?," *O'Reilly Radar*, 30 November, http://radar.oreilly.com/2009/11/what-would-jane-austen-have-tw.html.

Mitchell, William, Alan Inouye, and Marjory Blumenthal. 2003. *Beyond Productivity: Information Technology, Innovation, and Creativity*. Washington, DC: National Research Council of the National Academies, National Academies Press.

Mitrovica, Anthony. 2009. "The New Freedom Fighters," *University of Toronto Magazine*, Autumn: 27–31. Available online at www.magazine.utoronto.ca/back_issues/autumn09.pdf.

MKW (Wirtschaftsforschung GmbH). 2001. *Exploitation and Development of the Job Potential in the Cultural Sector in the Age of Digitization: Final Report*. Commissioned by European Commission DG Employment and Social Affairs, MKWCmbH, Berlin, June.

MobileTracker. 2005. "Mobile Phone Users to hit 2 Billion This Year," 18 January. Accessed from www.mobiletracker.net/archives/2005/01/18/2-billion-mobile-phones 10 December 2006.

Mommaas, Hans. 2004. "Creative Clusters and the Post-Industrial City: Towards the Remapping of Urban Cultural Policy," *Urban Studies* 41(3): 507–32.

Montgomery, Lucy, and Michael Keane. 2006. "Learning to Love the Market: Copyright, Culture and China," in P. Thomas and J. Servaes (eds.), *Intellectual Property Rights and Communications in Asia*. New Delhi: Sage, pp. 130–48.

Moore, Christopher. 2005. "Creative Choices: Changes to Australian Copyright Law and the Future of the Public Domain," *Media International Australia* 114, February: 71–82.

Morozov, Evgeny. 2011. *The Net Delusion: How Not to Liberate the World*. New York: Penguin.

Morrison, Chris. 2012. "Super Whales: Top Game Spenders Pay More Than $10,000 Apiece in Virtual Goods," *Inside Social Games*, www.insidesocialgames.com/2010/06/10/super-whales-spend-money-virtual-goods. Retrieved 13 November 2012.

Mosco, Vincent. 1996. *The Political Economy of Communication*. Thousand Oaks, CA: Sage.

———. 1997. "Citizenship and the Technopoles," *Javnost (The Public)* 4(4): 35–46.

———. 2000. "Webs of Myth and Power: Connectivity and the New Computer Technopoles," in A. Herman and T. Swiss (eds.), *The World Wide Web and Contemporary Cultural Theory*. New York: Routledge, pp. 37–60.

———. 2004. *The Digital Sublime: Myth, Power and Cyberspace*. Cambridge, MA: MIT Press.

———, and Catherine McKercher. 2008. *The Laboring of Communication*. Lanham, MD: Rowman & Littlefield.

MTI (Ministry of Trade and Industry). 2003. *Economic Contributions of Singapore's Creative Industries*. Singapore: Government of Singapore.

Murdock, Graham, and Peter Golding. 2004. "Dismantling the Digital Divide: Rethinking the Dynamics of Participation and Exclusion," in A. Calabrese and C. Sparks (eds.), *Towards a Political Economy of Culture: Capitalism and Communication in the Twenty-First Century*. Lanham, MD: Rowman & Littlefield, pp. 244–60.

Murphy, Brian Martin. 2002. "A Critical History of the Internet," in G. Elmer (ed.), *Critical Perspectives on the Internet*. Lanham, MD: Rowman & Littlefield, pp. 27–45.

Murray, Gil. 2003. *Nothing On but the Radio: A Look Back at Radio in Canada and How It Changed the World*. Toronto: Dundurn Press.

Murray, Janet H. 1997. *Hamlet on the Holodeck: The Future of Narrative in Cyberspace*. Cambridge, MA: MIT Press.

Musser, John, and Tim O'Reilly. 2007. *Web 2.0: Principles and Practices*. San Francisco: O'Reilly Radar.

Mussio, Laurence B. 2001. *Telecom Nation: Telecommunications, Computers, and Governments in Canada*. Montreal: McGill-Queen's University Press.

Nardi, Bonnie. 2010. *My Life as a Night Elf Priest: An Anthropological Account of* World of Warcraft. Ann Arbor, MI: University of Michigan Press.

Nakamura, Lisa. 2000. "'Where Do You Want to Go to Today?' Cybernetic Tourism, the Internet, and Transnationality," in B. Kolko, L. Nakamura, and G.B. Rodman (eds.), *Race in Cyberspace*. New York: Routledge, pp. 15–26.

National Endowment for the Arts. 2010. *Audience 2.0: How Technology Influences Arts Participation*. Washington, DC: NEA.

Nayak, Malathi. 2013 "FACTBOX—A Look at the $66 Billion Video Game Industry," Reuters, 10 June. Accessed from http://in.reuters.com/article/2013/06/10/gameshow-e-idINDEE9590DW20130610 29 September 2013.

Negroponte, Nicholas. 1995. *Being Digital*. Sydney, AU: Hodder & Stoughton.

Negus, Keith, and Michael Pickering. 2004. *Creativity, Communication, and Cultural Value*. London: Sage.

Neilsen, Inc. 2010. "Americans Using TV and Internet Together 35% More Than a Year Ago," *NeilsenWire*, 22 March 2010. Accessed from http://blog.nielsen.com/nielsenwire/online_mobile/three-screen-report-q409 11 November 2010.

Newson, Emily. 2006. "Celebrity Mags Embrace the Internet," Cardiff University Online Journalism, http://journalism.cf.ac.uk/2007/online/index.php?id=parse-195-0-0-251&article=551&author=Emily+Newson, posted 15 December. Accessed 6 May 2007.

Newman, James. 2002. "The Myth of the Ergodic Videogame," *Games Studies* 2(1): 1–8.

Nie, Norman, and Lutz Erbring. 2000. *Internet and Society: A Preliminary Report*. Stanford, CA: Stanford Institute for the Quantitative Study of Society.

Nielsen, Jakob. 2000. *Designing Web Usability*. Indianapolis, IN: New Riders.

Nielsén, Tobias. 2004. *Understanding the Experience Economy: A Swedish Perspective on Creativity*. Stockholm: QNB Analys & Kommunikation AB.

Nip, Joyce. 2006. "Changing Connections: The News Media, the Government and the People in China's SARS Epidemic," in A. Romano and M. Bromley (eds.), *Journalism and Democracy in Asia*. London: Routledge, pp. 28–40.

Noam, Eli. 1991. *Television in Europe*. New York: Oxford University Press.

Nonnenmacher, Tomas. 2001. "History of the US Telegraph Industry." EH.Net Encyclopedia, 14 August, edited by Robert Whaples, http://eh.net/encyclopedia/article/nonnenmacher.industry.telegraphic.us.

Nora, Simon, and Alain Minc. 1981. *The Computerization of Society*. Cambridge, MA: MIT Press.

Norman, Donald. 1998. *The Invisible Computer: Why Good Products Can Fail, the Personal Computer Is So Complex, and Information Appliances Are the Solution*, figure, page 30, © 1998 Massachusetts Institute of Technology, by permission of The MIT Press.

Norris, Pippa. 2001. *Digital Divide: Civic Engagement, Information Poverty, and the Internet Worldwide*. Cambridge, UK: Cambridge University Press.

Northfield, Dianne. 1999. *The Information Policy Maze: Global Challenges—National Responses*. Melbourne: Centre for International Research into Communications and Information Technologies.

Nussbaum, Bruce. 2005. "Get Creative! How to Build Innovative Companies," *Business Week*, 1 August, www.businessweek.com/magazine/content/05_31/b3945401.htm#. Accessed 29 December 2005.

Oakley, Kate. 2004. "Not So Cool Britannia: The Role of the Creative Industries in Economic Development," *International Journal of Cultural Studies* 7(1): 67–77.

O'Brien, Damien. 2007. "Viacom v. YouTube and Google: Copyright Challenges for User Generated Intermediaries." Paper presented to ECUPL-QUT Legal and Policy Framework for the Digital Content Industry Conference, Shanghai, 28–29 May.

O'Connor, Justin. 1999. "Popular Culture, Reflexivity and Urban Change," in J. Verwijnen and P. Lehtovuori (eds.), *Creative Cities*. Helsinki: University of Art and Design Publishing Unit.

——, and Xin Gu. 2006. "A New Modernity? The Arrival of 'Creative Industries' in China," *International Journal of Cultural Studies* 9(3): 271–83.

OECD (Organisation for Economic Co-operation and Development). 1996. *The Knowledge-Based Economy*. Paris: OECD.

——. 1999. *The Economic and Social Impacts of Electronic Commerce: Preliminary Findings and Research Agenda*. Paris: OECD.

——. 2003. *The e-Government Imperative*. Paris: OECD.

O'Neil, Mathieu. 2006. "Rebels for the System? Virus Writers, General Intellect, Cyberpunk and Criminal Capitalism," *Continuum: Journal of Media and Cultural Studies* 20(2): 225–41.

O'Regan, Tom. 2002. "Too Much Culture, Too Little Culture: Trends and Issues for Cultural Policy-Making," *Media International Australia* 102, February 9–24.

O'Reilly, Terry, and Mike Tennant. 2010. *The Age of Persuasion: How Marketing Ate Our Culture*. Toronto: Vintage Canada. Copyright © 2009 Terry O'Reilly and Mike Tennant. Reprinted by permission of Knopf Canada.

O'Reilly, Tim. 2005. "What is Web 2.0? Design Patterns and Business Models for the Next Generation of Software," www.oreillynet.com/pub/a/oreilly/tim/news/2005/09/30/what-is-web-20.html, posted 30 September. Accessed 17 March 2007.

——. 2006. "Web 2.0 Compact Definition: Trying Again," O'Reilly Radar, http://radar.oreilly.com/archives/2006/12/web_20_compact.html, posted 12 October. Accessed 17 March 2007.

Orlowski, Andrew. 2005. "On Creativity, Computers, and Copyright," *The Register*, www.theregister.co.uk/2005/07/21/creativity, published 21 July. Accessed 22 May 2007.

Ortiz, Christina. 2012. "World's Fastest Supercomputer Brought to You by Game Tech," *ReadWriteHack*, 2 November. Accessed from http://readwrite.com/2012/11/02/worlds-fastest-supercomputer-brought-to-you-by-gaming-technology 2 November 2012.

Ortutay, Barbara. 2012. "For Facebook, 'Hacker Way' Is Way of Life." *USA Today*, 4 February. Available at http://usatoday30.usatoday.com/tech/news/story/2012-02-04/facebook-the-hacker-way/52959640/1. Accessed 19 January 2013.

Orwell, George. 1949. *1984*. London: Secker & Warburg.

Osborne, Thomas. 2003. "Against 'Creativity': A Philistine Rant," *Economy and Society* 32(4): 507–25.

Ó Siochrú, Seán. 2004. "Civil Society Participation in the WSIS Process: Promises and Reality," *Continuum: Journal of Media and Cultural Studies* 18(3): 330–44.

——, and Bruce Girard, with Amy Mahan. 2003. *Global Media Governance: A Beginner's Guide*. Lanham, MD: Rowman & Littlefield.

Outing, Steve. 2005. "The 11 Layers of Citizen Journalism," www.poynter.org/content/content_print.asp?id=83126&custom=, posted 11 June. Accessed 28 April 2007.

Papacharissi, Zizi. 2002. "The Virtual Sphere: The Internet as a Public Sphere," *New Media and Society* 4(1): 9–27.

Paré, Daniel. 2003. *Internet Governance in Transition: Who is the Master of this Domain?* Lanham, MD: Rowman & Littlefield.

Park, Myung-Jin, Chang-Mai Kim, and Byung-Woo Sohn. 2000. "Modernization, Globalization and the Powerful State: The Korean Media," in J. Curran and M.-J. Park (eds.), *Dewesternizing Media Studies*. London: Routledge, pp. 111–23.

Parnell, Brid-Aine. 2013. "Twitter Must Unmask Racist French Twits or Face $1,300-a-Day Fine," www.theregister.co.uk/2013/01/25/twitter_france_user_details_hate_speech. Accessed 26 January 2013.

Peck, Jamie. 2005. "Struggling with the Creative Class," *International Journal of Urban and Regional Research* 29(4): 740–70.

Penfold, Carolyn. 2003. "Global Technology Meets Local Environment: State Attempts to Control Internet Content," in K.C. Ho, R. Kluver, and K.C.C. Yang (eds.), *Asia.com: Asian Encounters the Internet*. London: RoutledgeCurzon, pp. 83–96.

Penley, Constance, and Andrew Ross. 1991. *Technoculture*. Minneapolis, MN: University of Minnesota Press.

Perelman, Michael. 2002. *Steal This Idea: Intellectual Property Rights and the Corporate Confiscation of Creativity*. New York: Palgrave.

Phillips, Walter P. 1879 [1975]. *The Phillips Code, Telephone and Telegraph Age*. New York. Accessed from www.radions.net/philcode.htm 29 December 2009.

PMSEIC (Prime Minister's Science, Engineering, and Innovation Council, Australia). 2005. *Imagine Australia: The Role of Creativity in the Innovation Economy*, 2 December.

Podolny, Joel, and Karen Page. 1998. "Network Forms of Organization," *Annual Review of Sociology* 24: 57–76.

Poletti, Teresa. 2010. "Can Research In Motion Climb out of Its Slump?" *Marketwatch*, 1 July. Available at www.marketwatch.com/story/research-in-motion-caught-in-a-perfect-storm-2010-07-01.

Pool, Ithiel de Sola. 1983. *Technologies of Freedom*. Cambridge, MA: Belknap Press.

Porter, Michael. 1998. "Clusters and the New Economics of Competition," *Harvard Business Review* 76(6): 77–91.

Poster, Mark. 1990. *The Mode of Information: Poststructuralism and Social Context*. Cambridge, UK: Polity Press.

———. 1995. *The Second Media Age*. Cambridge, UK: Polity Press.

———. 2001. *What's the Matter with the Internet?* Minneapolis, MN: University of Minnesota Press.

———. 2005. "Culture and New Media," in L. Lievrouw and S. Livingstone (eds.), *Handbook of New Media*, 2nd ed. London: Sage, pp. 134–40.

———. 2006. *Information Please: Culture and Politics in the Age of Digital Machines*. Durham, NC: Duke University Press.

Postman, Neil. 1985. *Amusing Ourselves to Death: Public Discourse in the Age of Show Business*. New York: Penguin.

———. 1993. *Technopoly: The Surrender of Culture to Technology*. New York: Vintage.

Potts, Jason. 2003. "The Prometheus School of Information Economics," *Prometheus* 21(4): 477–86.

Powell, Walter W., and Kaisa Snellman. 2004. "The Knowledge Economy." *Annual Review of Sociology*: 199–220.

Pratt, Andy. 1998. "A 'Third Way' for the Creative Industries?," *International Journal of Communications Law and Policy* 4(1), www.digital-law.net/IJCLP/1_1998/ijclp_webdoc_4_1_1998.html. Accessed 29 May 2007.

Prensky, Marc. 2001. "Digital Natives, Digital Immigrants," www.marcprensky.com/writing/Prensky%20-%20Digital%20Natives,%20Digital%20Immigrants%20-%20Part1.pdf. Accessed 2 December 2006.

PriceWaterhouseCoopers. 2012. *Global Entertainment and Media Outlook: 2012–2016*. Available at www.pwc.com/gx/en/global-entertainment-media-outlook/segment-insights/video-games.jhtml. Accessed 18 December 2012.

Putnam, Robert. 1995. "Tuning In, Tuning Out: The Strange Disappearance of Social Capital in America," *Political Science and Politics* 28(4): 664–88.

———. 2000. *Bowling Alone: The Collapse and Revival of American Community*. New York: Simon & Schuster.

Quah, Danny. 2003. "Digital Goods and the New Economy," in D.C. Jones (ed.), *New Economy Handbook*. Amsterdam: Elsevier, pp. 289–321.

Rainie, Lee, and Peter Bell. 2004. "The Numbers That Count," *New Media and Society* 6(1): 44–54.

Ramsay, Randolph. 2007. "GDC '07: Chris Taylor Says 'No More Overtime'," Gamespot AU, 8 March. Accessed from http://au.gamespot.com/news/6167123.html?msg_sort=1 7 April 2007.

Ravensbergen, David. 2008. "Be Nice to the 'Creative Class'!" *The Tyee*. Accessed 5 August from http://thetyee.ca/Views/2008/08/05/CreativeClass.

Raymond, Eric. 1998. "The Cathedral and the Bazaar," *First Monday* 3(3), http://firstmonday.org/ojs/index.php/fm/article/view/1472/1387. Accessed 28 December 2003.

Redden, Guy. 2003. "Read the Whole Thing: Journalism, Weblogs and the Re-Mediation of the War in Iraq," *Media International Australia*, 109: 153–65.

Redhead, Steve. 2004. *Paul Virilio: Theorist for an Accelerated Culture*. Edinburgh: Edinburgh University Press.

Reed, Brad. 2012. "Google Has a Whopping 7100 People Working on Maps Alone." Yahoo! News, 21 September, http://news.yahoo.com/google-whopping-7-100-people-working-maps-alone-000541085.html. Accessed 13 November 2012.

Reeves, Byron, and Clifford Nass. 2002. *The Media Equation: How People Treat Computers, Televisions, and New Media Like Real People and Places*. Cambridge, UK: Cambridge University Press.

Rennie, Elinor. 2003. "'Trespassers are Welcome': Access and Community Television Policy," *Javnost (The Public)* 10(1): 49–62.

———. 2006. *Community Media: A Global Introduction*. Lanham, MD: Rowman & Littlefield.

Rheingold, Howard. 1994. *The Virtual Community: Finding Connection in a Computerized World*. London: Secker & Warburg.

———. 2002. *Smart Mobs: The Next Social Revolution*. Cambridge: Perseus.

Rice, Ronald. 1999. "Artifacts and Paradoxes in New Media," *New Media and Society* 1(1): 24–32.

———. 2002. "Primary Issues in Internet Use: Access, Civic and Community Involvement, and Social Interaction and Expression," in L. Lievrouw and S. Livingstone (eds.), *Handbook of New Media*. London: Sage, pp. 105–29.

———, and Carolyn Haythornthwaite. 2005. "Perspectives on Internet Use: Access, Involvement and Interaction," in L. Lievrouw and S. Livingstone (eds.), *Handbook of New Media*, 2nd ed. London: Sage, pp. 92–113.

Ricks, Christopher. 1968. "McLuhanism," in R. Rosenthal (ed.), *McLuhan: Pro & Con*. Baltimore, MD: Penguin.

Rifkin, Jeremy. 2000. *The Age of Access: How the Shift from Ownership to Access is Transforming Modern Life*. London: Penguin.

Rimmer, Matthew. 2003a. "Virtual Countries: Internet Domain Names and Geographical Terms," *Media International Australia* 106, February: 124–36.

———. 2003b. "The Dead Poets Society: The Copyright Term and the Public Domain," *First Monday* 8(6), www.firstmonday.org/issues/issue8_6/rimmer/index.html. Accessed 25 August 2003.

Ring, D.H. 1947. "Mobile Telephony—Wide Area Coverage," Bell Laboratories Technical Memo #TA4 47-1 60-37, 11 December 1947.

Robins, Kevin, and Frank Webster. 1999. *Times of the Technoculture: From the Information Society to the Virtual Life*. London: Routledge.

Robinson, Evan. 2005. "Why Crunch Mode Doesn't Work: 6 Lessons," International Game Developers Association—Articles, www.igda.org/articles/erobinson_crunch.php. Accessed 7 April 2007.

Robinson, Ken. 2001. *Out of Our Minds: Learning to Be Creative*. Oxford: Capstone.

Rogers, Everett. 2003. *Diffusion of Innovations*, 5th ed. New York: Free Press.

Rogers, Mark, Michael Epstein, and Jimmie Reeves. 2002. "*The Sopranos* as HBO Brand Equity: The Art of Commerce in the Age of Digital Reproduction," in D. Lavery (ed.), *This Thing of Ours: Investigating* The Sopranos. New York: Columbia University Press, pp. 42–57.

Romano, Angela. 2003. *Politics and the Press in Indonesia: Understanding an Evolving Political Culture*. London: RoutledgeCurzon.

Romer, Paul. 1994. "The Origins of Endogenous Growth," *Journal of Economic Perspectives* 8(1): 3–22.

———. 1995. "Interview with Peter Robinson," *Forbes* 155(12): 66–70.

———. 2007. "Economic Growth," in D. Henderson (ed.), *The Concise Encyclopedia of Economics*, www.econlib.org/library/enc/EconomicGrowth.html. Accessed 14 February 2007.

Rosen, Jay. 2000. "Questions and Answers about Public Journalism," *Journalism Studies* 1(4): 679–83.

———. 2007. "PressThink: Ghost of Democracy in the Media Machine," http://journalism.nyu.edu/pubzone/weblogs/pressthink. Accessed 28 April 2007.

Rossignol, Jim. 2006. "Sex, Fame and PC Baangs: How the Orient Plays Host to PC Gaming's Strangest Culture," *PC Gamer UK*, http://rossignol.cream.org/?p=284, 4 January. Accessed 15 July 2007.

Rossiter, Ned. 2006. *Organized Networks: Media Theory, Creative Labour, New Institutions*. Amsterdam: NAi Publishers, Institute of Network Cultures.

Rowland, Wade. 2006. *Spirit of the Web: The Age of Information from Telegraph to Internet*. Toronto: Thomas Allen Publishers.

Rudden, David. 2010. "Canada Boasts the Third-Largest Video Games Industry." *Network World*, www.networkworld.com/news/2010/040610-canada-boasts-the-third-largest-video.html. Accessed 3 April 2013.

Rushkoff, Douglas. 1996. *Playing the Future: How Kids' Culture Can Teach Us to Thrive in an Age of Chaos*. New York: HarperCollins.

Rutter, Jason, and Jo Bryce (eds.). 2006. *Understanding Digital Games*. Thousand Oaks, CA: Sage.

Sale, Kirkpatrick. 1995. *Rebels against the Future: The Luddites and the War on the Industrial Revolution—Lessons for the Computer Age*. Reading, MA: Addison-Wesley.

Sassen, Saskia. 1991. *The Global City: New York, London, Tokyo*. Princeton, NJ: Princeton University Press.

———. 1999. "The State and the New Geography of Power," in A. Calabrese and J.-C. Burgelman (eds.), *Communication, Citizenship, and Social Policy: Rethinking the Limits of the Welfare State*. Lanham, MD: Rowman & Littlefield, pp. 17–31.

———. 2001. *The Global City: New York, London, Tokyo*. Princeton, NJ: Princeton University Press.

Sawyer, Ben. 2002. "The Next Ages of Games Development," *The Adrenalin Vault*, Developer's Corner, www.avault.com/developer, 30 September. Accessed 28 October 2002.

Schabas, Paul B., and Erin Hoult. 2012. "Canada Rolls out Welcome Mat for Libel Tourists," *Inforrm's Blog*, April 18. Retrieved from http://inforrm. wordpress.com/2012/04/18/news-canada-rolls-out-welcome-mat-for-libel-tourists-paul-b-schabas-and-erin-hoult 26 January 2013.

Schell, Jesse. 2010. "Seeing," Augmented Reality World 2010 keynote address. Accessed from http://augmentedrealityevent.com/2010/08/25/are2010-keynote-by-jesse-schell-augmented-reality-will-define-the-21st-century 2 February 2013.

Schaffer, Jan. 2007. "Citizen Media: Fad or the Future of News? The Rise and Prospects of Hyper-Local Journalism," www.kcnn.org/research/citizen_media_report. Accessed 6 May 2007.

Schiller, Dan. 2000. *Digital Capitalism: Networking the Global Market System*. Cambridge, MA: MIT Press.

———. 2006. "Digital Capitalism: A Status Report on the Corporate Commonwealth of Information," in A.N. Valdivia (ed.), *A Companion to Media Studies*. Malden, MA: Blackwell, pp. 137–56.

Schiller, Herbert. 1995. "The Global Information Highway: Project for an Ungovernable World," in J. Brook and I.A. Boal (eds.), *Resisting the Virtual Life: The Culture and Politics of Information*. San Francisco: City Lights, pp. 17–33.

Schuler, Douglas. 1996. *New Community Networks: Wired for Change*. Reading, MA: Addison-Wesley.

Sclove, Richard. 1995. *Technology and Democracy*. New York: Guilford Press.

Scott, Allen. 2004. "Cultural-Products Industries and Urban Economic Development: Prospects for Growth and Market Contestation in Global Context," *Urban Affairs Review* 39(4): 461–90.

Scott, Ben. 2005. "A Contemporary History of Digital Journalism," *Television and New Media* 6(1): 89–126.

Scott, John. 1986. *Capitalist Property and Financial Power: A Comparative Study of Britain, the United States, and Japan*. Brighton, UK: Harvester Wheatsheaf Press.

———. 1991. *Social Network Analysis: A Handbook*. London: Sage.

Seaman, Bruce. 2000. "Arts Impact Studies: A Fashionable Excess," in G. Bradford, M. Gary, and G. Wallach (eds.), *The Politics of Culture: Policy Perspectives for Individuals, Institutions and Communities*. New York: New Press, pp. 266–85.

Sell, Susan. 2002. "Intellectual Property Rights," in D. Held and A. McGrew (eds.), *Governing Globalization: Power, Authority, and Global Governance*. Cambridge, UK: Polity Press, pp. 171–88.

Seltzer, K., and T. Bentley. 2000. *The Creative Age: Knowledge and Skills for the New Economy*. London: DEMOS.

Shanker, Daya. 2006. "Copyright, Competition Policy and Prevention of Monopolistic Abuses in the TRIPS Agreement," in P.N. Thomas and J. Servaes (eds.), *Intellectual Property Rights and Communications in Asia: Conflicting Traditions*. New Delhi: Sage, pp. 79–102.

Shapiro, Carl, and Hal Varian. 1999. *Information Rules: A Strategic Guide to the Network Economy*. Boston, MA: Harvard Business School Press.

Shaw, Gillian. 2012. "Dial Phone Rented for Decades," *Vancouver Sun*. Accessed from www .vancouversun.com/Dial+phone+rented+ decades/7191670/story.html 26 January 2013.

Shaw, Russell. 2005. "Web 2.0? It Doesn't Exist," http://blogs.zdnet.com/ip-telephony/?p=805, posted 17 December. Accessed 17 March 2007.

Shearmur, Richard. 2010. "Space, Place and Innovation: A Distance-Based Approach," *The Canadian Geographer/Le geographe canadien*, 54, no. 1, pp. 46–67.

Shenton, Karla, and Todd McNeeley. 1997. *The Virtual Communities Companion*. Albany, NY: Coriolis Group Books.

Shirky, Clay. 2003. "Social Software and the Politics of Groups," http://shirky.com/writings/group_politics.html, 9 March. Accessed 8 November 2005.

———. 2009. *Here Comes Everybody: The Power of Organizing Without Organizations*. New York: Penguin.

———. 2010. *Cognitive Surplus: Creativity and Generosity in a Connected Age*. New York: Penguin.

Sholle, David. 2002. "Disorganizing the 'New Technology,'" in G. Elmer (ed.), *Critical Perspectives on the Internet*. Lanham, MD: Rowman & Littlefield, pp. 3–26.

Sibary, Shona. 2011. "The Boys Who Made £100,000 from a 57-Second YouTube Clip: How Parents

Are Cashing in on Family Moments Caught on Camera," *Daily Mail*. 2 December. Retrieved from www.dailymail.co.uk/femail/article-2068938/Charlie-bit-finger-The-boys-100k-57-second-YouTube-video.html 19 January 2013.

Silver, David. 2000. "Looking Backwards, Looking Forward: Cyberculture Studies 1990–2000," in D. Gauntlett (ed.), *Web.studies: Rewiring Media Studies for the Digital Age*. London: Arnold, pp. 19–30.

Simeonov, S. 2006. "Metcalfe's Law: More Misunderstood than Wrong?" Posted 26 July at http://blog.simeonov.com/2006/07/26/metcalfes-law-more-misunderstood-than-wrong.

Siwek, Stephen. 2002. *Copyright Industries in the US Economy: The 2002 Report*. International Intellectual Property Alliance, Washington, DC.

———. 2004. "Copyright Industries in the US Economy," prepared for the International Intellectual Property Alliance, Washington, DC.

Slater, Don. 2002. "Social Relationships and Identity Online and Offline," in L. Lievrouw and S. Livingstone (eds.), *The Handbook of New Media*. London: Sage, pp. 533–46.

Smith, Anthony. 1991. "Towards a Global Culture?," in M. Featherstone (ed.), *Global Culture, Nationalism, Globalization and Modernity*. London: Sage, pp. 171–92.

Smith, Richard. 2004. "A Model for the Study of Clustering: A Case Study from New Media Firms in Vancouver," in L. Morel-Guimaraes (ed.), *Key Success Factors for Innovation and Sustainable Development*. Oxford: Elsevier.

———. 2006. "New Media Industry in Vancouver." Proceedings of the 5 November 2005 Colloque de l'Association d'Économie Politique (AÉP): La Compétitivité Urbaine à l'ère de la Nouvelle Économie: Enjeux Et Défis, Montreal.

——— and Ellen Godfrey. 2009. "Foundation for the Future: Establishing Baseline Measures for Assessing the Impact of Broadband in BC Communities," Vancouver, CPROST Report 2009–06.

Smythe, Dallas. 2001. "On the Audience Commodity and Its Work," in M.G. Durham and D.M. Kellner, (eds.), *Media and Cultural Studies: KeyWorks*. Hoboken, NJ: Wiley-Blackwell, pp. 253–79.

Sood, Ashish, and Gerard Tellis. 2005. "Technological Evolution and Radical Innovation," *Journal of Marketing* 69, July: 152–65.

Stadler, Felix. 2006. *Manuel Castells and the Theory of the Network Society*. Cambridge, UK: Polity Press.

Standage, Thomas. 2007. *The Victorian Internet: The Remarkable Story of the Telegraph and the Nineteenth Century's On-line Pioneers*. New York: Walker & Company.

Stavely-O'Connell, Sarah. 2009. "Libel Tourism Laws: Spoiling the Holiday and Saving the First Amendment," 4 N.Y.U. J.L. & Liberty 252–64.

Stein, Joel. 2007. "Have Something to Say? I Don't Care," LATimes.com, www.latimes.com/news/printedition/opinion/la-oe-stein2jan02,1,918996.column?track=rss&ctrack=1&cset=true, 2 January. Accessed 28 April 2007.

Stein, Laura, and Nikhil Sinha. 2002. "New Media and Communication Policy: The Role of the State in the Twenty-First Century," in L. Lievrouw and S. Livingstone (eds.), *Handbook of New Media*. London: Sage, pp. 410–31.

Sterling, Bruce. 2005. *Shaping Things*. Cambridge, MA: MIT Press.

Sternberg, Robert (ed.). 1999. *Handbook of Creativity*. Cambridge, UK: Cambridge University Press.

Stevenson, Deborah. 2004. "'Civic Gold Rush': Cultural Planning and the Third Way," *International Journal of Cultural Policy* 10(1): 119–31.

Stevenson, Nick. 1995. *Understanding Media Culture: Social Theory and Mass Communication*. London: Sage.

Stillman, W.J. 1891. "Journalism and Literature," *The Atlantic Monthly* 68(409), November, pp. 687–98.

Stokman, Franz, Rold Ziegler, and John Scott. 1985. *Networks of Corporate Power: A Comparative Analysis of Ten Countries*. Cambridge, UK: Polity Press.

Stoll, Clifford. 1995. *Silicon Snake Oil: Second Thoughts on the Information Highway*. London: Macmillan.

Storper, Michael. 1997. *The Regional World*. New York: Guilford.

Streeter, Thomas. 1987. "The Cable Fable Revisited: Discourse, Policy, and the Making of Cable Television," *Critical Studies in Mass Communication* 4: 71–97.

———. 2004. "Romanticism in Business Culture: The Internet, the 1990s, and the Origins of Irrational Exuberance," in A. Calabrese and C. Sparks (eds.), *Towards a Political Economy of Culture: Capitalism and Communication in the Twenty-First Century*. Lanham, MD: Rowman & Littlefield, pp. 286–306.

Streitz, Norbert, and Paddy Nixon. 2005. "The Disappearing Computer," *Communications of the ACM* 48(3): 33–5.

Strickler, Yancey. 2012. "Response to a Quora Inquiry," www.quora.com/Kickstarter/Proportionally-how-many-gaming-projects-in-Kickstarter-are-videogames-and-how-many-are-board-games. Accessed 13 November 2012.

Stueck, Wendy. 2007. "Club Penguin Founders Strike It Rich," *Globe and Mail*, 2 August. Accessed 30 June 2010 at www.theglobeandmail.com/news/technology/article774336.ece.

Suh, Bongwon, Gregorio Convertino, Ed H. Chi, and Peter Pirolli. 2009. *The Singularity Is Not Near: Slowing Growth of Wikipedia*, WikiSym'09, 25–7 October, Orlando, FL.

Sunstein, Cass. 2002. "The Law of Group Polarization," *Journal of Political Philosophy* 10(2): 175–95.

Supreme Court of Canada. 2002. Théberge v. Galerie d'Art due Petit Champlain Inc, 2 SCR 336.

Sutton-Smith, Brian. 1997. *The Ambiguity of Play*. Cambridge, MA: Harvard University Press.

Sweeny, Alistair. 2009. *BlackBerry Planet: The Story of Research In Motion and the Little Device That Took the World by Storm*. Toronto: Wiley.

Tapscott, Don. 1998. *Growing Up Digital: The Rise of the Net Generation*. New York: McGraw-Hill.

Taylor, Peter, D.R.F. Walker, and Jonathon Beaverstock. 2002. "Firms and their Global Service Networks," in S. Sassen (ed.), *Global Networks, Linked Cities*. New York: Routledge, pp. 93–115.

Taylor, T.L. 2012. *Raising the Stakes: E-sports and the Professionalization of Gaming*. Cambridge, MA: MIT Press.

Tellis, Gerard J., and Peter G. Golder. 1996. "First to Market, First to Fail? Real Causes of Enduring Market Leadership," *Sloan Management Review* 37(2): 65–75.

Terranova, Tiziana. 2004. *Network Culture: Politics for the Information Age*. London: Pluto Press.

Thiessen, Brian, Andrea York, and Skye Friesen. 2012. "Supreme Court Recognizes Employee Privacy in Workplace Computers." Accessed at http://blakes.com/english/view.asp?ID=5581 on 26 January 2013.

Thompson, Graham. 1990. "Sandford Fleming and the Pacific Cable: The Institutional Politics of Nineteenth-Century Imperial Communications," *Canadian Journal of Communication*, 15(2).

Thompson, Grahame. 2003. *Between Hierarchies and Markets: The Logic and Limits of Network Forms of Organization*. Oxford: Oxford University Press.

Thompson, John. 1991. *Ideology and Modern Culture*. Cambridge, UK: Polity Press.

——. 1995. *The Media and Modernity: A Social Theory of the Media*. Cambridge, UK: Polity Press.

Thoreau, Henry David. 2000 [1882]. *Walden*. vol. 1. Boston: Houghton Mifflin.

Throsby, David. 2001. *Economics and Culture*. Cambridge, UK: Cambridge University Press.

Thussu, Daya Kishan. 2006. *International Communication: Continuity and Change*. London: Arnold.

Toffler, Alvin. 1970. *Future Shock*. New York: Random House.

——. 1980. *The Third Wave*. New York: Bantam Books.

Tofts, Darren. 2005. *Interzone: Media Arts in Australia*. Melbourne: Craftsman House.

Toronto. 2008. "Creative City Planning Framework", accessed 19 December 2013 at www.toronto.ca/legdocs/mmis/2008/ed/bgrd/backgroundfile-11189.pdf

Townsend, David A. 2004. *Report on the National Antenna Tower Policy Review*. Ottawa: Industry Canada, www.ic.gc.ca/eic/site/smt-gst.nsf/eng/sf02037.html.

Trading Economics. 2012. *Canada Balance of Trade*. Retrieved from www.tradingeconomics.com/canada/balance-of-trade 19 January 2013.

Tsagarousianou, Roza, Damian Tambini, and Cathy Bryan (eds.). 1998. *Cyberdemocracy: Technology, Cities and Civic Networks*. London: Routledge.

Turban, Efraim, Jae Lee, David Kung, and Michael Chung. 2000. *Electronic Commerce: A Managerial Perspective*. 1st Edition, © 2000, p. 64. Reprinted by permission of Pearson Education, Inc., Upper Saddle River, NJ.

Turkle, Sherry. 1997. *Life on the Screen: Identity in the Age of the Internet*. New York: Touchstone.

Turner, Graeme. 1990. *British Cultural Studies: An Introduction*. Boston: Unwin Hyman.

——. 1999. "Tabloidisation, Journalism and the Possibility of Critique," *International Journal of Cultural Studies* 2(1): 59–76.

——. 2004. *Understanding Celebrity*. London: Sage.

——. 2005. *Ending the Affair: The Decline of Television Current Affairs in Australia*. Sydney: UNSW Press.

UNCTAD. 2004. "Creative Industries and Development," www.unctad.org/en/docs/tdxibpd13_en.pdf. Accessed 10 May 2007.

———. 2005. "World Investment Report 2005: Transnational Corporations and the Internationalization of R&D," United Nations, New York and Geneva.

UNESCO. 2003. "Culture, Trade and Globalization: Questions and Answers," www.unesco.org/culture/industries/trade/html_eng. Accessed 4 June 2003.

United Nations. 1948. *Universal Declaration of Human Rights*, adopted by the General Assembly of the United Nations, 10 December, www.un.org/Overview/rights.html. Accessed 5 May 2007.

US Trade Representative (2010). *Statement of ACTA Negotiating Partners on Recent ACTA Negotiations.* Washington. US Government. Available online at http://www.ustr.gov/about-us/press-office/press-releases/2010/june/office-us-trade-representative-releases-statement-act

Vaidhyanathan, Siva. 2001. *Copyrights and Copywrongs: The Rise of Intellectual Property and How It Threatens Creativity*. New York: New York University Press.

———. 2004. *The Anarchist in the Library: How the Clash between Freedom and Control Is Hacking the Real World.* New York: Basic Books.

———. 2006. "Critical Information Studies: A Bibliographic Manifesto." *Cultural Studies* 20(2/3), March/May: 292–315.

Van Dijck, José. 2009. "Users Like You? Theorizing Agency in User-Generated Content," *Media, Culture, and Society* 31.1: 41.

Van Dijk, Jan. 2012. *The Network Society*. London: Sage Publications.

Vastag, Brian. 2004. "Does Video Game Violence Sow Aggression?" *Journal of the American Medical Association* 291(15): 1822–4.

Veak, Tyler. 2006. *Democratizing Technology: Building on Andrew Feenberg's Critical Theory of Technology*. Albany, NY: State University of New York Press.

Venturelli, Shalini. 2005. "Culture and the Creative Economy in the Information Age," in J. Hartley (ed.), *Creative Industries*. Oxford: Blackwell, pp. 391–98.

von Hippel, Eric. 1988. *The Sources of Innovation*. New York: Oxford University Press.

———. 2005. *Democratizing Innovation*. Cambridge, MA: MIT Press.

Vulliamy, Ed. 2001. "Empire Hits Back," *The Observer*. 15 July. Retrieved 19 January 2013 from www.guardian.co.uk/books/2001/jul/15/globalisation.highereducation.

Wagstaff, Jeremy. 2004. "Korea's News Crusaders," *Far Eastern Economic Review*, 7 October, pp. 34–7.

Walterscheid, E.C. 2005. "Understanding the Copyright Act of 1790: The Issue of Common Law Copyright in America and the Modern Interpretation of the Copyright Power." *J. Copyright Soc'y USA* 53: 313.

Wang, Jing. 2004. "The Global Reach of a New Discourse: How Far Can 'Creative Industries' Travel," *International Journal of Cultural Studies* 7(1): 9–19.

Ward, Ian. 2003. "An Australian PR State?" *Australian Journal of Communication* 30(1): 25–42.

Wardrip-Fruin, Noah, and Nick Montfort. 2003. *New Media Reader*. Cambridge, MA: MIT Press.

Warnica, Richard. 2012. "Vancouver's Video-Game Industry Is Slowly Disappearing," *Canadian Business*, 19 September. Accessed 26 January 2013 at www.canadianbusiness.com/business-news/industries/technology-industry/vancouvers-video-game-industry-is-slowly-disappearing.

Warren, Christina. 2010. "Facebook Teams Up with British Government to Curb Deficit," *Mashable!* 9 July, http://mashable.com/2010/07/09/uk-government-facebook-deficit. Accessed 9 July 2010.

Wasserman, Stanley, and Katharine Faust. 1994. *Social Network Analysis: Methods and Applications*. Cambridge, UK: Cambridge University Press.

Webster, Frank, and Basil Dimitriou. 2003. *Manuel Castells*, 3 vols., Sage Modern Masters in Social Thought Series. London: Sage.

Weinberger, David. 2007. *Everything Is Miscellaneous: The Power of the New Digital Disorder*. London: Macmillan.

Weiss, Glenn. 2007. "Glenn Weiss: Architecture, Design and Public Art," www.glennweiss.com. Accessed 5 May 2007.

Wellman, Barry. 2001. "Physical Place and Cyberspace: The Rise of Personalized Networking," *International Journal of Urban and Regional Research* 25(2): 227–52.

———. 2004. "The Three Ages of Internet Studies: Ten, Five and Zero Years Ago," *New Media and Society* 6(1): 123–29.

———, and Milena Guila. 1998. "Virtual Communities as Communities: Net Surfers Don't Ride Alone," in M.A. Smith and P. Kollock (eds.), *Communities in Cyberspace*. London: Routledge, pp. 167–94.

———, and Carolyn Haythornthwaite. 2002. "Moving the Internet out of Cyberspace: The Internet in

Everyday Life—An Introduction," in B. Wellman and C. Haythornthwaite (eds.), *The Internet in Everyday Life*. Malden, MA: Blackwell, pp. 3–41.

———, Anabel Haase, James Witte, and Keith Hampton. 2001. "Does the Internet Increase, Decrease, or Supplement Social Capital? Social Networks, Participation, and Community Commitment," *American Behavioral Scientist* 45(3): 436–55.

Westerway, Peter. 1990. *Electronic Highways: An Introduction to Telecommunications in the 1990s*. Sydney, AU: Allen & Unwin.

Whitton, Nicola. 2010. *Learning with Digital Games: A Practical Guide to Engaging Students in Higher Education*. New York: Routledge.

Wikipedia contributors. 2007. "Mod (computer gaming)," Wikipedia, The Free Encyclopedia, http://en.wikipedia.org/wiki/Mod_%28computer_gaming%29, modified 6 April. Accessed 7 April 2007.

Williams, Raymond. 1965. *The Long Revolution*. London: Chatto & Windus.

———. 1974. *Television: Technology and Cultural Form*. London: Routledge.

———. 1976. *Keywords: A Vocabulary of Culture and Society*. London: Fontana.

Williams, Robin, and David Edge. 1996. "The Social Shaping of Technology," *Research Policy* 25(4): 865–99.

Williamson, Oliver E. 1975. *Markets and Hierarchies*. New York: Free Press.

———. 1985. *The Economic Institutions of Capitalism*. New York: Free Press.

Windschuttle, Keith. 2000. "The Poverty of Cultural Studies," *Journalism Studies* 1(1): 145–59.

Winner, Langdon. 1986a. "Technologies as Forms of Life," in L. Winner, *The Whale and the Reactor: A Search for Limits in an Age of High Technology*. Chicago: University of Chicago Press, pp. 3–18.

———. 1986b. "Do Artifacts Have Politics?," in L. Winner, *The Whale and the Reactor: A Search for Limits in an Age of High Technology*. Chicago: University of Chicago Press, pp. 19–37.

Winseck, Dwayne. 2002. "Wired Cities and Transnational Communications: New Forms of Governance for Telecommunications and the New Media," in L. Lievrouw and S. Livingstone (eds.), *Handbook of New Media*. London: Sage, pp. 393–409.

Winston, Brian. 1998. *Media Technology and Society—A History: From the Telegraph to the Internet*. London: Routledge.

WIPO (World Intellectual Property Organization). 2006. WIPO *Patent Report 2006: Statistics on Worldwide Patent Activities*, www.wipo.int/ipstats/en/statistics/patents/pdf/patent_report_2006.pdf. Accessed 27 May 2007.

Witt, Leonard. 2004. "Is Public Journalism Morphing into the Public's Journalism?," *National Civic Review* Fall: 49–57.

Wolf, Gary. 1996. "The Wisdom of Saint Marshall, the Holy Fool," *Wired* 4(1), www.wired.com/wired/archive/4.01/saint.marshal.html. Accessed 29 May 2007.

Wolfe, David. 2009. *The Geography of Innovation: Twenty-First Century Cities*. Ottawa: Conference Board of Canada.

Woods, Tim. 1999. *Beginning Postmodernism*. Manchester, UK: Manchester University Press.

Woolcock, Michael. 2001. "The Place of Social Capital in Understanding Social and Economic Outcomes," ISUMA: *Canadian Journal of Policy Research* 2(1): 11–17.

Woolgar, Steve. 2002. "Five Rules of Virtuality," in S. Woolgar (ed.), *Virtual Society? Technology, Cyberbole, Reality*. Oxford, UK: Oxford University Press, pp. 1–22.

World Bank, The. 2003. "Social Capital for Development," www.worldbank.org/poverty/scapital. Accessed 10 January 2004.

———. 2010. "Indicators," http://data.worldbank.org/indicator. Accessed 10 September 2010.

Wray, Richard. 2002. "First with the Message," *The Guardian*, 16 March. Retrieved 7 September 2013 from www.theguardian.com/business/2002/mar/16/5.

WSIS Civil Society Plenary. 2003. "Shaping Information Societies for Human Needs: Civil Society Declaration to the World Summit on the Information Society," Geneva, 8 December.

Wu, Tim. 2010. *The Master Switch: The Rise and Fall of Information Empires*. New York: Random House.

Yeon-Ho, Oh. 2004. "The Revolt of 727 News Guerillas," http://english.ohmynews.com/articleview/article_view.asp?no=153109&rel_no=1, published 19 February. Accessed 5 May 2007.

———. 2007. "10 Preconditions for the Value of User-Generated Content," OhMyNews CEO Oh Yeon-Ho's address on the 7th anniversary of OhMyNews, http://english.ohmynews.com/articleview/article_view.asp?article_class=8&no=347268&rel_no=1, published 26 February. Accessed 28 April 2007.

Yoo, Christopher S. 2008. "Network Neutrality, Consumers, and Innovation." *University of Chicago Legal Forum*, vol. 25, pg. 179.

———. 2009. "The Convergence of Broadcasting and Telephony: Legal and Regulatory Implications," *Communications & Convergence Review*, vol. 1, December, p. 44.

YouTube. 2013. *Statistics*. Retrieved 19 January 2013 from www.youtube.com/t/press_statistics.

Young, Sally. 2006. "Not Biting the Hand that Feeds? Media Reporting of Government Advertising in Australia," *Journalism Studies* 7(4): 554–74.

Yúdice, George. 2003. *The Expediency of Culture: Uses of Culture in the Global Era*. Durham, NC: Duke University Press.

Zelizer, Barbie. 2004. *Taking Journalism Seriously: News and the Academy*. Thousand Oaks, CA: Sage.

———. 2005. "The Culture of Journalism," in J. Curran and M. Gurevitch (eds.), *Mass Media and Society*, 4th ed. London: Arnold.

Zetie, Carl. 2004. "Convergence or Divergence: What's Next for Mobile Devices?" *InformationWeek*, 15 May, www.informationweek.com/story/showArticle.jhtml?articleID=18311545. Accessed 12 December 2006.

Zhang, Xiaoming. 2006. "From Institution to Industry: Reforms in Cultural Institutions in China," *International Journal of Cultural Studies* 9(3): 297–306.

Zhang, Yonghua. 2006. "China's Efforts for International Cooperation in Copyright Protection," in P. Thomas and J. Servaes (eds.), *Intellectual Property Rights and Communications in Asia*. New Delhi: Sage, pp. 149–63.

Index